Toward a Global Idea of Race

BORDERLINES

For more books in this series, see page vi.

Toward a Global Idea of Race

DENISE FERREIRA DA SILVA

BORDERLINES, VOLUME 27

 University of Minnesota Press

Minneapolis

London

Published by the University of Minnesota Press
111 Third Avenue South, Suite 290
Minneapolis, MN 55401-2520
http://www.upress.umn.edu

Library of Congress Cataloging-in-Publication Data

Silva, Denise Ferreira da.
    Toward a global idea of race / Denise Ferreira da Silva.
        p.   cm. — (Borderlines ; 27)
    Includes bibliographical references and index.
    ISBN-13: 978-0-8166-4919-8 (hc : alk. paper)
    ISBN-13: 978-0-8166-4920-4 (pb : alk. paper)
    1. Race relations.   2. Globalization—Social aspects.   I. Title.
    HT1521.S47 2007
    305.8—dc22
                                                    2006030304

Printed in the United States of America on acid-free paper

The University of Minnesota is an equal-opportunity educator and employer.

15 14 13 12 11 10   10 9 8 7 6 5 4 3 2

Contents

BORDERLINES

Acknowledgments

I have been very fortunate in receiving support as I wrote this book. I would not have completed the research and the writing of this book without financial and institutional support. The Ford Foundation (through the LASPAU Afro-Brazilian Studies Doctoral Scholarship), the University of Pittsburgh (through the Minority Fellowship Program and the Andrew Mellon Predoctoral Fellowship), and Hartwick College (through the James Jimeson Teaching Fellowship Program) provided the necessary resources for preparing this work as a dissertation. The University of California–San Diego's Faculty Career Development Program, the University of California Humanities Research Institute, and the Ford Foundation (through the Research-in-Residence Group "Re-Shaping the Americas") provided the necessary financial and institutional conditions for turning the dissertation into a book. The Department of African and African-American Studies of Yale University provided access to much-needed secondary and primary materials housed at the Beinecke Library.

Throughout these several years, many people provided invaluable intellectual, institutional, and personal support: Asale Ajani, Pal Alhuwalia, Adrienne Andrews, George R. Andrews, Doug Armato, Ayşegul Baykan, Patrick Bellegarde-Smith, Vera Benedito, Lauren Berlant, Kim Butler, Lisa Cacho, Hazel Carby, Drucilla Cornell, David Covin, Rod Ferguson, John French, Peter Fry, Rosemary George, Jon Goldberg-Hiller, Ted Gordon, Susan Gotsch, Greg Grandin,

James Green, Charlie Hale, Michael Hanchard, Angela Harris, Burkhart Holzner, Lisa Iglesias, May Joseph, Grace Kim, Nicole King, Vera Kutzinsky, David Lehman, Lisa Lowe, John Markoff, John Marquez, John Marx, Renisa Mawani, Michael Mitchel, Margareth Montoya, Stewart Motha, Athena Mutua, Mieko Nishida, Kate O'Donnell, Colin Perrin, Keisha-Khan Perry, Josh Price, Seth Racusen, Andrew Stein, Mick Taussig, Adam Thurschwell, Frank Valdez, Joao Vargas, Robert Westley, Tiffany Willoughby-Herard, Lisa Yoneyama, Iris Marion Young, and Abebe Zegeye. I thank Avery Gordon, Ray Allen, and Carrie Mullen for their faith in this project from the very beginning; David Campbell for supporting this project; David Theo Goldberg for pushing me to write the book I could; and Doug Armato for taking the risk to publish it.

My work is a bit less than, a bit more than, and the sum of everything I have learned from my teachers. I thank Roland Robertson for subtle and generous intellectual guidance, trust, and friendship, and Carlos Hasenbalg and Yvonne Maggie for everything and forever. My work has also (in no small measure) been affected by the rare intellectuals I have met along the way: I acknowledge Cedric Robinson for his radical intellect and generous spirit, Sherene Razack for a sharp intellect in the service of social justice, Peter Fitzpatrick for a cutting-edge intellectual craft dedicated to pressing political questions, Mike Shapiro for his truly revolutionary intellectual drive, and Tayyab Mahmud for his friendship, support, and passionate commitment to the collective project of global justice. Without Tayyab and Mike, this book would never have been.

At the University of California–San Diego, I have had the privilege to encounter an amazing staff and student body. I acknowledge the Ethnic Studies Department staff—Jackie, Patty, Juanita, Noe, Theresa, Bill, and Yolanda—for helping me navigate institutional waters. Very special thanks to our undergraduate and graduate students (especially Theo, Jore, Nga Miget, Cecilia, and Madel) who daily remind me of the ethical and political stakes of any intellectual enterprise. I thank Julie Hua, Neda Atanaso, Emily Cheng, and Jinah Kim for reading and commenting on early versions of the manuscript. My colleagues at UCSD have made this an exciting intellectual space, both in Ethnic Studies and beyond. Very special thanks to Liza Park and David Pellow for their principled support, to Ross Frank for generously reorienting me when I felt lost in the institutional maze, to Jane Rhodes for her wise words and gentle soul, to Charles Briggs for home fires and intellectual nourishment, and to Yen Le Espiritu for holding my heart as she reminded me of the reasons why we do this work.

Throughout these many years, I was fortunate to count on folks who provided emotional haven. I am forever grateful to Philip Mabry, who kept me reaching for clarity and conciseness while I wrote the dissertation that is the basis of this book, and whose love and friendship held me through the most difficult moments. Special thanks to Paula Chakravarty and Gianpaolo Barocchi for their radical hearts; to Veronique Voruz and Stewart Motha for making London much more than an intellectual home; to Brett St. Louis for reminding me to remember to look forward to looking back; to Silvia Del Cid, Clara Mantini-Briggs, Oyèrónké Oyěwěùmi, and Boatema Boateng, for being, doing, and saying all those things big sisters are, do, and say; and to my little sisters, Marcia Lima and Laura Moutinho, for not letting me go even after so many years away. As I prepared the final versions of this manuscript, I received a rare gift: my life and intellectual partner, Mark Harris, came home at last.

I am so lucky for having my brother Denis, who keeps the best of both of us, and for his children, Daniel, Lucas, and Ilka Maria, who bear my hope. From my parents, Maria Amélia Ferreira da Silva and José Araújo da Silva, comes the force that produced the following pages. Mãe and Pai, I thank you for this gift by dedicating it to you.

Preface: Before the Event

Our generation died when our fathers was born.
— BRUNO, BLACK MALE, AGE 18 (MID-1990s)

That moment . . . between the release of the trigger and the fall of another black body, of another brown body, and another . . . haunts this book. What is there to do? To capture, to resignify as one remembers, reconfigures, and disassembles what lies *before* those elusive moments. Perhaps if one formulates questions, names a problem. Which accounts have come together? When did it become a matter of course—a scientific truth—a fact of global existence that generations died sometime in the early 1960s? How did so many generations die when I was born? Who died? Why? There are too many answers to these questions. Just listen . . . read me. . . .

I am dead.

You are black and young. You live in a neighborhood where crime thrives. We take guns out of the streets, arrest dangerous criminals. You happen to live in a place that has the highest rates of homicides and rapes. We do our job right. We approached your building, you looked suspicious; we stopped, got out of our cars with our guns, and told you to put your hands up. We shot. We are the police. We have been very well trained to do our jobs.

I am an immigrant. I work. I have my papers. I live here because it is cheap. I belong to an African elite family. Why have you killed me?

You are black, male, and young. We do not know about African elites. In Africa blacks live in huts, hunting and gathering during the day, eating and chanting at night, killing each other all the time. No tomorrow. You are better off here. Why are you dying? You are black and young; you are in jail or on probation. The liberals say that America is a racist society. They say that black and brown people are either totally out of jobs or concentrated in the lowest-paying ones; they say employers will not hire young black males. You are the underclass: people without a future, people who do not know how to behave properly because the institutions—families, businesses, churches, and so on—have left the ghettos with the middle class, who took advantage of affirmative action to take better jobs and find better places to live. You deal drugs. You are a rapist. You are a criminal. You may even be a terrorist. We will keep you off the streets. If we do not arrest you, we will fire at you, as many bullets as necessary.

I am Fulani.

You are in America now. This is not Asia or Africa. Here it is different. Some radicals say that people like you have no chance. You are black. We do not like blacks. They say that America is the land of white supremacy. It is not just that we will not hire you. You help us to create a bond among white Americans. You make the system work.

But if I do that . . . why kill me? If you just keep me in the ghetto, if I don't have a decent school, a decent-paying job, welfare rights. You have all the answers. You know me. Why do you still need to kill me? Isn't being white enough?

Being white has never been enough. Not without being black.

I was dead before my father was born. Why me?

In this book, I introduce an engagement with the knowledge apparatus—the scientific tools of racial knowledge—that produces the subject of this question. Radically departing from the prevailing ways in which we understand racial subjection, it provides a reformulation of the figure at the center of modern ethical accounts, the notion of *homo modernus,* that is, the global/historical consciousness. Against the assumption that the historical constitutes the sole ontological context, I examine how the tools of nineteenth-century scientific projects of knowledge produced the notion of the

racial, which institutes the global as an ontoepistemological context—
a productive and violent gesture necessary to sustain the post-
Enlightenment version of the Subject as the sole self-determined
thing. While this statement refigures, as it reconstitutes, the whole
field of modern representation, its most immediate effect is to demonstrate how the knowledge arsenal, which now governs the global
(juridic, economic, and moral) configuration, institutes racial subjection as it presupposes and postulates that the elimination of its
"others" is necessary for the realization of the subject's exclusive
ethical attribute, namely, self-determination.

Why and how is exposed throughout this book as I review how
I have excavated modern representation as I have sought—against
self-righteous denials of its ontological irrelevance—to capture the
productive role the racial plays in post-Enlightenment conditions.
Each part of the book describes a particular moment of this undertaking. First, I consider its context of emergence, the unresolved ontological problem that haunted modern philosophy from the early
seventeenth century until the early nineteenth century, which was
to protect *man,* the rational being, from the constraining powers of
universal reason. This reading reveals that it was accomplished with
the writing of the subject as a historical, self-determined thing—a
temporary solution consolidated only in the mid-nineteenth century,
when man became an object of scientific knowledge. Second, my
analysis of the regimen of production of the racial shows how the
sciences of man and society tackled this founding ontological problem by deploying racial difference as a constitutive human attribute.
This solution institutes the core statement of racial subjection: while
the tools of universal reason (the "laws of nature") produce and
regulate human conditions, in each global region it establishes mentally (morally and intellectually) distinct kinds of human beings,
namely, the self-determined subject and its outer-determined others,
the ones whose minds are subjected to their *natural* (in the scientific
sense) conditions. Precisely this statement, I argue, informs the core
argument of the sociology of race relations, that is, the causes of
the subordination of the others of Europe reside in their physical
and mental (moral and intellectual) characteristics and the postulate that the solution to racial subjection requires the elimination
of racial difference. Finally, my analysis of its effects of signification shows how this statement and the scientific tools that sustain it

would inform the prevailing constructions of the U.S. and Brazilian subjects. In these writings, historical and scientific symbolic tools both produce the national subject as a self-determined being and circumscribe the subaltern (outer-determined) moral region inhabited by the non-European members of the national polity.

Behind this book is the desire to comprehend why and how, after a century of moral refutation of statements that deny it any role in modern existence, the most consistent effect of the racial seems to govern unchallenged the contemporary global configuration. I hope my critique of modern representation demonstrates that the political force of the racial resides in the fact that it consistently (re)produces the founding modern ontological statement. Each deployment of the racial consistently articulates man's unique attribute, self-determination, as each brings into existence, and disavows, that which signifies "other"-wise, announcing its necessary elimination. Because the prevailing account of racial subjection also follows this ontological mandate, it is not surprising that today it is deployed to explain away the violent deaths of people of color, as endless social scientific evidence renders them not only expected (as the outcome of juridical and economic exclusion) but also justified (as the forecasted end of the trajectory of an outer-determined consciousness). I hear the question, How does social scientific knowledge justify the murder of people of color? My reply is, How does its arsenal explain it? I offer the following pages as a provisional answer to both questions.

Glossary

When describing my analysis of the trajectory of the racial, I use terms already available in the literature and introduce new ones. Below I provide brief definitions for the latter in the hope that they will make this book more accessible. The reader should feel free to revisit these brief definitions any time he or she finds it helpful.

affectability: The condition of being subjected to both natural (in the scientific and lay sense) conditions and to others' power

affectable "I": The scientific construction of non-European minds

analytics of raciality: The apparatus of knowledge manufactured by the sciences of man and society (see Silva 2001)

history (the field): The region of modern knowledge that assumes time as the privileged ontoepistemological dimension, that is, as in history and the humanities

interiorized nomos: Formulations that state that reason is an exterior regulator that operates from the confines of the rational mind

interiorized poesis: Philosophical formulations that describe reason as the productive force that operates first and foremost from the confines of the rational mind

modern text (historical, national, and scientific text): A term used here to capture the specifically modern economy of signification

productive nomos: The conception of reason that describes it as the producer or regulator of the universe

scene of regulation: The account of how reason performs its sovereign role as a regulating power

scene of representation: The account of how reason performs its sovereign role as a productive power

science (the field): The region of modern knowledge that posits space as the privileged ontoepistemological dimension, that is, as in disciplines such as classical physics and chemistry

stage of exteriority: The mode through which scientific knowledge describes the setting of natural phenomena

stage of interiority: The setting in which philosophy (as well as history and other humanities disciplines) places human phenomena

strategy of engulfment: The scientific concepts that explain other human conditions as variations of those found in post-Enlightenment Europe

strategy of intervention: The methods, techniques, and procedures of the sciences of man and society, highlighting how they apprehend other modes of human existence as variations of post-Enlightenment conditions

strategy of particularization: The categories of human beings deployed by the sciences of man and society

transcendental poesis: Hegel's rewriting of reason as a transcendental force

transparency thesis: The ontoepistemological assumption governing post-Enlightenment thought

transparent "I": Man, the subject, the ontological figure consolidated in post-Enlightenment European thought

universal nomos: The first, nineteenth-century, physics conception of reason as the exterior regulator of the universe

universal poesis: The formulation of reason as the sovereign interior producer of the universe

Introduction: A Death Foretold

Not only can man's being not be understood without madness, it would not be man's being if it did not bear madness within itself as the limit of his freedom.

— JACQUES LACAN, *ÉCRITS*

What does Nietzsche's madman already know when he yells, "I seek God"? What does he mean when he says that the "murder" of God unleashed a history "higher than all history hitherto?" Why does he ask, "Are we not straying as through an infinite nothing?" and "Is not night continually closing in on us?"[1] What he knows—and what his listeners do not care to hear—is this: that the great accomplishment, the culmination of the victorious trajectory of reason that instituted man, the Subject, also foreshadowed his eventual demise. He knows that the philosophical conversation that instituted Man at the center of modern representation also released powerful weapons that threatened his most precious attribute. Why? Because that which falls prey to Reason by becoming its object has no place in the realm of Freedom.

While Nietzsche's madman recognizes that the arsenal that manufactured the transparent "I" threatened his freedom, he seems to ignore that reason, the powerful force that signaled that man had gone beyond the horizon of his finite existence, produces more than a limited human being. For this productive "Will to Truth" authorizes the "creation" of various and diverse kinds of human beings, as it has instituted subjects that stood differentially before universality when it deployed the powerful weapon, the concept of the racial, which manufactured both man and his "others" as subjects that gaze on the horizon of their finite existence. Many contemporary critics of modern thought, like the madman, show a limited engagement with modern thought when ignoring the role the racial has played in manufacturing man. From the other side of the critical terrain, contemporary race theorists also provide a partial critique when inquiring into how the productive narratives of science and history have consistently contained the others of Europe outside the trajectory of the subject that emerged in post-Enlightenment Europe. None, I think, engage the task at hand, which is to consider how both productive narratives—History and Science—of modern representation have worked together to institute the place of the subject. Put differently, in neither stream does the analysis of the racial guide a critique of the whole field of modern representation.

Why undertake such an insane task? the reader may ask. Why return to old moral and intellectual anxieties? My answer is simple: I find no moral or intellectual ease in quick dismissals of the racial as a scientific concept. I am convinced that the most crucial challenge for critics of modern thought requires displacing history's privileged ontoepistemological standing by engaging with science as the proper domain for the production of the truth of man. What is required, I think, is a radical gesture that clears up a critical position by displacing transparency, the attribute man has enjoyed since his institution as the sole self-determined being; consequently, it also requires creating a critical arsenal that identifies science and history as moments in the production of man without rehearsing either the logic of discovery or the thesis of transparency.

What the reader will find in the following pages is my attempt to meet this challenge, that is, a critique of modern representation guided by the desire to comprehend the role the racial plays in modern thought. I trace various philosophical, scientific, and national statements to identify the signifying strategies that have produced both man and his others. In other words, I provide a mapping of the *analytics of raciality:* a description of its context of emergence, its conditions of production, and the effects of signification of the conceptual arsenal generated in scientific projects that sought to discover the truth of man. In tracing the analytics of raciality, I identify the productivity of the racial and how it is tied to the emergence of an ontological context—globality—that fuses particular bodily traits, social configurations, and global regions, in which human difference is reproduced as irreducible and unsublatable. With this, I challenge the ontological privilege accorded to historicity and offer an account of modern representation that refigures the subject as *homo modernus*. That is, I demonstrate how the productive weapons of reason, the tools of science and history, institute both man and his others as global-historical beings.

Initially, I began this project because of my dissatisfaction with the way the sociology of race relations "explains" racial subjection. The matter became all the more urgent to me when I realized how the sociological account of racial subjection continues to govern the contemporary global configuration: cultural difference, the mode of representing human difference presupposed and (re)produced by the sociology of race relations, has become the obvious basis for framing demands for global justice and for punishing the global subaltern as well. From my desire to understand the conditions of emergence of this double-edged weapon, and seeking to avoid rehearsing the dominant ideology thesis, I have generated an account of racial subjection, which can no longer be distinguished from global subjection, that refuses to either resurrect the (universal) subject or write its others as dormant, innocent, particular (historical) beings. Instead, I argue that the markers of the death of man—the proliferating subaltern (racial, ethnic, postcolonial) "ontologies and epistemologies"—indicate how the powers of the subject remain with us, that the strategies of the modern Will to Truth, the tools of science and history, remain the productive weapons of global subjection.

THE BURIAL GROUNDS

St. Anselm's "ontological argument" goes more or less like this: if a supreme, infinite and eternal, perfect being can be conceived, and if God is an infinitely and eternally perfect being, God must exist. Even before the first signs of its demise, however, the subject—the self-determined being that would finally occupy the seat of "perfection" at the close of the eighteenth century—could never be described in the same way. Although self-evidence would become man's exclusive attribute, neither infinity nor eternity could be ascribed to him precisely because he is thoroughly a worldly, global, finite being. And yet, when the rumors of his death began to be heard, many seemed taken by surprise, as if they had forgotten their inheritance. Following the demise of the divine author and ruler in late eighteenth-century Europe, as the madman laments, should we not expect that a lesser entity would eventually share in the same fate? For one thing, the philosophical statements that transformed reason from an exclusive attribute of the mind into the sovereign ruler of science and history—the sole determinant of truth and freedom—situated this process entirely within the spatial and temporal borders of post-Enlightenment Europe. Furthermore, although it has been said that the process that found completion with the realization of man's transcendental "essence" has always already comprehended other modes and moments of being human, never and nowhere, the apostles of reason proclaimed, has a figure akin to man ever existed. Hence, if the Subject, the thing that actualizes reason and freedom, had been born somewhere in time, would it not also eventually die?

What was probably less self-evident, perhaps, was that the subject's passing would not result in its complete annihilation. I am not referring here to how the former private holdings of the subject, Truth and Being, were being invaded by its others, because it was precisely their "fragmentation" that led many observers to announce his death. What has yet to be acknowledged, however, is how this invasion belies the productive powers of the very tools that carved and instituted the place of the subject. To wit: "learning" about his passing in college in the 1980s, I was annoyed by the nostalgic accounts of that unseemly and untimely death. The metanarratives of the subject seemed too far removed from what was at stake in my corner of the globe. Freedom and reason had an immediate significance that seemed lost in most accounts of his passing. I could not quite comprehend the relevance of this loss for those of us engaged in the struggle to overthrow a nineteen-year-old military dictatorship in Brazil. I was young then. Also young were the transformations accompanying the announcement of the subject's death. And what we did not immediately realize was how this Brazilian moment was part of an event unfolding in so many elsewheres. Lyotard's (1984) crisis of the metanarratives of Western culture and Vattimo's (1992) announcement of the "end of modernity" were playing out everywhere: black activists in Rio, along with graffiti artists in New York, First Nation leaders in Vancouver, and people of color elsewhere had somehow changed knowledge in its production and circulation; black feminist writings in the United States were advancing new statements of "truth" and "being," challenging scientific and literary canons while defending the validity of their local narratives (Carby 1887; Collins 1989; Wall 1991); hip-hop artists, rappers, and break dancers, in addition, had surely participated in bringing about the loss of culture's "integrative" role; in "looking to getting paid" (Kelley 1997), they commodified culture, helping to rewrite the logic of capitalism (Jameson 1991) and the grounds for knowledge (Lyotard 1984). We had something to do with the crisis of science; we, the others of man, were upsetting history: our words and deeds unleashed the predicament of the "modern order."

In seeking to comprehend this Global event, however, writers of postmodernity and globalization could only announce the death of the subject.[2] Not surprisingly, social analysts described these circumstances as the onset of a new site of political struggle—the politics of representation, that is, the struggle for the recognition of cultural difference—that registered the demise of the metanarratives of reason and history that compose modern representation. Looking back, it seems a matter of course that, in reading this event as a proliferation of smaller "reasons" and "histories," social analysts would describe it in terms of the ascension of culture. After all, culture was the one thing they had ascribed to these suddenly speaking others, the peoples formerly described as lacking reason and placed outside history. Expectedly, anthropologists, the manufacturers of culture as a scientific concept, were the first to respond, recognizing the threat to their craft. Some welcomed the crisis as a relief, providing them with an opportunity to rewrite the discipline's project (Marcus and Fisher 1986).[3] Finally, the anthropologist could share her burden with her object: the "natives" of today could and should represent themselves, we were told, and she could finally (critically) inhabit her own position of privilege (Clifford 1988).

The problem, however, was that this epistemological emancipation seemed out of sync with the concept's ontological inheritance. As Lisa Lowe (1996) notes, culture has "become the medium of the *present* [and] the site that mediates the *past,* through which history is grasped as difference, as fragments, shocks, and flashes of disjunction" (6, italics in the original). Nevertheless, the speech of the other could never be a thoroughly *historical* "voicing," because cultural differ- ence is also a product of the scientific tools of reason. Hence, a truly emancipatory recrafting of the cultural also requires a critical engage- ment with how scientific universality institutes spaces of history, a radical move that few seem willing to make. Michael Taussig (1987) captures this necessity when he argues, "With European conquest and colonization, these spaces of death [symbolic spaces instituted by terror and torture] blend into a common pool of key signifiers biding the transforming culture of the conqueror with that of the con- quered" (5). Postmodern anthropologists have succeeded in rewriting culture out of fixity, boundedness, and "ethnographic authority," a move that places the objects of anthropological desire in the comfort- able ontological niche historicity rules, but one that can be celebrated only if one forgets the discipline's complicity, how its tools (concepts, theories, and methods) participated in the production of these "spaces of death."

For most sociologists, on the other hand, the passing of the sub- ject threatened a terrifying ontoepistemological crisis.[4] But, unlike many of their anthropological cousins, most sociologists decided to hold onto the bars of their disciplinary cage, rejecting postmodern descriptions of the demise of the "modern (social or moral) order," that is, the universal-historical order.[5] Not surprisingly, epistemolo- gy and ontology would follow more familiar paths, for the divide here is between competing accounts of the emerging social or moral order, a global order—accounts that produce the world as a small community or a fragmented moral whole. Regardless of the posi- tions taken, however, writers of globalization, global culture, and consumerism would describe a process that echoes Durkheim's ac- count of the emergence of "modern civilization," one tied to the spread of mass media, expanded means of transportation, and grow- ing consumption (Featherstone 1990, 1991). Unlike anthropologists who engaged in a battle to redefine the discipline's project, then, most sociologists held fast to their disciplinary grounds,[6] revisiting debates that seem to belong to a past long gone.

Many of my undergraduate students, some actively involved in the struggle for global justice, stare blankly at my mention of the death of the subject. "The death of whom?" they ask, demanding clarification. After my initial surprise, I usually find myself trying to explain why the political significance of his death derives precisely from the ontoepistemological irrelevance of his death: the subject may be dead, I tell them, but his ghost—the tools and the raw material used in his assemblage—remain with us.

AN UNHOLY GHOST

Each time I attempt to explain to my students how the productive narratives of the subject render his death irrelevant, I become more convinced that the power of cultural difference lies in its reconfiguration of the racial and the nation, concepts that instituted the political subjects described in accounts of postmodernity and globalization.[7] After all, their generation witnessed a return to political economy unleashed by mobilizations against the neoliberal reorganization of the global economy[8] coincident with the institutionalization of postmodern and global accounts of cultural change, as reflected in recent international governmental and nongovernmental organizations' stipulations that multiculturalism and diversity should now constitute the new standard for social justice. What one finds in this new global juridical-moral agenda that gives women's rights and cultural rights the same ethical weight attributed to the original declarations of human rights are not only outlines for government initiatives, such as affirmative action and diversity policies. It also defines an ethical mandate that legal and social reforms be informed by multiculturalism, that is, that public policy include racial and ethnic minorities, not merely juridically and economically, but also as bearers of cultural difference.

What is it that connects those "small [historical] narratives" that now crowd the symbolic postmodern saloon, those whose noisy emergence both announced the fall of the nation and reinstituted it as a political force, if not the laborers that sustain the global economy and those whose traditions are now the new target of global crusaders fighting in the name of freedom and human rights? What is it that links *maquiladora* workers in Tijuana; undocumented immigrants and refugees from Asia, Africa, Latin America, and the Middle East who hang under the high-speed trains that cross Europe; their Mexican counterparts who sneak under barbed wire fences and dodge bullets along the border of the southwest United States; villagers starving in refugee camps in Sudan and Angola; the Palestinian mother mourning the death of another son; black and brown teenagers killed by police officers in Los Angeles, Rio de Janeiro, and Caracas? In exasperation, I ask myself, Why is it not self-evident that, despite the pervasiveness of cultural difference, the racial and the nation still govern the global present precisely because of the way each refers to the ontological descriptors—universality and historicity—resolved in the figure of the Subject?[9]

I contend that we fail to understand how the racial governs the contemporary global configuration because the leading account of racial subjection—the sociohistorical logic of exclusion—(re)produces the powers of the subject by rewriting racial difference as a signifier of cultural difference, an argument I will return to and elaborate in chapter 7. What characterizes this construct is the fact that it presupposes what Foucault (1980) terms the juridical-political conception of power, informing both liberalism and historical materialism, which, I argue, entails a view of subjection (domination or oppression) as exclusion from universality resulting from unbecoming sociohistorical (cultural or historical) strategies motivated by physical (sexual or racial) traits. As a consequence, the racial subaltern is always already inscribed as a historical subject who finally comes into representation as a *transparent "I"* when articulating an emancipatory project. In this way, this formulation rehearses transparency, the modern ontological presupposition, when deploying universality and historicity as the privileged modern ontological descriptors: it suggests that racial emancipation comes about when the (juridical and economic) inclusion of the racial others and their voices (historical and cultural representations) finally realizes universality in postmodern social configurations.

My task in what follows is to demonstrate how this account deploys the authorized modern ontological descriptors—that is, as exclusion from universality and historicity—to construct the racial as an improper aid to otherwise appropriate strategies of power. I also seek to demonstrate how its "explanation" of social subjection merely describes how the racial, along with other social-historical categories, produces exclusion without really explaining how or why it does so. In what follows, I describe this tendency shared by feminist and critical race studies scholarship that has its origin in their reliance on the sociohistorical logic of exclusion and its account of social subjection.

The Bounds of Historicity: Race and Class

In "Race, Articulation, and Societies Structured in Dominance," Stuart Hall ([1980] 1996) advocates the use of Gramsci's conception of social formation in the study of race because it enables an analysis of the "historical specificities" of racism that are lost when the latter is conceived of as a universal and unchanging structure: it enables an examination of how racism functions in different settings with different histories of colonialism and slavery, how it changes in time, and how it operates in tandem with other social relations. More important, this perspective enables one to challenge conventional explanations of the relationship between racism and economic structures by demonstrating, for instance, how the needs of slavery can explain the emergence of attitudes of racial superiority rather than the other way around. In this formulation, racism would no longer be conceived as something that needs to be explained away. Instead, it is recentered as a theoretical device necessary for any analysis of multiracial societies.

Following the spirit of Hall's proposal, critical analysts of racial subjection have produced a significant body of work that, while still tied to the main concepts and formulations of the sociology of race relations, provides a distinctly different approach to racial subjection. Their work does not fall into a particular subdisciplinary field—to be sure, it is consistently interdisciplinary—but it remains sufficiently coherent to be identified as a field of scholarship I call the critical field of racial and ethnic studies (CRES). Michael Omi and Howard Winant's (1994) *Racial Formation in the United States* is by far the watershed intervention in this field. The authors define racial formation as the "socio-historical" process through which racial categories and racial meanings are constantly produced and challenged in ongoing political struggle about how society should be organized, ruled, and represented.[10] "Race," they argue, "is a concept which signifies and symbolizes social conflicts and interests by referring to different types of human bodies"; it is "an unstable and 'decentered' complex of social meanings constantly being transformed by political struggle" (55). To address how race links social structure and representation, the authors introduce the concept of "racial projects," defined as "simultaneously an interpretation, representation or explanation of racial dynamics, and an effort to re-organize or redistribute resources along particular racial lines" (56). That is, racial projects are competing ideologies deployed in the political arena; they also provide the basis for common-sense "racial identification" and explanations for differential positionings in the U.S. social structure.

Though Omi and Winant's historical-materialist rewriting of race as a sociohistorical concept postpones the descriptive manner in which the term is used in the United States, the privileged onto-epistemological status attributed to historicity poses a problem: if every historical (cultural or ideological) principle always interprets something structural, what would a racial project's structural, material referent be?[11] After all, Omi and Winant are not merely stating that race exists solely in the minds of badly educated individuals who misrepresent racial differences or that it is the product of zealous, profit-hungry capitalists. For them, race is a principle of social configuration, a social signifier, a symbolic construct that identifies certain social conditions as "racial formations." My point is this: if racial difference precedes race, the sociohistorical concept, either it is an empirical referent (as construed by quantitative analysts) or it is tied to another signifier. Even as they attempt to avoid it, Omi and Winant construct racial difference as a substantive bodily trait, an empirical (as opposed to material) referent of social signification. Thus, in repeating the ethically correct gesture, that is, in denying race any biological (scientific) soundness, they fail to demonstrate why racial difference, which is already an appropriation of the human body in scientific signification, should constitute a central dimension of social representation.

When incorporated into historical analysis, then, racial difference— otherwise conceived of as ("empty") irrelevant bodily difference— becomes phenomenon: the empirical referent of social scientific signification. And when framed in this way, the critical social analyst, suspicious of empiricism as he or she is, has no other choice than to write the racial as an unbecoming symbolic aid to what are otherwise properly modern (sociohistorical) mechanisms of exclusion from economic and juridical universality. This is evident in Hall's ([1980] 1996) description of race as a qualifier of class: "Race," he argues, "enters into the way black labor, male and female, is distributed as economic agents at the level of economic practices, and the class struggles which result from it; and into the way the fractions of the black laboring classes are reconstituted, through the means of political representation . . . , as political forces in the 'theater of politics'—and the political struggles which result; and the manner in which class is articulated as the collective and individual 'subjects' of emerging ideologies—and the struggles over ideology, culture, and consciousness which result" (55).[12] That is, while no more guilty than other historical theoretical perspectives, historical materialism resists any account of the racial as an inherently modern (post-Enlightenment) strategy of power. The bounds of historicity are similarly evident in Balibar's genealogy of racism, which reduces it to an element of nationalism and class. The author argues that the idea of race, initially a signifier of caste that circulated among the European aristocracy, now circulates among the working classes, where racism "tends to produce . . . the equivalent of a caste closure at least for one part of the working class," providing the "maximum possible closure where social mobility is concerned" (Balibar and Wallerstein 1991, 212). Thoroughly capitalist, from the nineteenth century on, racism would be added to other symbolic mechanisms of class exploitation as an excessive ideological device the dominant class imposed upon the exploited.

What troubles the account of racial subjection informing the CRES project is that its analysis of the racial in post-Enlightenment social configurations simultaneously embraces the post–Second World War moral command to erase it from the modern political lexicon. Because the sociohistorical logic of exclusion assumes that racial difference and the exclusionary symbolic (cultural or ideological) strategies it entails are extraneous to the modern ethical landscape, it can write the racial only as an unbecoming aid to (economic) class subjection. In saying this, it may seem that I have already thrown out the proverbial baby because, rather than joining those who excavate contemporary social configurations to collect specimens of racism, I have decided to engage precisely this "false" (ideological or cultural) construct, racial difference, that critical social analysts disavow by placing scare quotes around the term *race*. I could justify this choice by listing CRES statements, by unpacking arguments, to demonstrate how they repeatedly deploy the underlying account of racial subjection described here. But instead, rather than engage in such a superficial exercise, I seek to demonstrate how this investment in exclusion limits our understanding of how the racial works along with gender, that other crucial critical device also haunted by bodily difference. As I will argue, this follows from feminist scholarship's own investment in the sociohistorical logic of exclusion.

An Odd Coupling: Race and Gender

Feminist scholars have been struggling to develop adequate accounts for how race and gender work together to institute subaltern social subjects.[13] I suspect that part of this difficulty lies in the fact that gender addresses exclusion (from juridical universality) more comfortably than the racial, precisely because of how female subjection is articulated in the founding statements of modern thought:[14] while the female's role in (physical) reproduction would seem to immediately explain her incarceration in domesticity, gender subjection rests on the liberal rewriting of patriarchy as a juridical-moral moment ruled by "natural (divine) law," a political domain subordinated to the "laws of society." From Locke's formulation of the "political society" to Hegel's account of "civil law," patriarchy as a mode of power circumscribes the domestic sphere, where females are locked away, yet within the political body created by the rational political subject, the male owner of property, ruler of the household, and citizen (Pateman 1988). In so articulating the female role, these founding statements postulate female subjection according to (divine) conceptions of the natural and the universal. This notion was subsequently displaced by nineteenth-century articulations of "laws of nature" when reason was consolidated as the privileged ground for modern ontoepistemological accounts. Hence, although the female body would also come under the scrutiny of scientific tools in the nineteenth century, biological difference would remain a secondary basis for gender subjection, that is, though grounded on "naturalization," gender subjection, unlike racial subjection, does not presuppose a scientific account of bodily difference.[15]

For this reason, feminist scholars in the 1960s and 1970s could assume (with moral ease) that sexual difference served as the self-evident universal (empirical) basis for female subjection.[16] However, during the 1980s, at the height of the politics of representation, when feminist scholars deployed "experience" and "difference" to rewrite gender as a sociohistorical category—thereby retrieving it from the dangerously "naturalizing" waters of sexual difference—their project was immediately unsettled by denunciations of gender's own universalizing tendency.[17] Western and non-Western feminists of color refused the absorption of their difference into a universal female experience, insisting that race, class, and culture also be recognized as axes of subjection,[18] a move nicely captured by one of the keenest critics of Anglo-feminism, Chandra Mohanty (1991b), who proclaimed: "I want to recognize and analytically explore the links among the histories and struggles of third world women against racism, sexism, colonialism, imperialism, and monopoly capital. What I am suggesting, then, is an 'imagined community' of third world oppositional struggles, . . . with divergent histories and social locations, woven together by the political threads of opposition to forms of domination that are not only pervasive but also systemic" (4). While relatively brief, then, the trajectory of theorizing gender has covered considerable ground, from the divine and natural category of "woman," which produces the excluded female global subject via naturalization, to the analytic conception of gender, where sociohistorical constructions of difference and experience delimit female exclusion and seek to include female trajectories determined by other exclusionary mechanisms. It has also witnessed a productive debate about the representation of the gendered subaltern subject.

What has yet to be acknowledged, I think, is the troublesome coupling of gender and race, how these principles of social exclusion form a strangely compatible pair: both identify sociohistorical processes, both refer to supplemental cultural or ideological mechanisms that subordinate women and people of color, and each captures a particular way in which women of color experience that subordination. Nevertheless, this match made in patriarchal hell, I argue, has hindered the theoretical labor necessary to capture how they produce the female of color as a subaltern subject.

During the past twenty years or so, a large library has been built by scholars using difference and experience to address the combined effects of race and gender. Few dare to deploy one without gesturing toward the other, for it has become conventional wisdom that neither can adequately capture all dimensions of a subject's sociohistorical trajectory. Even fewer scholars go beyond the assertion that these categories operate as exclusionary principles—that is, most analyses can be catalogued in terms of analyzing the effects of gender on race or of race on gender—for the social trajectories of women of color.[19]

That is, when coupled with gender, race produces additional gender exclusion and, when coupled with race, gender produces additional racial exclusion, and so on.[20]

What I am suggesting is that precisely this sociohistorical logic of exclusion that makes the racial and gender such a suitable pair also hinders our understanding of how gender and race work together to institute a particular kind of subaltern subject. As Joan Scott (1991) argues, the conception of historicity has informed writings of the experience of women, blacks, and homosexuals limits our understanding of the trajectories of these subaltern collectivities. Because most analyses that privilege experience and difference fail to address discursive power, she contends, they reproduce the very logic that instituted the authority of the subject, the epistemological figure against which they write the other in history. Noting that this derives from the separation between language and experience, which leads to the naturalization of the former, she advocates a strategy of historical interpretation that "historicizes the terms by which experience is represented, and so historicizes 'experience' itself" (795). Put differently, the subject's transcendental manta and the subalterns' immanent (naturalized) experience are made of the same "essentialist" threat, for prevailing critical strategies produce the latter as a specimen of the "individual," the liberal-historical being.

Beyond the theoretical quandary the racial creates for contemporary critical analyses drawing from historical materialism—the labor of slaves and indentured workers, for instance, has been considered productive and yet never fully integrated into the historical-materialist arsenal—the most troubling aspect of examinations of the intersection of race, class, and gender is that they deploy these categories as descriptive devices. For this reason, rather than attempting to avoid the accusation of ignoring gender and class by recounting the ways each furthers racial exclusion, I have decided to follow Scott's suggestion. In doing so, however, I will not revisit history to indicate how, in various sociohistorical moments, alone and in combination with class and gender, the racial brings about exclusion from universality. Rather, I seek to engage in the kind of analytical groundwork necessary for a critical account that moves beyond listing how each excludes and, instead, examine how the racial combines with other social categories (gender, class, sexuality, culture, etc.) to produce modern subjects who can be excluded from (juridical) universality without unleashing an ethical crisis. Because a guiding question here is why, despite its moral ban, the racial still constitutes a prolific strategy of power, it is also necessary to chart the symbolic terrain the racial shares with the other tools the narratives of history and science have deployed to carve the place of the subject.

THE SYMBOLIC TRINITY

Which of the two meanings of culture should one employ when analyzing collective practices and products? Should it be the normative meaning, the one that refers to standards and values, products and practices (classical music, the opera, etc.) that distinguish modern culture? Or should it be the descriptive meaning, the one that refers to particularity, which writes a collectivity as a unified (geo-historical) consciousness? Following Bourdieu's (1984) lead, I argue that one can understand the meaning of culture, in either sense, only by engaging the anthropological sense, where one finds that the normative and the descriptive refer to two other concepts with which the cultural shares the task of instituting modern subjects, namely, the racial and the nation. For centuries they have been used to describe human collectives. Nevertheless, as modern signifying devices—as signifiers in the text of science and history—they have a shorter trajectory, one whose pace has increased so dramatically over the last fifty years that it has become difficult to establish their signifying boundaries and combined effects.

Much of what I do in the following chapters, mapping the analytics of raciality, is an attempt to unpack this conceptual mess by delimiting the signifying boundaries of the racial, establishing how it differs from the cultural and the nation by delineating the regions of signification—science and history—in which these modern productive tools thrive. This strategy, a crucial task for any critique of their effects of signification, enables us to trace their post-Enlightenment trajectories. In doing this, I demonstrate how in the mid–nineteenth century, (a) the scientists of man deployed an arsenal that produced self-consciousness as an effect of scientific determinants (the laws of "fecundity" and "heredity") and (b) the nation was consolidated as the concept that instituted modern polities as historical (moral) subjects, that is, as bound by principles expressed in its common language, religion, art, and so on, and how in the twentieth century

(c) the cultural emerged as a scientific concept that wrote the mind as a historical thing, but insofar as it produced moral relief, it did not displace, but actually repeated the effects of signification of the racial (Stocking 1968). In short, because the cultural is neither the racial nor the nation under an assumed name, the ontoepistemological placing of the cultural, in both senses identified by Bourdieu, determines effects of signification that overflow the borders it shares with each.

What makes this critical analytical groundwork necessary is precisely the fact that in the late twentieth century the cultural seems to have displaced the nation and the racial to become the governing political signifier. Prior to this, the racial and the nation guided constructions of the foremost modern political subject, namely, the nation-state, and both were appropriated worldwide by subaltern subjects in transnational and transcontinental alliances against colonialism and imperialism (Von Eschen 1997; Brock and Fuertes 1998). It was not until the late 1960s, however, that the nation would frame projects of racial emancipation. For example, many have identified how the anticolonial wars in Africa influenced the Black Power, Chicano, American Indian, and Asian American (nationalist) movements in the United States, which sought not merely inclusion but a radical transformation of the U.S. social configuration. As far as I am aware, however, no one has asked why the racial could not become the sole basis for an emancipatory project that could, for example, reclaim what Ture and Hamilton ([1967] 1992) refer to as "[black] history and our identity from what must be called cultural terrorism" and "the right to create our own terms through which to define ourselves and our relationship to the society, and to have these terms recognized," which is "the first necessity of a free people, and the first right that any oppressor must suspend" (35). It seems that precisely because these movements aimed beyond inclusion toward that ever-receding promised land of self-determination—that is, transparency—race (the social scientific signifier) could not sustain their projects. Instead, in the 1960s black, Chicano, American Indian, and Asian American activists and intellectuals deployed the nation, the historical signifier, to write the trajectory of the racial subaltern subject as a transparent "I." Whether this was the inevitable course of the racial and the nation it is not clear. But the extent to which they were bound to meet each other in twentieth-century political statements is relevant only because of how short-lived these emancipatory struggles were, joining concepts that refigured different modes of representing modern subjects.[21]

During the next two decades, the cultural would fill in the gaps of earlier nationalist projects, guiding attempts to recuperate the particular "histories" of racial subaltern collectivities. In the 1970s, for instance, U.S. blacks would gesture toward Africans and the black populations of Latin America and the Caribbean, claiming slavery as a common historical past, to manufacture a black "culture" that spread beyond the borders of the United States (Karenga 1993; Asante 1987; and Howe 1998; among others). Facing these sweet gifts of 1960s nationalist struggles, however, was the bitter fate of thriving in a conjuncture that no longer supported "essentialist" projects. In the 1980s, the heyday of the politics of representation—after this nationalist desire had been discarded along with many other promises of the 1960s—the cultural would be consolidated as the racial's historical companion (Gilroy 1993a and 1993b; Baker et al. 1997; Kelley 1997). During those years, cultural politics met innumerable challenges, the most serious of which, multiculturalism, now moves forcefully ahead as it guides the official agenda for global justice.[22] This liberal appropriation of multiculturalism is especially troubling because it embraces the sociohistorical logic of exclusion as the correct account of social (racial, ethnic, gender) subjection and accepts the emergence of claims for recognition of cultural difference as proof of the failure of assimilation (Mabry 1996; Silva 2005): it simultaneously normalizes claims of cultural difference in arguments that are seemingly critical of the earlier project of "assimilation" while retaining the earlier sociology of race relations argument concerning the extraneousness of the others of Europe that the biologic of racial difference is superseded by a sociologic of cultural difference to incarcerate the others of Europe in bounded transparency. As postmodern accounts sent the earlier formulation of the cultural to join the racial in ethical exile, the others of Europe embraced another doomed strategy of emancipation, namely, the project of producing and interpreting crafts that communicate their particular sociohistorical trajectories as subaltern travelers on the road to transparency.

The problem of cultural politics that undermines the postmodern emancipatory agenda is one of correlation: as any number cruncher knows, when two independent variables affect each other, the result of a linear regression is biased. In the same way, the equation of the racial and the cultural undermines cultural politics projects insofar as the effect communicated by both scientific concepts, which produce "meanings and beings" as effects of exterior determination, is oversignified. Therefore, although the postmodern rendering of the cultural has shed its "boundedness and fixity" when used to describe black cultural politics, not only does the old cultural resurface; it also resuscitates racial difference to produce a doubly "fixed" and doubly "bounded"—that is, a doubly determined—black culture. For instance, Gilroy (1993b) identifies this effect in what he calls the "ethno-absolutist" view of black culture.[23] Unfortunately, Gilroy's alternative does not fare any better. His "Black Atlantic," which he offers as an alternate approach to black cultural politics and is based on a transnational, trans-Atlantic, and consistently English-speaking formation, errs in the same (historical) direction. The early twentieth-century black U.S. American male intellectual trans-Atlantic travelers who, according to Gilroy, shared in the "desire to transcend both the structures of the nation state and the constraints of ethnicity and national particularity" (19), seemed to have wished nothing but these very things. In other words, the two trends Gilroy identifies rehearse the central themes of modern representation. I grant that he recognizes that the "politics of fulfillment" houses the "spirit" of the liberal project, namely, juridical universality. But why does he not recognize that his account of "the politics of transfiguration"—which marks "the emergence of qualitatively new desires, social relations, and modes of association within the racial community of interpretation and resistance and between that group and its erstwhile oppressors" (37)—produces a bit more than a transparent "I" in blackface? Without its nicely chosen postmodern or modern Habermasian communicating disguise, how different is his account of black culture compared to those he designates using terms of "cultural insiderism" or "ethnic absolutism"? Not much, I am afraid.

This, I argue, is the effect of the *transparency thesis,* the ontological assumption governing the social descriptors universality and historicity that has survived the death of the subject. The fact that it remains at the core of critical accounts of racial subjection and "post" mappings of the global configuration is clearly reflected in the postmodern refashioning of the cultural. Despite the patronizing project of giving "voice" or "agency" to their object, these anthropologists' intentions have (as always) been good. The critical reassessment of the fixity and boundedness of culture has also deflated the discipline's "ethnographic authority." Nevertheless, the cultural still authorizes (re)writings of the others of Europe, but now as incarcerated subjects of cultural difference.

Because they presuppose the ruling ontological premise, namely, transparency, ethnographic descriptions of the global subaltern as a cultural "other" (re)produce the racial's effect of signification, which is to write all that is particular to post-Enlightenment Europe as a signifier of the subject, the transparent "I." When deployed to address the products and practices of people of color, the cultural produces a kind of transparency that is self-defeating, as is the case with Gilroy's "racial community of interpretation" and its countercultural "politics of transfiguration." No matter how fluid, hybrid, or unbounded, when addressing a collectivity the racial has already inscribed as subaltern, the cultural acquires a descriptive sense that does not and cannot communicate interiority, as is the case with the nation, the historical signifier. It does not and cannot precisely because it remains fully within a scientific (anthropological) terrain of signification. As such, it reinforces the effects of signification of the racial: exterior determination. In short, it cannot institute a transparent (interior/temporal)—that is, self-determined—"I."

Perhaps we are (post)modern in more ways than we care to be. But does this give us license to be careless when specifying how this predicament guides our emancipatory projects? The pressing task, I believe, is to engage the racial as a modern political strategy rather than attempting, once again, to resuscitate the sociohistorical logic of exclusion. There are only so many ways we can recount the mechanisms and effects of exclusion. There are only so many ways to account for the failed emancipatory projects that use race, nation, and culture precisely because we are not quite certain what happens when these notions are deployed separately or in conjunction with one another. Certainly, the writing of racism as a modifier of proper historical (cultural or ideological) strategies of power has been productive. Unfortunately, this formulation retains the sociologic of exclusion, which transformed the exteriority the racial refigures as a scientific device into a substantive (preconceptual, prehistorical) marker of the outsideness of the others of Europe. More critical than this, however, as I argue elsewhere later, is how rendering the racial as a sociohistorical category reproduces the erasures that (trans)formed racial difference into a signifier of cultural difference: it (re)produces non-Europeans as others and (re)identifies the (instinctual, cultural, ideological) exclusionary strategies their presence evokes as extraneous to post-Enlightenment, modern, social (moral) configurations (Silva 2001).

For this reason, the necessary step for comprehending the present global configuration—necessary also for addressing the predicament of contemporary ("postmodern") critics of modern thought and race theorists—is to unpack how the racial, the cultural, and the nation institute modern subjects: by charting their contexts of emergence, describing their conditions of production, and delimiting their signifying effects. We need to abandon constructions of the racial as an add-on, an unbecoming device that reinforces the constitutive effects of otherwise appropriate modern political strategies, as it appears in Balibar's (1991) formulation of racism, which he defines as "a supplement internal to nationalism, *always in excess of it,* but always indispensable to its constitution and yet always insufficient to achieve its project" (Balibar and Wallerstein 1991, 54, my emphasis). For Balibar, racism and nationalism are principles that institute political collectivities through the binary of inclusion-exclusion: his formulation of the "historical reciprocity" of these principles constructs racism as enabling the constitution of the internal and external boundaries of a collectivity unified by nationalist ideologies and practices. However, foreclosed in this formulation—to which my summary does not do justice—are questions such as: Why should nationalism be supplemented by racism? What is it about the nation and the racial that makes them suitable companions? Why have they worked together even in circumstances where racial difference does not exclude, where the racial "other" is a bona fide national "same"? Why does the cultural so easily cross the borders it shares with both?

The relevance of these questions cannot and should not be dismissed in hoping for that moment of moral bliss, before and beyond the missteps of racism, when transparency will describe a social configuration where the racial no longer operates. Despite its laudable sentiments, this hope prevents our understanding the conditions of production of today's global subjects, of how they come into being. For we already know that the concepts used to describe them—the racial, the nation, and the cultural—fulfill the same signifying task of producing collectivities as particular kinds of modern subjects. Each, however, has very distinct effects of signification: (a) the racial produces modern subjects as an effect of exterior determination, which institutes an irreducible and unsublatable difference; (b) the nation produces modern subjects as an effect of historical (interior) determination, which assumes a difference that is resolved in an unfolding (temporal) transcendental essence; but (c) the cultural is more complex in its effects because it can signify either or both. In Bourdieu's second sense, the descriptive, the cultural is almost indistinguishable from the nation because it assumes that a "collective consciousness" is represented in artistic, religious, and other products. In the first sense, however, the cultural restores the racial in that the distinction between "high culture" and "low culture" presupposes "civilization," initially deployed by the sciences of man and society—the anthropology and sociology—to write the particularity of post-Enlightenment Europe (Elias 1982). The cultural, I repeat, is not a disguise of the nation, nor is it the racial under an assumed name, no matter how much moral relief may be found in replacing race with ethnicity; yet it reproduces the effects of signification of both. But this is something many of us ignore because we hope that the racial is politically relevant only because it operates as an added principle of exclusion in an otherwise thoroughly transparent social configuration governed by universality and historicity.

WHENCE THE RACIAL?

The Subject is dead! we have been told. So why is its most effective strategy of power still with us? The central task of this book is to map the analytics of raciality, to chart the contexts of emergence, to describe conditions of production, and to delimit the effects of signification of the arsenal that institutes self-consciousness as an effect of exterior (outer) determination. Although this road follows but one moment of the trajectory of the subject, the sole effect of interior (self-) determination, we will identify the most prolific modern strategies of power deployed to delimit its place, and this will show why its death, which has so many times been foretold, has not resulted in its complete annihilation. Hence, my first step is to elaborate my argument about how transparency hinders our understanding of racial subjection as a prelude to charting the context of the emergence of the analytics of raciality, of excavating the modern philosophical grounds that generated the statements used to assemble the transparent "I," the figure at the center of modern representation.

In Part 1 I introduce the idea of the *modern text* as an analytic strategy to describe modern representation as an ontoepistemological context composed of signifying strategies produced by two fields, namely, science and history. My excavation of the founding statements of modern thought identifies philosophical formulations that reproduce Descartes's outline of self-consciousness as the only existing being to enjoy self-determination—the ability to alone decide on its essence or existence—which requires the bold articulation and disavowal of the ontoepistemological relevance of extended things, that is, bodies. I then identify how this formulation of self-determination is threatened when two framers of modern science deploy a version of reason, *universal nomos,* the constraining ruler of the "world of things," that opens up the possibility of rewriting man as subjected to outer determination, namely, as an affectable thing. In seventeenth- and eighteenth-century statements, I identify the universal *nomos* and the *universal poesis* that emerged in social ontologies, which describe reason as the regulative and productive force, respectively. These are evident in the efforts of Locke, Leibniz, Kant, and Herder to (re)present the "I" as a self-determined being, seeking to postpone the threat introduced by the scientific rendering of universality. In their writing I identify statements that produce two scenes of reason, two ontological accounts of how it plays its universal regulative or productive role in the "world of men": the *scene of regulation,* which introduces universality as the juridical descriptor, and the *scene of representation,* which introduces historicity as a moral descriptor.

I argue that these statements that articulate and disavow extended things protect the mind's self-determination by designing two stages—interiority and exteriority—in which reason plays its sovereign role: in the *stage of exteriority* it operates as the exterior ruler of affectable things, and in the *stage of interiority* it is the force that guides the production of human knowledge and culture. Although these statements, most evident in Kant's notion of the Transcendental and Herder's formulation of the Historical, sought to secure interiority, the private holding man has always occupied in Western thought, none resolved the threat introduced in Descartes's founding statement that grounded the mind's ontoepistemological privilege on universal reason. It was only with Hegel's intervention, which consolidated modern representation, that the full delineation of self-consciousness resolved this threat. The key figure in this formulation is "Spirit," the transcendental (interior or temporal) "I," which guides his version of the play of reason, *transcendental poesis,* where I find the framing of the *transparency thesis,* the ontoepistemological assumption guiding modern representation. That is, Hegel refashioned the Subject as the transparent "I," the one whose emergence he located in post-Enlightenment Europe, where Spirit completed its self-actualizing trajectory. It is this tracing of subsequent refashionings of self-consciousness, and each version of universal reason this entails, that allows me to delineate the field of modern representation, the stage of exteriority, the context of emergence of the analytics of raciality—in sum, the arsenal that, in the nineteenth century, would finally write self-consciousness as an effect of the tools of scientific knowledge.

In Part II I identify another version of universal reason, *productive nomos,* introduced by the science of life, the project of knowledge that becomes a central element of the regimen of production of the analytics of raciality. Specifically, I show how it inaugurates the possibility of refashioning self-consciousness in the stage of exteriority when it describes how universal reason plays its regulative and productive role in a particular domain of nature—namely, living nature—that man shares with other living things. My focus here is on early scientific projects—the science of man, anthropology, and race relations—that deploy the tools of science to uncover the truth of man. Following the lead of the science of life, each deploys an arsenal that produces two kinds of modern subjects by tying certain bodily and mental configurations to different global regions: the subject of transparency, for whom universal reason is an interior guide, and subjects of affectability, for whom universal reason remains an exterior ruler. From its initial deployment in the science of man to race relations' rendering of the racial as a sociological concept, which introduces the sociologics of racial subjection, I trace the assemblage of the arsenal that describes the trajectory of the others of Europe as a movement toward obliteration. Put differently, my reading indicates that raciality, as a tool of productive *nomos*, constitutes an effective tool precisely because of the way its main signifiers—the racial and the cultural—provide an account of human difference, an account in which particularity remains irreducible and unsublatable, that is, one that would not dissipate in the unfolding of "Spirit." My reading also suggests that this arsenal, which belongs in the stage of exteriority, can no longer postpone the threat posed by universal reason, that it necessarily produces modern subjects as coexisting and relational beings. In doing so, the analytics of raciality institutes another ontological context, globality, in which the particularity of the mental and social configurations found in post-Enlightenment Europe can be sustained only in reference to those existing in other regions of the globe.

In Part III I turn to the analysis of the effects of signification of raciality, describing how it produces modern subjects. To do so I select those statements that sought to write early postcolonial polities—the United States and Brazil—as modern political subjects and identify strategies that belong to both ontological contexts, namely, historicity and globality. My reading of statements about the U.S. and Brazilian nations deployed between the 1890s and the 1930s indicates that the place of the national (interior/temporal) subject is established by the apparatus of the analytics of raciality to ensure that the affectable others of Europe inhabiting these polities do not determine their global position. In other words, I show how the racial subaltern subject is placed before (in front of) the ethical space inhabited by the proper national subject. In the United States, articulations of racial difference produce the particularity of the U.S. nation as a manifestation of a European (liberal) desire, and I trace how these articulations produce the logic of exclusion as a mode of racial subjection that places Indians, blacks, and Asians as subjects not encompassed by the principles that govern the U.S. social configuration, that is, universality and self-determination. In Brazil, miscegenation produces a national subject haunted by a desire for an always elusive object, namely, Europeanness (whiteness), and in my reading I indicate how the deployment of miscegenation as a historical signifier enables the writing of the Brazilian subject, the subject of democracy, against scientific statements of its inviability. From this solution emerges a mode of racial subjection governed by a logic of obliteration that cannot be apprehended using the prevailing sociologic of exclusion precisely because the latter is predicated upon the annihilation of raciality for the (re)institution of a modern transparent social configuration. By showing how scientific and historical strategies are appropriated in texts that institute both the national subject and its subaltern others, I then indicate how the political subjects addressed in accounts of postmodernity and globalization are constituted by the same tools that instituted the deceased subject. In doing so, this mapping of the analytics of raciality refashions the figure of the modern subject as *homo modernus,* the effect of signifiers that refer to the two ontological contexts—namely, historicity (the one figured in the nation) and globality (the one instituted by the racial)—that constitute modern (post-Enlightenment) representation.

1

The Transparency Thesis

They seem to me people of such innocence that, if we understood them and they understood us, they would become Christian soon; for they do not have nor understand any faith, it seems to me; and, therefore, if the banished, who will remain here, learn well their language and understand them, I have no doubt, according to the holy desire of Your Highness, they will become Christian and believe in Holy Faith, . . . for it is sure this is a good and humble people, which will absorb anything given to them; and Our Lord gave them good bodies and good faces, as to good men, and he, who brought us here, I believe, was not without a cause.

— PERO VAZ DE CAMINHA,

"CARTA A EL-REI DOM MANUEL"

Not the conversion of "such" peoples' souls, it would turn out, but the cataloguing of their minds, undertaken about three hundred years later, produced the strategies of power governing contemporary global conditions. Early colonial texts, like Pero Vaz de Caminha's letter of 1 May 1500 to King D. Manuel, are mostly tales of conquest: letters and diaries that provide the European traveler's point of view; write the "native" first as "innocent" and "brute," then as "irrational" and "savage"; and narrate the mishaps of the trips, the beauty and wealth of the newly appropriated royal lands, and the need to teach natives not to "reveal their *vergonhas* [sexual organs] with the same innocence they show their faces" and how to fear God. Each account narrates a political event, a double movement,

1

dislocation and engulfment, in which conqueror's and native's "be-ings" emerge as subjected to the divine author and ruler. Later ac-counts of European conquest would describe this political event as a moment in time, a fact of history. Nevertheless, Europe's conquest of the American continent has been first and foremost a spatial, that is, a global event—the dislocation of Europeans to the Americas and other parts of the planet and the engulfment of natives, their lands, and the resources of those lands. For this reason, because European juridical and economic appropriation of other lands and resources has from the outset required the symbolic appropriation of natives, the indigenous peoples, one cannot ignore that this beginning is al-ways already mediated by a rearrangement of the modern grammar and the deployment of projects of knowledge that address man as an object, which took place over the first three hundred years follow-ing the "first encounter." For it was only in the post-Enlightenment period, when reason finally displaced the divine ruler and author to become the sovereign ruler of man, that human difference became the product of a symbolic tool, the concept of the racial, deployed in projects to "discover" the truth of man, which (trans)formed the globe itself into a modern ontological context.

Before describing how I have charted modern representation to identify the context of emergence, conditions of production, and ef-fects of signification of the racial, in this chapter I indicate how the sociohistorical logic of exclusion splits the field of critique of mod-ern ontology into two halves: postmodern interventions and criti-cal racial theorizing. Both postmodern critics of modern thought and critical racial theorists, I think, engage the crucial challenge of describing how global subaltern subjects emerge in representation. Nevertheless, although they correctly address the symbolic as a privi-leged moment of modern power, the sociohistorical logic of exclu-sion prevents them from thoroughly unpacking modern mechanisms of signification and subjectification, a necessary move if one seeks to understand why an ethical crisis does not ensue from the consistent, numerous, and recurrent indications that the "others of Europe" are not comprehended by universality and self-determination, the prin-ciples governing post-Enlightenment social configurations. For it is because this prevailing account of racial subjection retains the pre-supposition that the racial is extraneous to modern thought that it prevents these proverbial twins from moving toward the point where they meet. Although this fracture could be attributed to theoretical-methodological differences, it seems to me that it reflects a profound similarity, which is the fact that, even in postmodern critical analyses that challenge transparency, the sociohistorical logic of exclusion (re)produces the post-Enlightenment version of the subject.

Throughout the last five centuries or so, Europeans and their descendants have crossed the globe over and over again appropriating lands, resources, and labor. No doubt these dislocations have instituted the global economic and juridical formations historical and social scientific literatures apprehend with the concepts of colonialism, imperialism, modernization, and globalization. Although we know so much about the sociohistorical determinants of racial subjection, we are at pains to describe how precisely the racial institutes the others of Europe as subaltern subjects. Failing to grasp how the racial produces modern subjects (even though we have no doubt that it does so), I think, results from how we know it. For underlying the sociohistorical logic of exclusion is the dismissal of the project of knowledge usually termed "race theorizing," "scientific racism," or "race theories" and the insistence on attributing the notion of race to the fact that, in nineteenth-century Europe,[1] science fell prey to "subjective" (psychological, cultural, ideological) elements, anachronistic and unbecoming "beliefs" or "prejudices" it erroneously validated (Stepan 1982). No doubt a rehearsal of the modern desire for freedom and truth, the statement that disqualifies and invalidates this early project of knowledge has failed to achieve its goal, that is, to erase the racial from the modern lexicon because it does not explore how it constitutes the modern grammar.

For this reason, I have chosen the less traveled road and address the racial as a scientific construct. Not, however, by assessing the "truth" of the statements of the scientists of man; I am not concerned with evaluation of methods and theories, nor do I follow the logic of discovery. My intent here is to address the apparatus the racial guides, the *analytics of raciality,* as a productive symbolic regimen that institutes human difference as an effect of the play of universal reason. My analysis of the context of emergence, the conditions of production, and the effects of signification of the racial shows how the writing of modern subjects in the post-Enlightenment period would also require the deployment of scientific tools, strategies of symbolic engulfment that transform bodily and social configurations into expressions of how universal reason produces human difference. By doing so, it provides an account of racial subjection that, by displacing historicity, the post-Enlightenment privileged context, situates the *transparency thesis,* that is, the ontoepistemological account that institutes "being and meaning" as effects of interiority and temporality. What this reading provides is the delineation of an other ontoepistemological context, globality, in which being and meaning emerge as an effect of exteriority and spatiality, a mode of representing human difference as an effect of scientific signification. By showing how the *transparent "I,"* which the representation of the subject historicity presupposes and (re)produces, emerges always already in a contention with others that both institute and threaten its ontological prerogative, my reading displaces the transparency thesis to refashion the modern subject as *homo modernus,* the global-historical being produced with tools yielded by both fields of modern representation, namely, history and science.

PARTIAL DEPARTURES

My point of entry into this fractured field is the ubiquitous question that, I think, concerns both postmodern critics and racial theorists: What sort of theoretical account of the contemporary political landscape, with its corresponding criteria for truth and ethical claims, would avoid repeating the exclusionary effects of modern grand narratives of science and history? When considering how postmodern remappings of the social that privilege plurality and contingency—such as, for instance, that of Laclau and Mouffe (1985)—would contribute to the understanding of racial subjection, I could not locate racial subaltern subjects in their portrait of the social.[2] Would they be "moments" (discursively instituted subject positions) or "elements" ("antagonistic parts") in their reframing of the social as a contingent "structured totality"? Under what conditions, what sort of "partial fixations," do they move into (as a "moment") and/or out (as an "antagonistic part") of this discursive field? Or is raciality a "total" fixation, that is, the sole always already feature of the field itself, which in this case would contradict their account of the social or force them to name it racial? With these unanswerable questions, I am not marking a failure of Laclau and Mouffe's theoretical project per se. For they introduce a notion of differentially constituted (open and incomplete) subjectivities or identities without attending

to whether and how the formulation of "difference" it deploys reinstitutes transparency, and with it the "the category of the 'subject' as a unified and unifying essence" (181), which they seek to
displace. This happens, I think, because the sociohistorical logic of
exclusion—and the transparency thesis it presupposes—conjures
up the subject when critical texts (re)produce the racial others as
already differentially constituted historical beings before their entrance into the modern political spaces where they become subaltern
subjects.

My point is that, without addressing the regimen of production
of such subaltern (postmodern) subjects, the subjects of cultural
difference, one ends up attributing to them a self-defeating kind of
transparency. For instance, in "Restaging the Universal: Hegemony
and the Limits of Formalism," Judith Butler (2000) returns to Hegel
to provide an account of hegemony that, displacing universality, rewrites the subject as an inherently social (historical or contingent)
thing. She charges Laclau and Mouffe's (1985) Lacanian rendering
of the "incomplete subject" with retaining a "quasi-"Kantian (formal or universal) foundation that colonizes their reformulation of
the notion of hegemony by reinstituting a given particular (the West)
as a universal limitation and excluding other particulars that sustain
it. Her solution is to return to Hegel, where she finds a reformulation of the universal I as always already committed to the plurality
that characterizes the social, the domain of the concrete, the particular, the contingent, and so on—which sustains her own (liberal)
version of hegemony.[3] The advantages of her Hegelian portrayal
of the postmodern landscape appear in Butler's description of how
it would resolve the challenge cultural difference poses to a global
feminist project.

Though she consistently insists that the excluded particulars constitute the Universal, Butler provides a partial reading of Hegel, one
that does not indicate how the excluded—the ones the Lacanian
quasi-universal bar fails to recuperate—figures in Hegel's account
of "true universality." Because she does not follow the trajectory
of Hegel's self-consciousness to the moment of resolution, the final
step in the trajectory of "Spirit," Butler argues that Hegel's notion
of individuality (concrete, contingent, etc.) immediately includes the
kind of (historic) particularity the notion of cultural difference institutes.[4] How? Through translation, she says: "Without translation,

the very concept of universality cannot cross the linguistic borders it claims," so any universal claim thus conceived—here she refers to international feminism—risks repeating a "colonial and expansionist logic." Not surprisingly, her deployment of cultural difference, one that celebrates historicity as the basis of an ethical (the intrinsically good, just) global political project, troubles her version of the global feminist discourse, which, unlike academic Anglo feminism, would "[override] the problem local cultures pose for international feminism [which] does not understand the parochial character of its own norms." Without explaining why open and fluid local cultures would need translation and how these "linguistic borders" have been produced, Butler moves on to place postcolonial critics at the forefront of the battle against imperialist feminism. From these self-knowing critics she seems to have learned that "by emphasizing the cultural location of universality one sees . . . that there can be no operative notion of universality that does not assume the risk of translation" (35).

Definitely, the postmodern debate seems stuck in modernity's constitutive oppositions. Where is the alternative when all that is offered is an old account of domination in which a self-described (abstract) universal precludes any transformative opposition through a founding exclusion of (concrete) local cultures and a new account of hegemony in which the political field is inhabited by already constituted culturally different others of the West who are dominated because of the identification of a particular local [Western] culture with the Universal? If one opts for the "abstract" universal, particularity becomes an annoyance, that which needs to be excluded for a universal account to be sustained; if one opts for the "concrete" universal, the particular will flourish, but a viable political project will need to rely on always already historic (linguistic or cultural) others who will aid in their own emancipation as "cultural translators" informing their universal (Western feminist) other by telling her how it works at home, in the recess of their "local cultures," where, before entering the political struggle for hegemony, her people rest peacefully in oblivious cultural transparency.

Whenever they alone guide the critical task, historic strategies such as culture and ideology necessarily produce transparent (interior-temporal) subjects while scientific constructs such as cultural difference proceed without disturbance to replace the others of Europe before transparency. That is, historicity cannot dissipate its own effects of power; it cannot institute subjects that signify otherwise. What I am suggesting is that racial subjection should not be conceived as a process of othering, of exclusion, in which an already historic racial or cultural other becomes the site of projection of unwanted attributes that, once specified, reveal the ideological (false or contradictory) basis upon which European particularity has been constructed. Without an examination of how the racial and the cultural institute (as scientific signifiers) the subjects crowding the global saloon, without a critical engagement with disciplinary (productive) power beyond the naming of the subjects of interiority Foucault traces, I contend, such critical remappings of the social will be at best irrelevant for the project of racial emancipation. For a relevant critique of the present global (juridic, economic, and moral) configuration in which raciality rules unchecked necessitates a full engagement with universality and historicity, one that would not stop at a critique of (the failure of juridical and economic) universality just to hold onto the promises of historicity. Instead of projects of inclusion, then, it would attempt to turn the transparency thesis on its head. For, I argue, it is precisely the failure to conceive the cultural and the racial as productive (scientific) signifiers that limits the understanding of how they govern the contemporary global configuration, instituting modern privileged and subaltern subjects.

"THE HISTORIC 'VEIL'"

Following the sociohistorical logic of exclusion, critical racial theorists write the racial subaltern as barred from universality and the conception of humanity (the self-determined subject of history) that the transparency thesis sustains. That would not be a problem if, as Fanon teaches us, the position this subject inhabits could be apprehended in the ontological accounts the transparency thesis authorizes. And yet, in writings of the black subject, one consistently meets a transparent I, buried under historical (cultural or ideological) debris,[5] waiting for critical strategies that would clean up the negative self-representations it absorbs from prevailing racist discourse.[6] No doubt symbolic and actual violence (enslavement, lynching, police brutality) marks our trajectory as modern subaltern subjects. Nevertheless, the privileging of historicity limits accounts such as Cornel West's (1997) construct of the "historic 'Veil'" that writes the black subject as an effect of the "interiorizing" of violence limited.[7] What is behind the veil? Is there a racial subject, a black sovereign that precedes our modern trajectories? If this is so—if before racial violence there is a pristine black subject fully enjoying its "humanity," thriving in self-determined (interior or temporal) existence, that can refuse to "interiorize" and actualize violence—why does it not do so? I think that this desire to lift the veil to reveal an original self-determined black subject fails to ask a crucial question: How did whiteness come to signify the transparent I and blackness to signify otherwise? Because it does not ask such questions, the metaphor of the veil rehearses the sociohistorical logic of exclusion, which writes blackness and whiteness as the "raw material" and not as the products of modern strategies of power. And, in the case of West's account, it (re)produces the black subject as a pathological (affectable) I, a self-consciousness hopelessly haunted by its own impossible desire for transparency.

My point is that the metaphor of the veil reproduces the effect of power of the sociohistorical logic of exclusion—which, as I show in Part 2, consists in a powerful tool of the analytics of raciality—which is to render racial emancipation contingent on the obliteration of racial difference. In *Against Race*, Paul Gilroy (2000) provides perhaps the best example of the perverse effects of this desire to recuperate the racial subaltern into an unbounded humanity. When advancing another claim for the erasure of the racial from modern political grammar, Gilroy announces that the demise of race is already under way, thanks to the radical alteration of bodies promised by genetic manipulation and the commodification of the black male body as an object for global and suburban white consumption. Any impulse to celebrate this "emancipation" from the (racial) body dies when one learns the answer to the question of how biotechnology ushers liberation from race in Gilroy's interpretation of "the tragic story of Henrietta Lacks," a working-class U.S. black woman whose cervical cells have been crucial to the advancement of cancer research, which exemplifies the passage from the "biopolitics of 'race'" to "nano-politics." For Gilroy, the fact that her blackness is irrelevant to medical research suggests a redefinition of the idea of humanity, for the "awareness of the indissoluble unity of all life at the level of genetic materials" displaces the idea of "specifically *racial* differences" (20, italics in the original). It would be all too easy to stop at pointing to the irony of how humanist desire needs science (genetics) to once again denounce race's scientific irrelevance. But it is more interesting, I think, to point to how this desire cannot reduce or sublate the *materiality* (body and social position) of the economically dispossessed black female, which resists the liberating powers of "transfiguration," "commodification," and biotechnology.

How did Henrietta Lacks's cervical cells become available to scientific research? Why did the cellular biologist at Johns Hopkins University see it as ethical to appropriate her cells without her consent? How has the use of economically dispossessed black neighborhoods as testing camps ensured advances in public health research at that university? What cells do not reveal is how the female racial subaltern has been consistently (re)produced as a kind of human being to whom neither juridic universality nor self-determination applies. Not only does her femaleness place Henrietta Lacks under patriarchal (divine or natural) law, away from the domain of the laws of the body politic. Her blackness also produces her as radically distinct from the kind of subject presumed in the ethical principles governing modern social configurations. Across the earth, women still die of cervical cancer despite the advances Lacks's stolen cells have enabled, but they do not die the same way. Economically dispossessed women of color, like Lacks, die with more pain and no hope. Not only do they lack the financial means to access even the basic technologies available for the prevention and treatment of cervical cancer; in many cases (as in the case of a Brazilian federal program for the treatment of economically dispossessed cancer patients), when given access to this technology they are treated as little more than test subjects. This is not because blackness determines the kind of cells that will grow in their bodies, but because it determines how they live with or die from cancer. That cancer cells do not indicate dark brown skin or flat noses can be conceived of as emancipatory only if one forgets, or minimizes, the political context within which lab materials will be collected and the benefits of biotechnological research will be distributed.

Whether inspired by humanism or not, any critical ontoepistemological account couched upon the transparency thesis will ignore the conditions of production of modern subjects, how the arsenal of the modern "Will to Truth," tools of reason, institute social (juridical, economic, ethical) subjects, the men and women who produce and reproduce (and the institutions that regulate) their own social trajectories. Whatever else can be said about the critical position Gilroy inhabits, it certainly holds onto the promises of historicity and universality, which animate postmodern humanist desires for a postracial, transparent future: "The spaces in which 'races' come to life," Gilroy laments, "are a field from which political interaction has been banished" (41). What would be left, I ask, to the project of social or global justice if modern subjects were freed from raciality? This is not just a rhetorical question. It requires a critique of modern thought that addresses scientific knowledge as a major productive site of power, one that addresses how the racial, the scientific signifier, produces social subjects who stand differentially before the institutions the transparency thesis sustains.

Perhaps it is evident now that the answer to the question of what lies behind the veil is more complicated than it appears to be. At least for the economically dispossessed racialized gendered person for whom, as for Henrietta Lacks, physical death is only the most evident effect of the post-Enlightenment desire for transparency and the historical and scientific signifying strategies that (re)produce it. What I am suggesting is that the moral ease with which the sociohistorical logic of exclusion captures racial subjection derives from how it (re)produces the transparency thesis by translating the obliteration of the kind of particularity the latter postulates into a demand for the obliteration of the signifier that institutes it, namely, the racial—a gesture that consistently reinstitutes the transparent subject of science and history, the proper name of the man. For this reason, I claim, only an excavation of modern thought, an analysis of the economy of signification governed by the transparency thesis and the analytics of raciality, will enable critical ontoepistemological projects and the ethical principle that usually accompany them, which can aid in the project of global justice.

THE NAMING OF MAN

Many racial theorists have recently undertaken this excavation, gathering instances of philosophical formulations of juridical universality and humanity that exclude the others of Europe. Although they remain in the grip of the sociohistorical logic of exclusion, they indicate why the answer to the question of how the racial operates as a strategy of power is buried in the founding texts of modern thought

(Fitzpatrick 1992; Goldberg 1993 and 2002; Mills 1997; and Eze 2002, among others).[8] Nevertheless, although these theorists have explored how the racial delimits the reach of the law and humanity, they have yet to ask how it produces the principles—universality and self-determination—these notions comprehend. How precisely does the racial (re)produce the universality of the law? How can the racial be reconciled with the ethical privilege, self-determination, historicity assures humanity? Asking these questions, I fear, would signal a questioning of universality and self-determination—a move too risky to make, it seems. With this statement, I am suggesting that postmodern critics of modern thought and racial theorists resist abandoning the transparency thesis, which so evidently undermines our understanding of how the racial operates as a strategy of power. But I am not intimating that they eagerly embrace transparency. For it is because they hold onto the sociologic of exclusion, I think, that the transparency thesis sneaks in on them.

Perhaps discussion of a text that could be placed at the very center of the critical field can help me to elaborate this point. In A Critique of Postcolonial Reason, Gayatri Chakraborty Spivak (1999) traces how the exclusion of the others of Europe from founding modern philosophical works has produced the ethical (cultural) narrative that has instituted the figure of man. What she finds in Kant's, Hegel's, and Marx's texts are rhetorical moves in which the articulation and expulsion of the "native informant"—what she refers to as the "rejection of [its] affect" (4–5)—instituted "the name of Man," the symbolic move that has sustained the various moments of European juridical and economic domination of other regions of the globe—colonialism, neocolonialism, imperialism, and so on. These "great narratives of ['German'] cultural self-representation," she argues, provide the material "for a narrative of crisis management," that is, "the 'scientific' fabrication of new representations of self and world that would provide alibis for the domination, exploitation, and epistemic violation entailed by the establishment of colony and empire" (7, my italics). What I want to highlight in Spivak's account is how she misses that these "master narratives" constitute the context of emergence of the racial when she immediately dismisses the latter as an "alibi"—an ideological construct, a false representation of the relationship between man and the "native informant"—for economic exploitation and juridical domination.

Why, I ask, was "'scientific' fabrication" necessary at all if the "master narratives" had already foreclosed the "other of man"? If "the (im)possible perspective . . . [of] the native informant" has been written (in "the source texts of European ethico-political self-representation") in its failure to replace the proper signifier of man (9), the "'scientific' [which the scare quotes cannot but name false] fabrication" of the other seems unnecessary. Unless, of course, what has been expelled in the master narratives had some sort of pristine (precolonial) "true" essence or existence before its foreclosure, prior to its becoming the "mark of expulsion" that false science would later fabricate.[9] For if one forgoes the desire for a Real that holds a historic (cultural subaltern) I and engages the Symbolic as the moment of production of the transparent I and its other, the scientific mill will have to be taken seriously as the very locus of production of the "name of Man" and of the "others" who fail to signify it and ask how scientific strategies, the alibis that sustain racial and colonial juridical domination and economic exploitation, populate the global space with a variety of modern subjects, who neither preceded nor are coetaneous with man, but have been produced using the same raw material assembled during the long period of his gestation.

When describing how they play out in the contemporary global configuration, Spivak belies how historical-materialist strategies, such as ideology, provided but partial critiques of modern (self-)representation. "In various guises," she contends, "they still inhabit and inhibit our attempts to overcome the limitations imposed on us by the newest division of the world, to the extent that, as the North continues ostensibly to 'aid' the South—as formerly imperialism 'civilized' the New World—the South's crucial assistance to the North in keeping up its resource-hungry lifestyle is forever foreclosed. In the pores of this book will be the suggestion that, the typecase of the foreclosed native informant today is the poorest *woman* of the South" (7, italics in the original). What I am suggesting is that only by relinquishing the desire to include "local cultures," through the unveiling of truth and/or the recognition of history, is it possible to address the questions racial subjection imposes: What is the ontological context inhabited by the transparent I and the others that institute and interrupt it? Under what conditions do they emerge as such, as dominant and subaltern, that is, as political subjects? Asking these questions would certainly prevent Spivak from fully embracing historical materialism, but it would also avoid a conflation that performs another troubling foreclosure. I am referring here to the conflation suggested in the immediate connection between ideology and political economy nicely compounded in her construct "axiomatics of imperialism," which evades an engagement with the heterogeneity of the "oppressed."

Before and beyond the gendered and self-interested economic alliances with imperialism and global capitalism, Spivak's global or postcolonial (economic and juridical) dominant and subaltern are also racial subjects, that is, effects of raciality. For the advantages of a critical position that scratches off the erasures, the place of silence, one that avoids the reinstitution of a transparent subject by rewriting the "native informant" as a "name for that mark of expulsion from the name of Man—a mark crossing out the impossibility of the ethical relations" (6, italics in the original)—can be lost if one does not acknowledge that the juridical and economic mapping of the global space is but one instance of the political relationship that institutes Europe and its others. While such a contentious relationship has been effaced by the common gendered self-interests of the colonizer and the colonized (I am not sure whether it is a curse or a blessing for feminist theorizing), the privileging of political economy and patriarchy misses the subtleties of the contemporary global political play.

How can one map a political context in which the U.S. political and economic interests both select (Islamic) Pakistan as an ally in their "war against (Islamic) terrorism" and the domination of Muslim women and allow for the continuing violence against Muslims in India and Palestine—while on the home front Christian Arabs, Latinos, light-skinned blacks, South Asians, and slightly darker Jews may fall prey to domestic "terror fighting"? Whatever "old" religious and geopolitical signifiers are brought to bear in the twenty-first century's renderings of "evil," the conspicuous figure of the (bearded or not) brown man on airplanes indicates how the racial all too easily overrides political-economic interest as well as national, regional, and global borders. What do Spivak's "postcolonial," "South," and "poorest woman of the South" have in common besides being economically exploited and juridically dominated by the "North"? How do the rhetorical strategies she identifies relate to the explicit exclusions noted by Goldberg (1993), Mills (1997), Eze (2001), and others?[10] Narcissus, I am convinced, ought never gaze at his own face. That the political-economic (capitalism in the shape of colonialism, imperialism, or globalization) and the political-symbolic (the racial and the cultural) engulfment of the globe produce the same peoples and places as "the oppressed," "the dominated," the subaltern, and "the South" seems a self-evident truth that should be left alone lest there remain no self-assured position for the critic to take. For the pervasiveness of the tools of the analytics of raciality in the contemporary global political grammar threatens the radicality of political-economic critiques and the righteousness of (anti-)racial statements in defense of "real," truly all-encompassing (as opposed to "ideological," "false"), universality and humanity, precisely because they consistently play the crucial role, which is to rewrite their indigenous place.

TOWARD AN ANALYSIS OF PRODUCTIVE POWER

Though I recognize the relevance of statements by Hobbes, Locke, Hume, Kant, and Hegel that explicitly place non-Europeans outside the trajectory of universal reason, I find the explicit exclusions they deploy insufficient to institute racial subjection. To map the locus of emergence of today's global subaltern subjects, one should ask: After the consolidation of the rule of reason in the nineteenth century, which new political-symbolic arsenal accompanied the apparatuses of juridical domination and economic exploitation of the others of Europe? My response is that, after the demise of the divine ruler and author rendered conversion an inappropriate mode of engulfment, what else if not scientific universality could produce an ethical position consistent with the attributes of universality and self-determination the early modern philosophers have given to man. My engagement with the founding statements of modern thought departs from postmodern critics' and racial theorists' approaches precisely because I am interested in the most subtle and yet powerful tools of racial subjection, the ones that the sociologic of exclusion (and its resilient metaphors "double consciousness," the "veil," and "the color line") can never capture precisely because of its privileging of historicity—that which nurses projects of a "postracial" future where the expansion of universality would finally include the others of Europe in the conception of being human that the transparency thesis produces. For racial subjection is as an effect of the desire that writes post-Enlightenment Europe in transparency and necessarily demands the obliteration of the others of Europe, historic strategies that cannot help the critical task.

Because I am convinced that the critical arsenal still lacks an engagement with modern representation that addresses this onto-epistemological context as a productive regimen governed by universal reason, the analytical strategy I introduce in the following chapter guides an excavation of modern thought through which I gather the statements that prepared the terrain for the formulation of the productive apparatus governing contemporary global political configuration. Much like Foucault's excavations of the modern episteme, the critical analysis of modern representation that I propose departs from Kant's definition of analysis because it considers not only the principles and conditions but also the consequences of knowledge, its political (productive) effects. When charting modern representation, like anyone who forfeits the comfortable grounds provided by a concrete and/or ideological outsideness, I am aware of the risk (and the necessity, I might add) of, as Jacques Derrida (1976) says, "falling back within that which is being deconstructed" (14). Taking from this risk the critical edge necessary to engage that which disallows anything from standing outside its determination, I gather certain statements that organize modern thought, which, set against each other, become useful tools for excavating the territory of transparency.

My small contribution to this task here is to situate the tools of the analytics of raciality, to describe the context of emergence, the regimen of production, and the effects of signification of the productive apparatus instituted by the scientific signifying strategies that transformed the descendants of yesterday's "natives" into modern subaltern subjects. With this I hope to unravel the contradiction haunting critical analyses of racial subjection, which, while recognizing the political significance of the racial, repeat the moral mantra that it is extraneous to modern ethicopolitical grammar. To do so, I pursue a question preempted by the lament for the scientific minds that let "prejudices" and "ideologies" colonize the domain of "truth": Why was it necessary, and why does it remain so, to deploy a concept that demarcates the limits of transparency if the latter's transcendental determinant is without limits, encompassing time and space, here and there, past and future, everything and everywhere?

This question, I think, requires that the racial be placed at the center of the critique of modern representation, which should begin with an account of how scientific universality institutes man. My point of departure is the acknowledgment that historicity is haunted. And it is not because man houses at his core the phantasm of an "other" historic "being." I deploy an analytical toolbox to decenter the transparency thesis, the ontological assumption that still governs the critical arsenal, to produce a modern contra-ontology, that is, an account of the transparent I that shows how it can emerge—in a relationship, always already contending with its others.

I

Homo Historicus

Ontology—once it is finally admitted as leaving existence by the wayside—
does not permit us to understand the being of the black man. For not only
must the black man be black; he must be black in relation to the white
man. Some critics will take it on themselves to remind us that his proposition has a converse. I say this is false. The black man has no ontological
resistance in the eyes of the white man.

—FRANTZ FANON, *BLACK SKIN, WHITE MASK*

What Fanon's account of the "fact of blackness" suggests is a formulation of the modern subject in which speech announces the precedence of the text, of language, of writing—a promise not undermined even when he refuses dialectics but embraces eschatology to reposit humanity at the horizon of racial emancipation. Holding onto this promise, I find in Fanon's ([1952] 1967) account of racial subjection indications for a rewriting of the modern play that would reconcile his seemingly contradictory statements: "The black man is *not a man*" (9, my italics) and "The Negro *is not. Anymore* than the white man" (231, my italics). Following the road Fanon sighted but would not pursue, I excavate the founding texts of modern thought, from which I gather the outlines of two ontoepistemological contexts: the one Fanon refutes, which the black man fails to signify, and the one the *analytics of raciality* produces, in which the black man and the white man emerge as signifiers of an irreducible difference. What I find in this excavation are precisely statements that allow me to situate the *transparency thesis,* the ontological assumption guiding modern representation, that is, the components of historical and scientific signification that would later be assembled in accounts of universal reason that emerged in the nineteenth century—Hegel's narrative of the trajectory of *"Spirit"* and the scientific projects that attempt to "discover" the truth of man—which consolidate reason as the sovereign ruler or producer of modern representation.

My description of the context of the emergence of the analytics of raciality suggests that the warnings of the mind without reason anticipate the version of the modern drama Fanon envisions but does not pursue. Though Nietzsche's madman probably guessed it, he never articulated that the killing of "God" condemned the subject to be haunted by universal reason. Modern philosophy has been moved by the need to reconcile a conception of reason as the new ruler of the universe with the most cherished attribute of man, that is, self-determination. Following the trajectory of self-consciousness from its initial outline, I indicate why the racial would constitute such a prolific strategy of power. I show how the statements that write it as the thing that thrives in the *stage of interiority* also delineate another ontoepistemological moment, the *stage of exteriority.* Not surprisingly, Hegel's *transcendental poesis,* which consolidates self-consciousness as an interior/temporal thing, the transparent "I," the one that always already knows that it houses that which is not itself, also renders the nineteenth-century deployment of the racial both possible and necessary. Without that other moment in which "being" is always less than, farther from, an "other being," that is, exteriority/spatiality, the ontological priority of the interior/temporal thing would be meaningless, as Derrida (1976) argues. For the racial emerges in projects of knowledge that presume scientific universality, for which universal reason plays the role of an exterior determinant; in modern representation, it governs an ontological context in which man emerges as an exterior or spatial thing, that is, globality, the one that escapes critical analysts of modern thought precisely because the ethical grip of the transparency thesis does not allow the decentering of historicity that its sighting demands.

In the following, neither a Foucauldian archaeological or genealogical exercise nor a straightforward use of Derrida's deconstruction, but somewhere between the two, I chart the context of the emergence of the analytics of raciality, the scientific arsenal that consistently rewrites post-Enlightenment European consciousness and social configurations in transparency. As I do so, however, I show how it accomplishes that which has haunted modern thought since the initial ascension of universal reason, namely, the writing of the mind in outer determination, that is, always already before, in a relationship, contenting with "others," a version of the self-determined "I" that necessarily signifies "other"-wise.

2

The Critique of Productive Reason

The ghost has its own desires, so to speak, which figure the whole complicated sociality of a determining formation that seems inoperative (like slavery) or invisible (like racially gendered capitalism) but that is nonetheless alive and enforced. But the force of the ghost's desire is not just negative, not just the haunting and staged words, marks, or gestures of domination and injury. The ghost is not other or alterity as such, ever. It is (like Beloved) pregnant with unfulfilled possibility, with the something to be done that the wavering present is demanding. This something to be done is not a return to the past but a reckoning with its repression in the present, a reckoning with that which we have lost, but never had.

—AVERY GORDON, *GHOSTLY MATTERS*

Following the ghost, seeking the lost treasures it announces, reason's accursed offerings that refigure no-thing, require an exploration of the grounds it haunts—the recuperation of the site where the *transparent "I"* and its "others" emerge as such, necessarily before each other. My task in this chapter is to describe analytical position and the toolbox I deploy to write modern representation "other"-wise. Both enable the refashioning of modern representation as the *modern text,* an account of the symbolic that describes how the "being and meaning" universal reason institutes are manufactured as byproductive strategies that both presuppose and institute a relationship—as presumed in Marx's (1956), Schmitt's (1976), and Foucault's (2003) renderings of the political in terms of contention, that is, as a moment

21

of human existence defined by (the possibility of) violence. What distinguishes my approach is the fact that it recuperates scientific signification to introduce a conception of political subjects as an effect of symbolic, productive violence. When doing so, it brackets the *transparency thesis,* thus abandoning the moral ban that entails fast rejections of raciality to show how, as a tool of productive reason, the racial produces both the transparent I and its others as modern political subjects.

When delimiting the analytical position and assembling the tools necessary to accomplish this task, I borrowed from the critical arsenal but more particularly from Foucault's critique of power/knowledge and Derrida's account of signification. Both allow me to show how the sovereign ruler of modern representation, universal reason, institutes the subjects inhabiting the contemporary global configuration. To those who may tremble before my reconciliation of Foucault's and Derrida's critical formulations, I can only say this: I am not reinventing gunpowder here. In *Society Must Be Defended,* Michel Foucault (2003) proposes an account of the political that indicates that these two postmodern critics were moving parallel to one another. In the lectures on which the book was based, he introduced the idea of a "race war" against both disciplinary power and the theory of sovereignty to capture another moment of modern power.[1] While many may read Foucault's "race struggle" as an immediate reference to the notion of the racial deployed in the nineteenth century—and he suggests as much—I prefer to read it as a metaphor that allows him to return the view of power as a "relationship of force," thus recuperating the possibility of violence as a dimension of the concept of the political. He asks, "If power is indeed the implementation and deployment of a relationship of force, rather than analyzing it in terms of surrender, contract, and alienation, or rather than analyzing it in function terms as the reproduction of the relations of production, shouldn't we be analyzing it first and foremost in terms of conflict, confrontation, and war?" (15). When entertaining a positive answer to this question, Foucault makes a move that suggests a mode of analysis of power that I find akin to Jacques Derrida's account of signification and Immanuel Levinas's critique of representation in that it conceives of violence as a dimension of power beyond the liberal formulation, which restricts the use of force to the state and considers only political acts of violence that target the state. This reconciliation is but a resolution of Foucault's notion of productive power, Derrida's notion of writing, and Levinas's rendering of representation as "partial violation." With these tools I delineate a critical position and assemble an analytical arsenal that addresses globality as an ontological context, whereas they describe the subject of universal reason as an effect of acts of productive violence, force, or power, as an outer determined thing always already in a relationship with (im)possible others.

THE CRITIQUE OF PRODUCTIVE "TRUTH"

In Michel Foucault's critique of modern thought I find the suggestion that attention to scientific signification can situate historicity (interiority-temporality), the ontological descriptor the transparency thesis authorizes. When addressing the modern episteme, modern representation, as the regimen of signification governed by the "will to truth," his analyses of power show how knowledge institutes the subject, that is, how the transparent I, the subject of freedom, is but an effect of the rules of production of truth, of the mode of power, which, Foucault (1980) argues, "produces effects" at the level of desire and knowledge (69). When describing how "discourses of truth" produce modern subjects—the fundamentally political things, which are "subjected to the production of truth and [yet] cannot exercise power except through the production of truth," and "we *must* speak the truth" (93, italics in the original)—he introduces a notion of productive power that brackets the juridical and economic moments privileged in the liberal and the historical-materialist ontology. Nevertheless, while his rendering of power/knowledge—which I term here *productivity*—suggests the possibility of addressing the racial as part of the arsenal of the modern regime of "truth," it has not animated such exploration because, beyond the explicit Eurocentrism many identify, Foucault's analyses of the power retains interiority as the distinguishing feature of man.

What I am arguing here is that Foucault limits his critique of historicity to an engagement with temporality, thereby addressing but one dimension of the transparent I. In *The Order of Things,* Foucault (1994) describes the modern episteme emerging with the deployment of an "analytics of finitude," the enveloping of the things of the world by temporality, which institutes man as the sovereign subject and privileged object of knowledge. Although he notes that the apprehension of the "things of the world" also results from that which in man is "finite"—the contingent, "empirical, positive (body and language)"—he stops at the realization that the positive is continuously brought back into the "figure of the Same" (315). Lost in the assumption that thought (reflection) returns, and reduces everything it addresses, to the temporality of the self-determined (interior) subject of knowledge—the knowing mind, man's transcendental moment—is an engagement with how knowledge (science) addresses human beings and social configurations as phenomena, as extended (exterior/spatial), "empirical" things. What has no place in Foucault's description of the "analytics of finitude," due to his decision not to navigate the territory opened up by his critique of modern ontology, is a consideration of how shifts in knowledge relate to economic and sexual moments of modern power/desire.[2]

Precisely because it addresses the intersection of two productive political moments—the economic and the sexual—of deployment of European desire across the globe, the racial indicates that any critique of the figure at the center of modern representation should engage interiority, the attribute it has exhibited since its articulation in the founding statements of Western thought. In *The History of Sexuality*, Foucault's (1978) considerations of race and sex as referents of power indicate why this is a thread he would not pursue. Although biopolitics indicates precisely the moment when the machinery of the racial and the arsenal of sexuality meet, he does not pursue the subject because, for Foucault, the racial belongs to another mode of power, the "symbolics of blood," one that does not operate via the production of minds. From "the second half of the nineteenth century," he argues, "the thematics of blood was sometimes called on to lend its entire historical weight toward revitalizing the type of political power that was exercised through the device of sexuality. Racism took shape at this point . . . it was then that a whole politics of settlement, . . . accompanied by a long series of permanent interventions at the level of the body, conduct, health, and everyday life, received their color and their justification from the mythical concern with protecting the purity of the blood and ensuring the triumph of the race" (149). What prevents Foucault from fully incorporating the nineteenth-century concept of the racial in his critique of modern thought, I think, is not an empirical limitation—though such limitations are significant, as indicated in

Stoler's (1995) examination of how the discourse of race participates in the formation of bourgeois European sexuality—but his partial engagement with modern representation.[3]

In his critique of "truth," Foucault challenges self-determination with the Kantian argument that, rather than the liberating ground, universal reason is the (interior) ruler or producer of freedom.[4] My point is that, because he locates that which escapes the reductive powers of the "Same" in a domain not yet charted by modern thought (the it-self, the unconscious, etc.), Foucault's excavations do not reach the place where European particularity is but an effect of the strategies of this productive ruler. For this reason, though a crucial contribution to the critique of modern representation, his own deployments of the thesis of productivity remain within its limits because he does challenge the ontological prerogative of interiority that guides accounts that locate man in transparency.[5] Had he relinquished interiority, Foucault would have contributed to our understanding of how the productive force of the racial ensues from the haunting spatiality he spots at the core of modern thought, but would never fully explore.[6]

THE HORIZON OF DEATH

What Foucault's analyses of power—as both disciplinary power and a "relationship of force"—signal but he does not explore is an analytical position that recuperates extension (exteriority-spatiality) from the statements that outline historicity as man's sole and exclusive horizon of existence. It is only from such a position that it is possible to dismantle interiority precisely because of how it addresses an ontological horizon that does not presuppose a "being" that precedes the context it shares with that which it is not, namely, "other beings." From what position does the transparent I contend with that which delimits its particular place? From the critical analytical position I delimited, I spot the ontological context where the Subject stands before the horizon of death. In globality, the ontoepistemological descriptor by which "the scientific" attempts to discover the truth of man, resides the racial. From there, I will show, it sustains the writing of post-Enlightenment Europe as the moment of transparency. As this critical position decenters historicity, the ontoepistemological context the transparency thesis institutes, it displaces interiority, the portal to self-determination,[7] to refashion modern representation as a productive context of power, the signifying strategies of which institute the subject as an effect of ontoepistemological contexts, namely, historicity and globality, instituted respectively by the texts of history and science.

In *Of Grammatology,* Jacques Derrida (1976) offers an account of signification that enables the carving out of this critical analytical position. His decisive move is to reject the symbolic prerogative of *interiority,* the assumption of an immediate connection (transparency) between speech and truth. By giving the trace—the unstable link between signifier and signified—signifying primacy, he provides an account of signification that indicates the possibility of recovering exteriority from the belly of Hegel's Transcendental Subject.[8] When proposing that spatiality (writing, *différance*) is the fundamental locus of signification and subjectification, Derrida adds to the critical arsenal a tool that refuses this absolute referent, the transcendental I, that precedes and institutes signification. With this, it rewrites the transparent (interior/temporal) I as an effect of differentiation or relationality, of the symbolic regimen where "being and meaning" emerge always already in exteriority and violence, out of the erasure of other (im)possible beings and meanings the trace hopelessly signifies. What spatiality offers is the possibility of recuperating from the debris of the founding statements of modern representation the effects of its productive violent acts, that which, according to the transparency thesis, the subject is not but without which it cannot be.

Through the reconciliation of Foucault's notion of productivity with his own framing of the political as a "relationship of force," which allows me to resolve both in Derrida's rendering of spatiality, I have identified an analytical position that centers relationship, outer determination, that is coexistence, contemporaneity, and contention. From this stance I engage modern subjects as the effect of a political-symbolic arsenal that situates them as always already before the horizon of death, the one instituted by spatiality that does not house I's and the others that can be resolved—reduced or sublated—in dialectical, phenomenological, or psychoanalytical accounts of negation or projection. Because "being and meaning" here result from the deferring, the postponement, the erasure of other possible "beings and meanings"—which can be spotted only in the trace that both produces and threatens signification—the ontoepistemological context that spatiality demarcates displaces interiority to establish exteriority as the ruler of signification. Before the reader attempts to resolve this position back into an account of nothingness, I repeat that I am not constructing death as negation, as always already comprehended by being—as in Sartre's ([1943] 1984) statement that "Being is *that* and outside of that, *nothing*" (36, italics in the original)—which would consist in another rehearsal of Hegel's narrative of "Spirit," which writes being, self-consciousness, as that which always already is everything that is not itself. Nor is it a "post"(colonial, modern, or racial) version of Hegel's lordship and bondsman passage because, it does not presuppose self-consciousness as a transparent I that has to contend with an always already racial or cultural transparent other. That is, I do not assume that those in contention, political subjects, precede their emergence in representation. Instead I conceive of them as political, because they emerge in signification, which, as Derrida suggests, itself presupposes and inaugurates a "relationship of force."

More specifically, I draw from Levinas's (1996) critique of modern representation the statement that the impulse to comprehend the "Other" *(Autrui),* necessarily establishes a relationship with another being that becomes both an "object of representation" and an "interlocutor." To speak of the Other, he states, presupposes the possibility of speaking to the Other; it is to invoke the Other, which, in itself, is a productive moment. In Levinas's statement, then, I find the suggestion that modern political-symbolic strategies can be read as productive acts that address (articulate and disavow) the Other and, in doing so, institute the "face of the other." Though this analytical position recognizes productivity as a dimension of scientific signification, it also reads it as a "partial" violent gesture, that is, as engulfment. Put differently, I read the other to mark the writing of the others of Europe in a mode of representation that privileges interiority. That is, I read modern representation as a regimen that produces beings that refigure, as they postpone, the Other—"the sole being whose negation can only announce itself as total: as *murder*"; this "Other . . . is that which escapes comprehension in the other *(autrui)* . . . that which I cannot negate partially, in violence, in grasping him within the horizon of being in general and possessing him" (9). I read modern representation not as a total appropriation or obliteration of the Other, that mode of being that remains outside representation, which it both threatens and institutes. Fully retained before the horizon of death, this Other, I claim, threatens another ontology it is the "Other of the [narrative of the] Same." As such, it refers to the mode of representation—before and beyond modern thought—to which the distinction between interiority and exteriority belongs, and for this reason, it indicates that universal reason can exercise its sovereign rule only as productive force.

When addressing the racial as the political-symbolic tool that institutes the global itself as an ontoepistemological signifier, I do not, as Chakrabarty (2000) does, read the other of man as another historical (interior-temporal) I. The critical analytical position I adopt does not presuppose preexisting or coexisting (interior) beings the (textual) erasure of which enables the writing of Europe in transparency. My intent here is to target what modern thought has defined as the moment of exteriority, that is, scientific signification, to chart the conditions under which the others of Europe can be represented as such, and to indicate why this exercise is necessary if one is to rewrite modern social configurations "other"-wise. What allows me to give analytical primacy to the horizon of death is precisely my refusal to rehearse the ethical condemnation of scientific signification as a moment of production of the truth of man. For the signifiers of death I gather refer precisely to that which modern thought deems the moment of outer determination, precisely because, as Derrida suggests, they produce an account of difference as neither sublatable nor reducible to the Transcendental I. That is, the I and the (actual, possible, or potential) others it institutes emerge before one another—in contention, in a relationship that always already presumes the horizon of death. For this reason, the retrieval of exteriority, of the moment of outer determination, allows a contra-ontological argument, one that reads modern representation as a political-symbolic apparatus, that is, as at once violent and productive.

When delimiting the ontoepistemological location the pair exteriority-spatiality institutes, I borrow and reformulate Roland Robertson's (1995) account of "globality" as a privileged site of differentiation, "the general conditions which facilitated the diffusion of general modernity" (27).[9] My rendering of the term, however, maintains but reverses the relationship between present ontoepistemological conditions and modernity that Robertson suggests. Instead of the context of deployment of claims for universalization and differentiation, I deploy globality to situate historicity, the authorized ontological stance, to refashion the latter as *one* moment in which one can trace the emergence of modern subjects. With this, I introduce a critical account that captures how scientific signifiers enable and unsettle the writing of the proper man, the post-Enlightenment European subject, the only one to enjoy the privilege of transparency. For I will show how in this ontological context, globality, the horizon of death, scientific signification has deployed the racial to produce modern subjects that emerge in exteriority/affectability and exist between two moments of violence: (a) *engulfment,* that is, "partial negation," the productive violent act of naming, the symbolic appropriation that produces them, inaugurating a *relationship* precisely because, in the regimen of representation interiority governs, it institutes unsublatable and irreducible subjects, and (b) *murder,* total annihilation, that which obliterates the necessary but haunting relationship between an I instituted by the desire for transparency (self-determination) and the affectable, always already vanishing others of Europe that the scientific cataloguing of minds institutes. When the racial writes Europeans and the others of Europe as subjects of exteriority, it institutes the body, social configurations, and global regions as signifiers of the mind. Therefore, the racial is an effect and a tool of the productive violent act that produces the global as a modern context of signification, one that refers to a mode of existing before historicity, the horizon of life, that the ontological context transparency thesis produces.[10] That is, the deployment of the racial as a political/symbolic weapon institutes globality as an *other* ontological context.

My critique of modern representation, then, recuperates the Global as a signifying context constituted by the materializations (effects and products) of scientific signifying strategies. Though I acknowledge the centrality of the human body, my reading of the science of man will show that, as a signifier of irreducible and unsublatable mental difference, the racial is relevant only to mark the difference between post-Enlightenment European and other contemporaneous, coexisting social configurations, when it transforms yesterday's religious conquerors and natives into modern subjects, racial (biological) things, to define the boundaries of that which has neither beginning nor end without displacing the transparency thesis. When describing globality as the horizon of death, I highlight how the ethical and ontological primacy of the transparency thesis, which emerges in Hegel's narrative of self-actualized "Spirit" that institutes beings and meanings that gaze solely at the horizon of life, both necessitates and rejects the I's and the others the *analytics of raciality* produces. For the racial constitutes an effective political-symbolic strategy precisely because the subjects it institutes are situated differently, namely, in globality. While the others of Europe gaze on the horizon of death, facing certain obliteration, the racial keeps the transparent I in self-determination (interiority) alone before the horizon of life, oblivious to, because always already knowledge-able (controlling and emulating) of, how universal reason governs its existence. Not surprisingly, critical analyses of racial subjection cannot explain the effects of power of the racial. Spreading before historicity, the effects of raciality are inaccessible to the arsenal that the sociohistorical logic of exclusion informs precisely because the latter assumes that the transparency thesis constitutes the sole modern ontological presupposition.[11]

READING "OTHER"-WISE

From the analytical position productivity and spatiality demarcate, I engage the racial as a modern political-symbolic strategy by asking what the reader may consider counterintuitive questions such as: What needs to be articulated in the text of man, but can never become his locus of emergence? What needs to be postponed, for otherwise it would erupt to render the speech of the transparent I troublesome? Relinquishing the moral shelter of historicity, these questions guided my tracing of the path of self-consciousness—from its outline in Descartes's inaugural statement, which maintains the mind in interiority, to its consolidation in Hegel's formulation of the Transcendental I—where I found that exteriority was consistently articulated to write its particularity but immediately disavowed lest its exclusive attribute, self-determination, vanish. What I gathered in this return to the founding statements of modern thought, then, were formulations that enabled me to locate the place exteriority occupies in modern thought. By reassembling these formulations, I was able to reconfigure modern representation as the modern text, for I show how the play of reason is described in two moments of signification, the *stage of interiority* and the *stage of exteriority,* the strategies of which constitute the "metanarratives" of history and science that bring modern subjects into representation.

What the modern text allows me to do is decenter the transparency thesis as I describe the signifying gestures—displacement, negation, and engulfment—that render exteriority an (im)possible ontological moment. When reading the founding statements of modern thought deployed between the seventeenth and the nineteenth centuries, I borrow Jacques Lacan's (1977) symbolic structures, "displacement" and "negation," symbolic tools that at once articulate and disavow signifiers of the Name of the Father, to describe the signifying gestures deployed to describe how universal reason plays its sovereign role.[12] Each allows me to show how the effort to secure the exclusive attribute of self-consciousness, self-determination—the ability to know and decide about one's essence and existence—resulted in the outlining of two symbolic regions, the stage of interiority and the stage of exteriority, in which universal reason plays its sovereign role. The challenge facing early modern philosophers, I will show, was how to sustain the writing of man as a self-determined (interior) thing in a mode of thought grounded on the assertion of the possibility of knowledge with certainty, that is, scientific universality, to establish that the mind has access to, relates to, and is affected by things other than itself, that is, exterior things, and yet the latter play no role in the determination of its essence or existence; that is, they consistently managed not to write the I as an affectable thing. In other words, this statement that inaugurates modern representation has held through the postponement—displacement and negation—of the moment of the "Thing," the "Other," that is, the recurrent articulation and disavowal of that which is not the *interior* thing, the writing of that which fails to signify self-determination, *exterior* things, as ontoepistemologically irrelevant. What I spot in these founding statements are the components of the two symbolic regions of modern representation: (a) the stage of exteriority, where reason plays its sovereign role, that of *universal nomos,* as the regulative (constraining) force that governs the things of the world that are subjected to outer determination, that is, affectable things, and (b) the stage of interiority, where universal reason plays its sovereign role as *universal poesis,* the productive (representing) power that founds the tools housed in the mind of man.

When I turn to Hegel's statements, I describe the consolidation of these two stages in the third symbolic gesture, engulfment, the one that transforms exteriority into a moment of the version of universal reason he deploys, that is, *transcendental poesis,* which consolidates the transparency thesis as the ruling ontoepistemological assumption.

This reconciliation, I contend, enabled the nineteenth-century projects of knowledge that would finally locate self-consciousness in the stage of exteriority. There I locate the emergence of the racial as a *strategy of engulfment*, the political-symbolic strategy that apprehends the human body and global regions as signifiers of how universal reason institutes different kinds of self-consciousness, that is, as an effect of productive tools that institute irreducible and unsublatable differences.

With the notion of engulfment, then, I describe how modern subjects emerge out of the simultaneous deployment of two signifying strategies that correspond to two regions of modern representation, namely: (a) the *field of history,* whose particular mode of signification I capture with the construct *historical text,* the one in which the subject emerges as an effect of the unfolding of transcendental poesis, in which historicity (interiority-temporality) constitutes the privileged ontological context, and (b) the *field of science,* whose particular mode of signification I capture with the term *scientific text,* in which self-consciousness and social configurations are represented as an effect of the tools of *productive nomos,* in which globality (exteriority-spatiality) constitutes the privileged ontological context. With the modern text, I propose a reading of modern representation that recuperates the racial as a political-symbolic weapon, a strategy of engulfment, whose crucial effect is to produce human bodies and global regions as signifiers of the productive play of universal reason. Each corresponds to a perspective from which I engage the analytics of raciality: (a) the analysis of its context of emergence, which I reconfigure by deploying the modern text in the excavation of the founding statements; (b) the analysis of its conditions of production, which I specify as the scientific text guides my analysis of the projects of knowledge of man and society that, deploying the racial as a tool of productive *nomos,* institute globality as an ontological context; and (c) the analysis of its effects of signification, which I gather when I deploy the historical text, which presumes historicity as the ontological context of emergence of modern subjects, in the reading of national narratives. What my analysis of postcolonial enfigurings of the juridical-historical thing—in a particular kind of historical text, namely, the *national text*—shows is how modern political subjects emerge through the simultaneous articulation of scientific and historical signifiers.

From an analytical position that engages modern representation as a political-symbolic context composed by strategies of engulfment, I show how the spelling of the proper name of man, the writing of the transparent I, is also an effect of raciality. For I choose engulfment to describe the productive effects of modern (scientific and historical) signifying strategies precisely because, as a spatial metaphor, it brackets the transparency thesis, the ontological assumption consolidated in Hegel's transcendental poesis. Because it situates power and desire in "the place of interval"—which, as Luce Irigaray (1993) proposes, conveys a sense of "the displacement of the subject or of the object in their relations of nearness or distance" (8)—engulfment as an account of productive power, "partial" violence, opens up a critical position that does not describe modern subjects and social configurations in transparency. Used here purportedly because it refers to one possible account of female power/desire, engulfment brackets the phallocentric narrative—informing conceptions of power as domination, penetration, and oppression—that writes post-Enlightenment Europe as the last act of the play of universal reason that resolves, hides, or dissipates everything else in the self-unfolding transcendental I.

For this reason, because the gesture that swallows, (trans)forms, without destroying, the critique of engulfment does not write yesterday's natives as *affectable "I's,"* nor does it uncover signs of what-was-before as resistances, a gesture that attempts to recuperate the native as always already self-consciousness, as a historical thing, an other minor transparent I. Because yesterday's conquerors and natives have been (trans)formed by the political-symbolic apparatus, the analytics of raciality, which carves them as global subjects, I hope this critique of modern representation shows how, precisely because it threatens and guarantees the coherence and consistency of the transparency thesis, the racial necessarily institutes the transparent I and its others as unstable subjects; therefore, it announces (the possibility of) ontoepistemological accounts that do not (re)produce the regions of transparency and the regions of affectability that compose the contemporary global configuration.

WHAT LIES AHEAD

I hope the following will show that my rejection of the sociohistorical logic of exclusion may constitute an ethical violation, but it is not a radical departure from modern representation. By refashioning it as the modern text, I move to erase the distinction forcing the choice (haunting "post" critiques of modern thought) between universality and historicity. Not because I deem it irrelevant, but because it becomes significant only when both are comprehended in the principle of transcendentality that Hegel's resolution of exteriority into interiority introduces. My point is that universality and historicity gain ethical authority only when transparency is assumed as an attribute of the collectivities they institute as modern subjects: as an attribute of reason, as the grounds for Habermas's speech acts, as an attribute of Butler's translatable "local cultures," or even as Laclau and Mouffe's new political subjectivities. That is, these writings of moral collectivities united by rationality (universality) or contingency (historicity) presume the transparency thesis, for they assume that interiority holds all that is necessary for the manufacturing of modern subjects.

For this reason, any radical remapping of the contemporary global configuration should neither rely on nor reassemble universality and historicity. Today's global subalterns inhabit the ethical place the arsenal of raciality produces. Facing the horizon of death, they stand perilously before the moment of transparency. Hence, the critical task is to engage the regimen of signification that composes this horizon of existence. For this reason, I acknowledge the productive powers of the modern "Will to Truth" and move to chart the modern text, the signifying context it produces, where I will gather the arsenal and effects of scientific signification. What I do in this mapping of the context of the emergence of the arsenal of raciality is to displace the transparency thesis, the ontological assumption informing both (a) critiques of juridical universality, which deploy the sociohistorical logic of exclusion to account for social subjection, and (b) critical racial analyses premised upon historicity, the ones that attempt to lift "the veil" and exhibit the racial subaltern in transparency. This gesture requires the retrieval of scientific universality from the waters of transcendental poesis, the one that institutes transcendentality as the ethical principle that guides the writing of post-Enlightenment European consciousness and social configuration in transparency. As I excavate the locus of the play of reason that scientific reason composes, the stage of exteriority, I find the regimen of production of raciality in the scientific projects that attempt to discover how the "laws of nature" produce mental and social configurations. I will show that without this political-symbolic arsenal it would be impossible to hold onto what transcendental poesis promises but cannot deliver because it is constrained by interiority, that is, the delimitation of the moment of transparency. For the arsenal of raciality does precisely that when it produces both (a) the affectable (subaltern) subjects that can be excluded from juridical universality without unleashing an ethical crisis and (b) the self-determined things who should enjoy the entitlements afforded and protected by the principle of universality said to govern modern social configurations.

Disregarding how scientific universality governs strategies of racial subjection enabled the 1980s celebrations or mourning of the demise of the Subject, which all too quickly and uncritically constructed the now "liberated" cultural others as minor transparent subjects. Two decades later, these cultural (historical) subalterns, still subjected to economic exploitation and dispossession, meet the force of law (juridical universality) almost exclusively in its punitive instantiation, in the policing of immigrants and refuges and the threat of self-righteous neoimperial violence. Haunted by what lies before it, this book spells out its own limitations. But I claim no innocence. My project is indebted to recent critiques of modern thought—here I include postmodern, poststructurist, and feminist contributions and the finest specimens of postcolonial writings (with all the overlappings) that decenter and "provincialize" Europe. I hope to push the critical task further, with an engagement with modern representation that does not remain prisoner to its terms. I do not claim to have located a critical position outside modern representation. I merely offer a modern contra-ontology, that is, a selective excavation of modern thought that seeks for what has to be postponed, but never obliterated, in fashionings of the transparent I, the *homo historicus,* to write its trajectory "other"-wise.

3

The Play of Reason

What I seek in speech is the response of the other. What constitutes me as a subject is my question. In order to be recognized by the other, I utter what was only in view of what will be. In order to find him, I call him by a name that he must assume in order to refuse to reply me. I identify myself in language, but only by losing myself in it like an object. What is realized in my history is not the past definite of what was, since it is no more, or even the present perfect of what has been in what I am but the future anterior of what I shall have been for what I am in the process of becoming.

—JACQUES LACAN, ÉCRITS

What does history realize when "becoming" unfolds before the horizon of death? Precisely because it introduces an answer to this question, Frantz Fanon's "Fact of blackness" offers a powerful point of departure for the critique of transparency. Not, however, as the ruling historicity imposes, because it describes a black or white subject of the frightened gaze trembling behind the veil of elusive transparency. Whatever blackness threatens to bring into (modern) representation will render the speech of man one, and just one, possible reference to the ontological context in which the black and the white man emerge as such. For if the subject of the "race problem" is a "double consciousness," as W. E. B. Du Bois describes it, it is only because he or she announces an "other" man, that is, one whose emergence, as Fanon's statement recalls, rehearses the haunting that institutes self-consciousness, inviting a return to the founding statements of

modern representation to retrieve the formulations that have outlined the subject.

My task in this chapter is to describe the first moment of this
excavation, the charting of the context of emergence of the *analytics of raciality*. Here I gather the assemblage of the horizon of
death in statements that describe how reason plays its sovereign
role. Following the early path of self-consciousness, beginning with
Descartes's inaugural statement, I trace the signifying gestures, displacement and negation, that have ensured the mind's ontoepistemological prerogative while securing its writing as an interior thing in a
universe of representation sustained by the scientific refashioning of
reason as a universal (exterior) ruler. What I do here is to show how
the articulation and disavowal of exterior things in ontoepistemological considerations postpone the threat that the mind itself would
be subjected to the new sovereign, *universal nomos,* that the framers
of modern science introduced into Western thought. When engaging
the predicament of self-consciousness, I find in seventeenth-century
philosophical statements how the displacement of exteriority is performed in the manufacturing of two scenes that describe how reason
plays its sovereign role, namely, the *scene of regulation,* where it
becomes *universal nomos,* a constraining or regulative force, the
one refigured by universality and the *scene of representation,* where
it becomes a productive power, the one that historicity refigures.
From each I gather the formulations that compose two ontoepistemological moments, the *stage of exteriority* and the *stage of interiority,* assembled by descriptions of how the mind and the things of
nature are situated before universal reason. Each corresponds to a
region of signification—respectively, *science* and *history*—that together compose modern representation. What I find in eighteenth-
century rewritings of the scenes of reason is another gesture, the
negation of exteriority, in the statement that universal reason acts
on the universe only because its tools of knowledge and pillars of
the morality reside in the human mind:[1] in Kant's reformulation of
the scene of regulation, it takes place when he locates the conditions
of possibility for scientific knowledge, for knowing with certainty,
in the understanding, and in Herder's rewriting of the scene of representation, it occurs in the postulate that reflection and language
constitute the conditions of possibility for moral unity. Here I gather
the montage of the stage of interiority, where the themes of the
Transcendental and the Historical consolidate universality and his-

toricity as the privileged ontoepistemological descriptors. Though in Kant's and Herder's rendering they acquire the attributes they refigure when deployed in modern ontoepistemological accounts, they are finally authorized when resolved in Hegel's formulations, which describe the play of reason as *transcendental poesis,* that is, the self-unfolding, self-representing, transcendental "I."

With this refiguring of modern representation it becomes possible to situate the epistemological rearrangement, the manufacturing of the analytics of raciality, when self-consciousness finally enters the stage of exteriority, in the projects of knowledge of man and society deployed about three hundred years after Descartes's inaugural statement. Neither version of the play of universal reason—as I will show in this and the next chapter—allowed for the possibility that the tools of scientific reason could be deployed to "discover" the "truth" of the interior thing. For the assertion of its ontoepistemological primacy depended not only on its intimacy with this new refiguring of the logos, but also on the fact that reason had to remain a universal (exterior) regulator from which modern representation derives its particularity. Not even Hegel's formulations that resolve the *nomos* and poesis in *transcendental poesis*—which, as I show in the next chapter, refashions self-consciousness as the *homo historicus,* the *transparent (interior-temporal) I*—fully dissipates this founding threat. Not surprisingly, a few decades after its deployment, the *homo historicus* would itself become an object of scientific reason in the projects of knowledge that attempted to discover the truth of man. What this charting of the context of emergence of the analytics of raciality does is to retrieve exteriority from Hegel's transcendental poesis. This is necessary groundwork that recuperates the *field of science* as a domain of production of modern political-symbolic strategies if one wishes to capture the effects of signification of the racial, to specify the role it plays when deployed in modern ontological accounts. From this reassembling of the founding statements of modern representation, then, I gather both ontological horizons, historicity and globality, to refashion self-consciousness as the *homo modernus,* that is, as the product of both arsenals—the narratives of history and science—of productive reason.

THE PREDICAMENT OF SELF-CONSCIOUSNESS

Though self-consciousness has been outlined in statements that dismiss metaphysical and religious considerations, the *homo historicus,* the transparent I, owes its privileged ontoepistemological position to how, over three hundred years, when attempting to keep the mind outside the determinations of all-powerful reason, modern philosophers consistently rewrote the defining premise of Western thought, namely, the ontoepistemological primacy of interiority. Western philosophy's self-attributed task has been to expose the "truth of things," which became possible after Parmenides distinguished between things as apprehended by the senses and things as entities [ón], as apprehended by the mind [nôus], and postulated a fundamental connection between the ón and the nôus. The statements that attribute ontoepistemological supremacy to the mind, the interior thing, would be consolidated into Plato's distinction of a world of phenomena (deceiving appearances) and a world of ideas (the "true being" of things) and Aristotle's specification of the tools necessary for knowing things as entities. From the very beginning, then, the prerogative of the mind as a knowing thing would rest on a postulated intimacy with the logos (reason and word), but it was rather late in its trajectory, in the writings of Stoics such as Epictetus and Cicero, and those of Augustine, that self-determination would be added as the rational thing's exclusive (moral) attribute. Precisely the need to secure this exclusive attribute, I argue, has occupied modern philosophers since the refashioning of reason as the secular ruler and producer of the universe, as an exterior (constraining or regulative) force, threatened to transform the mind into such an other thing of the world.

Following Aristotle's postulate that the happy life is the life of the "rational man," the Stoics declared that the "virtuous man" lives according to divine (rational) nature, that self-determination (self-sufficiency and self-discipline) distinguishes the good life.[2] In Stoicism, reason and freedom are joined because the mind participates in the nature of a divine author and ruler, which is "the vital force which created all things in this internally connected universe" and "the cosmic intelligence, which governs it from within" (Albert et al. 1969, 86). From that derives human beings' unique place among created things, for they alone can lead a "virtuous life," a rational, self-determined, and self-disciplined existence. In the fifth century, Augustine's merging of Stoicism and Catholicism rendered rationality (self-regulation) and will (self-determination) attributes exclusive to the soul, that interior dimension of human beings from which they access the now Judeo-Christian divine author and ruler. For Augustine, victory in the struggle for self-determination consists in a release from the passions of the body, for the rational soul finds freedom when the human will realizes itself in the supernatural creator's.[3] In the seventeenth century, the relationship between reason and freedom became central, as the mind's self-determination was resignified in a reformulation of the quest for the "truth of things,"[4] in which the grounds for knowing with certainty could rely neither on a supernatural ruler and author nor on common properties shared by the mind and other worldly things. Now man could rely solely on the mind's intimacy with reason, its exclusive quality as a self-knowing thing, to support the claim that he alone could decipher the ordered whole of created things, the universe designed by the divine rational will, namely, nature.

As I trace the trajectory of self-consciousness, I gather statements that ascertain the mind's self-determination and seek to secure it in interiority, unaffected by the determinations of the secular ruler and the extended things it regulates and controls, by rewriting its intimacy with universal reason. What I show is how this gesture itself inaugurates a haunting, the possibility that exteriority would acquire ontological priority because in science, the version of the quest for "truth" upon which modern thought grounds its particularity, knowledge with certainty, that is, "true" knowledge, rests on both (a) the use of the human body, that exterior dimension of the knowing subject through which it relates to the things it seeks to know, and (b) the rewriting of reason as the universal (exterior) foundation shared by the mind and these things. Because from early on Western thought has attributed to the body an inferior position and qualities (extension, matter, the concrete, etc.), while it has written the mind to signify the logos's proper qualities (thought, form, the abstract, etc.), it is not surprising that the rewriting of man in interiority has required the disavowal of the human body and everything else that shares its chief attribute, namely, extension.[5] Though consistent, and I concede necessary, this gesture has not been sufficient. Because the human body's ontoepistemological irrelevance had to be reproduced in each later statement, each would repeat this gesture by writing the mind in its difference from the human body and the things of the world. In doing so, each recalled that which remains without, outside, the seat of form or "spirit." Consequently, the statements that sketched the stage of interiority as the privileged holdings of self-consciousness also provided the blueprint of the stage of exteriority (nature), the domain inhabited by extended and therefore affectable things scientific knowledge addresses, that is, the one that threatens to assign a place to man, to undermine his writing in (rational/self-determined) interiority.

The Interior Thing

What I find in the outlining of self-consciousness is a statement that establishes the ontoepistemological primacy of *interiority,* once again reasserting that the mind's ability to know with certainty rests on its intimacy with the logos. In his *Meditations,* René Descartes ([1641] 1986) inaugurated the modern account of the self-determined mind in a statement that conflates being and knowledge when he gives ontoepistemological primacy to the *res cogitans,* the thinking thing, the only existing thing whose essence lies in its ability to determine, to decide upon, its own essence and existence. Put differently, Descartes's inaugural statement unites being and truth when ontology and epistemology are resolved in a purely interior (formal) act, namely, thinking. This was an accomplishment that required a bold signifying gesture, the displacement of exteriority, the declaration of its ontoepistemological irrelevance, in two formulations that articulate and disavow extended (exterior/affectable) things. In the first formulation, Descartes reasserts the ontological irrelevance of that which in man does not share in the mind's privilege, namely, the human body. Though he describes man as a mind-body composite, he postulates that "simply by knowing that I exist and seeing at the same time that absolutely nothing else belongs to my nature or essence except that I am a thinking thing, I can infer correctly that my essence consists solely in the fact that I am a thinking thing. . . . Accordingly, it is certain I am really distinct from my body and can exist without it" (54). This statement at once articulates and disavows the human body, for it recognizes its need to define, but affirms its inability to signify, the essence and existence of man.

Nevertheless, the assertion of the ontological primacy of the interior thing, the mind, does not settle Descartes's main concern, that is, to establish its ability to know with certainty the extended (material, sensible, etc.) things. The second formulation, the postulate that everything outside of and distinct from the mind plays no role in the determination of being and truth, that is, the declaration of the ontoepistemological irrelevance of extended things, requires three other steps that further establish the thinking thing's epistemological supremacy: (a) the statement that the human body's and the things' *affectability* renders them, respectively, an unreliable tool and the basis of knowledge; (b) the assertion that thinking (reflection, understanding, judgment) alone plays the determining role in knowledge; and (c) the determination of a formal criterion for truth and its justification. The assertion of interiority's ontoepistemological primacy requires that knowledge depend neither on a human body through which the subject relates to what it seeks to know, by receiving impressions from them—that is, being affected—nor on the exterior things themselves. First, Descartes postulates that what can be known with certainty are not the changeable, unreliable attributes of things—shape, taste, odor, and so on—which are known through the senses, but their lasting (abstract) qualities of being "extended, flexible, and movable," which only the rational mind comprehends. "For knowledge of the truth about such things seems to belong to the mind alone," he argues, so he errs when he threats these impressions "as reliable touchstones for immediate judgment about the essential nature of the bodies located outside us" (57). Second, Descartes also dismisses volitions and emotions, postulating that the question of certainty in knowledge, of "truth," concerns the intellect alone. Hence, he moves to establish why truth or falsity relates only to judgments, that is, the operations of intellect. These alone fall within the scope of his resolution of the problem of certainty. Third, when determining the criterion and basis of truth, Descartes postulates that the sole criterion for truth resides in what the mind can perceive as "clearly and distinctively" as it perceives itself and mathematical ideas. Nevertheless, because the thinking, interior thing, man, is an imperfect and finite formal substance, he cannot constitute the sole ground for asserting truth. For this, the mind depends on the divine author and ruler, now transformed into a rational figure, that is, the idea (form) of perfection, the essence and cause of that which is clearly and distinctively apprehended by the mind, that is, the true. From this "supreme substance" the mind receives the clear and distinct perceptions, the abstract attributes of extended things (length, shape, motion, etc.), mathematical objects, and so on (48).

When outlining self-consciousness, Descartes refashions the mind as the formal "I," the thinking thing, the sole ground for ontological and epistemological accounts. This recentering of the mind, the interior thing, is accomplished through three moves that perform the displacement of exteriority: (a) the ontological disavowal of the human body in the argument that thinking alone defines the existence and essence of man; (b) the epistemological disqualification of the human body and the things that affect it; and (c) the ontoepistemological disavowal of the "matter": of knowledge, the extended (exterior or affectable) things, the essence and existence of which is determined by the divinity that, now stripped from supernaturality, becomes form. What these formulations that articulate and disavow exterior things indicate, in a text concerned with the conditions of the possibility of knowing the "truth of things," is why it was necessary to write the failure of exteriority to signify the proper ("true") mode of being of man: the attribution of affectability—man's lacking the ability to decide on his essence and existence—that is, outer determination. Put differently, Descartes needs to articulate extended things (the human body and the sensible objects of knowledge) to write their ontoepistemological irrelevance lest man, the subject of knowledge, also become a thing whose existence and essence is determined from without, that is, an affectable thing. Nevertheless, man is a thing of the world, for his body locates him in that which cannot be resolved in the mind's distinguishing quality, interiority; he also belongs in exteriority, where he is and exists as any other affectable worldly thing; that is, because man neither is nor exists without his body, exteriority would remain a ghost haunting every later refashioning of self-consciousness.

Neither the Greek disregard for nor the Christian dismissal of the human body, to be sure, precluded exteriority's "return" in the interventions that reensure the mind's ontoepistemological primacy, nor would Descartes' inaugural displacement of exteriority prevent it from retuning in later refashionings of the I, for the simple reason that without the idea of exterior things, the mind's distinguishing attribute, interiority, cannot be articulated. Until the seventeenth century, this necessity appeared in the oppositional pairs—mind/body, reason/sensation, form/matter—that establish the mind's access to the sovereign of being and meaning, the Logos or God. In modern philosophy, however, this necessity became a threat that could be postponed only in statements that ensured the mind's intimacy with universal reason by keeping it out of the stage in which it performs the play of power. This is so because modern thought is sustained by an approach to truth, scientific knowledge, that relies on the very possibility of engaging exterior things; put differently, in modern thought, the ontoepistemological disavowal of exteriority becomes a necessity.[6]

Scientific Reason

After the "discoveries" of Copernicus, Galileo, and Kepler, the "Will to Truth" would neither address the things themselves nor contemplate the intentions of the author of the universe. Seeking more than to describe the texture of the universe, in science, knowledge would address the motions (affections) of things, that is, the (material) effects of the actions, of the play of the rational will that orders the universe. Although they do not reject Aristotle's postulate that knowledge should address principles, conditions, and causes, the writers of scientific reason are not concerned with "being," "essence," and "final causes." Instead, the statements that delineate the field of science establish that the knowing subject is interested in that which determines that the "world of things" appear as it does, seeking to discover how its governing power or force, universal reason, works because it would help the project of submitting existing things to the human will. What I find here is the montage of the stage of exteriority, where reason plays the role of the exterior (constraining or regulative) force governing how things appear, that which causes a thing to affect itself (change) and others (motion). That is, in this first articulation of reason as a secular sovereign, universal *nomos*—that is, in scientific universality—the knowing subject remains outside the scope of knowledge, for the truth of self-consciousness remains beyond the reach of the tools of knowledge. Nevertheless, because to know the world of things, the subject of knowledge counted with that which he shares with them, his body, the possibility is open that the self-consciousness could also be subjected to the powerful ruler, to be refashioned as an affectable thing. A possibility that would be explored only about two centuries later, by the writers of raciality, after Hegel resolved "causes" into "essences," "truth" into "being," and, more important, exteriority into interiority, when he refashioned the mind of man as the product, tool, and raw material of a transcendental mind. Neither a thing as any other nor the receptacle of divine information, in the outline of the field of science, the mind appropriates the impressions collected by the affectable body and combines the unique powers it receives from the divine author and ruler, understanding and will, to discover the tools, the "laws," the latter uses in the ordering of its lesser creations, that is, the things of nature.

In his *New Organon,* Francis Bacon ([1620] 1960) provides a general plan for the scientific journey. Explicitly dismissing ancient and medieval concerns with metaphysics and religion,[7] he argues that the aim of knowledge is to advance human power, to discover the "formal causes" operating in the world of things in order to render the replication of their effects possible. "For though in nature nothing really exists beside individual bodies performing pure individual acts according to a fixed law," he states, "yet in philosophy this very law, and the investigation, discovery, and explanation of it, is the foundation as well of knowledge as of operation. And it is this law, with its causes, that I mean when I speak of Form" (119–20). In order to uncover this law, the knowing subject counts with what it shares with the phenomena it addresses its own affectable body, which here becomes a tool of the rational mind. "The sense, which is the door of the intellect," Bacon argues, "is affected by individuals only. The images of those individuals—the impressions which they make on the senses—fix themselves in the memory, and pass into it in the first instances entire as it were, just as they come. These, the human mind proceeds to review and ruminate; and thereupon either simply rehearses them, or makes fanciful imitations of them, or analyses and classifies them" (292–93). Unlike the Cartesian formal I, who thrives in oblivious abstraction to apprehend the order of the universe, the scientific subject welcomes immersion into the confused, indistinct world of exterior things. For this reason, because in scientific signification affectability—which I use here to refigure change or motion—plays a central role, the displacement of exteriority as an ontoepistemological moment could be performed only in two dangerous formulations, which rewrite nature as the scene of regulation. First, the human body is at once called on and disavowed as a necessary instrument of knowledge. To engage the play of appearances, the subject of knowledge counts with its body—more accurately, the senses—which now become the appropriate tools to use to gather in the phenomena of the universe, the impressions the mind would use to discover the laws governing the world of things. Second, the immediate objects of knowledge, phenomena, the observation of which would give access to the order of nature, are also at once named and dismissed as mere "effects." That is, because it seeks the hidden, invisible, fixed causes, physics portrays the world of things, the domain of matter, as inhabited by affectable things, that is, beings subjected to outer determination. What emerges here is a conception of causes, laws of nature, as constraining commands, the tools of reason, the exterior (objective or abstract) forces, that affect things and determine how they affect each other. When rewriting reason as the secular regulative force acting on every existing thing, the framers of science transform nature into the holdings of a power that acts solely as law, that is, universal *nomos*.

From now on, the thinking thing can discover the secrets of nature but also translate them into the abstract (mathematical) instruments it has confectioned only because it is made of the same stuff the divine ruler deployed to order the universe. Not only is the knowing subject now interested in what it gathers with the senses, in experience, that is, the confused and contingent happenings of the world of things; it conceives of these events as the manifold, particular effects of general causes, the laws of nature, the forces deployed by the rational (divine) will. When turning its attention to moving (affectable) matter, the knowing subject seeks to decipher the regularities—the particular expressions, the effects of the acts of universal *nomos*—but it is not determined by nor does it determine what it seeks to know; knowledge remains the result of the abstract (formal) tools the mind produces to discover how reason, as an *exterior* (universal) force, controls and regulates the motions (the affections) of the things of the world. That is, exteriority governs scientific signification. In his *Principia,* Isaac Newton ([1686] 1995) translates the movements of the universe into the abstract language of knowledge, mathematics, which becomes the crucial instrument of physics, the study of the efficient causes governing the play of appearances. Physics, or "experimental philosophy," Newton states, is concerned with causes and effects; it moves from the particular to the universal, aware that nature may hold greater mysteries than the laws of motion, but those are beyond its scope. "In this philosophy," he posits, "particular propositions are inferred from the phænomena, and afterwards rendered general by induction. Thus it was that the impenetrability, the mobility, and the impulsive force of bodies, and the laws of motion and of gravitation, were discovered. And to us it is enough that gravity does really exist, and act according to the laws which we have explained, and abundantly serves to account for all the motions of the celestial bodies, and of our sea" (3).

What I gather in the statements that fashion reason as universal *nomos,* the law (the sovereign will), is the writing of the world of things, the manufacturing of nature as the stage of exteriority: the plenum is now inhabited by moving things, bodies, which obey the invisible forces or powers that determine how they affect and how they are affected by other bodies. That is, it introduces a conception of the universal as law (regulation) and a conception of the particular in which things matter not in themselves, but as objects of the exterior will that regulates or controls their motions (affections). Nevertheless, though privileging affectability, scientific universality constructs the relationships it observes in phenomena as the deed of a universal ordering (constraining or regulative) force, that is, law. In other words, in scientific signification, exteriority rules both postulates: (a) the defining statement of modern thought, that is, that reason is the exterior, hence universal, sovereign of the world of thing and an attribute of the mind of *man;* and consequently, (b) the defining statement of scientific knowledge, that is, that nature, now approached as the universe ordered by a secular force, is inhabited by affectable, outer-determined things, that is, those whose internal and external affections, change (inner motions) and movement (outer motions), result from the sovereign acts of their common ruler. Though confirming the mind's ability to know with certainty, which it derives from being the only existing thing with reason, even if it could be certain only of the causes of motion (affection), the discovery of the laws of nature marks the beginning of the ascending movement of universal reason, which inaugurates a threat, the henceforth thinkable possibility that order in the world of men is but an effect of an exterior (regulative and constraining) will.

THE SCENES OF REASON

When describing Descartes's outline of self-consciousness I highlight how the possibility of knowing that which lies outside itself—exterior things—with certainty sustains the writing of the mind's self-determination. Such a possibility, however, would be established only when the framers of scientific signification removed the divine ruler and producer from considerations of knowledge by asserting that the thinking thing could decipher the workings of the secular ruler of the world of things. Because the early formulators of scientific universality deployed the version of the play of reason as universal *nomos,* their radical gesture was to forfeit inquiring into questions of essence and being. Expectedly, the same move that would inaugurate a radically distinct moment in Western thought, modern philosophy, did not preclude—actually, it immediately required—considerations of how universal *nomos* operates in the "world of men," of how it operates in the collective entities constituted by the only rational existing thing.

In my reading of seventeenth-century refashionings of self-consciousness, under this new configuration of Western thought I identify two accounts of how universal reason performs its sovereign role: namely, through the scene of regulation and the scene of representation. Each corresponds to the attributes of the divine sovereign—will and design—whom, at this moment, reason had just begun to remove from the arena of truth. In both, the displacement of exteriority and the reasserting of its ontological irrelevance are performed in statements that rationality, the divine's gift to man, ensures that, unlike merely affectable things, the thing of interiority knows and emulates the will or design of the creator. In Locke's version of the scene of regulation, the deployment of the version of the play of reason as the workings of universal *nomos* enables the formulation of another rendering of universality, juridic universality. Still an exterior ruler, universal reason here constrains or regulates rational things that have two powers the objects of scientific knowledge lack, namely, understanding and will; that is, they can comprehend and decide to follow and emulate divine will. While the framing of juridical universality enables a social ontology that displaces the king's claim of divine power and asserts human beings' ability and right to decide on the basis and direction of their social existence, the idea that in exterior regulation, law, rests the possibility of collective life seriously threatens the very attribute of "inner freedom" that the mind acquires in Stoic morality. This is no small threat. In Leibniz's statements I identify the outline of the scene of representation, in which this threat is addressed through a return to considerations of "final causes"—to "essences" and "being." What we find here is another version of the play of reason, *universal poesis,* in which existing things (man and the things of the world) become the actualization of the self-producing "force" and the unique "essence," which the divine author places in the interiority of each created thing, that is, "souls" or "monads."

What I identify in these scenes of reason are outlines of the two descriptors—universality and historicity—that correspond to the social ontologies which, from the nineteenth century on, would guide accounts of the modern social configuration, the ones that constitute the modern political subject as the juridical-moral thing. Both descriptors were consolidated separately in the eighteenth century, when Kant and Herder rewrote these scenes to situate the play of universal reason fully in interiority, but they were reconciled when Hegel's version of the play of reason, transcendental poesis, resolved regulation into representation, *nomos* into poesis, the solution that consolidates the *transparency thesis* as the privileged modern onto-epistemological assumption.

The Scene of Regulation

When self-consciousness is fashioned as a juridical subject, the "individual" emerges as the basic ontological unit, the rational will that embraces *exterior* regulation to protect its life and self-determination.[8] In his *Two Treatises of Government,* John Locke ([1690] 1947) specifies the particular way in which the will of the divine author and ruler operates in the "world of men," the "political society." Not, however, before, in the *First Essay,* dismissing the argument that grounds political authority on a divine mandate and, in the *Second Essay,* precluding any possibility of conceiving the ordered world of men along the same lines as scientific signification produces the world of things. Against Hobbes's description of the "state of nature" as wrought by competition among individuals moved by uncontrolled desire, Locke offers an account of the conditions under which the political emerges, in which *man* is already subjected to a kind of universal regulation, the divine law of "self-preservation." Not, however, as the intrinsically affectable inhabitant of the world of things—the stage of exteriority—but as a self-determined thing, one able to know and follow the commands of his divine creator.

Three attributes of man, equality, freedom, and property, testify to the fact that the "natural law [divine will]" has endowed him with self-determination. First, Locke argues, before the institution of "political society," man existed in a state of "equality, wherein all the power and jurisdiction is reciprocal," where everyone is "born to all the same advantages of nature and the use of the same faculties" and "should also be equal one amongst another without subordination or subjection; unless the lord and master of them all should, by any manifest declaration of his will, set one above another, and confer on him by an evident and clear appointment an undoubted right to dominion and sovereignty" (122). Second, unlike in the world of things, where universal *nomos* operates from without—for things decide neither the application nor the direction of their intrinsic powers—in the world of men, regulation operates from within. In the "state of nature," Locke says, men are in a "state of perfect freedom to order their actions and dispose of their possessions and persons as they think fit, within the bounds of the law of nature, without asking leave or depending upon the will of any other man." For man in this state of perfection has the right, given by reason, Locke argues, to ensure "his own preservation" and that of "the rest of mankind," a right he will use only for self-protection (126). Third, from the argument that each human being is ruled solely by the "[divine] law of nature"—for "every man has a property in his own person; this nobody has any right to but himself"—Locke derives a notion of private property, which, besides life and freedom, includes every thing a particular human being modifies in his surroundings. "The labor of his body and the work of his hand," Locke argues, "are properly his. Whatsoever then he removes out of the state that nature has provided and left it in, he has mixed his labor with, and joined to it something that is his own, and thereby makes it his property" (134).

When describing these attributes, which are universal because the divine author and ruler gives them to all rational creatures alike, Locke introduces the notion of the "individual" as the basic moral unit—the one who decides and acts according to the divine will, which at this point remains the sole moral determinant, the measure of goodness and perfection. Because its action is restricted solely by the divine will, through the law of "self-preservation," the thinking thing retains self-determination. Here, however, the notion of self-determination gains another meaning. For just as the account of the universal *nomos* privileges the determinants of action, the writing of man's uniqueness required the statement that the mind also holds active powers, attributes it shares with the ruler of nature, namely, the will and the understanding. These, Locke argues, testify to man's freedom, which he ties to his power, his ability, to decide on (design and control) the course of—that is, to determine—his action. Not surprisingly, the founding question of this social ontology becomes Why does the self-determined thing subject itself to an exterior ruler, the "political society"? Because, Locke answers, acknowledging that an "individual" may desire to appropriate another's life, freedom, and possessions—instituting a "state of war" that may lead to "state of slavery," being under another's absolute power—individuals recognized the need for regulation beyond natural (divine) law. Because "freedom from absolute, arbitrary power is so necessary to and closely joined with a man's preservation that he cannot part with it but by what forfeits his preservation and life together," by freely deciding to sacrifice the power to execute the "law of self-preservation," the rational thing is doing no more than following divine determination. That is, the political body results from free, independent, rational acts, the objective of which is to ensure rather than hinder self-determination. "For law, in its true notion," Locke argues, "is not so much the limitation as the direction of a free and intelligent agent to his proper interest, and prescribes no farther than it for the general good of those under that law. . . . The end of law is not to abolish or restrain but to preserve and enlarge freedom; for in all the states of created beings capable of laws, where there is no law, there is not freedom" (132).

What one finds in Locke's description of the political society, the artificial body that individuals institute, is the articulation of the first modern ontological descriptor, *universality*. Here self-determination sustains a social ontology that produces the ordered world of men as the scene of (self-)regulation, that is, as a juridic (legal) unity. The "political society," Locke argues, ensues from "individuals'" consent, that is, rational and free decisions to create an artificial rational body, the "political society," the function of which is to enact and administer rules that will preserve individuals' property (life, liberty, and estate) by punishing acts of unrestrained wills. Nothing beyond the recognition that exterior (outer) determination is necessary for the preservation of life and freedom and property, no sense of metaphysical or religious unity (of origin or ends), but judgment, which is but the obedience of the "natural [divine] law of self-preservation," leads individuals to institute the body politic. Though as a juridical (rational) body the "political society" holds the "authority to decide controversies between them and punish offenders" (163), Locke argues, political power derives from the "will and determination of the majority; for that which acts any community being only the consent of the individuals of it, and it being necessary to that which is one body to move one way, it is necessary the body should move that way whither the greater force carries it, which is the consent of the majority" (169). Because this sacrifice results from a rational (free) decision—namely, consent—being subjected to the expression of the will and determination of the majority, to exterior rules, which are so because they apply indiscriminately to all members of the body politic, does not constitute a relinquishing of self-determination, the ability to design, decide on, and control one's action.

In the scene of regulation, the displacement of exteriority occurs in the postulate that in rationality, the "natural" (God-given) distinguishing attribute of man, resides the condition of possibility for social existence. Though instituted laws constrain individuals' actions, preventing and punishing only those that affect another's freedom, the determinants of freedom reside inside man, in the mind, which, unlike the bodies of nature—the ones without thought, will, or volition—has been endowed with self-determination. Consistently, affectability has no ontological significance, because rationality, through instituted (universal) laws, mediates the relationships among the members of the political society. While imposed by an exterior will, the juridic (collective) body, the political society, is a mere institution, a creation of the thinking thing, the only one able to decide, because it recognizes and appreciates the necessity to subject itself to exterior (outer) determination. Thus, Locke's version of liberal ontology protects *man*'s self-determination by rewriting exterior determination as an effect of individuals' (interior and rational) decisions. Yet it does not dissipate the danger introduced by the writing of reason as universal *nomos*. Just as the framers of science abandon (the desire to discover the essence of) the thing in itself, in Locke's account the individual sacrifices more than the power to execute the divine mandate. For according to early and later critics of universal *nomos,* liberal ontology also forfeits the dearest divine gift to man, the one that testifies to the profound intimacy human beings enjoy both with the divine author and with each other.

The Scene of Representation

Precisely the talent that *his* participation in the divine nature favors in *man,* representation (autopoesis) is recuperated in the version of reason as a universal productive force. In Leibniz's statements, the universe becomes an effect of fundamentally interior things, "souls" or "monads," which share in the productive power of the divine author and contribute to the realization of its design, perfection, by actualizing, manifesting, and displaying the intrinsic and unique qualities with which it endowed them.[9] In various pieces collected in his *Philosophical Essays,* G. W. Leibniz (1989) recuperates what his contemporaries—Descartes, Newton, and Locke, among others— have forsaken when rejecting metaphysics. For seeking to know how divine will is deployed, he laments, they have missed why it is so. When exploring how divine motives are inscribed in the texture of the universe, Leibniz rewrites the play of reason as universal poesis in a statement that consolidates temporality as a proper ontoepiste-mological moment. Recuperating Aristotle's notion of simple sub-stances, Leibniz defines monads—"individual substances," "souls," or "spirits"—as the basic created things endowed with three inter-related attributes, namely, "intrinsic difference," "inner force," and self-productivity. All existing, exterior, things, he postulates, are ac-tualizations of self-representing (productive or developing), "intrin-sically different" "souls," effects of the deployment of their "inner forces," whose goal is perfection, that is, the realization of the divine design. With this he refashions the universe (the "world of things" and the "world of men") as the scene of representation, an account of the play of reason that describes how all existing things constitute actualizations of the "inner force" and "intrinsic difference" housed in their "souls" or "spirits." For "the universe," he postulates, "is in some way multiplied as many times as there are substances, and the glory of God is likewise multiplied by as many entirely different representations of his work" (42).

In this version of the play of reason, the ontoepistemological dis-placement of exteriority occurs as the universe becomes but the recep-tacle of all that is possible and potential, all that always already is in interiority. Not only does this statement fully recuperate interiority—

as "intrinsic difference" (inner particularity) and "inner force" (inner determination)—without dismissing affection. Also, because the determinants of motion now reside in the things themselves and self-production (development) displaces dislocation as change enters the horizon of time, affectability—an attribute of extended (exterior/spatial) things—plays no role in the determination (the account of the essence and existence) of things. In the scene of representation, the relationship between the universal (reason) and the particular (things) will change. "Intrinsic difference" corresponds not only to a position in, but also to that which each particular thing ("soul") adds to, the universal. More important, the universe is now the stage of actualizations, the rendering real of "intrinsic difference," which is an effect but of each particular thing's "inner force"; that is, existing things are not approached as "effects," as reactions to or consequences of the working either of an exterior force or of actual relationships with other things. While each particular thing is a product of a universal force, it is also self-producing and "inner-" determined, that is, affected solely by the force residing at its core. "Each substance," Leibniz postulates, "bears in some way the character of God's infinite wisdom and omnipotence and imitates him as much as it is capable" (42); each "includes once and for all everything that can ever happen to it" (44). And, more important, each "is like a world apart, independent of all other things, except for God, thus all our phenomena, that is, all the things that can happen to us, are only consequences of our being" (47). Further, he states, each particular thing is a "unit of multiplicity," both as each comprehends and represents from a particular position all the existing things of the universe and as each houses all future (possible and potential) ones. Not only does each correspond to a particular mode of representing the universe, but they affect one another only as pieces of an infinite puzzle, because substances "act upon one another and are required, so to speak, to accommodate themselves to one another" (48). Finally, Lebiniz's nature is not static, but rather is an unfolding and contingent order composed of independently self-producing, self-transforming things. Here reason becomes universal poesis; it plays the role of a productive power, the principle that guides the temporal realization, the coming into existence, of the unique force it places in the interiority of each particular thing.

When considering how universal poesis operates in the world of

men, Leibniz introduces the second ontological descriptor, historicity, the one which renders social unity contingent upon morality, the
collective principles that each human being houses in its particular
intelligent "soul" or "spirit." The "intelligent soul," Leibniz postulates, "knowing what it is—having the ability to utter the word 'I,'
a word so full of meanings—does not merely remain and subsist
metaphysically, which it does to a greater degree than the others,
but also remains the same morally and constitutes the same person.
For it is memory or the knowledge of this self that renders it capable
of punishment or reward" (65). In the scene of representation, a social ontology emerges in which the I gains attributes ignored in the
Cartesian outline and displaced in Locke's appropriation of universal *nomos*. On the one hand, it acquires an "essence," "intrinsic difference," and "inner determination." Being self-producing while at
the same time encompassing the whole of existing (actual), possible,
and potential things and their transformations, the interior thing
is no longer a mere abstract, formal (thought) thing; it becomes a
thing that represents (reproduces) itself in time, that is, a temporal
thing. Not surprisingly, the disavowal of the human body is here as
ontologically decisive as it is epistemologically consistent. Having
virtually no relevance to knowledge, the human body now becomes
an aid in the realization of designs of the "soul." For Leibniz, the
body is that which is "accommodated to the soul for the situations
in which the soul is thought to act externally" (211). On the other
hand, in the scene of representation the individual is resolved in the
collective as "individual" freedom becomes always already an effect
of collective inner determination.

In his refashioning of the I as a self-representing thing, Leibniz
highlights three dimensions disregarded by the writers of the social as a juridic (self-regulating) body, namely, (a) *morality,* in the
view of self-consciousness as fundamentally accountable for its actions; (b) *representability,* in the conception of particularity, individuality, in which "intrinsic difference" corresponds to a particular
point of view, representation of the universe; and (c) *temporality,*
not merely as memory and insensible perceptions of continuity, the
past, but also in the sense in which each mind or soul always already
houses its future, that is, its possible and potential actualizations.[10]
With this, he outlines a social ontology premised upon historicity
(interiority-temporality). By resolving freedom into morality and
representability—"inner force" and "intrinsic difference," that is,

interiority—Leibniz rewrites self-consciousness, the I, as a moral thing without allowing for a consideration of the relationships among the members of the social whole. In the scene of representation, freedom (self-determination) becomes the "inner force" of the actualizations actualizing a divine "end" ("intrinsic difference"). Every existing thing, but the rational thing in particular, neither is nor exists as an effect of outward determination, for each and every existing thing moves toward the actualization of its interior (exclusive) force. Morality, as conformity to the divine design, guides ontological accounts that construct human actions and ideas as the actualizations of divine wisdom, not as the expressions of divine will. What this version of the play of reason as universal poesis introduced was the ontological descriptor *historicity,* which would later concern moral philosophies and projects of knowledge that, in the following centuries, would search in the facts and representations of the human past for the actualizations of the "ends," that is, the principles guiding human action (Taylor 1975).

From this initial excavation of the context of emergence of the analytics of raciality, the modern text, I gathered, in the scenes of reason, statements that secure self-consciousness in interiority through the displacement of exteriority, that is, statements that deny exterior things any ontoepistemological relevance. Though in both scenes universal reason remains a manifestation of the figure of the divine ruler and creator, in each the assertion that self-consciousness is a thing with reason sustains the mind's ontological prerogative. Each protects the mind's self-determination from the possibility introduced in the framing of scientific reason, containing the threat it announces with signifying gestures that produce affectability as the effect of one and only one exterior *(nomos)* or interior (poesis) determinant, namely, universal reason. When, in the following century, Enlightenment philosophers chose universal *nomos* over universal poesis to announce the culmination of the trajectory of man, new versions of the scenes of reason were deployed that, by consolidating the interior as the location from which universal reason plays its sovereign role, secure the mind's self-determination without forfeiting that which distinguishes modern thought.

THE STAGE OF INTERIORITY

No one disputes the assertion that the Age of Enlightenment consolidated scientific reason as the force of intellectual, moral, and economic "progress" and "development" (Cassirer 1951).[11] Reading Condorcet (1995) and other French Enlightenment philosophers, who despised the metaphysics lingering in the Cartesian thinking thing and praised the accomplishments of the English framers of science, one comes across many statements that announce the demise of the divine ruler and author, celebrating the fact that universal reason is finally alone to guide the human mind on the road to "progress" and "happiness."[12] My charting of two statements that consolidate universal reason's greatest accomplishment, Kant's formulation of the Transcendental and Herder's account of the Historical, highlight another bold gesture, the negation of exteriority, that is, the affirmation of its inexistence as an ontoepistemological moment. While each rewrites a particular version of the play of reason—universal *nomos* and universal poesis, respectively—and the corresponding scene of reason that explicates how it operates in the universe, both declare the nonexistence of exteriority when postulating that it is precisely because of how it operates in interiority, as an attribute of the mind, that the secular ruler and producer of the universe constitutes the sovereign master of epistemological and ontological accounts. Put differently, Kant's and Herder's formulations consolidate, respectively, universality and historicity as the privileged descriptors of modern social configuration, the montage of the stage of interiority, in statements that assert that reason plays the part of a universal regulative or productive force because of how it does so in (the mind of) man.

Nevertheless, my reading will show that neither Kant's identification of the tools of the transcendental nor Herder's naming of the pillars of the historical would provide a definite solution to the threat of affectability, because neither could relinquish exteriority. For both Kant's knowing subject and Herder's moral subject fashion the mind as always already mediated by the universal (exterior) determinant, namely, universal reason. So what they accomplish is to postpone this threat by postulating once again that because man is a thing with reason, because he is affected only by something that lies inside himself, he remains the only thing of reason that enjoys self-determination. My point, then, is this: neither can relinquish the grounding of freedom on reason, which is both necessary and unstable precisely because it requires the full montage of the stage of exteriority—a deed accomplished in the following century by the framers of the analytics of raciality—where it is possible to situate, to represent (think and imagine), post-Enlightenment Europe as just an "other" moment (spatial-temporal locus) of human existence, the task the racial has performed since the nineteenth century.

The Tools of the Transcendental

When refashioning universal *nomos* as transcendental (pure) reason, Kant ensures the universality—"objectivity and necessity"—of "truth" statements even as he locates the tools of scientific reason fully in interiority. In his *Critique of Pure Reason,* Kant ([1781] 1990) ascertains reason's sovereignty in a statement that unceremoniously, though very systematically, once again dismisses the divine author and ruler as well as metaphysics from epistemological considerations. More important, by locating the conditions of possibility of knowledge before and beyond sense perception, postulating that terms such as *time, space, substance, totality,* and so on are the tools "pure reason" provides to the understanding, he establishes that now scientific knowledge could progress independent of subjective (psychological) and purely empirical concerns and without principles derived solely from either of them. With this he settles the questioning of certainty Hume reopened to assert not only the mind's ability to know "laws" governing the play of phenomena, to "discover" the acts of reason in the stage of exteriority, in nature, but to know them a priori, that is, before and beyond experience. "That all knowledge begins with experience, there can be no doubt," Kant states at the opening of the First Critique. But he adds that "it by no means follows that all arise out of experience." His self-attributed task, then, is to describe the conditions of the possibility of a kind of knowledge "altogether independent of experience, and even of sensuous impressions" (1). Needing no common physical (body), supernatural (the divine author and ruler), or metaphysical ground for the mind that knows and the things to be known, this kind of knowledge, a priori, depends but on mediators, the tools of universal *nomos,* which exist only in the mind.

In this reading of Kant's rendering of the universal *nomos,* I am interested in his statements regarding scientific universality. More precisely, I gather in his rewriting of the scene of regulation the outline of the stage of interiority as the proper and sole location from which reason plays its role as the regulative force of the "world of things," insofar as they concern knowledge. Taking place here is not a dismissal of affectability as a crucial moment in scientific knowledge but its resolution in interiority in the statement that the necessary conditions for sense perception, the "pure intuitions" of space and time, reside in the mind. "Time," Kant postulates, "is the formal condition, *à priori,* of all phenomena whatsoever. Space, as the pure form of external intuition, is limited as a condition *à priori* of external phenomena alone. On the other hand, *because all representations, whether they have or have not external things for their objects, still in themselves, as determinations of the mind, belong to our internal state;* and because this internal state is subject to the formal condition of the internal intuition, that is, to time—time is a condition *à priori* of all phenomena whatsoever—the *immediate* condition of all internal and thereby the *mediate* condition of all external phenomena." Although he postulates that space is the condition of possibility for representing external (exterior) things, the objects of knowledge, Kant further renders knowledge an effect of interiority when he places all phenomena in time. "If I can say *à priori,*" he proceeds, "'all outward phenomena are in space, and determined *à priori* according the relations of space,' I can also, from the principle of the internal sense, affirm universally, 'all phenomena in general, that is, all objects of the sense, are in time, and stand necessarily in relations of time'" (30–31, italics in the original).

In his *Prolegomena to Any Future Metaphysics,* Kant ([1783] 1950) more explicitly postulates that as a condition for knowledge, exteriority is always already an effect of the tools of the mind. His crucial move is to render the senses (the human body) all but irrelevant to knowledge when he states that, because the things that affect the senses, phenomena, are already modified by the "pure intuitions" of time and space, experience addresses things as "objects of possible experience," such as nature, which encompasses "the existence of things, so far as it is determined according to universal law" (44); or better, that which "denotes the conformity to law of determinations of the existence of things generally" (45). For even before being seen, touched, or felt by the human body, and even before displacing, obliterating, of changing another thing, insofar as they are objects of knowledge, exterior things are already an effect of regulating reason. In these statements, I find a radical gesture, the negation, the declaration of the ontoepistemological inexistence of, exterior things, that is, the affirmation that, as objects of knowledge, phenomena, they constitute but effects of the interior tools of "pure reason."

Two other formulations mark the disavowal of exteriority as a dimension of knowledge. First, Kant postulates that exteriority in itself does not concern knowledge, because the latter addresses phenomena, which is an effect of the "pure intuition" of space. No longer an attribute of the thing itself, spatiality now belongs in the mind; it is the "pure intuition" that enables us to conceive of an "object as without us," to have a sense of exteriority. It is, in short, the (interior) condition of possibility for phenomena. "If," Kant states, "we depart from the subjective conditions, under which alone we can obtain external intuition, or, in other words, by means of which we are *affected* by objects, the representation of space has no meaning whatsoever" (26, my italics). With this statement, Kant dismisses Bacon's statement that affectability, unmediated sense perception, is a first necessary moment in scientific knowledge. Without the rational observer, no discrete bodies, no extended (exterior/affectable) things, nothing that could affect or be affected by the knowing subject or any other existing thing has any relevance to knowledge. Second, the negation of exteriority is further accomplished when Kant locates the subject of scientific knowledge itself in time. For Kant, the "pure intuition" that enables the mind to conceive of coexistence, succession, change, and motion also provides the very experience of interiority; hence, it is not just a condition of phenomena, but the condition of possibility for representation in general. "Because all representations," he posits, "whether they have or have not external things for their objects, still in themselves, as determinations of the mind, belong to our internal state; and because this internal state is subjected to, determined by, the formal conditions of their internal intuition, that is, to time—time is a condition *à priori* of all phenomena whatsoever—the *immediate* condition of all internal, and the *mediate* condition of all external phenomena" (30, italics in the original). With this Kant introduces an account of self-consciousness as the knowing I in which self-determination itself is always already an effect of universal *nomos*'s most powerful tool, that is, time.

In the account of the interiorized *nomos,* self-consciousness is once again conceived as a formal thing but, unlike in Descartes' outline, this not because it has thought, but because the mind is also determined by a tool of the transcendental, namely, the "pure intuition" of time.[13] "If the faculty of self-consciousness is to apprehend what lies in the mind," he observes, "it must affect that, and can in this way alone produce an intuition of self. But the form of this intuition, which lies in the original constitution of the mind, determines, in the representations of time, the manner in which the manifold representations are to combine themselves in the mind, since the subject intuits itself immediately and spontaneously, but according to the manner in which the *mind is internally affected,* consequently, as *it appears,* and *not as it is*" (41, my emphasis).

With this statement, Kant fashions both self-consciousness and exterior things, the objects of knowledge, as always already phenomena, as subjected to a universal ruler that operates in the mind. Hence, along with the possibility of knowing things in themselves, he submits the mind's self-determination to universal *nomos,* for the declaration of the essence and existence of the Cartesian formal I is also an effect of a tool of scientific reason, that is, the "pure intuition" of time. From the point of view of the trajectory of universal reason, this is a victorious statement that seems to unite self-consciousness and the things of the world in a way that does not challenge the former's exclusive attribute; after all, the universal foundation of truth now resides fully in interiority. To the self-determined thing that starts its trajectory contending with the threat, outer determination, introduced by its need to declare itself (essence and existence) a thing of reason, that is, that it shares the same ground with the things after all, there could not be a bitter victory.

The Pillars of the Historical

From the point of view of the trajectory of self-consciousness, Herder's greatest contribution was the reformulation of universal poesis, which also recaptures precisely the attributes of the mind, feelings and sensations, left out of accounts of universal *nomos.*[14] What I see in his formulations is a revision of the scene of representation in which he refashions self-consciousness as a moral thing when he introduces a social ontology that attributes social bounds to language, religion, culture, and so on. Focusing on collective "self-development," Herder's version of the play of reason performs the negation of exteriority when it (a) submits individual and collective inner determination and difference to the guiding or unifying principles actualized in cultural products and institutions and (b) introduces a social ontology grounded on the Historical, one that institutes the subject, the nation, or the people as an effect of temporality. In the pieces collected in his *Philosophical Writings,* Herder (2002) repeatedly charges modern philosophy with failing to perform its most important task. Not mesmerized by the achievements of scientific reason, its spiritless logic of understanding and its concerns with the rules of the world of things, he advocates a philosophy of the "healthy understanding," one that recognizes that "the people" have a sense of the good and right, and it is their self-attributed task to contribute to "the moral [self-]development *[Bildung]* of ('spirit of the) people.'" What this moral theory, which aims at the full development of the human "spirit" and not just the perfection of the understanding, looks like one learns in Herder's rewriting of the play of universal poesis, in his delineation of history as the movement of life, as "self-development" (self-representing), in which the centering of language in the fashioning of self-consciousness produces the thinking thing as a being with "spirit," that is, one endowed with inner (productive) force.

When rewriting the scene of representation, Herder outlines historical signification when describing the moral subject as always already the effect of the principles that guide a people's temporal trajectory, the "forces and inclinations" expressed in language and symbols, that is, cultural products. I have selected three statements that indicate how his version of the universal poesis writes the moral subject as a historical (universal, interior, or temporal) thing. First, he adds language to reflection and freedom to mark the uniqueness of human beings, a gesture that refashions self-consciousness as an intrinsically moral (social) thing. Herder (2002) argues that language and reflection are necessities because, as a social thing, the human being needs to communicate its sensations, feelings, and passions (66) and, because the senses of human beings are "inferior in sharpness," their "forces of representation" and need for representation are more ample (83). This incompleteness, he argues, determines that reason, freedom, and language must constitute human "intrinsic difference," rendering self-consciousness, the interior thing, a thing of reflection and representation (language) (87). Though he postulates that universal poesis—or "mother nature," to use his language—

produces human beings as things *with* feeling and sensation, Herder does not construct them as things *of* feeling and sensation.[15] "I cannot think the first human thought," he states, "cannot set up the first aware judgment in a sequence, without engaging in dialogue, or striving to engage in dialogue, in my soul. Hence the first human thought by its very nature prepares one to be able to engage in dialogue with others! The first characteristic mark that I grasp is a characteristic word for me and a communication word for others!" Here the negation of exteriority results from both the placing of the conditions for social or moral unity in the mind and the rewriting of sensation not as the effect of things upon the human being but as a moment of its own representation: the "sensing human being feels his way into everything, feels everything from out of himself, and imprints I with his image, his impress" (97).

Second, Herder firmly establishes temporality as the moment of actualization of the "inclinations and forces" that distinguish and unify a given people or nation. On the one hand, he delineates the historical as the terrain in which humanity actualizes its "intrinsic difference," the one that gathers how each particular nation has contributed to human *Bildung*. With regard to the human species, Herder (2002) postulates, "nature has linked a new chain: traditions from people to people! 'In this way arts, sciences, culture and language have refined themselves in a great progression of the course of the nations'—the finest bound of further formation that nature has chosen" (160). For this reason he advises the historian to seek among the diversity of people's cycle "a thread and plan of formation *[Bildung]* for developing in the human heart little by little certain inclinations and forces for which people previously and on another path saw no clear trace" (269). For the philosophy of "healthy understanding" aids in human formation (self-development) by tracing the various creations of each particular people, throughout its trajectory, to identify the inclinations that respond to its fate. When naming his project a "geography of humanity" or a "physics of history," Herder suggests that, although these creations are spread through the globe, they are fundamentally things of time; the historical alone comprehends the universality of differentiation.

Third, then, to comprehend these spatially and temporally separated actualizations of human self-productive force, Herder reintroduces the figure of the divine author as an "exemplary model," which sustains his view that an interiorized authority provides the basis for both a given nation's and humanity's moral unity. By conflating the two moments of the divine, author and ruler, resolving them into "the family," he indicates how patriarchal authority ensures moral unity. "Wherever the original father has his cognitions, inclination, and ethics from," he states, "whatever and however few these may be, round about a world and a world of posterity has already formed itself, and formed itself to firmness, in these inclinations and ethics merely through the quiet, forceful, eternal observation of his divine example!" (274). With this, he accounts for human (moral) difference without reinstating exteriority as the determinant of the universality of differentiation.

The negation of exteriority, the declaration of its impossibility as a determinant of a nation's particularity ("intrinsic difference"), occurs in Herder's postulate that the principle of patriarchal authority—informing a people's tradition—governs human history, that is, "the progress in the inclination of the human species," which begins in the despised despotic "Orient," where he locates the "infancy of humanity," the origins of moral unity, in the "so-called prejudices and impressions of upbringing" (276). There he finds the "*foundation pillars* of everything that is supposed to be built upon them later, or rather already through and through the *seeds* out of which everything later and weaker, however glorious it may be called, *develops*" (277, italics in the original). From there he follows the upward steps humanity has taken as exemplified in Egypt's creation of agriculture, the Phoenicians' invention of trade, the Greeks' appreciation of beauty and reason, up to the Roman world, which provided humanity with "an art of statecraft, military art, and international law of peoples" (290). Though in each of these historical moments Herder notes how specific geographical circumstances modified inherited achievements, what concerns him is how each people transform them according to their own particular (new) inclinations. Beginning in its "infancy" in the Orient, he describes humanity's "intrinsic difference," self-representation, as marked by the appropriation and transformation of products of collective invention, its tradition, according to a collectivity's particular inclinations.

What I gather in Herder's statements is the building of the pillars of the historical, the consolidation of historicity as a modern ontological descriptor, through the recuperation of feelings, emotions, and inclinations, in the refashioning of self-consciousness as a moral (rational or representing) I. In Herder's version of *universal poesis,* in which reason guides the productive force of human "self-development," the Historical becomes the signified of both universal (humanity's) and particular (nations' and individuals') *poesis.* Though sharing the universal (human) mark, "self-development," the realization of the "inclinations" and "dispositions" of the "human heart," are modified according to external facts of "land" and "place," as each nation, having "its center of happiness in itself," will develop its own. Moreover, this universalization of differentiation also furthers the unity of the nation. From contacts with other peoples arise "prejudice," the role of which, Herder argues, is to "force peoples together into their center, [to make] them firmer on their tribal stem, more blooming in their kind, more passionate and hence happier in their inclinations and purposes" (297). In this rendering of the scene of representation, the particularity of each nation constitutes but a possible and potential effect of human "intrinsic difference."

Recall that Herder is writing against "enlightened" Europe's celebration of sickly scientific reason; hence, his account of universal poesis is a rewriting of the notions of humanity and "progress," the favored themes of his contemporaries, one that he offers against what he sees as the latter's own articulation of European "prejudice." Is the "universal, philosophical, human friendly tone of our century," he asks, "such a unique judge as to pass judgment on, condemn, or beautifully fictionalize their ethics according to its own measure alone?" (299). What is noble in this version of the play of reason becomes apparent against the Enlightenment's arrogant self-definition as the end (the final goal) of human history and its claim that it had the ability to comprehend history in its entirety as a work of a universal *nomos.* What I want to highlight is how Herder's formulation of the Historical occurs in the statement that rewrites the play of reason by locating universal poesis in the mind of man. Therefore, his fashioning of self-consciousness consistently manages to defer affectability through the interiorizing of poesis, by conceiving of the social, moral unity, as an effect of guiding principles that are first and foremost products of the mind's ability to represent. For this reason, because he resolves the "unity and diversity" of nations (and their particular cultures) in interiority, neither Herder's recourse to geography as a basis for national "intrinsic difference,"

nor his notice of Enlightenment's arrogance, and not even his recognition of the deadly effects of the colonial projects it upholds,
could prevent his version of historicity from being appropriated in
the twentieth-century anthropological reformulation of the cultural
in a later moment of European colonial desire.

THE GIFT OF REASON

In his outlining of self-consciousness, Descartes reasserts the interior things' ontoepistemological prerogative and secures it in self-
determination, in the statement that the rational thing could alone
uncover how reason institutes (founds and orders) nature, the construct that encompasses everything it seeks to know—the earth and
the cosmos, the body and the soul, rules and principles—that is, the
ordered (created) universe. When the framers of science refashioned
reason as universal *nomos,* the claim to knowledge with certainty
was sustained by the assertion that the subject can "discover" the
forces, "fixed laws," governing the motions of the extended (exterior and affectable) things of the world. Now this access to the
truth of the world of things depends on that which man shares with
the things he seeks to know, his affectable body—a necessity that
threatens to submit man, the mind-body composite, to outer determination. Neither the scene of regulation nor the scene of representation produced under the seventeenth century's versions of the play
of reason, universal *nomos* and universal poesis, engages this possibility, because each resolves their respective principles of unity, law
and morality, in the powers of the mind, the thing with reason.

At the closing of the Age of Enlightenment, through the articulation of signifiers that indicate otherwise—the senses, the things of
the world, and the feeling subject itself—the revisions of the play of
reason returned it to interiority without relinquishing its construction as the ruler and author of the universe. Nevertheless, something was lost, for experience and nature were resignified as effects
of the tools of science and feelings and emotions were resolved as
the pillars of history. In both accounts, human beings' relationship
to things (Kant) and each other (Herder) is mediated by a regulative (tools of the understanding) or productive (forces of tradition)
power that, though housed in the mind, constitutes the universal
ontoepistemological ground. Foucault (1994) locates the emergence
of the modern episteme, modern representation, at this moment,

when, after Kant's manufacturing of the transcendental, the "being" of the things of the world would be captured in a temporality of the knowing subject, acquiring their own historicity. I would add that it was so also because of how Herder's formulation of the historical consolidates the locating of human difference in temporality. What happened then? How would the themes of universality and historicity merge in such a way that the it-self (interior) of things would be articulated in the same gesture that writes the thing itself as a moment of man?

When answering this question, Foucault (1994) focuses primarily on the new projects of knowledge in which man emerges as both a subject and an object of investigation. Because it is in the "new empiricities" ("labor," "language," and "life") that he locates the placing of man at the center of the modern ontoepistemological accounts, he could not but ignore a crucial question: What was the process through which the consolidation of the ruling of universal reason resulted in things' acquiring their own interiority, now subordinated to the temporality of the interior I? For Kant's account of universality could not expand Augustine's achievement, because it is not interested in the interiority of things. The condition of possibility for this achievement does reside, as Foucault argues, in Kant's Transcendental—and, I add, in Herder's Historical—but, as we will soon see, it was not an immediate effect of either. It could be achieved only by the version of universal reason that unites the exterior and the interior, the Transcendental and the Historical, by resolving *nomos* and poesis in transcendental poesis. Though Hegel's solution resolves "truth" into "being" by transforming cognition into recognition and reason into freedom, the rewriting of reason as "spirit," the Transcendental I, would not dissipate the threat that is the gift of universal *nomos* to modern thought.

4

Transcendental Poesis

Civil society is the [stage of] difference which intervenes between the family and the state, even if its formation follows later in time than that of the state, because, as [the stage of] difference, it presupposes the state. . . . Moreover, the creation of civil society is the achievement of the modern world which has for the first time given all determinations of the Idea their due. If the state is represented as a unity of different persons, as a unity which is only a partnership, then what is really meant is only Civil society. . . . Since particularity is inevitably conditioned by universality, the whole sphere of Civil society is the territory of mediation where there is free play for every idiosyncrasy, every talent, every accident of birth and fortune, and where waves of every passion gush forth, regulated only by reason glinting through them. Particularity, restricted by universality, is the only standard whereby each particular member promotes his welfare.
— G. F. W. HEGEL, *PHILOSOPHY OF RIGHT*

Refashioning the modern subject without the desire that renders racial emancipation contingent on something hidden behind an ideological veil—just waiting for the "right" tools to "free" it from the alienating debris over which modernity was built—is not the declaration of the death of the "other of modernity." By approaching the racial as the productive tool of reason that writes the "I" and its "others" before the horizon of death, I seek to understand the ways in which what has gone remains. For I am convinced that it exists in another fashion, that it does so because, as Jean-Luc Nancy (1993)

69

says, "the 'West' is precisely what designates itself as limit, as demarcation, even when it ceaselessly pushes back the frontiers of its imperium," hence it cannot but "open the world to the closure that is," to representation, to "what determines itself by its own limit," and, more important, that not only the "West" itself but also the "irrepresentable" it delimits "is also an effect of representation" (1). With the notion of the *modern text,* I approach modern representation as the ontoepistemological context in which engulfment constitutes the privileged (violent) productive act. My goal here is to capture how scientific knowledge mapped the trajectory of yesterday's "natives" and European conquerors after the "first encounter." That is, it enables me to trace how the modern "will to truth" has transformed both "knowledgeable" conquerors and yesterday's "innocent creatures" into modern political subjects that stand differentially before transcendentality and themes, universality and self-determination, with which it governs modern social (juridic, economic, and symbolic) configurations.

My task in this chapter is to complete the excavation of the context of emergence of the *analytics of raciality,* the critical analyses of the statements that consolidated the modern text, through the description of how Hegel's version of the play of reason, *transcendental poesis,* resolves the threat writers of self-consciousness have contended with since Descartes's inaugural statement. In Hegel's version, the possibility that it could contemplate the horizon of death, of becoming a thing of outer determination—*affectability*—will no longer threaten the *interior* thing because, in the *scene of engulfment,* exteriority becomes a moment of the trajectory of the transcendental (interior or temporal) subject. What I find in Hegel's statements is the completion of the figure of self-consciousness, which now becomes the *transparent (interior-temporal) "I,"* the only one that overcomes the founding dichotomy, interiority/exteriority, when recognizing that the universal foundation it shares with exterior things has always already been it-self. My analysis of Hegel's formulations shows how, when assembling the horizon of life, he manufactures the ethical principle transcendentality, and introduces a notion of freedom (self-determination or inner determination) as transparency, the one that provides the ground for modern ontological accounts and is the basis of ruling conceptions of the right and the good, that is, of justice.

Although the critical field is packed with denunciations and re-jections of transparency and intimations that transcendental poesis restricts the transparent I to the boundaries of post-Enlightenment Europe, none relates this version of the play of reason to nineteenth- and twentieth-century scientific projects that attempt to "discover" the truth of man. My reading shows that these result from the fact that Hegel's statement resolves but does not dissipate exteriority and the ontological context it announces when it describes how reason plays its productive role in the scene of engulfment, in which it be-comes a desiring, living, or productive force. Because from the begin-ning scientific reason has established the mark of modern thought, Hegel's, like previous versions of the play of reason, engages the *stage of exteriority* even as it reduces it to a moment of self-unfolding "spirit." Nevertheless, because engulfment apprehends but does not obliterate what it appropriates, it is possible to retrieve the stage of exteriority from the waters of transcendental poesis.

THE SCENE OF ENGULFMENT

Whatever other motives may have animated Hegel's project, it was constrained by the fact that, after almost two centuries, modern philosophy would not relinquish the figure whose outline marks its inauguration. Nor could self-consciousness retain its privileged place as the ground for ontological and epistemological accounts if its intimacy with universal reason was denied. Hence, if self-consciousness could not be transformed, if forfeiting the markers of its particularity, reason and freedom, would result in the loss of what distinguishes modern thought, which, by the late eighteenth century, already organized the post-Enlightenment portrait of mod-ern social configurations, the solution had to be, once again, to re-write the play of reason. Hegel's successful reformulation produced an account of the trajectory of self-consciousness in which inner determination and self-productivity become the two attributes it shares with universal reason. Put differently, drawing from Kant's and Herder's interiorizing of universal reason, Hegel reconstituted the Kantian formal ("pure reason") universal, the transcendental, as a historical (desiring or living) thing, namely, productive (interior-temporal) force, "Spirit," the transcendental "I." By resolving Reason into Freedom, Nature into History, Space into Time, things of the world into the (thinking, knowing, acting, desiring, or living) subject, Hegel rewrote the play of reason as transcendental poesis, thus consolidating the fields of modern representation, namely, science and history, the productive contexts that provided the signifying strategies that composed post-Enlightenment ontoepistemological accounts.

Nevertheless, I will show that the operative signifying gesture, here, engulfment, comprehends but does not obliterate exteriority, and in doing so it merely pushes back the horizon of death even as it recuperates that whose renunciation sustained the assertion of the possibility of knowing with certainty, the search for the in it-self ("final causes" or "essences") of things.[1] After almost two hundred years, one could easily read this accomplishment as a necessary outcome of the trajectory of self-consciousness. Perhaps this is so, but it would not have been possible if Hegel had not rewritten *universal poesis* itself in such a way that it precluded the return of Leibniz's notions of contingency and infinity and Herder's conception of tradition. Had he retained the former, his version of self-consciousness would not have retained self-determination, for it would have been unable to claim that it knows all that it could become or all possible and potential future modifications of things. Had he retained the latter, his reformulated self-consciousness would have been unable to alone decide its essence and existence, for it would have remained bounded to principles emerged in the "infancy of humanity." Neither an unbounded nor a predetermined temporality could preserve that which had been ensured by universal reason. To this effect, Hegel rewrote the acts of universal reason as the play of engulfment—the dialectical formulation of temporality that ties together beginnings, means, and ends—to produce a teleology that did not fall back into supernatural or secular metaphysics.[2] In Hegel's transcendental poesis, the theater of reason became the arena of history as the universe became the product of the temporal trajectory of a self-producing and self-moving transcendental (interior-temporal) I, namely, "Spirit," that in which form and content, essence and existence, the substance and its modifications, cause and effects are resolved. Though everything that is and can become is at once its raw material, instrument, and goal, only one thing, the one that shares reason's powers, the mind, can recognize that this is so.

What I find in Hegel's formulations is the statement that secures self-consciousness in self-determination by bridging the difference between regulation and representation in the moment of transparency, when self-consciousness recognizes that nothing is exterior to itself because, like itself, every existing thing is a moment, an actualization of spirit, the cause and end of the universe with which it enjoys a profound intimacy. With this Hegel addresses, because it is crucial for securing self-determination, the question of how to sustain the mind's ability to know extended (exterior-affectable) things: How can we resolve the immanent (material, concrete, and contingent) nature, the universe that stands before the mind, into the transcendent (the formal, abstract, and necessary) without recourse to universal reason as an exterior or interior constraint or focus on unmediated relationships that would retrieve *affectability?* That is, how can we preclude the eruption of that which the trace contains, whose deferment enables the writing of self-consciousness as an interior thing and which previous accounts of universal reason had kept at bay by risking self-determination itself? When addressing these questions, Hegel introduces two notions, namely, actualization and recognition, the effect of which is to provide an account of the trajectory of Spirit as the temporal (self-productive) process through which self-consciousness learns of a profound intimacy between itself and things. Though both are crucial to the writing of the "Same," each gains a particular meaning when deployed in Hegel's account of how self-consciousness is positioned in relation to the "world of things," the one given to it, and the "world of men," the one it produces. Through the engulfment of exteriority, in the movement of actualization and recognition, the version of the play of reason as transcendental poesis institutes the *transparency thesis,* the ruling modern ontoepistemological assumption, while allowing for projects of knowledge that produce modern subjects that remain before it.[3]

In *Phenomenology of Spirit,* Hegel ([1807] 1977) describes how self-consciousness comes to recognize that the profound intimacy between itself and exterior things resulted from the fact that both constitute distinct moments of the actualization of spirit. By recuperating knowledge's concerns with being or essence, the metaphysical mistake Locke criticizes, Hegel reunites the self-determined thing and that which stands before it—the external, the exterior, the extended—in an account that (trans)forms the thinking thing into a desiring thing. For Hegel, the "antithesis of its appearance and its truth has, however, for its essence only the truth, viz. the unity of self-consciousness with itself; this unity must become essential to self-consciousness, i.e. self-consciousness is Desire in general. Consciousness, as self-consciousness, henceforth has a double object: one is the immediate object, that of sense-certainty and perception, which *for self-consciousness* has the character of a *negative,* however; and the second, viz. *itself,* which is the true *essence,* and is present in the first instance only as opposed to the first object. In this sphere, self-consciousness exhibits itself as the movement in which this antithesis is removed, and the identity of itself with itself becomes explicit" (105, italics in the original). Here "abstract" essence and "concrete" existence of objects (things and other I's) do not constitute limits to self-determination, for both need to be engaged for the completion of self-consciousness' trajectory toward freedom, which occurs when it moves from "simple universality," the moment of "being in-itself," in its initial shape in the Cartesian outlining, into "true universality" at the completion of its trajectory—after it recuperates death, negation, as a dimension of itself—the moment of "being for-itself," that is, the moment of transparency.

When rewriting previous fashionings of consciousness, Hegel introduces an ontological account, the scene of engulfment, which reconciles the *scene of representation* and the *scene of regulation.*[4] In it, self-consciousness learns that scientific reason has misapprehended the play of phenomena, that knowing things consists in the recognition that the universe is the stage of actualization of a transcendental consciousness, the self-determining because self-producing force whose "essence" it shares. Through this movement of engulfment— actualization (exteriorization) and recognition (interiorization)— self-consciousness becomes the subject of transcendental poesis; its function is to actualize the possibilities and potentialities of Spirit, to bring it into existence by realizing its "inner force" (essence). Here the knowing subject is a desiring thing because the realization of its "intrinsic difference," self-determination, requires that first it move outside of itself, where it finds negation, the moment of regulation in things, and then recuperate them back into interiority, now conceived fully in the scene of representation. In this account, mediation takes a different role: the means of knowledge are neither the human body nor the tools of scientific reason, but the things to be known, namely, consciousness and exterior things, which are external to each other only as long as consciousness ignores that its truth is to become consciousness for-itself, that is, when it recognizes that self-regulation is only a vanishing moment in its trajectory toward recognition.

Previous versions of the play of reason preempted affectability, outer determination, that is, the possibility that self-consciousness is situated before the horizon of death, in statements that articulate and disavow exteriority to establish its ontoepistemological insignificance. In Hegel's account, exteriority is but a moment in the temporal trajectory of the self-producing thing, which ends with its emergence as an independent, transparent consciousness, that is, as self-consciousness. Further, self-consciousness is again able to access the thing-in-itself, essence, precisely because it acknowledges that the thing in-itself is but a moment of universal reason that is not yet aware of itself, that does not know that it is Spirit. In this montage of the stage of interiority, the play is the mode of production, for the principle of transcendentality (and the narrative it guides) produces the scene of engulfment (actualization and recognition) that resolves regulation into representation. Here the deferment of affectability results from an account that recuperates exteriority, the ontological moment negated in the statements that located the tools of universal *nomos* and the pillars of universal poesis in the mind, and redefines the pairs universal-particular, universality-historicity, exteriority-interiority, and space-time by resolving the first term into the second as the former becomes a vanishing step of the temporal trajectory of the transcendental I. Regarding exteriority, the attribute the human body shares with the objects of knowledge, it becomes a "vanishing," necessary but not determining moment of the movement of transcendental poesis. For immediate recognition cannot fully sustain the I's claim to know the world of things unless it risks becoming an object of universal *nomos*. Hegel introduces a notion of particularity that encompasses the material, contingent, immanent moments that need to be engulfed for consciousness to recognize the cause and end of every existing, possible, and potential thing as Spirit. Hegel's style constitutes but a deployment of his own dialectics; the structure of every section, part, and chapter of his *Phenomenology* rehearses the trajectory it writes. Instead of seeking for examples in appropriate passages in various moments of his text, I read his account of "observing reason," scientific reason, to show how he redefines the scene of regulation as the "Fall," the moment of dead reason, which is necessary for the realization of spirit, and his account of "world history," which engulfs the globe, which becomes the space where spirit deploys, represents, the effects of its productive play.

DEAD REASON

Throughout the little over one hundred years since Newton's and Locke's formulations, the search for the truth of things has been free of any concern with "being"—a move that constituted the emergence of science itself. Hegel's transcendental poesis returns to considerations of "being," establishing the task of knowledge as bringing about the realization of the Spirit's goal, which is the moment of actualization, when it comes into exteriority to become its own object. His is not an easy project. This accomplishment requires something that modern thought has rejected since at least Descartes, that is, extension needs to be brought back into, recognized by, and reconciled with thought. It demands an eternal engagement with exteriority (a sacrifice, Hegel acknowledges), which robs the mind of the certainty that it is the sole determinant of human conditions but necessary for learning that Spirit is "the absolute notion" that unites human consciousness and the things of the world. For this reason, Hegel's account of scientific reason enabled attempts to discover the "truth" of self-consciousness. This is so because it articulates exteriority as a necessary moment of the self-unfolding spirit, for it can complete its trajectory only in successive moments of contention with and sublation of immanence. The movement of Spirit is an eternal engagement with its own exterior self, namely, nature, that is, with extension ("pure negativity," death), which is a limit at the core of the transcendental I. Precisely because Hegel's account defers exteriority by apprehending it, his version of modern representation, the one that consolidates the modern text, provides the point of departure for a reading of the racial, the scientific signifier that produces self-consciousness as an effect of exteriority, which produces a modern contra-ontology.

When Hegel ([1807] 1977) describes the moment of scientific reason, he names it a vanishing moment in the process of actualization of spirit, when universal reason finds itself in the world as a "Thing," self-consciousness learns of objectification—that is, it becomes aware that the independent other, the thing, is also itself, but it does not know that thingification is a crucial aspect of "ethical life." For though "observing reason" conceives the "outer" (external or exterior) as the "expression" of the "inner" (the interior or thought) and mistakes the former for the latter, Hegel postulates, it fails to acknowledge that the one is necessarily the other. At this point, Hegel states, reason acts instinctively. It observes, describes, and experiments with the goal of showing how the existing things express the operation of universal (exterior) determinants, that is, laws. Because at this moment the law is immersed in the things as they exist, the universal appears only as immediate, even though consciousness now learns of the notion of law itself and of two other notions that indicate the proximity of the realization of "Spirit," namely, "matter" and "End." With the notion of "matter," it learns that law, universal *nomos,* is not merely "sensuous" and that things have universality, while with the notion of "End," it captures the idea of teleology, of the fact that what seems to be merely necessary is the culmination of a process that is a return to the beginning. Yet scientific reason sees only cause and effect, an external relation between two independent things, not recognizing that that which comes into being—the "effect" or "End"—was always already *in* there. Moreover, here "observing reason" learns the notion of self-consciousness, which "likewise distinguishes itself from itself without producing any distinction" (157). Mis(self)-recognition has serious consequences.

Through this mistake, scientific reason performs a double displacement: the "End" is conceived as exterior to the thing and as exterior to consciousness itself. In the first case, "the instinct of reason" fails to *recognize* that the "essence" of the thing is the act of becoming what it has always been, that is, that this action is not something produced by an exterior force, but is the thing itself. This "activity" is, according to Hegel, "nothing but the pre-essenceless form of its being-for-itself, and its substance, which is not merely a determinate being but the universal, or its End, does not fall outside of it" (159). Hence, instead of capturing that essential being of the thing, its "Notion," consciousness separates the two, conceiving the "Notion" as the "inner" and the actuality (the realized thing) as the "outer," and "their relation produces the law that the outer is the expression of the inner" (160)—that is, the "inner" becomes the universal, and the "outer" is its particularization.

What the "instinct of reason" does not comprehend in the observation of organic (living) beings, for instance, is that the "outer," the actual, is the manifestation, the actualization properly speaking, of the "inner," which, according to Hegel, is the proper mode of establishing their connection. In scientific reason, he concludes, the thing is "only something 'meant'"; "and if Reason can take an idle interest in observing this 'meant' thing, it is restricted to the description of the 'meanings' and fanciful conceits it finds in Nature" (179). In short, in scientific reason the relationship between the universal (interior, "essence") and the particular (the existing [extended] thing) is still conceived in terms of exteriority. Hegel deplores this moment of reason because, even though it has found universality, it has been unable to understand the true relationship between the universal and the particular. The particular remains immersed in immanence, a shape, a fixed form, not yet a moment of a self-transforming, living thing. In the second case, regarding consciousness, the assumption of exteriority entails another mistake. Failing to recognize that the "laws of thought" are part of the movement of thought itself, "observing" self-consciousness "converts its own nature into the form of being"—that is, it approaches itself as an object, as in Kant's formulation (181). The mistake is that "observing reason" takes the actual thinking "individual" on the one hand and the world on the other, severing the two without recognizing that whatever the thinking individual is is but a manifestation of given conditions of the world, that "individuality is what *its* world is, the world that is its own" (185, italics in the original).

For Hegel, "observing reason," dead reason, cannot know actuality other than as an external thing, as exteriority. "Observing reason," scientific reason, does not know Spirit. Hence, it views shapes as signs and conceives of the "outer," the exterior, the extended, as the expression of the "inner," of the interior, of thought. Failing to conceive what exists and is given to knowledge as temporality, as actuality, it reads it as a fixed, independent, particular thing. That is, science can uncover the universal laws that determine how things appear; it can even conceive of force as something internal, and perceive that infinite appearances of things can be captured by artificial constructs—mechanical instruments, mathematical instruments, the categories of understanding. However, because what experience presents to self-consciousness is extension, the things of the world as they affect each other according to universal laws, the scientific consciousness does not know of temporality; it can only conceive of thought as another fixed thing, an unmoving universal, as a form (an intuition) of the thing. This, Hegel proclaims, is alienated reason, and "this final stage of Reason in its observational role is its worst; and that is why its reversal becomes a necessity" (206). Awaiting consciousness, after the "Fall" of reason in complete thinghood (that of the existing independent thing and its own independence as self-consciousness), is the realization that self-moving reason is itself "reality."

This fall into nothingness precedes the moment when free self-consciousness finds itself objectified in an "other" free self-consciousness, when the liberal (Lockean "individual") subject finally realizes that the sacrifice that institutes the political, the collective, is no sacrifice. The moment of recognition, when in the particular "individual" it is recognized that "this existence unchangeable essence [the nation] is the expression of the very 'individuality' which seems opposed to it; the laws proclaim what each individual is and does; the individual knows them not only as his universal objective thinghood, but equally knows himself in them, or knows them as particularized in his own individuality, and in each of his fellow citizens" (213). No need for mediation. Unlike in Kant's Transcendental and Herder's Historical, in Hegel's Transcendental the merging of both recuperates exteriority to resolve it into interiority, in that which Augustine called the privilege of the rational soul. Thought is the "essence" of everything that exists, but only insofar as the interior thing also recognizes itself as a thing—not as an extended thing, for we just saw that at this point it still thrives in alienation—but as a thing that is fundamentally of time, always actuality, because it enjoys a profound intimacy, transparency, with that universal force that comes into being in time as it engulfs space, the Transcendental I, namely, "Spirit." This is the moment of "world history."

THE STAGE OF LIFE

Whatever answer is given to the question What is history? will more likely than not resonate with Hegel's philosophical account of "world history," the one in which history "reaches its culmination in a community which is in conformity with reason; or we could also say, one which embodies freedom" (Taylor 1975, 389). With this, I am not repeating Hegel's formulae to reduce every or any statement on history to a manifestation of the (Hegelian) "Same." My point is simpler. From the earlier delineation of the scene of representation, which remains at the basis of later rewritings of universal poesis and is at the core of the concepts—such as the nation, culture, ethnicity—designed to capture a historical consciousness, the descriptor *historicity* presupposes an ethical principle, transcendentality, the foundation and end, actualized in a collectivity's temporal trajectory. In his blueprint of the arena of history, Hegel sidesteps both grounds for social ontologies, the universal *nomos,* in which the basic moral entity, the "individual," sacrifices its "natural freedom" (God-given self-determination), and universal poesis, in which freedom is also an attribute of the moral collectivity to which he belongs. Rejecting Kant's formalism, Hegel refashions transcendental (pure) reason as "Spirit," that is, he rewrites it as transcendental poesis, which, as living form and content, will and action, is not merely the ground and guide but self-determination (freedom) itself. With this, he rearranges history itself, which now becomes not only an account of past facts and deeds, but the scene of life, which, along with the products of creative imagination (culture, arts, science, religion, etc.), constitutes the actualization of "Spirit."

What I find in Hegel's revision of the scene of representation, which replaces the divine ruler and author with the self-determining and self-producing figure of "Spirit," is a social ontology in which transparency becomes the "end," the final purpose, when the designs of the new author and ruler, Spirit, are actualized in human institutions and products. For, unlike other existing things, the human being has the ability to measure the rightness and goodness of its actions; as a thing with free will, it can decide whether its activity will bring the realization of the "Ends" of the ruler or producer of the universe. In Hegel's rendering of the scene of representation, *perfection* corresponds to the moment when Spirit becomes fully realized in social conditions, an accomplishment of human action that only the thinking thing can recognize. From this rewriting of representation as the scene of engulfment (actualization and recognition, exteriorization and interiorization) results a narrative of history in which, though assuming that it is its eternal and infinite inner force, the temporal unfolding transcendental subject has an "End," but it is not exactly the one to which Hegel refers in the earlier critique of scientific reason. Hegel writes modernity as marking a qualitative shift in "world history."

In the version of reason as transcendental poesis, human consciousness and action are conceived as things of reason and freedom, the actualizing instruments Spirit deploys to bring the possible and potential into actuality, which here is but man's recognition that Spirit is the "inner [transcendental] force" guiding his history and that self-determination is its nature and purpose. Nevertheless, it happens only in post-Enlightenment social (juridic, economic, and symbolic) configurations, when freedom is claimed as the sole ground for thought and action, when universality is actualized in law and morality. When every product of human poesis—social institutions and cultural products—is recognized as also a product of Spirit, when it acknowledges that profound intimacy with the transcendental productive force, self-consciousness achieves the moment of transparency.

In his *Lectures on the Philosophy of History*, Hegel (1900) argues that the cause and force, the shape of consciousness operating in "world history," has always been self-consciousness, that is, "Spirit." Since "Spirit" is the very movement of coming into being, History as its theater does no more than bring Spirit into being, to render it actual, to realize the "Notion," that is, reason as freedom. Perhaps it would not be an overstatement to say that Hegel's greatest accomplishment was no more than to deploy a common ground for man and the things of the world that the apologists of universal *nomos* had insisted on keeping at bay. However, from Hegel's statement that the "thinking Spirit only *began* with the revelation of divine essence" (17, italics in the original), it would not be a mistake to say that his privileging of reflection, as opposed to the "feelings and inclinations" Herder prefers, sidesteps any religiosity that is not conceived under the idea of universal reason. This would account for the fact that Hegel reformulates the question that sets up Herder's account of history. Instead of asking about the "origins" of the force actualized in human temporal trajectory, he returns to Leibniz's question about the "purpose of the world." With this, he moves from a conception of history as mere repetition of an "original" authority, which takes hold of human hearts and souls from the outset, to an account of history as constituted by the many steps of the struggle of an "absolute power" that moves in and out of itself in order to learn what it has been all along, namely, everything that comes into being. Though the religious connection that is spotted as spirit can achieve its purpose only in human action, what changes is the fact that Spirit comes into existence not as a supernatural author and ruler taking a particular human shape and sacrificing itself to prove its power, but in the actions of every human being who knows reason. "The realm of Spirit," Hegel postulates, "consists in what is produced by man" (20). Not that which is produced by any and every human being, but only that which is by those who recognize freedom as the distinguishing human attribute. Hegel's Spirit, the productive force, the cause, effect, and content of human history, is a thing of interiority. "Spirit," he explains, "is Being-within-itself (self-contained existence). But this precisely is Freedom. For when I am dependent, I refer to myself as something else which I am not. I cannot exist independently of something external. I am free when I am within myself." Spirit is "I." It is still a Cartesian subject: "This self-contained existence of Spirit," Hegel proceeds, "is self-consciousness, consciousness of self" (23).

How does Spirit achieve this goal in time? According to Hegel, spirit uses three means for its realization, namely, the individual, the state, and the people. Each reveals Spirit's nature in a particular manner, but the individual is the starting point for the other two. For Hegel "individual" will is that which renders actual the law, the principle, the concept of "world history." "The will, man's activity in general," renders "Spirit" real (active, actual) because "it is only through this activity that the concept and its implicit ('being-in-themselves') determination can be realized, actualized; for of themselves they have no immediate existence" (28). Nevertheless, when explaining how it is possible, Hegel rewrites Kant's moral law by resolving inner regulation into self-actualization. Through actions geared toward particular, subjective aims, the self-interested rational will becomes the "subject of history." Regardless of its immediate moral implications—good or bad, selfish or sacrificial—an individual's action is not "necessarily opposed to the universal," because individual action just fulfills that which is in the nature of the universal, which is that it "must be actualized through the particular" (35). The universal, that which exceeds subjective determinants of action, is a juridical and a moral moment of the unfolding spirit. "In the course of history," Hegel states, "two factors are important.

One is the preservation of a people, a state, of well-ordered spheres of life. This is the activity of individuals participating in the common effort and helping to bring about its particular manifestations. It is the preservation of ethical life. The other important factor, however, is the decline of the State. The existence of a national spirit is broken when it has used up and exhausted itself. World history, the World Spirit, continues on its course. . . . This is the result, on the one hand, of the inner development of the Idea and, on the other, of the activity of individuals, who are its agents and grin about its actualization" (38–39).

The state and the people constitute two distinct modes through which human will and action actualize the designs of Spirit, but Hegel does not separate the two. He conceives of the constitution as a formalization of a people's stages of "spiritual development," which is but a moment of "its consciousness of itself, of its own truth, its own essence, the spiritual powers which live and rule in it" (52). Although the "Idea" (reason as freedom) is that which is to be brought into being, the state is its externalization, its mode of existing as exteriority. Hegel argues that it is "the union of the universal and essential with the subjective will, as such it is *Morality*" (50, italics in the original). That is, in Hegel's formulation, the state includes both a juridical dimension (law, the constitution) and a moral dimension (the particular spirit of a people): it "is rational and self-conscious freedom, objectively knowing itself" (60). Here again the reunion of form and content comes into being in human collective activity. "The universal which appears and becomes known in the state, the form into which is cast all reality," Hegel teaches, "constitutes what is generally called the culture of a nation. The definite content, however, which receives the form of universality and is contained in the concrete reality of the State, is the spirit of the people. The true State is animated by this Spirit in all its affairs, wars, institutions, etc. But man must himself know of this—his own—Spirit and essence and give himself the consciousness of his original union with it. For we said that all morality is the unity of subjective and general will. The Spirit, then, must give itself an express consciousness of this unity, and the center of this knowledge is religion. Art and science are only different aspects of this very same content" (63–64).

In Hegel's account of "world history," in which the Global becomes the Transcendental I's exhibition hall, the subject of transcendental poesis does not merely mediate between the knowing self-consciousness and the things it seeks to know (in science), the rational will and the things it wills (morality), the rational agent and the things it acts upon (action), the rational sovereign and the laws it creates. It comes into being in mediation, because science, morality, action, and law are its modes of existence. "World history," then, rewrites the scene of representation as the scene of engulfment, the movement of the realization of "Spirit" in time in the living and dying of states, the emergence and obliteration of ethical (juridical-moral) wholes that result from the actions of individuals who are the means for the actualization of these collectivities' particular essence, that is, the people (the nation), who represent a particular stage of "Spirit." Individuals' minds, Hegel sates, "are full of it and their wills are their willing of these laws and of their country. It is this temporal totality which is One Being, the spirit of One People. To it the individuals belong; each individual is the son of its people and, at the same time, in so far as his state is in development, the son of his age. No one remains behind it; no one can leap ahead of it. This spiritual being is his—he is one of its representatives—it is that from which he arises and wherein he stands" (66). For Hegel, the purpose of "world history," the past, present, and future accomplishment of man, is the realization of Spirit, the self-determined, inner-determined, transcendental I, which can become aware that it is everything only in time, the only condition for a claim for being the absolute; if it were a thing of space, it would be a thing only among others.

As noted before, the temporal self-realization of Spirit is a dialectical process. In the scene of engulfment, human [auto]poesis brings Spirit into existence, that is, the being whose "truth" is becoming is neither Sisyphus nor Job; it is not condemned to fruitless, dead repetition. The direction, the goal of "world history," is "Progress." "Only the changes in the realm of Spirit," Hegel argues, "create the novel. This characteristic of Spirit suggested to man a feature entirely different from that of nature—the desire toward perfectibility" (68). When universal reason becomes transcendental poesis, self-consciousness assumes the shape of the *homo historicus,* which, when playing its productive role, actualized in post-Enlightenment social (juridical, economic, and cultural) configurations, recognizes that it has always already been Spirit, that each individual's thoughts and actions participate in the nature of the absolute (temporal) subject. "Spirit," Hegel postulates, "is essentially the result of its own activity. Its activity is transcending the immediately given negating it, and returning into itself" (94).

Unlike Herder's account, which resolves all spatial difference into the always already interior, the Historical, the productive signifying gesture here, engulfment, introduces a fundamental but sublatable and reducible difference when it circumscribes the place of the realization of spirit. For it writes post-Enlightenment European social configurations as the only ones in which it has completed its trajectory in its recognition of universality and self-determination. What this gesture institutes is the principle informing the transparency thesis, namely, trancendentality. When producing the scene of engulfment, Hegel builds the stage of life when he identifies the various moments of the trajectory of spirit: the "East," the "Greek World," the "Roman World," the "German World," and finally modernity, which compose a rather small portion of the world. Neither precolonial America nor Africa participates in this trajectory; only the "East" and "Europe" represent distinct moments of the actualization of spirit, while the new nations erected by Europeans on the American continent are not yet important actors in the stage of temporal reason. In the East and in Europe, then, Hegel finds expressions of the unfolding "Spirit": "The History of the World travels from East to West," he says, "for Europe is absolutely the end of History" (103). Nevertheless, only a few events in history, that is, the Reformation, French Revolution, and the emergence of the state, mark the realization of transcendental poesis, that is, moments when individual self-consciousnesses recognize their fundamental intimacy with the subject of *nomos* and poesis. In post-Enlightenment Europe, Spirit "first arrives at an abstract knowledge of its essence, ethical life is submerged in the formal universality of legality or law" (265); it divides itself into two domains, "culture" and the "realm of essential being," and takes hold of both. "They are," as Hegel describes them, "confounded and revolutionized by the insight [of the individual] and the diffusion of that insight, known as Enlightenment [returning into] self-consciousness, which now in the form of morality, grasps itself as the essentiality and essence of the actual self; it no longer places its world and its ground outside itself, but lets everything fade into itself, and as conscience, is Spirit that is certain of itself" (265). All other regions of the globe remain elsewhere in time, either awaiting or hopelessly unable to recognize that human mind and action are but the raw materials, tools, and products of Spirit.

THE MARK OF TRANSPARENCY

Both in his account of transcendental poesis and in the explicit exclusions that restrict the play of reason to the geographic limits of European space and the temporal boundaries of Greco-Judeo-Christian thought, Hegel writes post-Enlightenment social (juridical, economic, moral) configurations as the place of realization of "Spirit," that is, the moment of transparency. His decisive contribution to modern representation, I argue, is not to establish how post-Enlightenment European configurations depart from other previous and coexisting ones, but to establish why this is so. In Hegel's formulations, modernity is not just the most advanced stage of the human trajectory. It is the culmination of a temporal trajectory, the moment where human consciousness realizes its intimacy with the transcendental (active, self-productive, and self-determined) reason—that is, the moment in which individual consciousness and social (juridical, moral, and economic) conditions reveal themselves as the actualization of transcendentality. This is the place of transparency, where the transcendental subject is now conscious of itself as a (interior and exterior) thing of the world, and the (interior and extended) things of the world are recognized as the transcendental subject. How was it accomplished? How could the recognition of transcendentality be limited to particular human beings located in a rather small corner of the globe?

In transcendental poesis, the reunification of self-consciousness and the things does not presuppose the kind of universality provided by a divine author and ruler—Locke's "[divine] law of nature," Leibniz's "divine wisdom," and Herder's "divine example." For though the idea of divinity includes a fundamental equality or inequality among all created beings derived from how close a creature is to the perfect being, it also assumes a profound intimacy, the knowledge of which is contingent on the supreme being, that is, revelation. In Hegel's account, on the other hand, the shape-shifting self-consciousness not only thinks and acts, even if unaware, as a moment and the instrument of Spirit; it also holds the privilege of revealing to itself and to Spirit that the latter is the matter and the form of the world. "Spirit," Hegel (1900) posits, "being the *substance* and the universal, self-identical, and abiding essence, is the unmoved solid *ground* and *starting-point* for the action of all, and it is their purpose and goal, the in-itself of every self-consciousness expressed in thought. This substance is equally the universal *work* produced by the action of all and each as their unity and identity for it is the being-for-self, the self, action" (164, italics in the original).

Which self-consciousness? Whose actions? Whose works? Entertaining these questions will reveal how Hegel asks and answers the question of why post-Enlightenment European consciousness and social configuration mark the "end" of the self-unfolding "Spirit." What guides my reading of Hegel's answer is his distinction between two kinds of universality, universal reason (as *nomos* or poesis) and the "true" universality (universal reason as "Spirit"), namely, transcendentality. Precisely here the particular violent productive force of engulfment, the signifying gesture performed in Hegel's version of the play of reason, becomes all the more evident, of course, if one agrees with Žižek's (1999) statement that "Hegel is fully aware that the positive form in which this abstract universality gains actual existence is that of extreme violence: the obverse side of the inner peace of Universality is the destructive fury towards all particular content, that is to say, the universality 'in becoming' is the very opposite of the peaceful neutral medium of all particular content—only in this way can universality become 'for itself'; only in this way can 'progress' take place" (94). In my view, then, it is precisely because the resolution of regulation in representation does not destroy exteriority but surrounds and encloses it between "abstract universality" and "true universality"—between self-consciousness just before the moment of the lordship and the bondsman and self-consciousness in the moment "ethical life," rendering it the "stuff" of which the further unfolded "Spirit" is made—representation, as Levinas (1991) postulates, remains but a "partial violation," that is, the play of engulfment. For had Hegel privileged "actual existence"—as Marx did later when he rewrote History as an eschatology—the account of transcendental poesis would not have provided a symbolic (universal or historical) appropriation of the global, which was later remapped by the racial. In the narrative of universal poesis, the signifying gesture, engulfment, institutes modern representation by resolving universality and historicity in transcendentality and provisionally containing

the threat introduced in the outlining of self-consciousness in a figure, the *homo historicus,* which is both the producer of science and
a producer or product of history, that is, the transparent I, the self-
determined subject of universality.

When Hegel consolidates the structures of the stage of interiority,
social configurations also become moments of actualization of the
coming into being of self-consciousness as such—as a thing of reason
as freedom. Precisely because this writing of history establishes a
fundamental connection between consciousness and the products of
human action, Hegel's formulations enable the identification of the
main dimensions of the particularly modern mode of signification—
the one that, Foucault (1994) argues, has placed the temporality of
man at the core of exterior things. By postulating the recognition
of Spirit as the cause and end of human will and action, Hegel once
again postpones the threat posed by the grounding of freedom upon
reason. The move here is to rewrite Nature and History as stages
where the play of engulfment is enacted. For engulfment is nothing
but a productive and violent act of spirit, the process through which
the mind relates to itself and to what lies outside (here including other
consciousness) as it continuously engages exterior things, which it
recognizes as a moment of itself (as an exteriorization/actualization),
which it takes back (through interiorization/recognition) until it finally realizes that universal reason (thought or science) and freedom
(action or history) are one and the same thing. To repeat, the solution
here is a reconciliation produced by the resolution of the universal
nomos into universal poesis that results from actualization, which
transforms the particular into the exteriorized universal, and recognition, in which the particular is interiorized, resulting in a transformation of the ("pure') universal into the "truly universal," that
is, the transcendental. In other words, in "world history" the *homo
historicus,* the free, rationally acting individual consciousness, is a
thing of "Spirit."

For Hegel, post-Enlightenment Europe testifies to the realization
of "Spirit" when the "Idea," reason as freedom, is realized in social
configurations, when "Spirit" is recognized as the transcendental
(ruler and producer) I, when self-consciousness learns its cause and
essence, namely, transcendentality, that is, at the moment of "ethical
life." In other words, when Hegel refashions self-consciousness as
the *homo historicus*—the self-determined (interior-temporal) thing,

the one whose will and action actualize but "Spirit"—he also establishes that universality and historicity constitute the principles that mark post-Enlightenment Europe's "intrinsic difference." Hegel's social subject is quite distinct from the Lockean and the Kantian formulations of the liberal subject; the "individual" is the moral entity alone in the presence of the divine and civil laws and the determinations of morality. In place of Locke's rational agent, the self-interested entity, we find a living I, a particular self-consciousness, whose "truth," whose freedom, always already resides in a transparent (interior-temporal) collective I. Instead of Kant's ([1788] 1993) subject of duty, who feels the moral law as a constraint because he is not thoroughly ruled by universal reason, still subjected to the affections of the body and inclinations of the will, we find a self-knowing, desiring consciousness that, unlike Herder's moral thing that remains subjected to patriarchal authority, has learned that affections and inclinations are but the means to its self-realization, as that which actualizes the fundamental attributes of the higher (secular) consciousness.

Far from rejecting earlier social ontologies, Hegel builds the stage of life in his description of "ethical life," which, by unifying them in transcendentality, recuperates universality and historicity as the "intrinsic difference" and establishes the particularity of post-Enlightenment social configurations. His account of "world history" as the coming into being of the living "ethical substance" resolves human consciousness into the particular "Spirit" of a people. No doubt Hegel was not the first to deploy a conception of history that conceives of the political subject by combining *nomos* and poesis in the notion of the nation; Vico's "new science," Montesquieu's historical account of the nature of laws, and Bousset's and Voltaire's writings are a few examples of similar attempts. Similarly, as discussed earlier, Herder and other German ("romantic") critics of the Enlightenment introduced a conception of language and history that poses a "concrete" universality of differentiation against the idea of "abstract" humanity celebrated by the apostles of scientific reason. Nevertheless, post–World War II examinations of modern political conditions have stressed the irrationality of the German romantic account, pointing—as they obviously emerged in the post-Nazi period—to the risks of a conception of moral unity that is not exclusively and explicitly premised on the universal *nomos*. What they do not systematically consider is why the nation, the historical-transcendental signifier, would so easily share with the racial (the scientific signifier) statements that institute the body politic as a "spiritual" (moral) unit. To address this question, I intend to describe the conditions of the production of the racial by engaging the projects of knowledge that deployed the tools of scientific reason to uncover the truth of man.

II

Homo Scientificus

A new species would bless me as its creator and source; many happy and excellent natures would owe their being to me.

—MARY SHELLEY, *FRANKENSTEIN*

When mourning the death of his best friend, Dr. Frankenstein recalls that he "had never sympathized in my tastes for natural science, his literary pursuits differed completely from those which had occupied me" (Shelley [1818] 1991, 53). Evoking Clerval's historic preferences, his interest in the East, religion, and language, Victor Frankenstein laments his own tragic choice. As his now deceased family, friend, and fiancée often reminded him, his scientific pursuits entailed hours, days, and weeks locked in his laboratory or searching for suitable body parts in hospitals and morgues—a life spent away from the warm world of the living in the cold caves of the dead. What is the path of the scientist if not the search for gifts of death, an unholy ambition elevated neither by a desire to find a cure for the diseases that threaten the bodies of the living (the work of the physician) nor by a dedication to relieve the troubled souls of the dying (the work of the clergyman)? His path to "truth" ignores human beings' most cherished attribute ("spirit"), subordinating them to the forms of lifeless things whose only noble destiny was to return to the cycle of life. What had Dr. Frankenstein accomplished? The creation of a monster, a murderer, assembled with pieces of dead bodies, a ghost, the silhouette of the threat that, since about two centuries before the publication of Shelley's novel, had haunted the interior thing. A deed so dangerous that not even the writers of *universal nomos* had dared to propose, nor had the framers of *universal*

poesis ever contemplated, one that assumes that in the body of man resides the causes for the emergence of the self-determined "I," the one they carefully contained when maintaining that the mind relates only to the regulative or productive force of the universe through the fundamental immateriality—as form or "spirit"—it shares with it.

Not until the second half of the nineteenth century, after Hegel had written the trajectory of self-consciousness as a self-productive path of a self-determined (interior-temporal) thing, could projects of knowledge of man and society emerge that deployed the tools of scientific reason not to create a rational living thing but to show how the tools of universal *nomos,* the "laws of nature," produce the mind of man. For without resolving *affectability,* without transforming the contents (the "substance" and the "matter") of transparency into effects of universal *nomos,* the particularity of the post-Enlightenment European subject and social configuration would "vanish" as the *transcendental "I"* continued its self-actualizing trajectory. Here I employ an analytical tool, the scientific text, which shows how this possibility is deferred when scientific projects that seek to "discover" the "truth" of man rewrite the mind as an object of scientific reason. This is possible, however, only after the science of life, the first scientific project that addresses man as a thing of nature, has introduced a new version of the play of reason, productive *nomos,* as a regulative-productive power. Yet I show how, even as *productive nomos* (trans)forms everything it reaches into exteriorizations of the tools of universal *nomos,* the "laws of nature," when it refashions the transparent "I" as a specimen of the *homo scientificus,* it rewrites its bodily and social configurations as signifiers of transcendentality.

When describing the regimen of production of the *analytics of raciality,* the text of the sciences of man and society, I show how they deploy productive *nomos* to manufacture a political-symbolic weapon, the analytics of raciality, which accomplishes precisely that which *transcendental poesis* prescribes but does not ensure: it delimits the borders of the moment of transparency, completing the fashioning of the transparent I by rendering it both a temporal and a spatial thing. How? When the main productive tools of the analytics of raciality, the racial and the cultural, engage extension, writing self-consciousness as an effect of exteriority-spatiality, they do so by ensuring that the transparent I would not become an affectable thing. Nevertheless, while here resides its effectiveness as a political-symbolic weapon, the analytics of raciality necessarily brings to the fore that which has from the outset threatened the writing of the interior thing's self-determination. For when the sciences of mind and society refashion self-consciousness as the *homo scientificus,* an effect of the laws of nature, they institute globality as a modern ontoepistemological context in which both the transparent I and its irreducible and unsublatable "others" emerge in outer determination, together facing but the horizon of death.

My goal here is not to measure how far or how close these scientific projects are to that which they pursue, that is, the truth of man. By approaching them as scientific texts, I recognize that they presuppose a ground for truth, productive *nomos,* which combines both the logic of "discovery" (universal *nomos*) and the *thesis of transparency* (transcendental poesis). With this mapping of the regimen of the analytics of raciality I pursue something neither the critics of the racial nor the celebrators of the cultural consider: how the racial and the cultural, the *strategies of engulfment* governing the contemporary global configuration, circumscribe the place of operation of transcendentality, the principle guiding modern conceptions of justice, to the material (bodily and social) configurations these framers of the *homo scientificus* write to signify transparency. In so doing, I add to the critical arsenal an account of modern representation that recognizes that scientific signification plays an ontoepistemological role as the site of production of political-symbolic tools deployed in the writing of modern subjects.

5

Productive Nomos

Everything in nature, in the inanimate as well as the animate world, happens according to rules, although we do not always know these rules. . . . All nature is actually nothing but a nexus of appearances according to rule; and there is nothing at all without rules. When we believe that we have come across an absence of rules, we can only say that the rules are unknown to us.
— IMMANUEL KANT, *LOGIC*

So, it is the rules of right, the mechanisms of power, the effects of truth or if you like, the rules of power and the powers of true discourses, that can be said more or less to have formed the general terrain of my concern.
— MICHEL FOUCAULT, *POWER/KNOWLEDGe*

My charting of the context of the emergence of the *analytics of raciality* in the previous part of this book shows how both versions of the play of reason, *universal nomos* and *universal poesis,* retain self-consciousness secure in interiority, subjected solely to its "inward determinations." No writer of the scenes of reason addresses the mind as an affectable thing, that is, as subject to outer determination. Not even the formulators of scientific universality ever questioned the mind's self-determination; none dared to bring it into the scrutiny of the tools of universal *nomos.* Not until the account of *transcendental poesis* reconciled the versions of universal reason by resolving the transcendental into the historical, reason into freedom, transforming self-consciousness and the things into moments of a transcendental "I." Nevertheless, although it spells out the particularity of the subject and social configuration that emerged in post-Enlightenment Europe, Hegel's transcendental poesis leaves open the possibility that this particularity would vanish in the unfolding of "Spirit." What transcendental poesis promises but cannot deliver—that to which the purchase the *transparency thesis* enjoys in the critical field testifies, that which modern thought has always counted on as an impossibility—is the establishing of the limits of temporality, the assurance that, though as a thing of unbounded *time,* the *transparent "I"* exists solely within the spatial-temporal limits of post-Enlightenment Europe. Because it describes the moment of transparency as a temporal event, transcendental poesis does not establish European particularity with certainty, as an "objective" and "necessary" fact. For these post-Kantian criteria of sovereign reason could be met only with an account that privileges space—the moment of irreducible and unsublatable difference or, to use Foucault's (1994) terms, one that also comprehended the finitude man shares with other existing things.

My task in this chapter is to describe the version of the play of reason, the productive *nomos,* that transforms the mind into an object of scientific reason without, however, undermining Hegel's fashioning of self-consciousness as the transparent I, that is, a self-determined thing. When the human body and the social are finally comprehended in scientific universality, the powers of universal reason, regulation and representation, are resolved in an account that addresses precisely that which had to be postponed lest it would undermine that which marked modern thought's version of the intimacy that the mind has with the logos. From this results the final delineation of modern representation with the complete assemblage of the *stage of exteriority,* which now becomes the dominion of Productive Reason, the regulative-productive force that authorizes any ontoepistemological statement. Though Kant's formulation of the transcendental suggests the idea of productive regulation—what I think leads Foucault (1994) to argue that it has rendered the "analytics of finitude" possible—it lacks a crucial dimension that Hegel's temporalizing of reason provides. In transcendental poesis, the merging of universal reason's regulative and productive powers writes the *scene of engulfment,* where exteriority is not only rendered ontoepistemo-

logically irrelevant but, because already a moment of a transcendental productive force, it also becomes product and effect, the stuff
without which "Spirit" cannot fulfill its essentiality, that is, to come
into existence.

I show how the science of life, the scientific project that rewrites
the play of reason as the acts of productive *nomos,* inverts but does
not displace Hegel's account when deploying two guiding notions,
the "laws of the condition of existence" and the principle of "natural selection," to capture how time itself is inscribed in that which
Western thought has conceived of as things of space, namely, extended (exterior-affectable) things. This is a transformation that
becomes possible only after transcendental poesis writes regulation as self-representation, which conceives of existing things as
both always already ordered by something that has a fundamental
interiority—not, as Kant postulates, as an effect of an exterior (universal) tool, the "pure intuition" of time, but as the interior tool
that is exteriorized as Spirit manifests itself as space. At the core
of productive *nomos,* then, I find a rewriting of the play of engulfment, which, rather than merely describing extended, that is, spatial
(exterior-affectable) things as yet-to-be sublated moments of spirit,
reads them as always already exteriorizations of the transcendental
force in the "essence" of which they always already participate. That
is, the science of life delimits a region of nature as the stage of actualization of a productive and regulative force, productive *nomos,*
with the "law of conditions of existence" that turns representation
into an effect of regulation, and the "principle of natural selection,"
which transforms regulation into an instrument of representation.

With this analysis of the science of life, then, I begin my mapping
of the regimen of the production of the analytics of raciality, the description of the political-symbolic arsenal that transforms the Global
into a modern ontological context. What I do here is primarily to
identify the presuppositions and the signifying strategies deployed in
the scientific projects—the science of man, anthropology, and (the
sociology of) race relations—which apprehend the mind as an effect of the tools of scientific reason, the ones that deploy the two
political-symbolic weapons, the racial and the cultural, which institute self-consciousness as a global (exterior-spatial) thing without
threatening the writing of the transparent I in self-determination.
Finalizing the account of scientific signification, the delineation of

the stage of exteriority, already begun in the previous part of the book, here I deploy the notion of the scientific text, the analytical tool that addresses the moment of modern representation in which ontoepistemological statements are governed by the rules of scientific signification. I do so by describing the conditions of production of the signifying strategies, intervention, engulfment, and particularization, that transform certain things, the self-moving bodies of nature, into exteriorizations of productive *nomos*.

My analysis of these scientific text accounts, then, shows how they reproduce the scene of engulfment, in that the rules of the production of words and their arrangement presume that the post-Enlightenment European space constitutes the moment of transparency. This, I will show, results from how their *strategies of engulfment* transform that which is exterior, the effects of the universal *nomos,* into products, moments, "other" manifestations of the fundamental interiority that distinguishes the *homo historicus.* Such transformation, which has to be performed over and over again to contain exteriority's other effect, results from the *strategies of intervention,* which consist in the laws, the modes through which the universal *nomos* constrains and produces human conditions, which are expressed in bodily and social configurations corresponding to particular kinds of consciousness. Finally, that precisely because these deployments of the productive *nomos* assume that post-Enlightenment Europe constitutes the moment of transparency, the perfect actualization-exteriorization of universal reason, they locate it at the top of the classificatory schema they produce, which is used in statements that describe, explain, and interpret the present global configuration. These *strategies of particularization* constitute the lexicon, the words that address human beings as exterior things, the ones that cannot but belie the ontoepistemological basis of the universe of signification in which they are devised because they cannot obliterate that "Other" theater, spatiality, the one that these scientific projects consistently postpone by resolving the particularities they chart into moments of the productive *nomos,* the destiny of which is to remain engulfed in accounts that narrate the movement toward transparency.

This reading shows why the science of life's unique strategies of intervention, Cuvier's law of conditions of existence and Darwin's principle of natural selection enabled signifying strategies that produce the human bodies, social configurations, and the global itself as expressions of the "laws of nature" without displacing the ruling principle of transcendentality; that is, how they ensure the (re)placing of the transparent I within the spatial-temporal boundaries of post-Enlightenment Europe. For though deployments of productive *nomos* would institute an ontological context, globality, in which man appears as an exterior-spatial thing, the analytics of raciality once again postpones the threat of *affectablity,* outer determination, by writing post-Enlightenment European bodies and social configurations as the sole signifiers of actualized universal reason, that is, as the "original" place of emergence of the transparent I.

"LAWS OF CONDITIONS OF EXISTENCE"

In *The Animal Kingdom,* Georges Cuvier (1863) rewrites natural history as the science of life when he states how this project of knowledge could emulate Newton's experimental philosophy. More precisely, the rupture with natural history, which, he argues, relies on the "simple laws of observations," occurs in the identification of a very different kind of "law of nature." "Particular Physics, or Natural History," Cuvier notes, "has for its object to apply specially the laws recognized by the various branches of General Physics, to the numerous and varied beings which exist in nature, in order to explain the phenomena which they severally present" (2). Nevertheless, given the fragility characteristic of its objects, "which do not allow for rigorous calculation, or precise measurement in all their parts," he concedes that natural history could not be strict in its employment of the tools of *scientific reason.* "Natural History," he adds, has "a principle on which to reason, which is peculiar to it, and which it employs advantageously on many occasions; it is that of the *conditions of existence,* commonly termed *final causes.* As nothing can exist without concurrence of those conditions which render its existence possible, the component parts of each must be so arranged as to render possible the whole living being, not only with regard to itself, but to its surrounding relations; and the analysis of these conditions frequently conducts to general laws, as demonstrable as those which are derived from calculation and experiment. It is only when the laws of general physics, and those which result from the conditions of existence are exhausted, that we are reduced to the simple laws of observation" (2–3, italics in the original). What this strategy of intervention, the "laws of conditions of existence," does is to split the "world of things" into two as it divides nature into a domain inhabited by the movable bodies, the objects of "general physics," and one constituted by self-moving bodies, the objects of the science of life. When it does so, Cuvier's statement introduces a strategy of engulfment, Life, which captures how the self-moving things of *nature,* animated bodies, the ones which resembles man's body, express, as they exteriorize-actualize, the productive-regulative power of the universe.[1]

In the science of life, a method used by eighteenth-century naturalists, comparative anatomy is deployed to map the inner ordering and movement to be used in the charting of a whole domain of nature, that is, the "animal kingdom," which is a rewriting of the naturalists' grid of specification, as strategies of particularization. From now on the knowledge of nature will result from observations whose goal is to determine degrees of differentiation, complexity, and specialization of parts and movements, that is, how it approaches and departs from universality and self-determination, which guide the placing of a given animal in a class or subdivision.[2] In *Lectures on Comparative Anatomy,* Cuvier (1802) instructs the reader how to proceed in this charting of living nature. Recognizing that it is impractical to observe every existing animal, and rejecting the option of establishing a priori criteria for their classification, he teaches that to verify the specificity of an organ it is necessary to observe how it affects a "function." "The only forms and qualities fitted for [furnishing characters that will identify those organs belonging to the first rank]," he argues, "are those which modify, in an important manner, the function to which the organ belongs; those which may be said to give it a new direction, and to produce new results. All the other considerations to which an organ, whatever its rank, may give rise, are of no importance so long as they do not directly influence the functions it exercises" (64–65). That is, the operations of the "laws of conditions of existence" can be observed only through the examination of parts (organs) and movements (functions) enabling the maintenance, growth, and reproduction of living bodies. "This general and common motion of all the parts," Cuvier teaches, "forms so peculiarly the essence of Life, that the parts which are separated from a living body soon die, because they possess no motion of their own, and only participated in the general motion produced by their union" (5–6). Neither a random nor a passive effect of bodily arrangements, each exteriorization of life, each particular kind of living thing, exists because of the regularity (rationality) of its internal arrangement, because the forms of its organs and the goal of its motions (functions) have to be perfectly combined.

What I find in the scientific version of the scene of engulfment, the science of life, is the rewriting of universal reason as a productive and regulative force, that is, productive *nomos*. Not only is life a cause; it is also a producer. That is, "the laws of conditions of existence" are both exterior (outer) powers and the interior (inner) force, the regulating and (re)producing sovereign of this domain of natural things. On the one hand, regulation (order) produces life. Because life, Cuvier teaches, "presupposes organization in general, and the life proper to each being presupposes the organization peculiar to that being, just as the movement of the clock presupposes the clock; and accordingly, we behold life only in beings that are organized and formed to enjoy it; and all the efforts of philosophers have not yet been able to discover matter in the act of organization, either of itself or by any extrinsic cause." On the other hand, life produces regulation. While it operates within the body, the plan at work escapes the elements it affects. Because "Life," Cuvier continues, is "exercising upon the elements which at every instant form part of the living body, and upon those which it attracts to it, an action contrary to that which would be produced without it by the usual chemical affinities, it is inconsistent to suppose that it can be produced by these affinities, and yet we know of no other power in nature capable of reuniting previously separated molecules" (6). That is, life is a scientific signifier, but one that describes the *scene of regulation* as a productive context. Not only does it govern the arrangement of various and diverse organs and their functions, but it also produces the particular organisms that compose living nature. That is, in Cuvier's version of the science of life, living bodies, the extended and self-producing things of nature, are exteriorizations, both products and "effects" of a tool of a universal reason, that is, life.

What distinguishes this version of the play of reason is precisely the deployment of the Enlightenment idea of "progress" into nature when it maps a portion of it by classifying its inhabitants according to the degree of differentiation, specialization, and complexity of its inhabitants, that is, their degree of perfection—in other words, when it establishes how a living thing's internal arrangement indicates how it exteriorizes the regulative-productive force of the universe, that is, productive *nomos*.[3]

More important, in the text of the science of life, the human body finally becomes an object of the tools of scientific reason. For its particular organization would be named the privileged signifier of the universal ruler-producer, productive *nomos,* that is, the living form that more perfectly expresses or actualizes the workings of universal reason. As Foucault (1994) states, the body of man becomes the measure of any account of living nature. "Man," Cuvier (1863) says, "forms but one genus, and that genus the only one of its order," and "his history is more directly interesting to ourselves, and forms the standard of comparison to which we refer that of other animals" (32). According to Cuvier, the human body owes this singular placing to its "upright position," unique movements, and the higher degree of differentiation, specialization, and complexity of its vital organs and functions but, more important, to mental processes that play no role in the emergence and preservation of the living body. "The more sophisticated" mental functions ("memory," "association of ideas," "abstraction," "reasoning," and "imagination"), Cuvier (1863) teaches, derive from modifications in those parts of the nervous system that are "more circumscribed as the animal is more perfect," that is, in man, the perfect animal. Unique to the human intellect, he argues, are "the power[s] of separating . . . accessory ideas of objects, and of combining those that are alike in several different objects under one general idea, the prototype of which nowhere really exists, nor presents itself in an isolated form; this is abstraction" (17). Justifying this supreme placing of the human body are its "higher" functions, mental processes, which emulate the universal (rational or temporal) force that regulates and produces the "world of things." Although constructing human "mental functions" as the perfect expression (signifier) of life suggests that the exclusive qualities of the interior thing are effects of a tool of reason, the "laws of conditions of existence," the writing of self-consciousness as a mere effect of an exterior (outer) determination is immediately closed off when Cuvier explains that man's unique "character," his "mental functions," give him a distinctive position in relation to the laws of life, providing him with an attribute all other living things lack, that is, self-perfectioning; that is, man is a perfect animal because he is not only subjected to, but also a subject of, productive regulation.

With this statement Cuvier deploys the tools of scientific signification to repeat what philosophers have proclaimed for centuries, namely, that what distinguishes man from other existing things is the fact that he is a thing with reason and self-determination. My point is that rather than the human body, man (Descartes's body-mind composite) would occupy the privileged place in the "animal kingdom" as the "highest order of the mammalians," the "first order animal." For, although his body is a product of the universal (exterior) laws of the "conditions of existence," man's mind testifies to the fact that he enjoys a productive power that, though an effect, is not constrained by these laws. What the strategy of engulfment, life, does is to rewrite the human body, which had been safely disavowed (displaced and negated) in the founding statements of modern thought, as a signifier of the mind. But as it does so, it reunites body and mind; man's organic parts and movements become the extended determinants of his mind's unique attributes, that is, (the ability to conceive of) universality and self-determination. In this early adventure of scientific reason into the domain of freedom, the proposition that in the spatial (exterior or affectable) dimension of man resides the cause of the rational mind's particularity introduces the possibility that the stage of exteriority should be considered ontologically relevant.

Nevertheless, affectability is immediately postponed in the statement that articulates the body as a double signifier of exteriority, as an extended (exterior/affectable) thing and as an expression or actualization of a tool of universal *nomos*. In the scientific version of the scene of engulfment, man, the living thing whose brain has reason, would not become an affectable thing, because life is a strategy of engulfment, that is, it transforms all the other living things into less perfect, less developed, versions of the body of man. For in the scientific rehearsal of transcendental poesis, the living thing that has a rational mind, the one with highly developed mental functions, "civilized" man, is placed within the (spatial-temporal) boundaries of post-Enlightenment European space. "Although the human species would appear to be single, since the union of any of its members produces individuals capable of propagation, there are, nevertheless," Cuvier notes, "certain hereditary peculiarities of conformation are observable, which constitute what we termed races. Three of these in particular appear eminently distinct: the 'Caucasian,' or white, the 'Mongolian,' or yellow, and the Ethiopian, or black. The Caucasian, to which we belong, is distinguished by the beauty of the oval which forms the head; and it is this one which has given rise to the most civilized nations—to those which have generally held the rest in subjection: it varies in complexion and in the color of the hair." The other two "races or varieties of mankind" are organically and geographically distinct from the "civilized Caucasian": "The Mongolian is known by his projecting cheek-bones, flat visage, narrow and oblique eyebrow, scanty beard, and olive complexion. Great empires have been established by this race in China and Japan, and its conquests have sometimes extended to their side of the Great Desert; but its civilization has always remained stationary. The Negro race is confined to the southward of the Atlas chain of mountains: its color is black, its hair crisped, the cranium compressed, and nose flattened. The projecting muzzle and thick lips evidently approximate it to the Apes: the hordes of which it is composed have always continued barbarous" (37–38). In sum, the living body that best expresses life is not the human body, but the body of post-Enlightenment (Caucasian, white) Europeans, the body of man, the *homo historicus,* the one whose ("highly developed") "mental functions" are inscribed in its social configuration, that is, "civilization."

Though incipient, this mapping of human bodies and the global space says that bodily and social configurations, as bases for differentiating human beings, are exteriorizations (products and effects) of productive *nomos.* Because they presuppose a strategy of intervention, the "laws of conditions of existence," which entail the particular organic configurations found in a given global location, the incipient strategies of particularization Cuvier deploys—the terms "Caucasian," "Mongolian," and "Negro"—presuppose the universality of differentiation as it is conceived in the version of universal reason as productive *nomos,* that is, as a transcendental (regulating-productive) I. Nonetheless, if each configuration of the human body found in distinct regions of the global space corresponds to a particular degree of social "development," "progress," which is but an actualization of the attributes of the mind, the possibility is now open for the deployment of the tools of scientific reason to "discover" the universal (exterior) determinants of self-consciousness.

Each particular bodily and social configuration would constitute but exteriorizations, that is, as a particular expression of the law of life and as an actualization of the particular mind it produces in a given region of the global space. (This possibility was not lost to the scientists of man, as we will see shortly.) What does not appear in this first version of the science of life, however, is the explicit writing of the "others of Europe" in *affectability,* an accomplishment that become possible only after the second version of the science of life introduced temporality as the distinguishing feature of living nature.

THE PRINCIPLE OF "NATURAL SELECTION"

Neither a concern with organic variations nor an account of the extent of the diversity of the living world lay outside the scope of Cuvier's formulation of the science of life. But he was more interested in mapping the forms of the living body than in traveling the world to assess the scope of life's productive powers. If in the first version, the "laws of conditions of existence" construct particular bodies as moments of actualization of universal *nomos,* the principle of natural selection deploys temporality at the core of nature to produce it as the stage of actualization of universal poesis. Here the whole of nature, at last, gains a Spirit whose end is to increase diversity and perfection on the globe; that is, the text of evolution successfully describes the stage of exteriority as a proper moment of the play of productive reason. In *The Origins of Species,* Charles Darwin ([1859] 1994) introduces a strategy of intervention, the principle of "natural selection," to capture precisely *why* and *how* life deploys its productive powers. With the principle of natural selection, Darwin expands the domain of investigation of the workings of life beyond any particular finite body to rewrite living nature as a self-regulating and self-producing totality, one in which the variations among living things become an effect of the regulating and pro ductive force whose "End" reaches beyond the existence of any particular exteriorization of life. "The structure of every organic being is related," Darwin argues, "in the most essential yet often hidden manner, to that of all other organic beings, with which it comes into competition for food or residence, or from which it has to escape, or on which it preys." Darwin deploys the construct of the "struggle for existence," which suggests a Hobbesian account of living nature, to capture the means through which the ends of natural selection are accomplished, namely, what Darwin refers to as "the preservation of favorable individual differences and variations, and the destruction of those which are injurious" (60).

In the second version of the science of life, the idea of evolution completes the formulation of productive *nomos*. In this the scientific version of the play of engulfment, the thesis of the "survival of the fittest" plays a crucial role when it situates the scope of life beyond the finite existence of any particular living body. "Variation," Darwin explains, "is a long-continued and slow process, and natural selection will in such cases not as yet have had time to overcome the tendency to further variability and to reversion to a less modified state. But when a species with an extraordinarily developed organ has become the parent of many modified descendants—which on our view must be a very slow process, requiring a long lapse of time—in this case, natural selection has succeeded in giving a fixed character to the organ, in however extraordinarily manner it may have been developed." The direction of this productive process is evident. "Although new and important modifications may not arise from reversion and analogous variation," Darwin proceeds, "such modifications will add to the beautiful and harmonious diversity of nature. Whatever the cause may be of each slight difference—and a cause for each must exist—we have reason to believe that it is the steady accumulation of beneficial differences which has given rise to all the more important modifications of structure in relation to the habits of each species" (132).

Not only particular bodies but the whole of created (living) things, which is spread throughout the global space, becomes the laboratory for the observation of the activity of a temporal regulative and productive force that actualizes itself by producing increasingly differentiated, specialized, and complex living things. "It may metaphorically be said," Darwin proposes, "that natural selection is daily and hourly scrutinizing, throughout the world, the slightest variations; rejecting those that are bad, preserving and adding up all that are good; silently and insensibly working, whenever and wherever opportunity offers, at the improvement of each organic being in relation to its organic and inorganic conditions of Life. We see nothing of these slow changes in process, until the hand of time has marked the lapse of ages, and then so imperfect is our view into long-past geological ages, that we see only that the forms of Life are now different from what they formerly were" (65–66). Not surprisingly, while Cuvier's undertakings kept him locked in laboratories of anatomy or forced him to spend his nights in cemeteries, as Stocking (1968) points out, Darwin's pursuits led him to travel to the most distant regions of the globe in search of specimens of the productivity of nature. For the project of the science of life now also demanded the reading of the materializations of time onto the global space (McGrane 1989). What the collection, examination, and cataloguing of organic structures capture are various and particular signifiers of the play of a regulative and productive force that operates in time, that is, productive *nomos,* the outcome of which is similar to that of the movement of "Spirit," namely, *perfection,* for it issues beings whose organic configurations not only express its determinations but also actualize its various moments.

Human beings, however, have no significant place in the statement that attributes a single "beginning" and a single "end" to the play of engulfment, that is, the text of evolution. Not only does Darwin provide no mapping of the human organic configuration, but he immediately places post-Enlightenment Europeans beyond the workings of productive *nomos.* Following the ruling principle of transcendentality, he states that self-determination places the interior/temporal thing beyond the means of natural selection. Expectedly, the self-productive thing, which moves against the determinations of natural selection, is not the human being in general but man. In *The Descent of Man,* Darwin ([1871] 1979) argues that the uniqueness of man, not the whole of the human species, is expressed in his social configurations—industry, arts, and political configurations—that is, "civilization," which now becomes an expression of the movement of a productive *nomos.* From human self-productivity, he argues, results the improvement of the general conditions of life, the modifications of the natural and social circumstances, which limit the action of natural selection by favoring the survival of the weakest individual. "Progress," he points out, "has been much more general than retrogression; that man has risen, though by slow and interrupted steps, from a lowly condition to the highest standard as yet attained by him in knowledge, morality and religion" (161). That is, the "civilized man's "intellectual and moral" attributes testify to his adaptive advantage over all other living things, including the "savage races." They account for how Europeans, the "Caucasian races," had sidestepped the "laws of variation," the means through which the principle of natural selection achieves its ends. "Modern civilization," Darwin argues, owes its emergence to "an increase in the actual number of population, in the number of men endowed with high intellectual and moral faculties, as well as in their standard of excellence. Corporeal structure appears to have little influence, except so far as vigor of body leads to vigor of mind" (156).

Although Cuvier's version of the science of life places man, the transparent I, at the submit of living nature and highlights how his superior, more perfect, organic arrangement is expressed in post-Enlightenment European social configurations, it provides no account of the relationship between the "races or varieties of men." When he explicitly writes the transparent I, the *homo historicus,* outside—always already the winner—of the "struggle for Life," Darwin introduces an element absent in previous (Eighteenth-century naturalists' and philosophers') descriptions of the global as a site of human differentiation, namely, *affectability.*[4] In the same statement, his version of the science of life safely places post-Enlightenment Europe in the moment of transparency and writes the "savage races" in the same way Newton has described the bodies of physics, as doubly affectable living things, that is, as doubly governed by exteriority, that is, the exterior regulating force (productive nomos) and coexisting more powerful human beings, that is, the "Caucasian races." In other words, they are always already losers in the "struggle for existence" against the European "races of men," the ones whose social configurations testify to their competitive advantage.[5] "At some future period, not very distant as measured by centuries," Darwin predicts, "the *civilized races of man* will almost certainly *exterminate,* and *replace,* the *savage races* throughout the world. At the same time, the anthropomorphous apes . . . will no doubt be exterminated. The *break between man and his nearest allies* will then be wider, for it will intervene between man in a more *civilized state,* as we may hope, even than the Caucasian, and some ape as low as a baboon, instead of, as now, between the negro or Australian and the gorilla" (172–73, my italics).

What my charting of the scientific text that introduces the version of reason as the play of productive *nomos* shows is how Darwin's version of the science of life successfully rewrites living nature as a stage of the unfolding of transcendental poesis, the ruling principle of modern representation. My point is that Darwin excluded human beings from *The Origin of Species* because, by the mid-nineteenth century, the ruling principle of transcendentality had already taken hold of modern thought, to which evolution (through the thesis of the "common origin" of every living thing) testifies. For this reason, when he finally addressed "human variation" he would not, like Cuvier, attribute European particularity to an exterior determinant, that is, Life as it is exteriorized in particular organic arrangements, as that which happens to man, that which escapes, though it is the condition of possibility for the deployment of, his productive ability. He does not follow Cuvier's suggestion that human visible physical traits correspond to variations in organic structure that account for differences in "mental functions." Instead, he assumes that the "civilized races" of man's highly developed "mental functions" and social configuration, "modern civilization," are the main signifiers of European *particularity*. Always already a self-determined thing, in Darwin's version of *productive nomos* the "civilized man" remains (as a transparent thing) fully in the *scene of representation,* from whence *he* defies the regulative and productive force of nature, beyond the means of "natural selection." He alone is self-producing; he alone enjoys the ability of self-perfection.

THE NATURAL MAN

Though it acknowledges the ontological prerogative of the transparency thesis, this charting of the conditions of production of the analytics of raciality—the scientific text and signifying strategies—does not fully rewrite the modern subject and social configurations back into transparency. Much of the groundwork necessary to situate my task was done in the previous part of the book, where I gathered from the founding statements of modern thought building blocks that allowed me to delimit the stages of the theater of reason, the *stage of interiority* and the *stage of exteriority,* which correspond to the two fields of signification, history and science, that constitute modern representation. What this chapter provides is a further delineation of the stage of exteriority, which I gather from the version of the play of reason, productive *nomos,* introduced in the text of the science of life.

My reading of Georges Cuvier's and Charles Darwin's versions of the science of life fulfilled two objectives.[6] First, I describe the main attributes of this version of universal reason, the one in which the centering of the stage of exteriority rewrites the subject of transcendental poesis as the agent of a productive *nomos*. This, I show, results from how a sector of nature is written as a stage where the scene of engulfment is performed when its inhabitants are apprehended as exteriorizations or actualizations, effects or products of the temporal play of the exterior power that regulates and produces them. In other words, when it extends the narrative of transcendental poesis to comprehend the "world of things"—or, to cite Foucault (1994), it deploys temporality in the world of things—by combining the notions of "progress" and "development," the science of life performs another appropriation of nature through a version of universal reason that merges universal poesis and universal *nomos* in such a way that the scene of regulation constitutes the privileged moment for examining the workings of universal reason. That is, although transcendentality constitutes the ruling principle, when the transcendental I plays its role as productive *nomos*, the world of (living) things becomes a stage of the scene of representation, but one in which reason plays its role as a productive power only when it can govern things, that is, through regulation. Second, I show how it does so by deploying and explicating the main signifying strategies of the scientific text—namely, strategies of intervention, strategies of engulfment, and strategies of particularization—the ones which show how, unlike the critics of the racial charge, scientific signification has consistently worked in tandem with historical signification.[7]

With this excavation I uncover the regimen of scientific signification, which by the second half of the nineteenth century deployed a strategy of engulfment, life, which describes how universal reason plays its productive role in nature by delimiting a microuniverse of sorts endowed its own "cause" and "end." This, I show, is an effect of the strategies of intervention, the laws of conditions of existence and natural selection, which write the self-moving and self-productive things of nature as organic beings, internally ordered and moving bodies. In this version of the play of reason, productive *nomos*, nature acquires a "final end" that guides the classificatory scheme, strategies of particularization, which assume that each living thing is governed by a productive power whose aims lie beyond the particular needs of each living thing or group of things of the same kind (genus, order, family, etc.). That is, these strategies of intervention write living nature as a stage of actualization of universal reason, a gesture that renders not only the effects of regulation but also the products of representation accessible to the tools of scientific reason.

This suggests that the stages of transcendental poesis, the temporal productive process culminating with the emergence of the post-Enlightenment European mind and social configuration, could be established by investigating man as an "empirical" thing. For "civilized man," once again, signifies the "ends" of the universal regulative and productive power, the mark of its full exteriorization in living nature. This writing of man as an effect of scientific signification, as a natural thing, was achieved with the articulation of a construct that, like all other tools of the science of life, was also deployed in the previous moment of modern thought, namely, the idea of "race or variety of mankind," a signifier of exteriority, connecting mental functions and social configurations. That is, the human body and social configurations are scientific signifiers, expressions of exterior determinants of the interior (mind's) productive powers that are unique to human beings. From the scientists of man's appropriation of these signifiers resulted (a) a concept, the racial, that would delimit (b) a whole power/knowledge apparatus, *scientia racialis,* which deployed a series of strategies that constituted the political-symbolic arsenal, the analytics of raciality, which would yield (c) representations of the human being governed by exteriority, the rule of science.

Yesterday's and today's critics of the science of man have rejected the concept of the racial, forgetting that the threat it announces is an effect of scientific signification, which, after the account of transcendental poesis, instituted the *homo scientificus,* that is, the refashioning of self-consciousness as a product or effect of the tools of universal *nomos.* Because productive *nomos* captures how universal reason performs its sovereign role when the scene of engulfment is shown in the stage of exteriority, it would enable the formulation of a science of the mind, the scientific texts—the science of man, anthropology, and race relations[8]—which brought the mind of man and his "others" into the stage of exteriority, where the transparent I becomes just an "other" mode of being human.

6

The Science of the Mind

The study of the natural history of man embraces almost every branch of human knowledge. . . . The subject is not man, considered as an abstract being: the inquiry extends to millions of men scattered over the earth, their physical peculiarities, their present and former relations to each other, and stretches back to a time when man scarcely left more traces of his existence than the savage beast which inhabited the same region. From the results obtained we must, then, draw inferences concerning the relations of the races of mankind to each other, their intermixture, their descent and propagation, their relation to other creatures, especially to the higher mammals; and also, the changes which air, climate, and mode of life, have produced in man in his struggle for existence.

—KARL VOGT, *LECTURES ON MAN*

From its initial outlining in Descartes's founding statement and in every later refashioning in the scenes of reason, self-consciousness, the self-determined thing, has been kept outside the *stage of exteriority,* the dominium of universal reason inhabited by the spatial (exterior/affectable) things. Before Hegel's resolution of regulation into representation, in which self-consciousness becomes the *transparent "I,"* neither the placing of man at the summit of nature nor the connection between bodily and social configurations allowed and/or necessitated projects of knowledge that deployed the tools of scientific reason to uncover the "truth" of the mind. What did not exist before the mid–nineteenth century, that which was both

115

impossible and unnecessary before *transcendental poesis* placed the post-Enlightenment European mind and social configuration in transparency, was a scientific machinery that included training of specialists, formation of research institutions, manufacturing of instruments, delimitation of sites of investigation, definition of objects, and dedication of specialized locales to study them.

My task in this chapter is to chart the regimen of production of the political-symbolic arsenal, the *analytics of raciality,* which accomplishes something transcendental poesis could only postulate, that is, placement of the moment of transparency exclusively within Europe. What my description of the scientific texts—those of the science of man, anthropology, which transform or form the mind into a thing of *productive nomos*—shows is how, when the science of the mind addressed the exterior dimensions (bodily and social configurations) of man's existence, the Global emerged as the privileged ontoepistemological context. Although this gesture keeps the transparent I in self-determination, I contend, it necessarily produced post-Enlightenment Europe's particularity as an effect of outer determination, that is, as the marker of an irreducible and unsublatable difference that could be captured only when placed alongside the "other" modes of being of man. This mapping of the conditions of production of the analytics of raciality has two moments.

My first move is to describe the first moment of the analytics of raciality, the science of man, to show how, although it inherited the eighteenth-century naturalists' correlation between global regions and bodily and social configurations, it is the first project of knowledge to write post-Enlightenment Europe's particularity by deploying the apparatus of scientific reason manufactured in the account of productive *nomos.* Its arsenal does this when it transforms race (a term previously employed to describe collectivities in terms of blood relationship) into the racial (a scientific concept), the *strategy of engulfment* that produces the human body as an exteriorization of productive *nomos.* In other words, it rewrites the manifoldness of human bodies into signifiers (exteriorizations) of the mind (intellectual and moral attributes), that is, as expressions of the "laws of conditions of existence," the "principle of natural selection," and the various social configurations found across the globe as actualizations of the different minds (interior things) these scientific tools produce. Through the deployment of strategies of engulfment that always already assume that post-Enlightenment European (white) bodies and (civilized) social configurations are not submitted to the regulative and productive force of universe, the science of the mind produces bodies and social configurations as signifiers—expressions and actualizations, respectively—of two kinds of minds, namely, (a) the *transparent I,* which emerged in post-Enlightenment Europe, the kind of mind that is able to know, emulate, and control powers of universal reason, and (b) the *affectable "I,"* the one that emerged in other global regions, the kind of mind subjected to both the exterior determination of the "laws of nature" and the superior force of European minds. What this refashioning of self-consciousness, which establishes the stage of exteriority as the arena in which to address human differentiation, accomplishes, I will show, is the production of an ontoepistemological context, globality, that constitutes a necessarily uneven political surface.

My description of the second moment of the analytics of raciality shows how, when twentieth-century anthropology deployed a scientific version of the cultural that returned the account of human difference to the *stage of interiority,* it colonized the latter with signifying strategies that instituted mental (moral) difference as an effect of exterior determinants. What distinguishes this moment, I show, is a deployment of historicity that presupposes globality as a stage of human differentiation. That is, even though throughout the twentieth century the cultural would be consolidated as the authorized signifier of human difference—an upward trajectory that has culminated in its present position as the guiding global political concept—it would not obliterate the political-symbolic force of the racial. Not only because, without the science of man's notion of racial difference, which here becomes the "empirical" basis for distinguishing between Europeans and their "others," the very delimitation of the exclusive object of anthropological investigation, the "primitive" mental and social configurations, would be impossible, but also because without globality, outside the scientific *stage of engulfment,* the cultural would not maintain the boundaries of transparency.

What I gather here is how both strategies of engulfment, the racial and the cultural, the main signifiers of the analytics of raciality, institute globality as an ontological context, the one in which self-consciousness becomes an effect of exteriority, where it emerges always already in contention with that which is not it-self, without transparency, that is, before the horizon of death. While each postpones the threat the human body has always signified, which is to write the thinking thing as an affectable thing by limiting it to the spatial boundaries of Europe, each also produces the self-consciousnesses and social configurations it describes as necessarily contemporaneous, coexisting, and contending, global (exterior/spatial) modes of being human. With this, I highlight something that neither racial theorists nor postmodern critics of modern thought consider because it is presupposed by the *transparency thesis* and the sociohistorical logic of exclusion that both (re)produce, that neither the racial nor the cultural violates modern ethical principles because, as modern political-symbolic weapons, they do more than supplement the transparency thesis, allowing the deployment of accounts that write the *affectability* of the others of Europe and post-Enlightenment Europe's transparency as "necessary and objective" effects and products of productive reason.

SCIENTIA RACIALIS

Seventeenth-century naturalist and philosophical texts deployed the phrase "races or varieties of men" to comprehend human differentiation. Missing in their statements, however, was the assumption that a regulative or productive force responded to the correlations they found between global regions and bodily and mental (intellectual and moral) traits. "Nothing" the naturalist Buffon (1997) argues, "can prove more clearly that the climate is the principle cause of the varieties of mankind, than this color of the Hottentots, whose blackness could not be diminished but by the temperature of the climate" (22). He further notes that, even if the "rudiments of blackness" are inherited, once "Negroes" are transplanted to a cold climate, blackness will disappear in a few generations (24). Notwithstanding the fact that natural history does not seek to "discover" the "laws of nature" determining human consciousness nor does it attribute permanence to the distinctions it maps, it does read visible physical traits as indexes of mental and social configurations. For instance, the eighteenth-century philosopher who doubts that experience could give access to the universal (exterior) determinants of nature, Hume ([1754] 1997), notes that the observable differences suggest that all other "breeds of men" are "naturally inferior to the white," for "there never was a civilized nation of any other complexion than white, nor even any individual eminent either in action or speculation. No ingenious manufactures amongst them, no arts, no sciences" (33). Even the philosopher who describes the interior tools of scientific reason, Kant ([1775] 1997), attributes human difference to "a predetermined ability or natural dispositions," that is, the God-given circumstances of climate and soil humans share with other created things. "This foresight of Nature to equip her creation with hidden inner furnishings against all sorts of future circumstances in order that it be preserved and suited to the variety of climate or soil," Kant notes, "is worthy of all wonder; and in the course of wanderings and transplantations of animals and plants it seems to produce new sorts which, however, are nothing more than deviations and races of one and the same genus" (43). Nevertheless, he notes that among "races of mankind," these "natural dispositions" may include more than external physical traits. For instance, Kant ([1764] 1960) notes that the difference between "Negroes" and whites is fundamental, "and it appears to be as great in regard to mental capacities as in color. The religion of fetishes so widespread among them is perhaps a sort of idolatry that sinks as deeply into trifling as appears to be possible to human nature" (111).

Writing a few decades later, Hegel (1900) also comments on "mental capacities" in a statement that places Africans outside transcendental poesis. For Hegel, the degree of mental differences is such that, in regard to Africans, "we must quite give up the principle which naturally accompanies our ideas—the category of Universality." "Negro" consciousness, he postulates, is underdeveloped, and the very notion of self-consciousness is completely foreign to members of that race. They "have not yet," he notes, "attained to the realization of any substantial objective existence—as for example God, or Law—in which the interest of man's volition is involved and in which he realizes his own being" (93). Not only does the "Negro" fail to distinguish between the individual and the universal dimension of his own being, which was reflected in a religion that lacked consciousness of a "Higher Power"; he argues that the "Negro" projects the spiritual dimension "into the world of phenomena by means of images" (94). Also lacking in the "Negroes," he argues, are conceptions of justice, morality, and political organization; they entertain no respect for authority or humanity, a conclusion he drew from their practices of "slavery" and "cannibalism," which he says reflect "the want of self-control [that] distinguishes the character of the Negroes. This condition is capable of no development or culture, and as we see them at this day, such have they always been" (98). For this reason, while acknowledging that slavery itself was unjust, because the "essence of humanity is Freedom," Hegel argued that for "the Negro" slavery could be a "phase of education—a mode of becoming participant in a higher morality and the culture connected with it" (99).

Nevertheless, philosophical statements drawing from natural history could not, as Thomas Jefferson lamented at the end of the eighteenth century, establish such connection with certainty as "objective" and "necessary," because there was yet to emerge an account of human differentiation formulated according to the rules of the field of science. In the previous chapter I argue that this became possible when the first version of the science of life deployed the *strategies of intervention*, the laws of conditions of existence and the principle of natural selection, which transformed universal reason into productive *nomos*. Using the science of life's arsenal, the scientists of man attempted to prove, to establish with certainty (as a "necessary" and "objective" fact), what eighteenth-century naturalists could only describe and the philosophers who framed man could only postulate. What I gather in this first moment of the analytics of raciality are the signifying strategies that, by apprehending man's extended (exterior-spatial) dimensions, the body and social configurations, have provided modern representation with a political-symbolic arsenal that writes mental and social configurations, the stuff of modern ontological accounts, as an effect and product of tools of universal reason.

The Science of Man

In the second edition of the *Instructions générale pour les recherches anthropologiques a faire sur le vivant*, prepared for the Societé d'Anthroplogie de Paris, Paul Broca (1879) describes the techniques and strategies of the science of man, the project of knowledge that displaced the eighteenth-century naturalist account of human difference. The manual contains detailed guidelines for conducting laboratory and field research for gathering, handling, and measuring information. Broca's main concern was to systematize anthropological research and to increase the quantity and quality of material collected about non-European peoples. Besides detailed descriptions of the contents of anthropological collections, it also includes instructions on how to gather, preserve, and identify the relevant body parts and how to prepare the *feuille d'observation* (a formulary to be filled with data obtained by observation and measurement, descriptions, drawings of instruments used in field and laboratory work and explanations of how to manipulate them); information about prices of instruments and where to purchase them; and enumerations, descriptions, and discussions of how to measure the most important characteristics used in the differentiation of the various "human races."

Although the Societé's manual includes extensive and detailed instructions on how to gather and preserve intact skulls and brains, due to the difficulty of collecting and preserving brains with their actual living size and volume, the skull constituted the primary object of research. The reason was simple. Measurement of skulls would provide information about the volume and size of the brain. "Among variations presented among the various human races," Broca instructs, "the volume and form of the brain can only be appreciated indirectly; instead of the brain itself, one has to study the skull." That is, craniology plays an important role in anthropological research because, Broca says, "any brain character[istic] is translated externally in the configuration of the skull bones," even though, he adds, "the study of the skull provides but a very insufficient knowledge of the brain" (15–16). Hence, even though he also instructed the anthropologist to carefully collect, preserve, and measure limbs as well as pieces of skins and hair samples to be classified according to the "color table," the privileged "morphological trait" used to distinguish "human races"—"Caucasian," "Mongolian," "Ethiopian"—was the features of the organ responsible for the "mental functions," namely, the brain. When explaining why the study of the skull is important Broca teaches: "The frontal part of the skull [is] the most important part . . . because in it one finds the noblest parts of the brain. To advance any opinion about the intelligence and the brain should be based upon the recognition that the frontal part is related to the highest faculties of the spirit, in individuals as well as in race, a relatively developed frontal brain constitutes a character of superior development" (146).[1]

The result of neither external factors such as climate and soil nor mere "natural dispositions" that testify to "divine nature's" creativity, the science of man's rewriting of natural history's "varieties of men" produced the mental (intellectual and moral) differences modern philosophers attributed to the "others of Europe" as effects of the particular configuration of their brains, which, they claimed, is signified in the forms of their heads. When approaching man as an "empirical" thing, writing his high mental powers as the effect of exterior determinants, the tools of productive *nomos*,[2] the science of man did not displace the transparent I from the top of the "animal kingdom." What it did was something that both the writers of the *scene of regulation* and the manufacturers of the *scene of representation* avoided, that is, situate the mind fully in the stage of exteriority. With this, it inaugurated a mode of representing the interior thing which, rather than replacing, complementing, or contradicting, supplemented the philosophical fashionings of self-consciousness. In *Elements d'anthropologie generale,* Paul Topinard (1885) specifies how the science of man addresses human variation. Anthropology, he argues, addresses human beings as members of collectivities characterized by resemblances, the continuity of which "in time [is] determined by heredity" and which produce a "unity within a succession of individuals more than of families" (195). Historical investigations, he argues, address different kinds of collectivities. "The nation or the nationality," he writes, "is a political association engendered by circumstances . . . favored by the unity of language, the unity of religion, cemented by habits, the memories and the glories of suffering." For the "notion of race is absolutely foreign to it"; anthropology "has nothing to do with the question of nationality" (212–13).

Though retaining the presuppositions and correlations established by naturalists' mappings of human variation, the science of man would deploy the signifying strategies of the science of life to chart the human body as a site of expression of productive *nomos.* In *Races and Peoples,* Daniel Brinton ([1870] 1901) states that anthropological research addresses the "internal structure of the organs," which determine the physical and mental differences among human groups, in order to "ascertain which of [them] are the least variable and hence of most value in classifying the human species into its general varieties and types" (18). The strategies of intervention of the science of life, the laws of conditions of existence and the principle of natural selection, are now deployed to address a particular sector of living nature. They guide the manufacturing of a grid of minds differentiated according to the degree of complexification, specialization, and differentiation of heads and social configurations. On the one hand, the shapes of the heads become expressions of levels of "development" of mental functions, that is, of how closely a "race's" intellectual and moral attributes approximated the attributes of the transparent I, the being Cuvier placed at the top of the animal kingdom. "When all or many of these (higher primates') traits are present," Brinton argues, "the individual approaches physically the type of the anthropoid apes, and a race presenting many of them is properly called a 'lower race,' where they are not present, the race is 'higher,' as it maintains in their integrity the special traits of the genus Man, and it is true to the type of the species" (48). When specifying the organic features relevant to the classification of "human races," these scientists of man combined those used by natural history and the one the science of life selected as the distinctive human characteristic. According to Brinton, the list includes the structure of the head bones (the skull, orbit of the eyes, aperture of nostrils, and projection of maxillaries); the color of the skin; the color of the eyes and hair; the muscular structures; and stature and proportion. Nevertheless, these are important, he argues, because they are "correlated to the psychological functions in such a manner as profoundly to influence the destiny of the nation" (39).

On the other hand, "civilization," the degree of "progress" of a particular social configuration, becomes an expression of the degree of mental (moral and intellectual) "development." As E. B. Tylor states: "Civilization actually existing among mankind in different grades, we are enabled to estimate and compare it by positive examples. The educated world of Europe and America practically settles a standard by simply placing its own nations at one end of the social series and savage tribes at the other, arranging the rest of mankind between these limits according as they correspond more closely to savage or to cultured life. The principal criteria of classification are the absence or presence, high or low development, of the industrial arts . . . , the extent of scientific knowledge, the definiteness of moral principles, the conditions of religious belief and ceremony, the degree of social and political organization and so forth" (cited in

Stocking 1968, 81). Mere observation of these signifiers of "civilization," as Darwin seems to believe, would not suffice. According to Tylor (1898), "one of the first questions that occurs is whether people who differ so much intellectually as savage tribes and civilized nation, show any corresponding difference in their brain. . . . The form of the skull itself, so important in its relation to the brain within and the expressive features without, has been to the anatomist one of the best means of distinguishing the races" (60). What the study of "civilization" indicates, then, is how life regulates or produces "human variation," how it institutes two basic types of mind: (a) the European type, the one whose actualizations, "modern civilization," most perfectly express its determinant, that is, the one the narrative of transcendental poesis locates in the moment of transparency, and (b) the non-European type, the one whose actualizations, "primitive" or traditional culture, correspond to those Herder locates near the "infancy of humanity," that is, the one that actualizes neither universality nor self-determination. However, to establish "the origin of these great varieties of races themselves, and exactly assign them their earliest homes cannot be usefully attempted in the present scantiness of evidence," Tylor recognizes, "it may perhaps be reasonable to imagine as latest-formed the white race of the temperate region, least able to bear extreme heat or live without the appliances of culture, but gifted with the *powers of knowing and ruling* which give them sway over the world" (113, my italics). For the scientists of man, social configurations, differentiated according to how their economic, juridical, and spiritual (cultural) dimensions express how the productive *nomos* operates on the human mind (that is, they are also signifiers of mental forms and functions, as "progress") indicate those that more perfectly actualize the temporal workings of universal reason.

With this, the science of man refashioned the mind as a scientific signifier, an expression of the laws of conditions of existence and the principle of natural selection. What in the narrative of *transcendental poesis* constituted actualizations of the subject of transcendental poesis now shape-shifted into exteriorizations of productive *nomos*. When writing bodily and social configurations as effects of productive *nomos*, these scientists of man (re)produced the boundaries identified in eighteenth-century (and even earlier) philosophy and natural history's taxonomy of the globe with statements that followed the rules of scientific signification, that is, the ones that instituted "beings and meanings" as effects of exteriority. Though external traits such as skin color, orbit of the eyes, and so on provided "characters" to be used in the classification of the "varieties of man," the project of the scientists of man could be sustained only if its delimitation of its object followed the rules of signification of the field of science. Through head measurements, a technique inherited from eighteenth-century phrenology, they produced a scientific (mathematical) representation of the link between the configuration of the skull (a proxy for the configuration of the brain) and mental operations. "Measurements," Boas ([1899] 1966) argues, "should always have a biological significance. As soon as they lose their significance, they lose also their descriptive value" (169 in original edition). According to Topinard (1885, 219–20), the numbers obtained through these measurements identify "ideal types," abstract constructions of the scientific mind not to be found in nature; they do not correspond to an existing "empirical race." That is, Broca (1879) argues, the instruments, techniques, and measurements of the science of man sought to construct abstract values (means) to be used in the comparison and distinction of the various types (185). Resulting from this translation of head shapes into numbers was a strategy of engulfment, "racial type," which would organize the whole arsenal of the science of man.

Homo Racialis

The concept of "racial type," first introduced by Nott and Gliddon (1854) in the United States in their statement that the various "races of mankind" are specimens of the "original," fundamental, "types of mankind," would become, a few years later, the strategy of engulfment of the project of knowledge that attempted to discover the "truth" of man by describing his mind, body, and social configurations as effects of productive *nomos*. In his *Phenomena of Hybridity in the Genus Homo,* Broca (1864) teaches that a "racial type" is not empirical [but] "fictitious, the description is an ideal one, like the forms of the Apollo of Belvedere. Human types, like all other types, are merely abstractions" (8). This statement writes the human body as the racial body. "After having by analytical process first studied the various races," Broca instructs, "we now subject them to a synthetic process, we soon recognize that there exist among them various affinities, which enable us to dispose them in a certain number of natural groups. . . . The ensemble of characters common to each group, constitute the type of that group." What this statement introduces is a scientific account of the "varieties of man" that produces the connection between head forms, visible traits, and global region as an effect of how the new universal sovereign regulates/produces human difference. According to Broca, "All the ["European races"] have the skin white, regular features, soft hair, oval face, vertical jaws, and elliptical cranium, etc. These points of resemblance give them in some sort a family likeness, by which they are recognized at once, and which caused them to be designated by the collective name of Caucasian races. The hyperborean races, and those of Eastern Asia, constitute the family of Mongolian races; the group of Ethiopian races equally comprises a large number of black races with woolly hair, and a prognathous head. The American and the Malayo-Polynesian races form the two last groups" (7–8). In the *scientia racialis,* the racial—not race, which, as Foucault (2003) reminds us, like the nation and class, preceded their nineteenth-century instantiations—would rule or guide the terms of the grid of specification of human beings that identified each particular bodily form and the corresponding type of mind (mental functions) as coming from a particular global region or continent.

What the formulation of the racial inaugurated is a mode of representing man, *homo scientificus,* which addresses man fundamentally as phenomena, as a spatial (exterior or affectable) thing. Consistently, however, this scientific signifier would not challenge the philosophical placing of post-Enlightenment Europeans, the "white (Caucasian) races," in transparency. Nonetheless, the human attribute it specifies, raciality, assumes that mental ("intellectual and moral") contents express productive *nomos.* The racial produces the human body and social configurations as both (a) signifiers of the exterior determinants (laws of conditions of existence and the principle of natural selection) of organic variation and (b) signifiers of the interior principles (consciousness) that mark a collectivity's "intrinsic difference." The racial situates post-Enlightenment European minds (the transparent I) and social configuration ("modern civilization") among (necessarily contemporaneous, coexisting) minds and social configurations found in other global regions. My point is that the science of man once again refashioned self-consciousness as *homo racialis,* rendering man (the body-mind composite) a thing for which globality (exteriority-spatiality) constitutes the horizon of existence. Because man can be known, determined in globality, only through the deployment of a scientific arsenal that explains and describes why and how his body and social configuration departs from or approximates others found on other continents, even as the science of man once again safely secured post-Enlightenment Europe in transparency, the transparent I did not escape the effects of scientific signification. As a strategy of engulfment, a tool of productive *nomos,* the racial places the transparent I, as a mind-body composite, alongside "other" mind-body composites in a signifying chain that allows no resolution, neither sublation nor reduction. With this, it manufactures a mode of representing man not governed by the rules of signification of history, one that does not presuppose historicity (interiority-temporality) as the horizon of the self-determining thing, *Dasein,* as Heidegger renamed it.

When assembling globality, the scientists of man rewrote two principles of classification inherited from natural history, "heredity" and "fecundity," as "laws of nature." Both operated as complementary strategies of intervention that sustain the two theses, namely: (a) the thesis of "permanence of characters," the one that stipulates the inheritance of racial characteristics, and (b) the thesis of "hybridity," the one that addresses their actual operation. Both strategies transformed the grid of "races of mankind"—which included the categories "Caucasian," "Mongolians," and "Negroes," to name the main ones—into a *strategy of particularization,* namely, classification according to racial difference. From then on, racial categories, as scientific signifiers of human difference, would presuppose the particular tools of scientific reason that regulate and produce a fundamental ("necessary" and "objective") connection between the human body, the global region (continent), and the mind. That is, they *expressed* how productive *nomos* operates in human conditions of existence: the life of the individual and that of the social body. With the scientific signifier *racial difference* it became possible to deploy statements that assumed that human difference is irreducible and unsublatable because it is an effect of the laws of nature that produce the existing variety of bodily and social configurations. On the one hand, heredity and the thesis of the permanence of characters established that the particular attributes of

Caucasians, Mongolians, and Negroes had emerged in the confinement of a particular global region where each of these *racial* types had "originally" formed. Precisely because they are hereditary, then, the characteristics unique to each "racial type" were seen as permanent; neither change of climate, as Buffon postulated, nor prolonged contacts with a different racial type could obliterate them (Knox 1850; Cope 1870; Ripley 1899). "The hereditary types," Topinard (1885) writes, "are physical, physiological or pathological, they are complementary and obey one another and the general law of heredity. . . . Continuity in time constitutes the characteristic trait of the notion of race. . . . Hence, two operations tend to establish the reality of race: first, the determination of the type from the analysis following the synthesis of characters; second, the proof of continuity in time" (194–95).

On the other hand, the laws of fecundity and the thesis of hybridity consolidated the grid of racial difference when establishing the negative effects of miscegenation or interbreeding. What measures of fecundity indicated, the scientists of man argued, was whether intercourse between individuals belonging to "distant races" could produce prolific offspring; and examinations of "human hybrids" enabled arguments on whether interbreeding produced degenerate offspring physically and mentally inferior to both "parent races." In Broca (1879) one finds the crucial questions to be asked by the anthropologists when considering the effects of interbreeding, which included questions as to whether the crossing of "distant races" produced fecund and healthy offspring, whether hybrids were able to constitute "a new racial type," what was the influence of each "original type" in the ensuing mixed offspring, and the moral and intellectual qualities of "mixed offspring." Highlighting the importance of global region in the determination of racial difference, to situate each of these questions Broca cites examples of mixed-race populations in regions of European colonization. For instance, when considering the influence of climate on the fecundity of European mixed-race individuals in Asia, he notes that "the pure European races are fecund among those of first generation, and are always non-fecund in the second generation. This does result from climate. And the sterility of *métis* produced by their crossing with the indigenous races, consequently depends upon the same cause" (209).

What these questions regarding the possibility of human hybrids

indicate is how miscegenation (hybridization) as a process complements racial difference. As a signifier of particularity, racial difference encapsulates the attributes of each racial type that emerged in
a distant past within the confines of a given continent. As a signifier
of containment, miscegenation operates, usually as an eschatological signifier to indicate the present and future impossibility of the
production of human beings that could not be assigned to the grid of
human variation organized by the signifying strategies of the *scientia
racialis* (Broca 1864; Vogt 1864). Agassiz's comments on nineteenth-
century Brazil indicate how miscegenation operates as a strategy of
containment. He notes that where "interrupted miscegenation" had
produced "a class of men in which the pure type has disappeared and
with him all the good physical and moral qualities of the primitive
races, leaving in its place a bastard people so repulsive as the mixed
dogs, with horror toward the animal of the same species, among
whom it is impossible to find one individual who has retained the
intelligence, the nobility, and natural affectivity which make the
pure bred dog the civilized man's preferred companion" (cited in
Augel 1980, 214). With these signifying strategies—racial difference and miscegenation—the science of man provided an account
of bodily and social configurations that would rewrite eighteenth-
century philosophers' postulate placing post-Enlightenment Europe
in transparency and of the "others of Europe" in affectability according to the rules of scientific signification.[3]

The Writing of Globality

From Georges Cuvier's initial enunciation of the "races of mankind"
in a scientific text to Paul Broca's instructions on how to classify
the various types of human "crossings," I trace the first moments
of manufacturing the analytics of raciality, the political-symbolic arsenal that transformed the categories employed by eighteenth-century
naturalists and philosophers into scientific signifiers that produced
the human body, social configurations, and minds as effects of the
tools of productive *nomos*. That is, the signifying strategies of the
scientia racialis produced a strategy of engulfment, the racial, as a
signifier of human difference that presupposed that scientific reason
accounts for the various existing modes of being human. When introducing the racial as a scientific signifier producing the body, the
social, and the global as modern signifiers, they wrote "Europeans

or Caucasians" as coexisting with, contemporaneous with, always already determined by what distinguishes them from and makes them approximate to "Mongolians" and "Ethiopians or Negroes." My point is that the deployment of the racial (as a signifier of human difference) in these post-Enlightenment scientific projects instituted globality as a modern ontological context, the content and borders of which presupposed productive *nomos* as a determinant of human "essence and existence."

When manufacturing raciality as a human attribute, the science of man introduced an account of self-consciousness, *homo scientificus,* which, combined with its philosophical version, *homo historicus,* completes the figure of *homo modernus,* the modern subject—at once producer and product and cause and effect—an effect of both scientific and historical signification. By rewriting post-Enlightenment Europe in transparency, raciality constructed European bodies and social configurations as signifiers (actualizations) of universality and self-determination, establishing as a "necessary" and "objective" fact what transcendental poesis could only describe. With this, introduced is a mode of representing self-consciousness in which exteriority (laws, the body, etc.) replaced interiority (culture, religion, etc.) as the basis for establishing the universality of (human) differentiation.[4] By doing so, it performed what had been carefully avoided in the founding statements of modern representation, discussed in the previous part of this book; it deployed in modern representation ontological signifiers that referred to that "Other," the (im)possible account of being in which self-consciousness would emerge as a situated, global (exterior-spatial), outer-determined thing.

From very early on, as noted before, the project of the science of man met moral challenges—which Stocking (1968) and Stepan (1982), among others, describe—that charged the racial with being a concept that robs man of his distinctive attribute, self-determination, to subject him to the "laws of nature." However, neither the notion of racial formation nor the postmodern reconfigurings of historicity in the "politics of representation" have been able to dissipate its productive effects or to write it out of the modern political grammar and lexicon. In the following I show that the racial's resistance to moral banishment also results from how it governs the ontoepistemological conditions of emergence of the twentieth-century sciences of the mind, anthropology and sociology, which deploy the cultural to relocate the study of human difference back in the stage of interiority without dissipating the unsublatable and irreducible difference raciality produces, the one in which the obliteration of the affectable "others of Europe" becomes the "necessary" and "objective" outcome of the play of productive *nomos*.

SCIENTIA CULTURALIS

In a 1904 address to the British Anthropological Association, Henry Balfour, then curator of the Pitt-Rivers Museum, described the methods Lieutenant Colonel A. Lane-Fox Pitt-Rivers had confected in 1851 in his study of the evolution of firearms among "primitive" British subjects. Both Balfour's (1906) descriptions of his own explorations of the "development of musical instruments" and his comments on Pitt-Rivers's depiction of an anthropological project follow the guidelines of Darwin's version of the science of life. Both scientists of man engaged in systematic examinations of weapons and musical instruments, respectively, mapping them according to the locus of origin and the particular "sequences of ideas" they were able to identify. Both noted that the arms and musical instruments of the "primitive peoples" were dramatically inferior to those found in Western Europe. Both confirmed the "direction" of evolution and the superiority of European culture. What called my attention to Balfour's account was precisely the interval separating the building of Pitt-Rivers's "ethnographical collection" and his own. During the fifty-five years separating their respective ethnological explorations, the anthropological project began a profound transformation, even as British anthropologists continued to encounter their object in their role as civil or military colonial officials of the British Empire. For Balfour's contemporaries would produce detailed descriptions of what they saw and heard among the surviving "natives" to display in a larger context, where the various signifiers of "human variation" they collected would be deployed in a global-epistemological configuration already mapped by the racial. At the dawn of the twentieth century, the age of historicity, the concept of the cultural would inform a scientific project for which man and his social configurations constitute the privileged object, namely, anthropology. Following the steps of its predecessor, the cultural would also operate as a signifier of globality, that is, as a strategy of engulfment, a political-symbolic strategy that hides and announces spatiality by writing the actual and possible relationships between the coexisting human collectivities it maps as governed by the productive *nomos*.

My task in this section is to identify the signifying strategies that re-signify the Cultural as a signifier that captures how the tools of the productive *nomos* institute distinct mental and social configurations. Though the scientific concept of the cultural has informed both the anthropological and the sociological projects, it has had rather distinct effects in each because of how *racial difference* delimits their zone of deployment. In anthropology, the cultural rewrites the others of Europe in *affectability* as the signifying strategies that replace the arsenal of the science of man would resignify racial difference as substantive difference, that is, as God-given bodily traits that correspond to continental borders and are immediate (preconceptual) indexes of the universal determinants of cultural particularity, which anthropological tools aim to "discover." What my reading shows are the effects of these twentieth-century appropriations of the productive *nomos* to account for "human variation." That is, it charts the conditions of production of the cultural as a scientific signifier, that is, the product of the tools of productive *nomos*.

What I do here is not to advance a critique of the anthropological project, nor do I point to inconsistencies or propose a reconfiguration of its conceptual arsenal. Instead I have chosen to read three major (re)formulations of the cultural as a scientific signifier, namely, (a) Émile Durkheim's project of a science of morality, which would become the basis for most twentieth-century versions of the anthropological and sociological projects; (b) Franz Boas's statements that deploy the notion of the "laws of thought and action," the one that would ground U.S. cultural anthropology; and (c) Radcliffe-Brown's version of British social anthropology, which addresses social (exterior) forms. I have chosen these because they apprehend two distinct sites, mental and social configurations, when examining how productive *nomos* institutes non-European minds, thus fashioning a consciousness radically distinct from the one transcendental poesis locates in post-Enlightenment Europe. When reading these classical versions of the anthropological text, my goal is not only to chart the conditions of production of the cultural, the strategy of the analytics of raciality that would inform twentieth-century statements on human difference. I am also interested in how their replacing the others of Europe in affectability is an effect both of the way globality defines the conditions of emergence of this particular social scientific project and of the very reformulation of the cultural as a scientific signifier. While both tasks indicate why the cultural is not just another name for the racial, only after I chart the text of the sociology of race relations in the next will it become evident why the writing of racial difference as a signifier of cultural difference hampers our understanding of how the racial operates as a modern political-symbolic weapon.

My point here is that the racial, the political-symbolic tool that produces globality, informed the conditions of production of these twentieth-century social scientific projects precisely because racial difference, now substantive (prescientific and prehistoric) difference, would constitute the "empirical" basis of the division of labor among the scientific projects that deployed the cultural to account for human difference. Not surprisingly, neither those who call for the moral banishment of the racial nor those who find moral solace in the cultural are able to comprehend how the analytics of raciality operates as a political-symbolic arsenal. No apostle of inclusion and historicity recognizes that the social scientific arsenal they deploy to explain racial subjection, the one that assumes that racial difference is a substantive signifier of cultural difference, always already both assumes and, as I show in the following, reproduces, an irreducible and unsublatable difference between the kinds of minds indigenous to Europe and those that originated in other global regions. That is, it is precisely because they presume globality that twentieth-century versions of the anthropological project could return the study of human difference to the stage of interiority without contradicting transcendental poesis and, consequently, without erasing the borders between anthropology, history, and sociology. The fact that anthropology's terrain is already prepared by raciality and carved with signifying strategies that follow the rules of scientific signification produced the subject of the cultural, the others of Europe, as doubly and safely incarcerated in affectability, as self-consciousness determined by the (exterior) "laws of nature," which now fully operates in interiority, and condemned to obliteration when in contact with "modern [European-white] civilization." Hence, as Fabian (1983) notes, in anthropology the cultural attributes to the others of Europe a temporality that is radically distinct from that which transcendental poesis assigns to man, which explains why, despite postmodern critics' best intentions, when deployed to name the racial subaltern, cultural difference cannot write transparent I's. For this reason, though the embracing of the cultural against the racial may provide moral solace, it dissipates neither the effects of the latter nor the cultural's own writing of the others of Europe in affectability.

The Science of Morality

Twentieth-century anthropologists and sociologists were dedicated to the gathering of samples of signifiers of non-European consciousness to produce their own mapping of the global space. Like the scientists of man, these scientists of the social were also carving a niche in the *field of science,* also claiming that their signifying strategies would add to what is provided by historical investigations. Not, however, because they would provide a scientific account of the object of history, but because when constructing their object, the tools they deployed to excavate their mental and social configurations necessarily postponed transparency for what they gathered was mediated by tools of scientific reason. What distinguishes their approach to the exterior (universal) determinants of the "diversity of cultures" from that of the science of man, then, is the fact that they locate "human variation" back in the scene of representation. Not only do they take the products of the human mind, symbols and tools, as the privileged object; their mapping of social configurations assumes that productive *nomos* regulates and produces human consciousness. In other words, their strategy of engulfment, the cultural, not only rewrites *interiorized nomos* and *interiorized poesis* as universal (exterior) producer or cause of an ordered (juridical and moral) "world of men"; it also addresses social configurations as actualizations of a consciousness thoroughly *subjected* to tools of universal reason. With this, the cultural performs what Kant avoids with the distinction between the "empirical" and "moral law" and what Herder despises and sidesteps by postulating that moral unity derives from human beings' innate need to communicate—that is, it writes morality and guiding principles as effects of the laws of productive *nomos.*

Certainly in the twentieth century the anthropological project retained many signifying strategies deployed in the previous century, such as those mapped by Morgan, Tylor, Fraser, and others and earlier versions of the science of the social, such as historical materialism, which would undergo readjustments without relinquishing its crucial features. Nevertheless, it cannot be denied that what distinguishes twentieth-century anthropology is the circumscription of the mind as a domain of operation of productive *nomos*. To this effect, the French sociologist Émile Durkheim's notion of "collective [common] consciousness" has been crucial because of how, by tying together representations, actions, and institutions, it produces or rewrites the cultural as a strategy of engulfment through the rewriting of interiorized *nomos* (moral law) and interiorized poesis (tradition) as markers of how universal reason regulates or produces the social. Durkheim's "science of morality" aims at the investigation of the objective, exterior, and constraining dimensions of human collective existence; it addresses the social as phenomena. Not surprisingly, then, a consistent distinction between "civilized" and "primitive" societies would organize his rendering of the cultural as a scientific signifier of consciousness.

In *The Elementary Forms of the Religious Life,* Durkheim ([1915] 1965) provides an account of the "origins" of "collective representations" that reproduces both Herder's description of the various phases of human moral development and Hegel's narrative of transcendental poesis. Nevertheless, instead of engaging these versions of historicity, he targets Kant's formulation of interiorized *nomos*. For Durkheim's project here is to demonstrate how the social (collective life) rather than the transcendental provides the tools human beings deploy when attempting to comprehend the "world of things" and the "world of men." Not only is the social the "higher representation" of nature—"The social realm is a natural realm which differs from the others only by a greater complexity," Durkheim writes (31)—society is the exterior producer and regulator of "individual" consciousness, whose exteriorization can be captured with the strategies of the science of morality, statistical models and descriptions of the social configuration. Further, a particular social configuration also actualizes interiorized *nomos* and poesis. That is, it is the stuff of "collective representations," which, Durkheim argues, "should show the mental states of the group; they should depend upon the way in which this is founded and organized, upon its morphology, upon its religious, moral and economic institution, etc." (28). "Collective representations," according to Durkheim, constitute man as

a "social being which represents the highest reality in the intellectual and moral order that we can know by observation—I mean
society" (29). In this statement, he provides a scientific rendering of
interiorized *nomos* and interiorized poesis in which both Kant's notion of moral law (inner regulation) and Herder's notion of tradition
(inner determination) become effects of given social configurations
and of the collective ideas and practices that provide that which
constrains and guides, regulates and produces—the principles and
norms (rules) actualized in individual's ideas and actions.

The project of a "science of morality," a science of the social, necessitates a strategy of intervention able to capture how productive
nomos institutes the variety of "collective representations" and the
particular "common consciousness" they signify. In the *Division of
Labor in Society,* Émile Durkheim ([1893] 1984) deploys a strategy of intervention, functionalism, modeled after the science of life's
notion of "conditions of existence." In this text he seeks to establish
the function of the division of labor in "modern civilization," which
he sets up by distinguishing between the types of "social solidarity,"
two forms of the social bond. For Durkheim, then, the social bond
is an effect of interiorized *nomos,* an effect of constraint, that is, of
customs and laws. Although it may "be objected that social relationships can be forged without necessarily taking on a legal form," he
argues, "[they do not] remain indeterminate; instead of being regulated by law they are merely regulated by custom" (25). With the
notion of "collective consciousness" he rewrites self-consciousness
as an effect of social regulation, that is, he introduces a version of
interiorized *nomos* in which individual consciousness becomes an
effect of beliefs, practices, and customs that indicate how productive *nomos* is expressed in a particular society. "There is in the consciousness of each one of us," he argues, two consciousnesses: "one
that we share in common with our group in its entirety, which is consequently not ourselves, but society living and acting within us; the
other that, on the contrary, represents us alone in what is personal
and distinctive about us, what makes us an individual" (84). If one
recalls that, like many late nineteenth-century scientists of society,
Durkheim is concerned with the effect of modern civilization on the
"spirit" of the peoples of Europe, this rewriting of poesis as *nomos*
that renders it an object of scientific investigation does not constitute an ironic outcome of the philosophical conversation followed

earlier. Recall that universality remains the guiding presupposition both of Herder's critique of sickly universal reason and his account of interiorized poesis and of Hegel's reconciliation of the universal or interiorized *nomos* and poesis into transcendental poesis. If this is so, Durkheim's only ethical violation here would be his rewriting of interiorized poesis, now resolved into interiorized *nomos,* according to the rules of scientific signification. Whether this outcome was a matter of course or an epistemological mishap becomes irrelevant because early sociologists' concerns with the moral effects of "progress" did not invite their fellow Europeans to emulate the social conditions found among "primitives." Why this would not happen becomes evident in the way Durkheim's explanation of the function of the division of labor explicitly responds to his contemporaries' concerns. The "most notable effect of the division of labor," he argues, "is not that it increases productivity of the functions that are divided in this way, but that it links them very closely. . . . [That is,] its role is not simply to embellish or improve existing societies, but to make possible societies which, without these functions would not exist" (21). When identifying the kind of society, the type of social bond, that the division of labor enables, he follows the racial mapping of the global space to distinguish between the kinds of "collective consciousness" corresponding to "primitive" and "civilized societies." What distinguishes these social conditions, he argues, is the strength of the hold of "collective consciousness" on individual consciousness. Among the others of Europe he finds a type of solidarity that resembles penal law, which punishes crimes against the moral collective. To this "type of solidarity," he argues, corresponds the kind of "common consciousness" characterized by "a certain conformity of each individual consciousness to a common type" (61), which precludes any conception of the individual as separated from the collectivity; "its real function is to maintain inviolate the cohesion of society by sustaining the common consciousness in all its vigor" (63). In post-Enlightenment industrialized Europe, on the other hand, "progress" has entailed a "type of solidarity" that corresponds to "contractual law," whose function is to produce submission to collectively upheld principles and where the presence of "society" is usually felt in the moment of the institution rather than in the application of the law. The form of collective consciousness it exemplifies is the one entailed by the division of labor, in which the social bond is based on cooperation rather than similarity and where a large, complex, and differentiated social configuration provides ample room for the development of individual consciousness. Whatever exteriority Durkheim's formulations attribute to "collective [common] consciousness" and "collective representations," when he describes them as fundamentally social or produces them by deploying the strategies of scientific reason they remain consistent with other deployments of the productive *nomos* that, as seen before, keep the post-Enlightenment European social configurations and the consciousness they actualize safely in the moment of transparency.

How explicitly the various versions of the anthropological and the sociological project indicate the influence of Durkheim's formulations becomes irrelevant when one—even one who would restore historical materialism, which I do not engage in this chapter, and one who would more explicitly follow Max Weber's sociological rendering of the cultural—acknowledges that he or she would respond to Durkheim's successful rewriting of the cultural as a signifier of interiorized *nomos* and poesis. What I am suggesting here is that one cannot immediately refute the argument advanced by many social scientists who identify Durkheim as the "forefather" of twentieth-century social scientific projects. Though I am not repeating this argument, I acknowledge that the versions of the science of the social analyzed in the following pages pursue his desire to render the social a scientific object, even when they explicitly advocate their departure from Durkheim's path.

The Vanishing "Mind"

Two more or less contemporaneous strategies of intervention, Franz Boas's laws of "thought and action" and A. R. Radcliffe-Brown's notions of "structure and function," delimit the particular way in which anthropology would apprehend how the productive *nomos* institutes human differentiation.[5] Though none claim that these strategies should be deployed only in investigations of the others of Europe, the notion of the cultural that they deploy both assumes and rewrites the consciousness they map as radically distinct from the one found in the post-Enlightenment European space. Although, as we will see shortly, the deauthorizing of the science of man's project was central to the rewriting of the cultural as a scientific signifier, early twentieth-century anthropologists did spend some time either challenging or circumscribing the explanatory validity of the racial. For the most part, while acknowledging the existence of a branch of the discipline—sometimes called "physical anthropology" and other times "biological anthropology"—dealing with the natural aspects of human groups, anthropologists set themselves the task of addressing the self-created dimensions of collective existence.[6] Nevertheless, racial difference remains crucial to the distinguishing of the object of ethnographic excavations.

For instance, when explaining the distinction between the historical and anthropological method, Radcliffe-Brown (1958) uses the following example to situate the complexity of the object of ethnological strategies of intervention. "You may find," he writes, "particularly on the western side [of Madagascar], many individuals of distinctively Negro, i.e., African type, in respect, I mean, of their physical characters. And quite a number of the elements of Madagascar culture seem to be African also. But closer examination shows that there are elements both of race and culture that are not African, and a study of these enables us to demonstrate without question that some of them have been derived from south-eastern Asia" (5). Precisely this matter-of-fact articulation of racial difference demonstrates that the effects of signification would remain an implicit determinant in the discipline's main strategy of engulfment, the concept of the cultural. That this was necessarily so is indicated by the fact that the major versions of the anthropological project moved toward a region of investigation of human conditions claimed by either sociology or history.

Fortunately for the practitioner, because the discipline's project was deployed in a global space and under an epistemological arrangement already mapped by the racial, the exclusively anthropological object fell within neither. Nevertheless, precisely the claim that the "vanishing native" was the proper object of the anthropological desire indicates how the various versions of the anthropological project would draw the discipline's epistemological borders.

In *The Mind of Primitive Man,* Boas (1911) introduces the strategy of intervention, the laws of "thought and action," which rewrites mental (intellectual and moral) difference as an effect of the workings of productive *nomos.* Before describing the scientific construct that would guide cultural anthropology, however, his crucial move is to dismiss the two main arguments of the science of man with evidence that questions the accuracy and appropriateness of its strategies of interventions. The productive move here is to rewrite raciality as a "natural," God-given human attribute, that is, as substantive difference. Though an immediate effect of this gesture is to delimit the object of anthropological excavations and the proper mode of approaching the peoples the racial writes in affectability, its most productive and most lasting effects, playing out in the present global configuration, have been to provide an account of racial subjection that assumes and produces raciality as foreign to the modern political grammar. The statement that deauthorizes the project of the science of man posits that neither the thesis of permanence of characters nor that of heredity explains the different paces of "cultural development" between "primitive" and European societies.[7] Nor does it derive from the "mental (biological) inferiority" of the former but from their particular natural environment, their social configurations, and the conditions under which their contact with more "advanced people" has taken place. The observable individuals' "variations" within the same "racial type" and between "civilized" and "primitive" societies, Boas argues, indicate the impact of the environment and social conditions, which is proved by the fact that heredity has a stronger influence on geographically isolated and less mixed peoples, that is, on the "primitive races" that remain isolated in their places of "origin." For Boas, the various degrees of variability of "physical traits" among "different races" derive from isolation. "When a people is descended from a small uniform group," he states, "its variability will decrease; while on the other hand, when a group has much-varied origin, or when the ancestors belong to an entirely distinct type, the variability may be considerably increased" (93). That is, the rejection of the science of man's theses did not implicate a complete dismissal of racial difference.

What had initially been a product of modern strategies of knowledge was transformed into a substantive signifier, the effects of "natural" processes on the human body. The connection between organic forms and geographic location is retained. But now geographic "isolation" and "inbreeding" would replace heredity and the permanence of characters as causes of the persistence of the fundamental types: Mongoloid, European, and Negro. Though the racial would lose its explanatory validity, its effects would remain at the core of the anthropological project as racial difference, now substantive difference constitutes the "empirical" basis for distinguishing between the "vanishing native" and the anthropologists' fellow Europeans and their descendants everywhere.

After systematically dismissing the premises, strategies, and conclusions of the science of man, Boas instructs the reader as to how anthropology should seek to discover the cause of the particular consciousness that emerges among peoples racially (biologically and geographically) distinct from Europeans. What Boas introduces is a project of the knowledge of man for which the exterior (universal) determinants of "human variation" belong to the stage of interiority. The proper anthropological objects, he argues, are "the activities of the human mind [that] exhibit an infinite variety of form among the peoples of the world" (98). "The organization of mind," he states, "is practically identical among all races of man; that mental activities follow the same laws everywhere, but its manifestations depend upon the character of the individual experience that is subjected to the action of these laws. It is quite evident that the activities of the human mind depend upon these two elements [heredity and the environment]." These universal (exterior) determinants do not produce the content, but they define the form of thought. "The organization of the mind," Boas proceeds, "may be defined as the group of laws which determines the modes of thought and of action, irrespective of the subject-matter of mental activity." What this strategy of intervention identifies, he continues, "are the manner of discrimination between perceptions, the manner in which perceptions associate themselves with previous perception, the manner in which a stimulus leads to action, and the motions produced by stimuli. These laws determine to a great extent the manifestations of the mind. In these we recognize hereditary causes" (102–3). Although the laws of "thought and action" produce particular forms of mind, anthropological excavations would gather specimens of beliefs, customs, and individuals' daily behavior, that is, the particular contents of the mind that express these laws and actions that actualize them. That is, "human variation" now becomes an effect of a productive *nomos,* the laws of "thought and action" that ensure the permanence, as they determine the form, of the "contents of the primitive mind." With this statement Boas delineates the zone of deployment of a scientific concept of the cultural in a scientific rendering of interiorized poesis that, unlike Durkheim's, neither presumes nor claims global applicability.

What I am suggesting here is that Boas's scientific rewriting of interiorized poesis is tailored exclusively for the investigation of "the primitive mind." For this reason, rather than accentuate the fundamental equality of mental processes, as Durkheim does before he moves on to describe European particularity, Boas highlights the fundamental inequality between "primitive" and "civilized" minds. "Lack of logical connection in its conclusions, lack of control of will," Boas notes, "are apparently two of its fundamental characteristics in primitive society. In the formations of opinions, belief takes the place of logical demonstrations. The emotional value of opinions is great, and consequently they quickly lead to action. The will appears unbalanced, there being a readiness to yield to strong emotions and stubborn resistance in trifling matters" (98–99). What distinguishes "civilized" and "primitive thought," he argues, are differences in the collective "habitual mental reactions" expressed in the ideas, customs, habits, and so on that individuals draw from when attempting to make sense of the world. That is, the distinctive traits of "primitive consciousness," such as incapacity for "abstract and logical reasoning," derive from the stronghold of traditional ideas, feelings, and emotions.

With this he rewrites as an effect of the productive *nomos* what Herder describes as the tools of universal poesis in a statement that appropriates the notion of tradition as signifier of the kind of consciousness prevailing among the others of Europe. For Boas, the signifiers of the affectability of the "primitive mind" are not organic forms, but mental forms, which explain its inability to rid itself of mental constructs formed in ancient phases of man's temporal development. Now European consciousness results from the "advance of civilization," which favors the emergence of a mental form, reflection, that enables the elimination of traditional mental contents. "There is an undoubted tendency in the advance of civilization," Boas argues, "to eliminate traditional elements, and to gain a clearer insight into the hypothetical basis of our reasoning. . . . With the advance of civilization, reasoning becomes more and more logical, not because each individual carries out his thought in a more logical manner, but because the traditional material which is handed down to each individual has been thought out and worked through more thoroughly and more carefully. While in primitive civilization the traditional material is doubted and examined by only a very few individuals, the number of thinkers who try to free themselves from the fetter of tradition increases as civilization advances" (206). The concept of the cultural that this formulation introduces not only assumes that the "primitive" mental forms express an exterior determinant, the laws of "thought and action"; it also assumes that the "primitive mind" is actualized in collective ideas, practices, and institutions, the excavation of which would reveal "contents of the mind of the primitive man." With this Boas writes the "primitive mind" as twice affectable, for it is determined by the laws of "thought and action" and by the traditional mental forms they produce, which remain unaltered as long as they remain in their places of "origin." Further, by redeploying the notion of "civilization" to mark the conditions of emergence and actualization of two distinct kinds of mind, "modern" and "primitive," Boas's rendering of the cultural reproduces the affectability of the others of Europe in the territory carved out by the racial.

Most contemporary analyses of racial subjection celebrate this transformation as the substitution of "historical" for "biological" constructions of cultural difference. What usually escapes these analyses is that, though arguing the particularity of the primitive mind as a product of (temporal-spatial) isolation, the anthropological text would establish that cultural difference derives from temporal processes always already mapped by the categories of racial difference it uses to distinguish between the civilized and primitive man. If anything, the cultural, as a strategy of engulfment that relocates human variation in the scene of representation, further reinscribes the effect of the racial by rewriting the affectability of the primitive mind in time, a statement that, against Herder's account of interiorized poesis and as the definitive scientific rendering of transcendental poesis, produces its temporality as fundamentally distinct from that of post-Enlightenment Europe. And yet, without the racial mapping of the global space, it would be impossible to distinguish anthropology from sociology and history, for these disciplinary undertakings deploy the cultural to capture how universal reason (in the shape of productive *nomos* and transcendental poesis, respectively) produces a collectivity's particular consciousness.

In *Structure and Function in Primitive Society*, Radcliffe-Brown (1952) introduces a strategy of intervention, sustained by the notions of "structure and function," that rewrites social configurations as effects of the tools of productive *nomos*.[8] When introducing the version of the anthropological project known as British social anthropology, however, he recalls that, in his inaugural lecture, James Frazer, the first British professor of social anthropology, defined anthropology as "the branch of sociology" that investigates "primitive societies." With this statement he supports his version of the discipline's project, which is distinct from historical approaches with which anthropology could be mistakenly identified. "In anthropology," Radcliffe-Brown states, "the study of what are called primitive or backward peoples, the term ethnography is applied to what is specifically a mode of idiographic enquiry, the aim of which is to give acceptable accounts of such peoples and their social life." What renders anthropology a distinct scientific enterprise is its method. "Ethnography," according to Radcliffe-Brown, differs from history in that the ethnographer derives his knowledge, or some major part of it, from direct observation of or contact with the people about whom he writes, and not, like the historian, from written records (2). Such records were not available to the anthropologists. The British school of social anthropology writes the anthropological enterprise as the study of social forms and defines the cultural as a dimension of the broader configuration captured in the notion of social forms. The primary aim of ethnographic work, Radcliffe-Brown argues, is to gather information that would enable the description, comparison, and classification of "the processes of social life." "The process itself," he explains, "consists of an immense multitude of actions and interactions of human beings, acting as individuals or in combinations or groups." Hence, he defines social anthropology "as the comparative theoretical study of forms of social life amongst primitive peoples" (4).

This construction of "primitive social life" presupposes the liberal version of self-consciousness as the self-determined thing who acts according to the determinants of his will but within the constraints of the forms of a higher consciousness, that is, "society." But Radcliffe-Brown did not have to be concerned with how his picture of the social submits individual freedom to universal (exterior) determinants. He defines the project of social anthropology as "the investigation of the nature of human society by the systematic comparison of societies of diverse type, with particular attention to the simpler forms of society of primitive savage or non-literate peoples"

(111). For the racial had already written the bodies of "non-literate" peoples to signify a consciousness emerging before transparency; the cultural would merely inscribe this effect of signification when describing "primitive" social configurations as actualizations of a consciousness that ignores the idea of universality, that is, one which has not moved beyond what Herder has identified as the "infancy of humanity." As Radcliffe-Brown notes, "In simplest forms of social life the number of separate cultural traditions may be reduced to two, one for men and the other for women." (5). Not surprisingly, in the description of the "social system" of "primitive peoples" the social anthropologist will privilege "the kinship systems," the study of which, until recently, many anthropologists identified as the key for understanding "primitive consciousness." Although I am sure the reader would not mind brushing up his or her recollections of the comparative method, the British school's main strategy of intervention, due to length and clarity constraints I will briefly mention a few dimensions of the "social system" of interest to the social anthropologist.

What interests me in Radcliffe-Brown's version of the anthropological project is how it both assumes the racial division between "advanced" or "complex" and "primitive" or "simple" societies and reproduces this division. That this division is a presupposition is established in the fact that anthropology investigates non-European social configurations. Following the founding characterizations of "primitive" and "modern" societies, Radcliffe-Brown (1952) starts from the assumption—which he seems to offer as a challenge to those who might believe otherwise—that "simple societies" are nothing but that, *simple*. Therefore, when examining legal dimensions (rights and obligations) of "primitive society," he notes the lack of distinction between rights over persons and rights over things. Writing the anthropological project as a scientific endeavor meant specifying the strategy of intervention with which to capture how productive *nomos* is exteriorized in "primitive" social configurations. When explaining his "comparative method," for instance, Radcliffe-Brown provides a description of the particular expressions of interiorized *nomos* and poesis, "norms and values," that the notion of totemism captures. He notes that in the pairing of social groups with natural entities "the resemblances and difference of animal species are translated into terms of friendship and conflict, solidarity and opposition," that is, that "the world of animal life is represented in terms of social relations similar to those of human society" (97–98). He deploys the notion of "basic structure," the "union of opposites," which he traces back to ancient Greek and Chinese philosophy, that is, a mode of productive *nomos* that cannot be captured with the historic signifying strategies. He defines the strategy of intervention, the comparative method, as "one by which we pass from the particular to the general, from the general to the more general, with the end in view that we may in this way arrive at the universal, at characteristics which can be found in different forms of human societies" (106). When deployed in the analysis of a "primitive" social configuration, the comparative method describes a social configuration in which totemism corresponds to a particular collective arrangement (families, clans, hordes, etc.) and to a conception of "rights and duties," which lack a conception of the individual.

Perhaps the search for a strategy of engulfment firmly secured in the field of science might have risked the anthropological frontiers with sociology and linguistics. Neither, however, was under as much threat as the line of separation between the proper anthropological zone of deployment and the discipline of history. Consistently and insistently, U.S. (cultural) anthropologists recalled the racial mapping of their field with references to the fact that "primitives" had written neither documents nor any other kind of inscriptions the historian found available in "civilized" archives. Even Boas, the celebrated "father" of cultural (historical) anthropology, was aware of the challenge facing his formulation of the anthropological project.

This problem may have been inherited from the German diffusionist school, to which Boas is said to have belonged, or derived from explicit choices made among U.S. American anthropologists who, like Kroeber, or Sapir, conceived of "cultural anthropology . . . as a strictly historical science" (cited in Radcliffe-Brown 1958, 12). In any event, the historical orientation of U.S. anthropology all the more required a scientific formulation of the cultural. Perhaps Herder and Hegel, earlier critics of scientific reason, are to blame for the fact that neither Boas's construction of cultural anthropology in the study of peoples written as without history and reason, nor even Kroeber's (1951) own definition of the "superorganic" or "sociocultural" as the fourth level of human existence, firmly secured the cultural in the field of science. For Kroeber, for instance, the "cultural phenomena"—the "customs and beliefs which hold primitive societies together" (118)—are ruled by specific principles, and the concept of culture is the abstract construct appropriate for capturing them. That culture is the "fourth level." That it presupposes what are then "more basic" dimensions of human existence (after "body," "psyche," and "society"), he argues, does not mean that it is subjected to them; it is culture that superimposes itself onto individual and collective organic conditions. Fundamentally human creations, he states, "cultural values," along with "cultural forms" that embody them and cultural contents, "exist only through man and reside in men" (129).

My own reading, however, suggests that the problem was rather one of refashioning the cultural as a strategy of engulfment. Resonating with the 1980s U.S. anthropologists' self-criticism, earlier cultural anthropologists were plagued with questions such as whether culture was a human universal or existed in particular thriving or "vanishing" cultures and whether, as Kroeber states, culture determines other dimensions of human beings or is responsive to them. They were also plagued by the persisting need to distinguish "cultural relativity," which examines a cultural element according to the principles of a given culture, from the idea of "cultural relativism," which suggests that every culture has its own regulating principles and therefore none hold the privilege as a universal parameter, an idea raised by Ruth Benedict's work. Generally speaking, formulations of the cultural deployed in the United States share a concern with the problem of "cultural integration," that is, one regarding the strength and nature of the bond between (individual) personality and (collective) culture. The predicament of cultural anthropology seems to reside, as Mead (1964) suggests, in that it is a rather peculiar science. "It is still fair to treat anthropology as a field science," she noted, "whose members work with fresh field material, studying living creature of living languages, excavating the earth where archaeological remains are still in situ, observing behaviors of real mothers' brothers to real sisters' sons, taking down folklore from the lips of those who heard the tale from other men's lips, measuring the bodies and sampling the blood of men who live in their own lands—lands to which we travel in order to study the people" (5). To claim a particular niche in the field of science, which includes more than the other two versions of the anthropological project just discussed, cultural anthropology strives to distinguish itself from history and sociology.

Nevertheless, because they address the dimensions resolved in the account of transcendental poesis, these earlier versions of the anthropological project—social anthropology, cultural anthropology, and structural anthropology—had to dehistoricize their approach to the region of the "empirical" that they share with sociology and history. In doing so, they relied on strategies of intervention that, like historical strategies, privileged the "contents of the mind," and that, like sociological strategies, addressed them only insofar as they are collective. Between these two camps, anthropology confected a strategy of engulfment, the cultural, that captures how productive *nomos* determines the particular interiorizing of *nomos* and poesis that characterizes primitive consciousness. That this particularity was already circumscribed by the signifying effects of the racial, and was produced through signifying strategies that (even if never quite sure) belonged to the domain of science, had the result that the subject of the cultural, the striving, "[ever-]vanishing natives," the objects of anthropological desire, remained fully (twice inscribed) in exteriority/affectability, as consciousness determined by the exterior "laws of nature," condemned to be *obliterated when engulfed by* "modern civilization."

MUNDUS SCIENTIFICUS

In "Race and History," Claude Lévi-Strauss (1961) recalls: "The original sin of anthropology [the science of man] . . . consists in its confusion of the idea of race, in the purely biological sense[,] . . . with the sociological and psychological products of human civilization." What anthropology had finally realized, he explains, is that the diverse "cultural contributions of Asia or Europe, Africa or America" derive not from the fact that these continents are "inhabited by peoples of different racial stocks" but from "geographical, historical and sociological circumstances" (220). Unfortunately, Lévi-Strauss notes, such acknowledgement had yet to reach "the man in the street." Before anthropology could eliminate the public's tendency to attribute "intellectual and moral relevance" to "black and white skin," it needed to answer a nagging question, which had survived the demise of the science of man. "If there are not innate racial aptitudes," he says the public might ask the anthropologist, "how can we explain the fact that the white man's civilization had made the tremendous advances with which we are all familiar while the civilizations of the coloured peoples have lagged behind?" To settle this question, he argues, anthropology should engage the "problem of the inequality—or diversity—of human *cultures,* which is in fact—however unjustifiably—closely associated with [the inequality of human *races*] in the public mind" (221, italics in the original).

His own answer is that the "diversity of cultures" does not so much result from geographic isolation as it is an effect of a "natural [psychological] phenomenon," "the ethnocentric attitude," which is the tendency "to reject out of hand the Cultural institutions—ethical, religious, social or aesthetic—which are furthest removed from those with which we identify ourselves" (224). Ironically, he notes, this universal "attitude of mind," which pervades "Western civilization," where it sustains statements that exclude "'savages' . . . from human kind, is precisely the attitude most strikingly characteristic of those same savages" (224–25). By repeating Herder's account of "prejudice," Lévi-Strauss seems to suggest that the "original sin" of the science of man was not so much to map the exterior determinants of human difference, "diversity and inequality." The greatest sin was to do so through an evolutionary logic that writes the cultures of yesterday's "'natives'" as instances of "stages of development" already superseded by "western civilization," which hides the fact that "progress" has always resulted from a "coalition of cultures," as is demonstrated by the fact that the cultures that had come into contact had "improved," while isolated cultures had remained "stationary" (225). Ethnocentric or not, the goodness of "progress" remains in the eyes of the European beholder.

Almost fifty years after Lévi-Strauss's statement, many of the postmodern critiques of modern thought lament the fact that "the ethnocentric attitude" still operating in twenty-first-century social scientific accounts of the "diversity of cultures" prevents the expansion of universality with the inclusion of females, homosexuals, and the others of Europe, which would entail a social configuration that would look like a "coalition of cultures." Faithful to Herder's thesis of the universality of differentiation, in one version of it they assert that whatever contributions a given "culture" has made to the human archive constitute instances of human autopoesis. Like Lévi-Strauss, however, they manage to forget that any scientific rendering of interiority will necessarily rehearse the play of engulfment. Twentieth-century anthropology and sociology substituted the two "universals," mental laws and social forms, for bodily ones, ethnographical excavations for the mapping of the human body, but never abandoned the scientific desire that rewrites universal reason as productive *nomos*. Though in both the cultural addresses interiority, in neither does it operate as a historical signifying strategy, that is, it cannot produce self-consciousness as a thing of historicity (interiority-temporality). Mostly, in the anthropological text where, by rewriting the others of Europe in affectability, the cultural writes a subject of poesis that is fully a thing of globality (exteriority-spatiality). My point is that the observation of Lévi-Strauss and the postmodern critics is a valid observation only because it applies to all twentieth-century versions of the anthropological project, including their own.

Not much intellectual art, I think, is necessary to acknowledge that the cultural necessarily produces its object as an affectable thing results from its being a signifier that operates according to the rules of scientific signification. Of that it is as guilty as any other social scientific concept, including class, which has never been blamed for performing the same kind of "epistemic violence," to borrow Spivak's famous phrase. Why would the cultural meet so much misgivings not even a hundred years after it was warmly welcomed as the scientific concept that did not violate the most cherished attribute of man? In this chapter I have shown why the cultural fails to write the minds of the others of Europe in historicity, because it is deployed in an ontoepistemological configuration mapped by the analytics of raciality, the political-symbolic arsenal of which it has also become a powerful weapon. The predicament of the cultural, I insist, issues not so much from supporting the Western observer's self-proclaimed "ethnographic authority," to name that which distinguishes its authentic "other," forever locked in its "difference" (Clifford 1988). Twentieth-century social scientific texts, as I argue in the first pages of this book, have been haunted by an "original sin," which has been as productive as the one said to have occasioned the fall from paradise. When deploying the cultural to incarcerate the others of Europe in their traditions and to safely keep post-Enlightenment Europe in the moment of transparency, these social scientific projects have already been approaching their objects as racial things. Not because these versions of these disciplines failed to refute the "original sin," the writing of man as an effect of the tools of productive *nomos,* scientific reason in the guise of Spirit, but because, as they did so, they incorporated racial difference as a substantive trait of the human body. Had this not been the case, it would not have been possible to carve their separate niches in such a way as not to distinguish them from history.

Not surprisingly, the consolidation of social scientific projects guided by the concept of the cultural, ones that approached difference as an effect of interiority, needed first to deny the racial explanatory significance. That was not a very difficult task given that, despite being so prolific, the racial has never been seated comfortably in the modern (moral) grammar, the one the transparency thesis governs. Certainly *homo culturalis* is not *homo racialis* under an assumed name, but the grid of particularization it indicates would be meaningless without globality, the ontological context the racial signifies. Nevertheless, it is precisely because the cultural necessarily refers back to the scene of representation—a task it performs beautifully in historical and literary texts, at least those not yet colonized by social scientific strategies—that it cannot displace the racial, for it would never satisfactorily perform the latter's primary role, which is to postpone, as it announces or betrays, any account of post-Enlightenment European particularity that would privilege that "Other" ontoepistemological instance, thus dissipating its founding presupposition, namely, the principle of transcendentality that ensures the locating of its particular mode of being human in transparency. For this reason, any critical analysis of the present global configuration should attend to how, in claims for fighting crime or terror, two social scientific signifiers once again (re)place the others of Europe before the principles said to govern Western European and the U.S. social configurations, universality (legality) and freedom.

7

The Sociologics of Racial Subjection

The essence of race relations [is] that they are the relations of strangers; of peoples which are associated primarily for secular and practical purposes; for exchange of goods and services. They are otherwise the relations of peoples of diverse races and cultures which have been thrown together by the fortunes of war, and who, for any reason, have not been sufficiently knit together by intermarriage and interbreeding to constitute a single ethnic community, with all that it implies.

— ROBERT E. PARK, *RACE AND CULTURE*

When Robert E. Park appropriates the "stranger" to describe "the problem of race relations," he does not inaugurate a project of knowledge that, as Yu (2001) poses, is "predicated on a definition of the exotic, of what is absolutely foreign and different about one place and another" (6). For the sociology of race relations was not the first social scientific project to write the "others of Europe" as "absolutely" (irreducibly and unsublatably) different. The figure of the stranger does no more than to refigure previous writings, those of the science of man and twentieth-century anthropology, of the others of Europe in *affectability*. My point is that precisely because the arsenal of race relations presupposes previous moments of the *analytics of raciality,* the ones that institute globality as an ontoepistemological context, the stranger as a spatial metaphor prefigures a strategy of intervention, the "race relations cycle," which predicates the obliteration of those who do not share in the spatial "origins"

153

of the *transparent "I."* For this reason, it does not—and this is an effect of racial difference—as it does in Simmel's version of sociology, signify a new type of "social relationship" that is resolved in temporality. In the text of race relations, "stranger" captures an incessant wave of affectable "strangers" coming from every corner of the globe to muddle an otherwise transparent social configuration, namely, that of the early twentieth-century United States.

My task in this chapter is to describe the conditions of production of the accounts of social subjugation, the sociologics of racial subjection, manufactured in this third moment of production of the arsenal of raciality. What I show is how, by rewriting racial difference as a signifier of cultural difference, the toolbox of race relations writes the U.S. social subject and social configuration in transparency and replaces the others of Europe in affectability. By so doing, it produces a particular kind of modern social subject, the racial subject, which does not actualize the principles of the transparent I, namely, universality and self-determination. With this, it adds to the political-symbolic arsenal that raciality introduces the statement that the presence of the others of Europe institutes in modern social configurations a kind of social consciousness that does not actualize the principle of transcendentality. In other words, I show how the sociologics of racial subjection presupposes the postulates that, in the presence of racial difference, European (white) subjects no longer occupy the place of the transparent I; they become affectable subjects, gazing at the horizon of death, the ones whose ideas and actions are always already determined by the presence of an inferior "other," a racial subaltern whose body and mind refer to other global regions.

My reading of the arsenal of the Chicago School of Sociology identifies a foundational statement on the causes of racial subjection in which globality constitutes the unacknowledged ontoepistemological referent that entails an account of racial subjection that renders exteriority a "natural" (in the sense of God-given) attribute of the others of Europe. It is the basis of two accounts of racial subjection: (a) the logic of obliteration, which writes the trajectories of the others of Europe as a movement toward annihilation, the necessary destiny of affectable consciousness because it is necessary that *transcendentality* return as the sole guiding principle of the modern social configurations they inhabit, which Brazil's postslavery conditions exemplify, and (b) the logic of exclusion, which deploys racial difference to explain why in certain transparent social configurations the others of Europe remain outside the scope of its governing principles, which the early twentieth-century United States exemplifies. What my reading uncovers, however, is that, even though the logic of exclusion would guide deployments of the arsenal of race relations, it remains subordinated to the logic of obliteration. More important, it shows that the prevailing sociohistorical logic of exclusion—which, as I show elsewhere (Silva 2001 and 2004b), emerged in post–World War II versions of race relations—fails to capture racial subjection precisely because, by incorporating the effects of previous moments of the analytics of raciality as an "empirical" given, they necessarily (re)produce the logic of obliteration postulated in the narrative of *transcendental poesis* and proved in the deployments of *productive nomos* that compose the analytics of raciality. Therefore, it also constitutes another weapon in the arsenal of the analytics of raciality, one that not only reproduces the affectability of the others of Europe but presupposes the failure of the logic of obliteration, the defining statement of race relations. For this reason, the critical accounts of racial subjection it sustains rewrite the racial itself as foreign—because of an excessive, unbecoming strategy of power—to modern social configurations.

THE "RACE RELATIONS CYCLE"

What is the "problem of race relations"? In the early twentieth-century United States, Robert E. Park identified two manifestations of this problem. In Northern and Western cities, where "progress" depended on the "cheapened" labor necessary to further capitalist accumulation, an increasing flux of Eastern and Southern European immigrants, Asian immigrants, and U.S. Southern blacks promoted a type of competition in which "individuals" were organized as "physically" identified "social groups," entailing the emergence of a type of social relationship informed by principles that depart from universality, the one "Anglo-Saxons" had actualized in the U.S. social configuration. Following the logic of raciality, the arsenal of the Chicago School of Sociology assumed that the transparent I would be the obvious victor in the struggle against its racial (physically and mentally) "others." This is indicated in its guiding *strategy of intervention*, namely, the "race relations cycle"—"conflict and

competition," "accommodation," "assimilation," and "amalgamation" or miscegenation—which, according to Park (1950c), "is apparently progressive and irreversible" (150).[1] Though it explained
the trajectory of certain immigrant groups, Southern and Eastern
Europeans, other subjugated "races and cultures," U.S. blacks, and
Asian immigrants were neither "assimilating" nor "amalgamating"
with the all-powerful "Anglo-Saxon." When accounting for this the-
oretically unexpected outcome, Park, his associates, and students deployed an arsenal that, guided by the assumption of the irreducible
and unsublatable affectability of the others of Europe, outlined the
strategies of the analytics of raciality that would govern twentieth-
century global configuration.[2]

Guiding the arsenal of race relations is a *strategy of intervention*
that refigures globality, the ontological horizon the racial produces,
when it writes the affectability of the others of Europe as the cause
of their subjection. In the introduction to his *Race and Culture
Contacts,* E. B. Reuter (1934) provides a summary of this social
scientific construct, which introduces a logic of obliteration that
explains the outcome of Europeans' juridical and economic appropriation of lands situated in other global regions. He identifies three
modes through which encounters between Europeans and their others take place: immigration, enslavement, and conquest. In all cases,
"contact" undermines the existing "social and moral orders," leading eventually to the destruction of the weaker order. In this brief
exposition of the "theory of race and culture contacts," Reuter identifies possible outcomes, "three universals" or "the basic facts and
the pattern of the subsequent processes," which operate at the racial, cultural, and individual levels, namely, "racial miscegenation,"
"mixture of cultural elements," and "personal disorganization." The
logic of obliteration is articulated in Reuter's description of the first
pattern, in which he shows how "the theory of race and culture contacts" transformed the science of man's notion of miscegenation into
an eschatological signifier that captures how the play of productive
nomos determines the outcome of "contacts" between Europeans
and the others of Europe. Although it occurs in every situation of
contact, the pattern of "racial miscegenation," he argues, will vary
according to the nature of the contact. In the case of immigration,
"the peoples in contact are relatively friendly and not too far apart
in physical appearance and social status, [and] intermarriage com-

monly goes on easily and without exciting opposition or comment"
(8). In slavery, "the difference in social status is such as commonly
to prevent any considerable amount of intermarriage" (8). Finally,
in cases of conquest, "where representatives of a powerful nation
impose themselves as a ruling group, exploiting the native resources
without enslaving the native people," he argues, "the mixture of
races generally goes on more slowly" (9). According to Reuter, the
second universal, "mixture of culture elements," is defined as "the
transfer of culture elements and the blending of heritages to the appearance of a new culture organization" that may result in "a hybrid
product quite unlike either parent culture." That is, the dominated
group's social (economic, juridical, and cultural) configurations are
annihilated in these situations. What this cultural "struggle for existence," this situation of competition and "conflict . . . between the
sponsors of the competing systems," entails are attempts to preserve
the "defeated" culture and the elaborations of "rationalizations" of
the process: "prejudices, discrimination, beliefs, doctrine, movements, and the other incidents of a changing order" (10–11). That
is, the presence of the affectable "native" troubles the otherwise
stable "dominant group." Finally, from this process of "cultural and
social change" results the disorganization and reorganization of "individual personalities," which are the markers of "progress" (14).
What the "theory of race and cultural contacts" does is to rewrite
the play of engulfment as an eschatological narrative, thus deploying
the logic of obliteration, which stipulates, as do the strategies of the
science of man and anthropology, that the racial (physical) difference
(via "miscegenation") and cultural (moral/social) difference (via assimilation) of the other of Europe will necessarily disappear.

From this account of the relationship between Europeans and
their others result the two logics of racial subjection that will guide
the political-symbolic arsenal that the race relations cycle organizes:
(a) the logic of obliteration, which postulates the necessity of the
disappearance of the racial and cultural differences of the others of Europe, and (b) the logic of exclusion, which captures the
situations in which racial difference halts the natural outcomes of
the encounters between Europeans and their others. Although the
logic of exclusion has become the prevailing account of racial subjection, the basic strategies of race relations, "race prejudice" and
"race consciousness," presuppose the logic of obliteration, for they

consistently (re)produce modern social configurations as actualizations of a transparent I and effectively produce as consciousness the others of Europe, whose intrinsic affectability will lead to their annihilation. When describing the political-symbolic arsenal that produces the sociologics of racial subjection, I show how the foundational statement of race relations deploys an account of the causes of the others of Europe that produces or assumes their affectability at three levels: (a) non-Europeans' visible physical traits, which are substantive signs of an "inferior" consciousness, which entail (b) "mores" and actions that depart from universality, resulting in the (c) *exclusion* of non-Europeans and their removal to regions of subalternity built at the core of the U.S. "modern civilization." The sociologic of exclusion entails the postulate that, in otherwise transparent social configurations, racial difference institutes affectable social subjects, those whose actions actualize ideas irreconcilable with universality and self-determination. The primacy of the logic of obliteration will become evident when I turn to accounts of the Brazilian social configuration, the one not troubled by the "problem of race relations." There I show how the eschatological narrative of the "race relations cycle" itself constitutes an effective strategy of racial subjection. What I introduce here is a reading of the text of race relations that indicates how the very strategies available to explain racial subjection constitute but another moment of the analytics of raciality, that is, they belong in the political-symbolic arsenal that produces the others of Europe as subaltern modern subjects.

THE PROBLEM OF RACIAL DIFFERENCE

In early twentieth-century U.S. sociology, the affectability of the others of Europe guided the elaboration of a political-symbolic arsenal that attributed racial subjection to the cultural difference signified in their bodies. According to Park ([1939] 1950), the "problem of race relations" emerged in the modern U.S. Northern industrialized cities because the conditions proper to a modern social configuration prevented the visibly different Asians and blacks from fulfilling their eschatological destiny.[3] "The chief obstacle to the assimilation of the Negro and the Oriental," Park argues, is "not mental but physical traits. It is not because the Negro and the Japanese are so differently constituted that they do not assimilate. If they are given an opportunity, the Japanese are quite as capable as the Italians, the Armenians, or the Slavs of acquiring our culture, and sharing our national ideals. The trouble is not with the Japanese mind but with the Japanese skin" (208). Unlike Southern and Eastern European immigrants, Park ([1928] 1950) argues, Asians and blacks exhibit "physical traits," signs of "social (moral) distance," that do not disappear in the second generation. These marks entail reactions on the part of the "native" group, ideas and practices expressing prejudices, that exacerbate the "race conflict," preventing the "assimilation" of the "newcomers" into the U.S. modern social configuration. That is, because they "fail" to lose the "visible" signs (racial difference) of cultural ("social/moral") difference, blacks and Asians are the "strangers" whose presence transforms an otherwise transparent social configuration into one that is pathological—not ruled by universality and self-determination—one that fails to fulfill the logic of obliteration prescribed in the "theory of racial and cultural contacts."

When describing how the halting of the "race relations cycle" institutes racial subjection, Park identifies a kind of social subject whose principle and actions actualize neither universality nor self-determination. For Park ([1924a] 1950), "race consciousness" is the differential attitude regarding those with whom one shares little or no "intimacy." Though "empathy" is also a "natural" (God-given) impulse among human beings, Park argues, it is prevented under certain circumstances, such as when "differences" produce "self-consciousness" and "fears" or a divergence of interests (257). What distinguishes this kind of self-consciousness is "race prejudice," which Park ([1917] 1950) defines as a "spontaneous, more or less instinctive defense-reaction, the practical effect of which is to restrict free competition between races" (227).[4] In other words, "race prejudice" is the instinctual reaction to "social/moral distance," the function of which is to ensure the dominant race's self-preservation. Without this particular kind of "strangers," the others of Europe, both the U.S. social configuration and the U.S. American social subject would return to transparency; that is, those engaged in competition would be "free and equal individuals" (juridical-moral things governed by universality and self-determination). Taking place here is a rewriting of raciality as an exclusive attribute of racial subalterns, whose bodies always already refer to "other" global regions, "other" social configurations, while the "native" (U.S. white Anglo-Saxon) racial group, and the social configurations they produce are rewritten as signifiers (actualizations and exteriorizations) of the principle of transcendentality.[5] The primary effect of signification here is the writing of the causes of racial subjection, the condition of the emergence of race prejudice, the social attitude that produces racial exclusion, as foreign to modern social configurations. For the racial became an element of the U.S. social configuration only with the arrival of strangers whose bodily configuration precluded the fulfillment of the "race relations cycle," that is, those whose racial difference prevents them from "assimilation" into, or "amalgamation" with, the racial group who had created a "modern civilization" in the United States.

What kind of subaltern consciousness did racial subjection institute? When answering this question, Park rewrites the racial other in affectability by describing a self-consciousness without transparency, that is, one fully situated before the horizon of death. In "Negro Consciousness as Reflected in Race Literature," Park ([1923] 1950) describes the trajectory of the racial subaltern subject as necessarily a movement of obliteration. This appears in the distinction between the "Negro folk songs" of slavery and the poetry of the "modernized Negro" of the Harlem Renaissance, which he sees as a loss of authenticity. Whereas in modern ontology self-consciousness emerges in transparency, in Park's reading of black literature it appears as a move away from Negro "essence," which is here again an effect of affectability, that is the loss of black authenticity entailed by contact with the "modern civilization." Each moment of "Negro literature," he argues, constituted distinct actualizations of black consciousness, for each transcribed a moment of "Negro life." However, presupposing that the others of Europe do not know of transparency, they have not kept pace with the movements of "Spirit," each of the moments Park captures, even the one in which he identifies "authentic" manifestations of "Negro race consciousness," is already mediated by whiteness, already an effect of outer determination. According to Park, the "primitive Negro literature" produced under slavery—the "folk songs"—constitute the sole authentic actualizations of the "Negro race consciousness." The "Negro folk songs," he argues, actualized the conditions of slavery, reflecting "life as [the slave] saw and felt it at that time" (185); they communicate a "racial dream" whose wordiness "indicated patience, humility; resignation in the life, mitigated by expectation of a glorious riot in the next" (288). In contrast, post-Emancipation cultural forms, such as the "militant" poetry of the Harlem Renaissance, fail to actualize "Negro consciousness." Why? Reflection, Park answers. "Writing," he argues, "enforces reflection. Reflection makes the writer self-conscious and destroys the natural spontaneity which is the essence of folk song" (289). This poetry reflects the Negro's need to deal with the contradiction posed by emancipation: freedom without citizenship, without equality; it was a compulsion to deal with the problem of being "at once a Negro and a citizen" (291).

For Park, this loss of authenticity underlies Du Bois's notion of "double consciousness," the condition of "always looking through the eyes of the others, that has made it difficult for Negro poetry to achieve a sincere expression of Negro life" (292). What these cultural products actualize is not a Negro tradition, but "a natural and inevitable reaction to race prejudice." For Park, this form of "Negro race consciousness" is not just an expression of blacks' subordinate position but also an "expression of Negro temperament under all conditions of modern life" (294). "Negroes," Park noted, "have been less interested in demonstrating their right as individuals to participate in the common cultural life about them; they have been more concerned, on the other hand, in defining their own conception of their mission as a race" (293). This form of "Negro consciousness," Park writes, emerged out of the necessity of collective action, the necessity that Negroes should cooperate to win for themselves the place and the respect in the white man's world that the Constitution could not give them, which has created among the Negroes of the United States a solidarity that does not exist elsewhere. Race consciousness is the natural and inevitable reaction to race prejudice (294). It results not only from whites' "race prejudice," which excludes blacks, but also from the fact that "Negro" existence takes place in a social configuration that actualizes a principle foreign to the black mind.

In Park's reading of the slavery songs and the Harlem Renaissance "Negro poetry," it becomes evident how the strategy of intervention of race relations, the "race relations cycle," constructs the racial subaltern as a subject of outer determination, as a consciousness always already immersed in affectability, not a transparent I. Though it writes this particular consciousness as the exteriorization of objective determinants of black subjection, it presupposes the erasure of how raciality as a scientific construct already maps the social configuration in which blacks emerge as subaltern social subjects. What Park's account of black consciousness indicates is the most powerful effect of the sociologic of exclusion. Because it assumes and rewrites the black subject as intrinsically affectable, it renders subalternity the proper social position of the other of Europe. How else to explain why Park read the modernized Negro as inauthentic and slave songs as authentic signifiers of black consciousness if not as statements of blacks' "unnatural" presence in a social configuration governed by transparency, one to which only the consciousness that houses universality and self-determination is indigenous.

The reader may consider this an overstatement, but, in the absence of any other qualifiers, Park's statement suggests that only subalternity provides the conditions necessary for "Negroes" to actualize their "true" being. Hence, the radical written literature of the incompletely modernized Negro reflects a loss of authenticity, for it resulted from reflection (an attribute of the interior thing, the one with reason) that he interprets as borrowed transparency, the impossible desire for identifying blackness with the surrounding white social space and its inhabitants. However, in his account, these moments of subjection—"isolated" enslaved conditions and segregated regions of the U.S. social configuration—reflect circumstances that, though determined from without, are not political because of the assumption of the ruling racial group's transparency and blacks' affectability. This argument suggests that complete assimilation would result in a total loss of an authentic Negro subjectivity. More important, it introduces the thesis that the fully modernized Negro would necessarily cease to be a Negro. By erasing the effects of power of the racial, ignoring the political-symbolic relationship it encapsulates, race relations has produced racial subjection as an effect of the fundamental impossibility of certain strangers' becoming transparent, of being modern. Not only does this produce blackness as an impossible basis for formulating any project of emancipation; it suggests that, because it is always already the exclusive attribute of a transparent I, the racial subaltern's desire for emancipation, for inclusion in the dominant (white Anglo-Saxon society), is fundamentally a desire for self-obliteration.

THE STRANGE CAREER OF MISCEGENATION

By now it will appear obvious that the counterpoint of Park's celebration of the destiny of the African in Brazil in his introduction to Pierson's *Negroes in Brazil,* was U.S. blacks' position as "a nation within a [U.S.] nation." But let there be no mistake here. What Brazil's, actually Bahia's, social configuration indicates is the promise of a postslavery social space free of "race segregation." The episode of "natural history" to which Park refers, "the career" of Africans in Brazil, was their certain (if slow) obliteration, taking with them the nonmodern "mores" their presence entails.[6] What escaped Park, and later students of race relations in Brazil, is that the career of Africans in Brazil has also been an effect of the strange career of the very natural history process, miscegenation, that he celebrates. In *Negroes in Brazil*, Donald Pierson (1942) describes a postslavery or postcolonial social configuration in which the race relations cycle had reached its culmination. To be sure, in Pierson's study one finds statements that reappear in later analyses of racial subjection in Brazil, where, more often than not, they were deployed to write the Brazilian particularity as a paradox. Moreover, his account of the Brazilian racial situation introduces the argument that class difference rather than racial difference explains dark-skinned *baianos'* social subjection. Finally, although Pierson's analysis already anticipates the historical take on the foundational statement, because it still deploys the Chicago School's version of sociology, I read it as still belonging with the early twentieth-century version of race relations.

What interests me in Pierson's description of the postslavery Brazilian social configuration is his answer to the question of why the political-symbolic strategies of race relations fail to capture its racial situation. More specifically, I am interested in how he rewrites miscegenation, "physical" and "cultural," to mark the return to transparency as predicated in the "theory of race and culture contacts." According to Pierson, the specific features of slavery in Brazil required the introduction of a large number of African slaves into the Brazilian space and forced the Portuguese to search for more effective means to create a modern social configuration in the southern part of the American continent. More precisely, according to Pierson, it produced "mild slavery," giving Brazilian slaves a much better lot than those in the United States and the West Indies: less violence, more manumissions, and a much more gradual and less conflictive process of emancipation. Not only did it enable the survival and expansion of African culture and the uncontrolled intimacy between masters and slaves, which produced a physical and cultural miscegenation that eliminated racial difference. It also facilitated the diffusion of European "blood" and "spirit," which would eventually eliminate African influence in Brazil. According to Pierson, the "social order" ensuing from this contact is governed by a "racial ideology" that, instead of emphasizing "social (moral) distance," produced the self-image of a society in which the elimination of racial difference constitutes its inhabitants as "one single people." "In Bahia," he argues, blacks and whites "do not stand over against each other as irreducible ethnic groups, differing only in appearance, which is obvious, but also in kind, and fated to remain separate and distinct. . . . Every citizen is considered first of all Brazilian . . . irreducible to racial origin" (218). In short, out of Brazil's "mild slavery" emerged a "social order" characterized by a "comparative absence of conflict and absence of 'race segregation,'" where Europeanness would be actualized in bodies and minds, but one in which "race prejudice" played no significant role in the social configuration.

The celebrated "career" of Africans in Brazil was then to slowly but surely disappear under the inescapable force of a European desire as miscegenation eliminated racial difference and ensured that, after slavery, the Brazilian social space was ruled by universality. "The most obvious effect of miscegenation," Pierson states, "is to eliminate the physical differences between the races. In Bahia intermixture has now, for more than four hundred years, been breaking down physical barriers and reducing the visibility which in the United States always serves to call out three traditional responses and is long associated with variations in social status" (124–25). In Pierson's account, Brazilian social configuration does not constitute an object of race relations precisely because miscegenation has eliminated racial difference.[7] Though his conclusions would remain at the core of explanations of the Brazilian solution to the "problem of race relations," the text of race relations would be systematically deployed only in examinations of the Brazilian social configuration after the Second World War.

The foundational statement establishes that racial difference entails a pathological social configuration, an expression of affectable (outer determined) self-consciousness, emerging in the presence in modern social configurations of groups whose racial differences halt the play of productive *nomos* as it is articulated in the "race relations cycle." Resulting from this is an account of racial subjection, the logic of exclusion, that assumes that only when reacting to the "social (moral) distance" signified in Asian and black difference does the native (white) group constitute itself as a nonmodern collectivity, a "racial group." That is, a proper modern social configuration actualizes but universality and self-determination, the exclusive attributes of the transparent I, to which it returns after the fulfillment of the logic of obliteration. This statement reproduces both transcendental poesis and the previous play of productive *nomos* described in the moments of the analytics of raciality, which write whiteness and "modern civilization" as signifiers of transparency and replace the others of Europe in affectability. Race relations adds three statements to the analytics of raciality: (a) in transparent (European or white) social configurations, the presence of the others of Europe entails unbecoming exclusionary ideas and practices that can be eliminated only with the fulfillment of the logic of obliteration, as post-slavery Brazil exemplifies; (b) the racial subaltern consciousness actualizes its position in a given social configuration, but because it results from race prejudice and other exterior determinants, when the racial subaltern subject emerges as a self-consciousness in the *scene of representation* it cannot but desire self-destruction; that is, the eschatology that in the historical materialist text brings about self-determination in the text of race relations produces social subjects that yearn for self-obliteration; and (c) postcolonial spaces where the logic of obliteration has been or was in the process of fulfillment, due to unhindered miscegenation, would not constitute an object of the sociology of race relations, because the absence of "racial conflict" and "competition" renders racial difference not sociologically relevant and, therefore, politically irrelevant.

BEFORE AND BEYOND TRANSPARENCY

What the logic of exclusion and historicity cannot capture is that though distinct, the United States' and Brazil's modes of racial subjection indicate how the racial, the signifier of globality, operates as a productive strategy of power. Throughout the twentieth century, the deployment of blackness and Africanity, in political projects such as the Garvey movement, Pan-Africanism, and Negritude, indicated that the racial operates as a global political concept that institutes political subjects whose subaltern position cannot be addressed solely by stating their exclusion from (juridical) universality and economic exploitation, because their place has been demarcated by signifiers of scientific universality. Nor can historicity account for the emergence of the black subaltern as an oppositional consciousness, along the lines of Laclau and Mouffe's "antagonic parts," Butler's "local cultures," or Bhabha's speaking postcolonial subjects, because the delimitation of their particular position, subalternity, necessitates the deployment of raciality. What I am suggesting is that the analytics of raciality renders self-defeating those deployments of the cultural in emancipatory projects that demand the recognition (inclusion) of the cultural difference of the others of Europe but assume that signifiers of transparency alone rule modern representation.

My description of the analytics of raciality shows how this modern political-symbolic arsenal, which transforms human bodily and social configurations into signifiers of the mind, produces the global as a modern ontological context. What the signifiers of productive *nomos* that it deploys, the racial the cultural, do is to produce globality as a configuration unevenly divided between bodies and regions of affectability and bodies and regions of transparency. What distinguishes this account from most critical racial analyses and postmodern critiques of modern thought is the fact that I am not so much repeating the argument that the others of Europe have been placed outside history and reason or claiming that they have been fixed in an earlier time or altogether outside time, as objects of "untruth"—"scientific falsifications," "prejudices," and "false beliefs." What I am highlighting is that, rather than producing the others of Europe outside of historicity and universality, the arsenal the racial guides engulfs them by writing their difference as an effect of the play of productive reason. By engaging scientific signification as a productive moment, I move away from prevailing critiques of the narratives of "progress" and "development," which for better or worse read the construction of non-Europeans' (racial/cultural) particularity as the effect of the spatializing of time, that is, as a "lag" or a "wait," which retains the modern construction of space as the moment of negativity. For instance, my view is unlike that of Homi Bhabha (1994a), who deploys this idea of a "time lag" in a critique of colonial discourse, which writes the emergence of the postcolonial subject as a sort of return of a repressed or oppressed historical subject. This idea corresponds to constructions of the colonial space as the *terra incognita,* the empty space, which enables the "emergence of modernity—as an ideology of *beginning, modernity as the new*" (246, italics in the original). Therefore, it is also already a product of modern representation and cannot be its irreducible condition (the resisting bar, that which would signify another mode of representation, another ontology) of possibility. What I am pointing to here is that effect of historicity, which is to immediately assume, without inquiring into its conditions of production, the (historic) "being" of the ("racial" or "cultural") "other" and dismiss as ideological ("falsifications") the scientific statements that produce these very names, namely, the racial and the cultural.[8]

In Bhabha's account, the racial or colonial "other" plays a disruptive role because he assumes that its "difference" has first been falsified in "stereotypical knowledge" and the writing of its global location as *terra incognita,* therefore allowing for the enunciation of the European subject in transparency, resolving the projects of domination and exclusion that contradict Western self-representation. Though self-defeating, because the being that, after denouncing "stereotyping," returns in the Symbolic cannot displace historicity, this is not an unexpected full-fledged return to historicity when one learns how Bhabha's project nicely complements Butler's and Spivak's. Bhabha describes his postmodern (inclusive) project as one that he hopes will do just that, that is, bring the postcolonial other into modern (historical) representation *"to establish a sign of the present,* of modernity, that is not that 'now' of transparent immediacy, and to found a form of social individuation where communality is *not predicated on a transcendent becoming."* Guiding his quest, he states, are the questions of a "contra-modernity" that address "what is modernity in those colonial conditions where its imposition is itself the denial of historical freedom, civic autonomy and the 'ethical' choice of refashioning" (241, italics in the original). Exactly here, Bhabha repositions the postcolonial or racial subaltern subject as a "fully fashioned identity," a thoroughly historic subject—in Herder's rendering of historicity—behind the ideological veil, as the other modernity, the modernity of unfreedom, which flourishes in another space, in the "postcolonial world" where "stereotyping" and the juridical and economic exclusions it sustains also reside. What I am pointing to here is how the sociohistorical logic of exclusion once again undermines the critical potential of poststructuralist strategies by rewriting the *modern text* as they rehearse the very historicity they challenge.

For this reason, instead of locating the place of emergence of racial subaltern subjects in a temporal slot by deploying a good version of historicity, which would include their "submerged histories," my option here has been to chart modern representation, where I locate the political-symbolic strategies that have produced the others of Europe as modern subaltern subjects. With this I am not dismissing postcolonial interventions as irrelevant. Instead, I write against the limits of (their critique of) historicity, which relies on the modern construction of distance as a temporal metaphor to circumscribe the place of emergence of the colonized as a transparent I. My hope here is to contribute to a complexification of this argument by recuperating the spatial connotation of distance, which is possible only if one reads the before, where the racial and the cultural write the others of Europe as an effect of signifiers of exteriority, of political-symbolic strategies to institute a particularity that does not belong to time, one that threatens history because it recuperates the relationship postponed in modern representation. Perhaps this choice renders my project closer to Foucault's than I claim—here I have in mind Bhabha's (1994) and others' comments on the pitfalls of Foucault's Eurocentrism—but I never stated that I engage European self-representation from a position that is textually outside of it. For only by reading modern representation against the grain does one learn that the particular temporality attributed to European bodies and social configurations results from how the racial, the signifier of globality, produces both self-determined and affectable consciousness.

Earlier I have stated that the sociohistorical logic of exclusion informs critical racial theorizing and remapping of the contemporary global configuration. Both inherit its main dimensions: (a) their signifying strategies further reproduce the effect of raciality, which is to write post-Enlightenment European social configuration as the actualization of a transparent I, which produces the cultural and ideological mechanisms of racial subjection and the subject they institute as effects of nonmodern foundations (beliefs, previous social configurations, "nature"); (b) they rewrite the others of Europe in affectability, extraneous to transparent social configurations; hence (c) because they fail to acknowledge that the transparent I is also an effect of the arsenal of raciality, they embrace the view that the elimination of racial difference—not as a physical trait but as a "false" *strategy of particularization*—would (re)institute transparent social configuration, the one (juridical) universality and historicity describe, which transcendental poesis produces. For this reason, as discussed earlier, they can guide only those racial emancipatory projects that assume that only historic signifiers, such as class, nation, or culture, constitute the acceptable signifiers of a racial subaltern consciousness.

When the global configuration demands a refashioning of the concept without which neither "native" nor postmodern critics of anthropology can live, I think it may be helpful to recall that the emergence of the concept of the cultural as the privileged *strategy of engulfment* and of ethnography as the proper strategy of intervention marked the entry of the others of Europe into temporality, the domain the racial reserves to bodies, social configurations, and the global locations that signify the transparent I. Though not a new statement, it needs to be repeated nonetheless, because today's claims for the obliteration of cultural difference—in statements that articulate it as something that needs to be both acknowledged and overcome through translation, as something that is left behind when, as Clifford (1988) says, "too many voices [speak] all at once" and "syncretism and parodic invention become the rule" (95), as necessary to populate the global space with "cosmopolitans" and "hybrids"—also forget that it is a product of the anthropological text. We owe the postmodern critique of "ethnographic authority" the emergence of this image of a global Tower of Babel that produces the present global configuration as a neoliberal multicultural polity, the one that includes never-before-heard languages that speak of never-before-heard things that actualize a never-before-known consciousness. The never-before-known could become relevant, however, only because postmodern anthropology writes the others of Europe as things with interiority (ones whose particular consciousness is immediately actualized in what they say and do) and because the new tools of scientific reason can reveal how whatever they say and do actualizes a transparent (interior-temporal) subaltern I. What postmodern writers do not acknowledge, however, is that the "new subjectivities" they capture are through and through an effect of productive *nomos*. My point is that current writings of the global subaltern have been authorized by earlier deployments of productive *nomos*. Like other products of scientific signification, they have become "nature" itself, objects and subjects of critical projects that, holding onto the desire to "discover" and "control" a yet-to-be-uncovered "truth" or "essence," refuse to engage their own effects. For this reason, I intend to map the regimen of production that releases these living ghosts, to chart the social scientific arsenal that reproduces or repositions the others of Europe in affectability.

III

Homo Modernus

STEPHANO: *Now forward with your tale. Pr'ythee, stand further off.*
CALIBAN: *Beat him enough. After a little time I'll beat him too.*
STEPHANO: *Stand further.—Come, proceed.*
CALIBAN: *Why, as I told thee, 'tis a custom with him*
I' the afternoon to sleep. There thou mayst brain him,
Having first seized his books; or with a log
Batter his skull, or paunch him with a stake,
Or cut his wezand with thy knife. Remember,
First to possess his books; for without them
He's but a sot, as I am, nor hath not
One spirit to command: they all do hate him
As rootedly as I. Burn his books.
He has brave utensils,—for so he calls them,—
Which, when he has a house, he'll deck withal.
And that most deeply to consider is
The beauty of his daughter; he himself
Calls her nonpareil; I never saw a woman,
But only Sycorax my dam and she;
But she as far surpasseth Sycorax
As great'st does least.

—WILLIAM SHAKESPEARE, *THE TEMPEST*

What, the reader may ask, can the tale of Prospero and Caliban teach about the effects of the writing of the "others of Europe" as affectable consciousness? When revisiting *The Tempest,* like other postcolonial critics, I read the play as an allegory of conquest. However I choose to read in the account of Prospero's magic—the circumstances it creates, its reach and limits, and the subject it creates—an outline of the modern grammar, I read *The Tempest* as an account of engulfment. Although I acknowledge that, unlike Shakespeare's play, which ends with a gesture of deference but not perhaps repentance as Prospero renounces his unbecoming power, after modern texts unleash their powerful words these utterances neither remain confined within the limits of the written statement nor become mere objects of conflicting interpretations. When appropriated in political statements, their political-symbolic tools produce "histories" and "biographies" of transcendentality and *affectability,* that is, the "spirits" of the books of science both resist and strive for closure. Each deployment of scientific signifiers not only retains their initial signification, but also reproduces that which distinguishes the context of signification that brought them into existence. What drives my project, as noted earlier, is the desire to gather the conditions of production of today's global subjects, both the newly audible "voices" that postmodern remappings attempt to include and the nation-states that both produce and are threatened by the recent juridical-economic reconfiguring of the global landscape.

Although the expected path would be to engage this present circumstance, the realization that the leading account of social subjection, the sociohistorical logic of exclusion, cannot address its more subtle and pervasive dimensions has forced me to take a step back, to engage the political texts in which today's global subjects are first articulated as political things. To do so, I have devised an analytical strategy, the national text, which displaces the *transparency thesis* when it captures how the writing of the national subject as a *transparent "I,"* a historical thing, necessitates the deployment of the arsenal of raciality. By gathering late nineteenth- and early twentieth-century statements that attempt to rewrite two postcolonial or postslavery polities, the United States and Brazil, as modern political subjects, I show that signifiers of raciality institute subjects that stand differentially before the juridical and economic dimensions of these modern social configurations. My reading shows how the strategies of the *analytics of raciality* institute an irreducible and unsublatable difference that cannot be resolved in the teleological trajectory of the nation subject. In each case, its tools institute both the national subject and its subaltern "others" when they resolve the geographic distance—bridge the American and the European continents—when they write the white body as a signifier of a transparent consciousness; that is, raciality produces a mental (moral) proximity to post-Enlightenment Europe, thus demarcating the place of emergence of the national subject as a specimen of the transcendental "I."

What I am describing here is *homo modernus,* an account of man in which self-consciousness emerges before both ontological horizons, historicity and globality, as it stands on the stage of life while facing the horizon of death. It does so for this reason: because man emerges always already in a relationship, in which transparency is not a given but the desired outcome of a political-symbolic act, engulfment, that is, "partial violation." Because the national text does acknowledge that modern political texts are rehearsals of both productions of the *scene of engulfment*—neither dismissing nor challenging historicity's ontological prerogative—it situates historical signification by indicating how scientific signification performs, because of its privileging of interiority, the version of the play of reason that *transcendental poesis* alone could not accomplish. Without recourse to *productive nomos,* without the signifiers that postpone the threat of an "Other" ontological context, globality, by producing the "others of Europe" as social configurations and consciousness as effects of a productive/regulative force but without the writing of post-Enlightenment European social configurations and consciousness as the perfect actualization and expression of productive *nomos,* which resolves contemporaneous coexisting modes of being human by stipulating that universal reason institutes them before the moment of transparency, the philosophical writing of the transparent social configuration and consciousness would not be sustained, for it would be hopelessly situated, determined by that which is not the same as itself.

In short, this reading captures the version of self-consciousness that emerged in twentieth-century modern representation, *homo modernus*—namely, the *global/historical* consciousness—the figure produced through the deployment of scientific and historic signifiers in modern ontological accounts. By doing so it shows why the choice of *good* historicity, and the dismissal of the racial as a "false" scientific tool, to realize the promises of universality is a rather limited basis for projects of racial and global emancipation. For it is only because the arsenal of raciality secures post-Enlightenment Europe's mind and social configuration in transparency, as it writes the others of Europe in a place not encompassed by transcendentality, that the latter subaltern positioning does not unleash the ethical crisis expected by those who argue that racial subjection contradicts modern ethical principles.

8

Outlining the Global/Historical Subject

What now was this particular social problem which, through the chances of birth and existence, became so peculiarly mine? At bottom and in essence it was as old as human life. Yet in its revelation, throughout the nineteenth century, it was significantly and fatally new: the difference between men; differences in their appearance, in their physique, in their thoughts and customs; differences so great and so impelling that always from the beginning of time, they thrust themselves forward upon the consciousness of all living things. Culture among human beings came to be and had to be built upon the knowledge of these differences.

—W. E. B. DU BOIS, *DUSK OF DAWN*

Why has the productive force of the *analytics of raciality,* which Du Bois already articulated in the 1930s, been missed in both critical racial theorizing and postmodern critiques of modern thought? Though I could explore how theoretical and methodological choices—actually, the impossibility of forfeiting these choices to explore how they have become the only ones available—limit their comprehension of the political-symbolic operatives in the contemporary global configuration, I will engage what I think is the most crucial determination, that is, the assumption that the racial is a "'scientific' fabrication," a signifier of colonial always already white anxiety and economic interests, that refigures neither universality nor historicity, the descriptors the *transparency thesis* authorizes. Holding onto the promises of historicity, which Renan articulated in the late nineteenth century, the works that compose the critical arsenal recuperate the universality of differentiation to write the "others of Europe" as always already historical subjects, and then move to capture a moment before racial subjection, where they are already historical, enjoying transparency before engulfment. While productive, this inclusive gesture has crowded the politics of recognition with numerous historical subjects parading and yelling their cultural differences. It has also shown that having a "voice," being heard as a subaltern *transparent "I,"* does not dissipate the effects of raciality.

Why? Because the crucial effect of the resolution of previous moments of the analytics of raciality, the science of man and anthropology, into the sociohistorical logic of exclusion, which writes the racial as an unbecoming (bad and dangerous) strategy of power, has been to "naturalize" racial subjection, that is, to write it as an effect of the "natural (divine) law"—namely, by placing the causes of racial subjection in that account of nature that precedes its appropriation in the various versions of the play of reason—*universal nomos, universal poesis, transcendental poesis, and productive nomos*— that is, in the theater of divine nature. For this reason, every later deployment of the tools of productive *nomos,* which address racial subjection, would rewrite racial difference as an "empirical" given, as something that needs not to be theorized, something belonging neither to the *scene of regulation* (universality) nor to the *scene of representation* (historicity), but an "individual" God-given attribute that has mistakenly (irrationally) become an operative factor in modern social configurations.

My task in this chapter is to describe how the national text recuperates the political subjects proliferating in the contemporary global configuration as specimens of *homo modernus,* an account of self-consciousness that acknowledges both historicity and globality as horizons of existence. Following Foucault's (1994) argument that the modern episteme emerged in the nineteenth century—and Hobsbawm's (1994a) account that registers the emergence of the complete outline of a modern political subject, the nation-state, in the late nineteenth century—I manufactured the national text to engage narratives of the nation as instances of the articulation of political subjects that necessarily combine strategies deployed in both fields of modern representation. That is, as a critical analytical tool, the national text rewrites national narratives as composed by the political-symbolic arsenal deployed in later versions of the play of reason, transcendental poesis and productive *nomos*.

What my reading of statements that write two early postcolonial polities, the United States and Brazil, as modern social configurations describes is how both historic and scientific strategies institute the national subject as a modern subject. Because both globality and historicity constitute the modern political (ontoepistemological) context, historical and scientific political-symbolic strategies produce the context of the emergence of the subject. While it is a historic text, one ruled by transcendentality, I show that the national subject constitutes a specimen of *homo modernus*, fully a product of modern representation, precisely because it is an effect of the nation, the historic (interior-temporal) signifier, one that institutes it as a particular subject of transcendental poesis and of the racial, the (exterior-spatial) signifier of globality, the one that produces the subject as an effect of the tools of productive *nomos*. What my reading shows is that the racial constitutes an effective political-symbolic strategy precisely because, when deployed in historic texts, it produces a moral context in which placing both the transparent I and the affectable "other" before the horizon of death does not entail the ethical crisis to be expected in the social configurations the transparency thesis describes.

WHENCE CALIBANS?

How does the national text depart from existing critical strategies? To answer this question, I briefly return to the tale of Prospero and Caliban, where I find a prefiguring of globality, the ontological context that could emerge only when universal reason was transformed into a productive and regulative force, that is, productive *nomos*. My first move here is to recognize the kind of power reason displaces, magic, as a productive strategy. When reading *The Tempest* one cannot miss how it describes the process Foucault (1994) calls the demise of resemblance, the kind of knowledge that magic signifies, which is how Prospero's sorcery and the subject it governs belong in the New World. Back in Naples, Prospero's unbecoming power has no utility, nor does he need his subject in exile, Caliban, the unbecoming (undesirable and improper) subject, whose deformed body, affectable mind, and dangerous *place* represent conditions that not only depart from those found in Europe but also have no significance for the exercise of Prospero's proper power at home. Nevertheless, if Caliban is nothing but a product of Prospero's magic, and if this power does not belong in Europe, one can argue that the relationship instituted in the "first encounter" on Sychorax's island, in that it produced a ruler and a ruled being, produced Prospero and Caliban as such. That is, if Caliban as a subject is a product of magic, the same productive power institutes Prospero as a master. This is not another version of Hegel's lordship and bondsman allegory, though. When Prospero is also conceived as an effect of the power of his books, not of his mind or his firearms, his proper place, his place of "origin," also becomes an effect of the magic that has instituted the political relationship between Prospero and Caliban. Put differently, I am suggesting that Prospero's particularity is also the effect of that what establishes his "difference" from Caliban, and so are his proper place and subjects. Perhaps the most crucial effect of the play is to produce Prospero's powers as signifiers of spatial distance, the ocean between Sychorax's island (America) and Naples (Europe)—and therefore Prospero's dislocation—which separates the powers that mark him as a political subject: the unbecoming power that produced him as Caliban's master and the blood relationship (his being Miranda's father) that will enable his exercise of his proper (patriarchal) power in his place of origin, the European space, through his heirs.

The postmodern or global reader may ask, What if Prospero abandons his unbecoming power and the subject it produces on Sychorax's island precisely because the spirits his magic mobilizes are indigenous to that place? Perhaps. Because Shakespeare was a very early modern writer, his plays and poems chronicle precisely the period during which the idols Bacon abjures and Don Quijote's windmills are written in the past, as belonging to the world of resemblance (Foucault 1994). Nevertheless, contra critical rewritings of reason as the force of "progress," I choose to appropriate the tale of Caliban's subjection as a metaphor that reads global subjects otherwise. Because they are products of "books," (i.e., *modern text*), which are as productive as Prospero's book, the "voices" crowding the postmodern salon at the apogee of the politics of representation can be "heard," comprehended. For they emerge in modern political grammar, in the political-symbolic moment of the nation-state, the foremost modern political subject—the juridical, economic, and moral collective that universal reason sustains—which now struggles for sovereignty in an increasingly Hobbesian global space. Throughout the twentieth century, under the rule of the principle of nationality, I contend, both former European colonial powers and the others of Europe (on the American continent, in the colonies of Asia and Africa, and in other areas never under official colonial subjection) deployed the historical signifier (the nation) and the global signifiers (the racial and the cultural) to write their particular version of the subject of transcendental poesis. Neither the citizen, the "individual," subject of the state and the juridical (universal) thing of liberal theorizing, nor the national subject, the moral (historical) thing, can describe them because the political things inhabiting the contemporary global configuration are global/historical subjects. To be sure, their political demands would not hold without the arsenal, the analytics of raciality, that circumscribes the region of application of the principles, self-determination and universality, presupposed in their demands for recognition.

What the strategies of engulfment of the arsenal of raciality, the racial and the cultural, accomplish is to resolve and reconcile the *places* of deployment of Prospero's powers by writing the difference between Europe and other global regions as an effect of that which has been claimed to mark post-Enlightenment Europe's particularity to sustain the claim that its social configurations actualize a self-determined transparent (interior-temporal) I. From the initial deployment of racial difference as a social scientific signifier, it has consistently rewritten post-Enlightenment European social configurations and social subjects in transparency. On the one hand, it constructs the heirs of yesterday's natives as modern Calibans, "strangers" whose racial difference produces the affectable (unbecoming/pathological) moral configurations bringing about their subjection. On the other hand, it entails signifying strategies that engulf the globe—namely, "civilization," "modernization," and "globalization"—which retain as a presupposition the science of man's writing of Africa, Asia, and Latin America as subaltern global regions. By addressing these effects of raciality simultaneously, I indicate that, rather than an effect of unbecoming (improper cultural or ideological) strategies of power, the racial configures the globe as a modern signifying context, and in doing so it announces-postpones the "Other" ontological horizon globality threatens to refigure, the horizon of death. For this reason,

welcoming the moral ease the sociohistorical logic of exclusion allows the critical "post" (-modern, -colonial, -Marxist, -structuralist)
writer to remain fully safe in the *stage of interiority,* suspicious of
scientific signification and yet reverent toward scientific claims of
innocence, as the refusal to engage productivity belies, he is unable to
engage globality as a modern ontoepistemological context.

What I am highlighting here is the predicament entailed by the
insistence of "post" critics of modern thought that historicity constitutes the only road to emancipation. Though I have advanced this
argument in the previous pages, I return to it here to indicate why,
instead of embracing historicity to articulate another demand for
the expansion of universality, I choose to displace both descriptors
not by rejecting them but by charting their context of emergence,
namely, the modern text. To situate my argument, I will engage a
recent addition to the critical library to explore other effects of embracing the transparency thesis. In *Provincializing Europe,* Dipesh
Chakrabarty (2000) introduces a version of historicity with which
he attempts to recuperate the Indian postcolonial trajectory from
what he calls the "ideology of historicism." At the core of this ideology, in which "historical time" becomes a "measure of cultural
distance," is the argument that "progress or 'development,'" which
started first in Europe, would, in time, necessarily reach all regions
of the globe (8). This argument locates the others of Europe in the
"not yet" of history, which Chakrabarty defines as the "global ideology" that facilitates European domination of the global space by
telling the colonized "to wait." In postcolonial scholarship, the pervasiveness of historicism, combined with a need to engage "secular universals" determined by their commitment to social justice,
prevails in accounts that treat local intellectual traditions "as truly
dead, as history." What his project of "provincializing Europe" provides, he argues, is a reconceptualization of history and the political
itself that captures "the experience of political modernity in a country like India" (6) because it advances a conception of the political
that includes the histories of "gods and spirits," the ones that enter
postmodern or modern historiography as always already outside the
movement of universal (rational-scientific) history.

When attempting to recuperate these histories of "gods and spirits," Chakrabarty returns to classical historical materialism, which,
stripped of its own version of the "stagiest theory of history" and

combined with Heidegger's concern with "questions of belonging and diversity," allow him to manufacture a strategy of historical analysis that will "destabilize this abstract figure of the universal human" that the ideology of historicism has inherited from the scientific construction of time (19). In Marx's account of capital, he identifies two histories: History 1, the empty history of capital, and History 2, which assumes that under the capitalist mode of production there exist "ways of being human [which] will be acted out in manners that do not lend themselves to the reproduction of the logic of capital" and allows for a "politics of human belonging and diversity" (67). Embracing "History 2," Chakrabarty recuperates Herder's *interiorized poesis,* through Heidegger's version of it, from the yoke of productive *nomos* and the disenchanted "master" and "subaltern" histories that it produces. If the reader has any doubt, I will make it explicit: we have reached a *better* history, not the one of the historians "from below," not Hegel's "true universality," but a *truly inclusive* history that, without mediation, without the assumption of universality (the universality of the productive *nomos,* that is), reconstitutes human beings as differentiated solely in terms of the "unities of multiplicity" that Herder's interiorized poesis produces. What this version of historicity produces, Chakrabarty argues, is a "pluralist history," one that includes histories in which "gods and spirits" are subjects, a history like that of the Bengali elites, for whom "Labor, as the activity of producing, is seldom a completely secular activity in India; it often entails, through rituals big and small, the invocation of the divine or superhuman presence" (72), the one that "secular histories" ignore because it is "disenchanted history, it is the idea of a godless, continuous, empty, and homogeneous time, which history shares with other social sciences and modern political philosophy as a basic building block" (75). What Chakrabarty's version of history allows, he claims, is a philosophical engagement with these "subaltern histories," "with questions of difference that are elided in dominant traditions of Marxism" (94).

With this invitation to contemplate the other ways of "being and belonging" and the histories they write, Chakrabarty fully returns to universal poesis. Never explicit, though it is suggested all along as he invokes Heidegger, Gadamer, Marx, Weber, and Nietzsche—all dissatisfied German "historicists" on their own terms, but never Leibniz or Herder—this invitation to reconsider my qualms with historicity dissipates as the limits of his historical rewriting of the others of Europe become more evident. How? When Chakrabarty defines precisely the kind of "subaltern history" he wishes to include in the scene of representation. What "subaltern pasts" capture are the histories of "gods and spirits," which "do not belong exclusively to socially subordinate or subaltern groups, not to minority identities alone. Elite and dominant groups can also have subaltern pasts to the extent that they participate in life-worlds subordinated by the 'major' narratives of the dominant institutions" (101). How would such a "subversive" history, Chakrabarty's own version of universal poesis, look like? He answers this question in the second part of his book, where he revisits the Bengali nationalist elite texts to write an "affective" history. I will not follow him all the way there. Instead I ask why he chose the Santals' rebellious god to construct the nationalist elites' history as a "subaltern past," one that invites us to contemplate other possibilities of being human, other modes of "being in the world," and to appreciate a history that belongs to "gods and spirits."

Perhaps this is the wayward social scientist in me, but she cannot be held responsible for my inability to appreciate and celebrate better historicity. She cannot explain why I agree with Spivak that the subaltern cannot speak, that when emerging in modern representation, through whatever version of the play of reason (universal *nomos,* universal poesis, transcendental poesis, or productive *nomos*), the subaltern is always already inscribed in the larger text, the context of signification in which the others of Europe acquire the names one deploys today even in the most radical and brilliant critics of the text that delimits their place of emergence. When sublating and reducing the peasant Santals into the Bengali elites' "history," Chakrabarty rewrites "subaltern history" as a sort of transcendental history. Because, much like universality, the descriptor *historicity* is resolved in transcendentality, it institutes the others of Europe (a) as "not yet" modern, (b) as always already anthropological subjects, or (c) as subjects of "resisting" or as enchanted subjects of "singular histories" of gods and spirits. My point is that reincarnating Herder via Heidegger to write "history" against Hegel or Marx's "History 1" is a smart trick, but it is no subversive magic. I hear Prospero's laugh as Caliban now rehearses his productive power by selectively reading his books. I hear Nietzsche's madman laughing at Nietzsche's own limited comprehension of the predicament he intuited. I find the dead subject, *homo historicus,* resuscitated in texts that aim to reenact his killing by choosing his (interior or historic) soul over his (exterior or scientific) body, his warm blood over his dead flesh.

The predicament of the postcolonial critic of modern representation resides not in that the interested disciplines—anthropology, sociology, and history—cannot forfeit productive *nomos* and will necessarily write the others of Europe as a contemporaneous *before;* it lies, instead, in an inability to fully engage their *now.* For, like the modern poet, they rewrite the scene of representation, from which they denounce "'scientific' fabrications." What this return to poesis, to a reopening of the universe of human possibilities—as Chakrabarty's own choice of literate elites indicates—assumes is no more than a conception of difference that is immediately translated back into a comprehensible grammar and lexicon, the text of interiority, which allows the forfeiting of the mediation of scientific universality. For the subject of "gods and spirits," written against or despite the subjects of productive *nomos,* remains a (modern) subject of historicity, for its "singularity" is only another example of humanity's (universal) productive force; it is a self-consciousness, a thing not determined from without, one that cannot signify the disturbing, deferring trace, as Chakrabarty hopes it will do, because it resists in "plurality and diversity," because it brings "others" into the scene of representation but never disassembles the theater it shares with the scene of (scientific) regulation. The politics of representation finds its limit in its own conditions of possibility, namely, the modern text. To embrace historical signification, to opt for writing the "subaltern past" against what is empty (chronological history and scientific signification), is but to add another version of the founding statements of modern thought, where the rewriting of the play of reason as transcendental poesis renders it evident that the transparent I, *homo historicus,* could not come into being without displacing, negating, or engulfing all that challenges its claim to self-determination, without statements that seek to comprehend anything that renders it but another mode of being human.

For this reason, because the choice between the universality of regulation and the universality of representation keeps "post" critics fully within the text they attempt to deconstruct, I have chosen to embrace this predicament. Instead of searching for other forms of poesis to once again challenge *nomos,* I have decided to indicate how the region of subalternity, the position of those who cannot be brought into modern representation without being resolved into one of these dimensions of modern representation, has come to be delimited. Not, as said before, by identifying other moments of exclusion but by reading the texts that reproduce their exteriority, the ones that, though never fully closing the possibility that they would participate in the rituals of modern political existence, the rituals of democracy, have ensured that they will never benefit from the entitlements it presumes. Although Chakrabarty's approach does address the kind of linearity introduced by scientific rewritings of history, his writing of historicism as an ideology that produces the colonized as eternally unprepared for self-determination stops short of the radical critique of modern ontology that it promises. What I am suggesting here is that Chakrabarty, much like other "post" critics I engaged earlier, for he moves toward an interpretation of Indian nationalist elites' history in which, rather than a contradiction, he finds a rejection of what he calls a "stagiest theory of history," reproduces the very distinction between modern political subjects that informs the kind of "historicism" he denounces. Put differently, from Indian particularity he moves on to describe this particular historical subject without further investigating the ways in which that particularity need not be translated, for it makes sense only in the grammar that institutes it. In short, before Indian could become a "nonmodern" historical subject, it had to be constructed as an other of Europe, a global subaltern subject, something to which India's elites may have contributed and from which they have certainly benefited, but it was neither of their own (nor of the British imperialist) making because it was the context within which their (racial/cultural) difference could be represented.

BEFORE HISTORICITY

What I am proposing here is neither a philosophy nor a theory of the subject. My modest move is to recuperate globality as a modern ontoepistemological context. Though, as noted earlier, I acknowledge the centrality of historical signification, I am convinced that without an engagement with scientific signification our critical strategies will remain at best irrelevant and at worst will add to the political-symbolic arsenal that consistently (re)produces the others of Europe as global subaltern subjects. To situate this critical strategy, I return to historical materialism, where instead of better historicity I find a critique of modern thought, a delineation of a social ontology that more productively challenges both the *scene of regulation* (Locke's version of universal *nomos*) and the *scene of representation* (in Herder's interiorized poesis and Hegel's transcendental poesis). Precisely because it does so by rewriting the scene of representation, historical materialism both promises to produce and avoids producing a social ontology that acknowledges that modern subjects presume both ontological contexts, namely, historicity and globality. Beginning with the "promises," I read the notion of material production as an attempt to recuperate exteriority from the entrails of transcendental poesis. Beyond the "inversion" of Hegel's dialectical account of history and the radicalizing of Adam Smith's conception of labor, the historical materialist rebuilding of the stage of interiority constitutes a powerful critique of modern thought precisely because of how it deploys scientific universality to produce a social ontology that centers *affectability*—one that addresses the relationships in which human beings engage in the (re)production of material (bodily and social) existence. What the rewriting of labor as a tool of productive *nomos* promises to fully explore but does not is the possibility that the stage of exteriority constitutes the privileged ontoepistemological moment.

Following the version of reason as productive *nomos,* the historical materialist critique of modern thought attributes the main role in the scene of engulfment to a tool of scientific reason, the laws of material production. By displacing transcendental poesis as an "ideal," "illusory" rendering of the force of history, historical materialism briefly moves self-consciousness to the stage of exteriority. At the center of this transformation is a union of nature and history through the notion of labor, which now as a concept (an abstract construct) writes human self-productivity as the universal, the objective, producer of wealth, because it is the actualization not of freedom but of necessity. Although it attacks transcendental poesis with its own tools to reveal the latter as "ideology," its task is to aid in the realization of history, serving as an instrument of the last revolutionary class. When mapping post-Enlightenment social configuration, by describing the instruments and relations of material (economic) production and the juridical (state) and cultural forms, the conditions under which "actual," "real" man "makes history," historical materialism follows the logic of discovery to deploy strategies that produce social phenomena as the effects of exterior determinants the operations of which can be made accessible and controlled by human beings, but which are not of their own making.

In *Grundrisse,* Karl Marx ([1857–68] 1993), anticipates the procedures he deploys in *Capital* ([1867] 1977) when he attacks the method of (liberal) political economic analysis. His first move is to deploy productive *nomos* to show how and why the social is a proper object of scientific reason. "The scientific correct method," he argues, is the one that assumes that economic categories already constitute a mental processing of "the concrete," representations of the "real subject" of history, society, where "individuals" are already differentiated according to their placement in material production (101), according to their particular "stage of [historical] development." That is, he introduces an account of relationship between knowledge and the "real" that is consistent with transcendental poesis, that is, as a movement of universalization. Not surprisingly, he chooses the United States as exemplary of a capitalist social configuration where there is "indifference towards any specific kind of labor [which] presupposes a very developed totality of real kinds of labor, of which no single one is any longer predominant" (104). The capitalist mode of production, "the most developed and the most complex historic organization of production," he argues—evidently substituting "economic development" for Herder's "moral development" and hijacking the Enlightenment notion of "progress,"—results from the laws of [material] development that account for the successive emergence and obliteration of the modes of production and social conditions that characterize the Marxist version of "world history." For it is precisely because this stage of material (economic) development, industrial production, results from exterior determinants that the "categories which express its relations, the comprehension of its structure . . . also allow insights into the structure and the relations of production of all the vanished social formation out of whose ruins and elements it built itself up, whose partly still unconquered remnants are carried along with it, whose mere nuances have developed explicit significance within it" (105). That is, in classic historical materialism, the universality of differentiation is the effect not of universal poesis, as in Herder, but of productive *nomos.*

Nevertheless, while productive *nomos* constitutes the "true" productive force of history, historical materialism does not write a social ontology premised on exteriority-spatiality. In *The German Ideology,* Karl Marx and Friedrich Engels's (1947) critique of early nineteenth-century Hegelian philosophers, the rewriting of History and self-consciousness as effects of a double exteriority—that is, that of universal regulation (laws of production) and social relationships— retains self-determination as the singular attribute of the *homo historicus.* Here they perform the famous inversion in which material (as opposed to spirit's, the "idea's") production—that is, the necessity of satisfying needs rather than freedom of will—becomes a universal productive force—the producer and product, cause and effect, of human self-productivity. "The way in which men produce their means of subsistence," they argue, "depends first of all on the nature of the actual means they find in existence and have to reproduce. This mode of production must not be considered simply as being the reproduction of the physical existence of the individuals. Rather it is a definite mode of life on their part. As individuals express their life, so they are. What they are, therefore, coincides with their production, both with what they produce and with how they produce. The nature of individuals thus depends on the material conditions determining their production" (8). For Marx and Engels, these conditions are those of the interdependent men and women who relate to each other in the production of their "conditions of existence," as the agents of History. With this statement they place relationships at the basis of history and refashion self-consciousness as a thing of "necessity," which is, as seen in Part 1, an attribute of that which is apprehended by the tools of the *nomos.* That is, it is "necessity," a mode of the regulating reason, that produces historical consciousness, the moral collectivities, which in Herder's version of universal poesis and in Hegel's transcendental poesis are guided by Spirit, the universal subject of poesis. "The production of ideas, of conceptions, of consciousness," they argue, "is at first directly interwoven with the material activity and the material intercourse of men, the language of real life. . . . The same applies to mental production as expressed in the language of the politics, laws, morality, religion, metaphysics of a people. Men are the producers of their conceptions, ideas, etc—real, active men, *as they are conditioned by a definite development of their productive forces and*

of the intercourse corresponding to these, up to its furthest form"
(18, my emphasis). Nevertheless, even as it writes self-consciousness
as an effect of the laws of history, as what expresses the "actual,"
conditions under which "individuals," as members of an economic
ensemble (a class) exist, historical materialism retains the construction of exteriority introduced in the account of universal *nomos,* but
now it both regulates and produces human beings' (re)production
of their "material"/"actual" (physical reproduction and economic
production, i.e., bodily and social) "conditions of existence" and,
consequently, human consciousness.

What does not take place here is the radical gesture that would
turn modern representation on its head. Historical materialism would
not inaugurate a social ontology premised on globality (exteriority-
spatiality), one in which the political would constitute an effect neither
of (constraining) self-regulation nor of (uniting) self-representation,
but of the relationships necessary for the production of conditions of
existence. For Marx and Engels's text retains the transparency thesis,
the ontological assumption that writes self-consciousness as a self-
determined thing. In the historical materialist's version of the play of
engulfment, the moment of transparency is postponed to the moment
when the proletariat recognizes the "true" nature of its existence as
the dominated/exploited class, when the movement of history—the
play of class struggles determined by the laws of production—comes
to an end. What I am suggesting is that, because historical materialism does not relinquish interiority, it rewrites self-consciousness in
transparency. In other words, its limits reside precisely in that, although classical historical materialism relies on the idea of law, universal reason as a constraining force (in its scientific instantiation)—
in its centering of materiality (of the laboring body [the principal
instrument] and of human relationships [at once agent and effect]
of production), the privileging of the "real/divided" society over the
"ideal/unified" nation, as the subject of History—retains recognition
as the sine qua non of proletarian emancipation.

My point is that Marx's critique of transcendental poesis retains
the promise of historicity, transparency, when reinstituting its limits
as it rewrites the social back into the scene of regulation. Not surprisingly, "post" critics such as Spivak and Chakrabarty, like Gramsci
and others before them, have no problem embracing better historicity. In the historical materialist montage of the scene of engulfment—

its resolution of historicity into scientific universality—the transparency thesis remains the ethical presupposition, as a promise, in the statement that the laws of material production, the tool of universal reason that entails universalization of "conditions of existence," became lived "reality" only in post-Enlightenment, post–Industrial Revolution social configurations. Only then, when the "true" productive forces (social labor) of History became transparent, did "actual" human beings achieve self-determination (self-consciousness) both (a) in the Cartesian/Lockean sense, as they actually decided upon their existence and essence and the juridico-economic conditions under which they existed as a collectivity, and, (b) in the Herderian/Hegelian sense, as they recognized that it was a product of their own self-productive capacity. Hence, the limits of historicity, its spatial/temporal termination, is once again reinstated in the deployment of scientific universality, which maintains that the moment of transparency has been achieved in the social configuration where the full development of material productive forces leads to the emergence of juridical (of law and the state) and cultural forms, and of a consciousness (self-consciousness) to which the "laws of history" have become transparent to its agents. Much like transcendental poesis, classic historical materialism locates the condition for this "world-historical" event, the proletarian revolution, and the new, just, social conditions it would entail, communism—the actualization of freedom—in Europe.

Nevertheless, classical historical materialism's rewriting of history as an effect of productive *nomos* indicates that, even though ruled by the principle of transcendentality, nineteenth-century writings of man and society as objects of scientific reason harbored a productive uneasiness. In the trajectory of the historical materialist project itself, the negative effects of this uneasiness appeared in self-defeating accusations of "scientificism" (determinism and positivism), which were returned with accusations of "historicism" (idealism and humanism), while its positive, productive effects appeared in twentieth-century rewritings that engaged precisely that which in the classic formulation remained incomplete, the need to address modern representation as a political moment, which became all the more central in the latter part of the nineteenth century, when the nation, which belongs to the scene of representation, became a necessary modern political signifier.[1]

My interest here is in the promises this uneasiness holds, the ones that appear in the historical materialist writing of the social as a domain of operation of power, which is neither a result of instituted laws, the ones "individuals" agree to obey, nor the product of self-consciousness already-in-the-moment-of-transparency. When writing consciousness as an effect of material production, Marx and Engels did more than introduce the social as an object of investigation, as teachers of sociology prefer to emphasize. More important, in the centering of "actual conditions," symbolic and actual relationships, the political moment opened up the possibility of a critical analysis of the social in which spatiality—where "being and meaning" emerge in exteriority-affectability—became the privileged moment of signification. Though, as noted before, it resolved this exterior-spatial in modern representation as an effect of universal (productive) *nomos,* by positing (social) relationships as also exterior producers of consciousness, it opened up the possibility that had been kept at bay as long as self-consciousness was not appropriated in the mode of signification ruled by exteriority, the field of science. By insisting that this is only a possibility, I acknowledge that the historical materialist critique remained fully within modern representation, for it ultimately reinstituted self-determination, the attribute of interior things, even though it came into being only after the dissipation of conditions of material production and the full realization (actualization) of the productive laws governing it. In Marx's account, affectability was once again resolved not through "partial" violence—displacement, negation, or engulfment of exteriority—but in a radical signifying gesture, an act of "total violence," the realization of the principle of death, which erased it as a possible ontological horizon, a mode of existence, as it could appear only in an account of History as an eschatology (Foucault 1994).

For this reason, because it takes exteriority as the starting point of an account that locates the moment of transparency after the destruction of the Stage of Life, while holding onto the promises of historicity that it extends beyond its "End"—where it points to what Jacques Derrida (1994) calls a hauntology—classic historical materialism peers into the theater of globality, the "Other" ontological context announced by exteriority, just to immediately enclose it between the a priori Law of Material Production (the necessity that moves History) and the a posteriori Life of Freedom (the social conditions emerging "after" history, i.e., communism). And yet, precisely because in doing so classic historical materialism offers exteriority as a powerful point of departure for the critique of modern representation, it charts a terrain for a critical analysis of the social itself, which neither presumes nor immediately returns to the mapping of modern social conditions as a territory constituted solely by representations ruled by the principle of transcendentality. My point is that, as classic historical materialism itself has become another producer of accounts of the self-consciousness that refuse to presuppose transparency, it also exemplifies the cruciality of an engagement with scientific signification, which has from its very moment of emergence, as Marx and Engels's revolutionary desire indicates, been involved in the symbolic mapping of the social configurations they investigated. In the following, I pursue the promises of classic historical materialism to propose a critical strategy of social analyses, a remapping of the modern social configuration, which displaces both the transparency thesis and the "ideological" argument that prevail in "post" critiques of modern thought, in critical racial theorizing, and in critical analyses of the nation.

AN OUTLINE OF THE GLOBAL/HISTORICAL CONSCIOUSNESS

With the critical device *national text* I describe narratives of the nation as political-symbolic contexts that refigure both globality and historicity as ontological contexts. Precisely because it takes scientific signification seriously and reads exteriority as a tool and an effect of modern signification, unlike the ideological argument, the national text guides a critique of modern representation that does not crumble before the critical task. Neither reflexively embracing historicity nor presuming an untapped reservoir of "truth," of "reality," for it assumes that the latter can be sifted with "truly universal," scientific or historic gestures, the national text, avoids the deadlock of postmodern historicity, which either presupposes or produces transparent (ethical) collectivities. Not, as noted before, by seeking outside modern representation that not-yet-tapped reservoir of "innocence," but by reading it against the grain; that is, much like Foucault, I read the desire for "discovery" as an instance of the production of modern political-symbolic strategies, one that explores the "Other" possible ontological context, the Global, as the privileged epistemological context for advancing a critique of modern representation, which is also a modern contra-ontology.

My chosen examples here are precisely the postcolonial nationalist statements that could not deploy "gods and spirits" to write the "singular" ways in which they are constituted as modern political subjects, as nation-states, as particular versions of the *homo historicus,* the transparent I. In my description of transcendental poesis, I indicate how, when Hegel refashioned the universal *nomos* and universal poesis, he identified the state and the nation as, respectively, the formal and substantive actualizations of the transcendental subject in the moment of the people or the nation. Precisely this version of the nation was consolidated in the last quarter of the nineteenth century. My argument here is that, though productive and consistent with the ontological privileging of interiority, Hegel's resolution has not been sufficient. For, as Arendt's (1979) analysis of imperialism and Hobsbawm's (1994a) history of the long nineteenth century suggest, the late nineteenth century saw the emergence of two distinct signifiers of human difference. In the period between 1875 and the 1930s, while the nation guided the reconfiguring of European borders, the racial would reorganize the global space. More important, the nation as a signifier of historicity would become a political signifier, for becoming a nationality, a transparent (interior-temporal) I would constitute a criterion for writing a collectivity as a modern political subject.[2] Following the prevailing tendency to write the racial as an unbecoming strategy of power, critical analyses of the nation (and nationalism) usually address its role as a political category that operates as a negative principle in narratives of the nation.

Most accounts of the "origin" of modern nation-states focus primarily on specifically European historical processes that culminated with the constitution of the territorial, economic, and political entities the world came to know in the nineteenth century (Tilly 1975). Nevertheless, even as they focus on "nationalism," the force producing the idea of the nation as an "objective entity," as the ideological strategy and write the nation as an "imagined community" or a "myth," critical analysts of the nation agree that by the end of the last century, producing a people as a national subject, as the product and agent of the temporal trajectory that actualizes its "intrinsic difference"—not as an isolated moral collective but as always already a moment, a particular actualization, of the transcendental I—would become central for defining their position in the global space. Under these conditions, the nation constituted a fundamental dimension of the modern political subject, because the construction of a collectivity as an interior-temporal thing, a transparent I, was central to support claims of sovereignty (self-determination), the juridical and military control of a given territory, and the right and ability to explore its economic resources, as well as the dominion of distinct peoples inhabiting the same territory and the colonial appropriation of other regions of the global space (Anderson 1983; Gellner 1983; Hobsbawm 1994b).

In *Imagined Communities,* Benedict Anderson (1983) describes the material (economic) and cultural conditions of emergence of these "imagined communities" of power, these "kingdoms of History." He defines the nation as a "cultural artifact" resulting from cultural transformations, such as European expansion, reformation, the Enlightenment, and the French Revolution, which entailed the demise of "religious community" and material transformations, such as "print capitalism," which enabled the emergence of a conception of "homogeneous, empty time." Though he provides an account of the emergence of the nation that more closely captures how it would constitute a privileged modern political category, as he identifies precisely the attributes of the nation spelled out in Hegel's and Renan's statements, the limits of Anderson's perspective become apparent when he turns to explain the emergence of national claims outside the European space. For instance, he argues that the post–Second World War "wave of nationalism" resulted from the "diffusion of the cultural and material conditions [of Europe] necessary for the emergence of this new form of community," which reflects the "achievements of industrial capitalism" that European imperialism had deployed in Africa and Asia. While this cannot be denied, Anderson's account fails to address the epistemological conditions under which the "diffusion" of European cultural (and material) constructs takes place, how the political-symbolic mapping of the global space determined the local appropriation of these "imports."[3] Much of the problem in comprehending earlier and later postcolonial national narratives derives, I think, from the pervasiveness of the sociohistorical logic of exclusion. Following the prevailing ethical rejection of the racial, critical analysts of the nation argue that the claim for "racial commonality" is a negative, an added ideological strategy to institute national homogeneity, which as noted before has resulted in its being considered a political category only when it operates as an exclusionary strategy.[4]

My reading of the U.S. American and the Brazilian national texts departs from this view, for I engage in a charting of the effects of the deployment of raciality in statements that write these nations' particularity. My objective is to show how the particular appropriations of the signifying strategies produced by the science of man, anthropology, and race relations have enabled the writing of these American subjects within the moment of transparency. With this, I introduce a critical strategy of social analysis that privileges the political-symbolic moment of modern social configurations. Instead of historicity, I read statements that write national subjects as political (historic) texts that include signifiers of historicity and globality. I hope to indicate how the historical subject is always already a racial "I"; it emerges situated, always already produced in relation to an "other," a racial "other," for both are produced in signifying contexts constituted by historic and scientific strategies. In other words, I read the national subject, the particular subject of transcendental poesis, as also a product of the analytics of raciality.

The national text captures a full-fashioned *homo modernus,* a specimen of the *homo historicus* that stands, as another specimen of the *homo scientificus,* before the *affectable I*'s the racial institutes— that is, a global/historical subject. That is, the national text addresses narratives of the nation as an instance of productive violent political statements that reproduce the "others of Europe" as affectable consciousness (fully submitted to the tools of *nomos*) in order to re-place the national (historical) subject in transparency. My reading shows how, when deployed in these historical texts, the arsenal of raciality authorizes projects of social (re)configuration as it prescribes how its inhabitants participate in the nation's present and how they will perform in its future without ever accounting for their being placed in its past; it shows how the analytics of raciality institutes historical subjects; how it delimits the teleology, the particular version of transcendental poesis; how its political-symbolic strategies produce the national subject as a specimen of the *homo modernus,* that is, as a global/historical subject.

9

The Spirit of Liberalism

To me most certainly the United States did not seem a foreign country. It was simply English with a difference.
— JOHN G. BROOKS, *AS THE OTHERS SEE US*

Notwithstanding the U.S. liberal-capitalist configuration, at the turn of the twentieth century Europeans still questioned whether their North American cousins were building a "modern civilization." Most doubted that its "progress," economic prosperity, and democracy actualized a particular historical collective, that the people of the United States constituted a "spiritual individuality," that is, a nation. In Brander Mathews's (1906) reply to an unnamed French journalist, he indicates that such doubting could not be taken lightly: what Europeans call a "money-making" attitude behind U.S. economic prosperity, he says, was inherited from Pilgrim settlers whose courage and aggressiveness were pivotal for the conquest of the wild American land. Many late nineteenth-century commentaries on the "American civilization" also noted the harmful effects of its juridical configuration, how "unlimited equality" affected the emerging American "spirit," how it would prevent the development of distinct moral and aesthetic principles. Linking political equality and the decline of "civilization" in this way was not new. Earlier in the nineteenth century, Tocqueville (1969) had observed that, of the principles U.S. Americans had inherited from their European ancestors, democracy

197

had been the one they had developed the most. "Equality of conditions," he recognized, was the necessary outcome of "progress," but the United States was the only "modern civilization" where democracy had a firm hold on institutions and "mores." Nevertheless, political equality threatened the nation's "spirit." The "power of majority," its heightened moral and political authority, he argued, posed a serious threat to "the institutions and the character" of the United States. Not only does majority rule hamper political dissent and, by concentrating power in the hands of lawmakers, considerably weaken the executive's authority; it also stalls artistic genius. "Literary genius," he observed, "cannot exist without freedom of spirit, and there is no freedom of spirit in America" (256).

What supported Europeans' statements on the ill effects of "unlimited equality" if democracy constituted the greatest gift post-Enlightened Europeans claimed to have given to humanity? Mathew Arnold's (1888) comments on the "civilization of the United States" suggest that they aimed at demarcating a *moral* distinction between the United States and Europe. The United States, Arnold recognizes, had answered the political and economic challenges of "modern civilization," but it had yet to achieve that which characterizes "civilization" itself, the realization of the higher "ends" of humanity. Precisely that which enabled U.S. Americans to accomplish the economic aims of modernity, Arnold notes, prevented the development of that quality necessary for "spiritual progress," the building of "complete human life" (3), that is, a "sense of distinction." Everything in America, Arnold claims, "is against distinction . . . and against the sense of elevation to be gained through admiring and respecting it. The glorification of the 'average man' . . . is against it" (9). Most probably, then, accusations of lack of "distinction," of "spirit," were reactions to U.S. Americans' celebration of their rapid accession to global political-economic hegemony. Regardless of the possible motives, these comments on U.S. Americans' "culture and civilization" are significant because, when deployed to differentiate U.S. Americans from Europeans, they conveyed an irreducible (spatial) difference to which writers of the U.S. American nation immediately responded.

My task in this chapter is to describe how the arsenal of the *analytics of raciality* enables articulation of the U.S. American subject as a *transparent "I"* as it dissipates the distance between the American and the European continent by writing the white (Anglo-Saxon) body as a signifier of a European consciousness. What my analysis of statements deployed between the 1880s and the 1930s will show is how the articulation of racial difference institutes an ontological account in which the bridging of this distance, which represents colonial dislocation, enables the writing of the U.S. "spirit" as a further developed manifestation of post-Enlightenment European principles. Following the narrative of *transcendental poesis,* the writers of the U.S. American nation deploy statements that produce a transparent I and a social configuration that actualize the principles this version of the play of reason sustains, namely, universality and self-determination. When doing so, however, they face a challenge that is only intimated in the European commentaries described earlier but that is explicitly articulated in their writings, which is the fact that, by the late 1800s, globality already informed fashionings of self-consciousness. For not only is the United States situated in a different global region; it also had to deal with the effects of early colonial deployments of European power and desire—more specifically, the appropriation of lands, resources, and labor, out of which the United States itself emerged—which produced social configurations Europeans were condemned to share with their "others."

It is not surprising that racial difference would become, and remains, a crucial political-symbolic strategy in ontologies of the U.S. subject and the guiding signifier of descriptions of the U.S. social configuration. Without the white body, the writers of the U.S. nation would not be able to resolve the distance that threatens to locate it in *affectability,* as European comments on its lack of "spirit" and "distinction" suggest, regardless of its economic and juridical accomplishments, nor would they be able to ensure that the U.S. social configuration, "progress" itself, actualizes a self-consciousness that could have and had emerged only in Europe; that is, they would not be able to write the U.S. American as a specimen of *homo historicus,* a transparent I. What I gather in these writings is an ontological account, the national text, in which self-consciousness always already emerges in contention, in a relationship that takes place at the level of the symbolic, one in which the transparent I be/comes (comes into being as a self-determined thing) against that which needs to be written as not the same as itself, that is, an affectable "other," the bearer of a difference that cannot be resolved (sublated or reduced) in time. In short, my reading shows how the U.S. national subject, the liberal "I" actualized in the U.S. social (juridical, economic, and moral) configuration, was manufactured at the same time and with the same political-symbolic strategies, the tools of raciality, that produced its subaltern "others." As I do so, I indicate that the unequal placing of the descendants of the "others of Europe" before the principle of universality, the one said to alone govern the U.S. juridical and economic moments, was not an immediate effect of their God-given racial traits—resulting from prejudice, false beliefs and ideologies, and acts of discrimination—but that racial difference, the *strategy of particularization* that has produced the U.S. American as a European being, has also governed these moments of the U.S. social configuration as it has established the ethical place, the one transcendentality rules, on which the latter alone stands.[1]

"WE, THE (ANGLO-SAXON) PEOPLE"

Madison Grant's call for action, unleashed in his introduction to Lothrop Stoddard's (1920) *The Rising Tide of Color against White World Supremacy,* conveys a message repeated in most statements on U.S. American particularity that proliferated in the first decades of the twentieth century. Hegel's "land of the future" was under a threat, invaded by Eastern and Southern European immigrants from the East, blacks from the South, and Chinese and Japanese from the West. In the thirty years preceding the First World War, the physical frontier was being replaced by the "rising of the industrial metropolis" (Paxton 1920).[2] Not only did this period see the appearance of the automobile, the introduction of Taylorism, city planning, the beginnings of suburbanization and urbanization, and the efforts to improve adult education and scientific farming; it also witnessed the first wave of Eastern and Southern European immigration. Between 1900 and 1910, three million foreign-born whites resided in the United States.[3] The demographic changes animating Madison Grant's call on the ("Anglo-Saxon") working class to maintain the "racial integrity" of the nation, which they eventually heard as the ambiguous alliances between organized labor, farmers, the federal government, and reformers of all kinds,[4] guaranteed the passage of a number of legislative acts that aimed not only to "restrict the voracity of big monopolies" and to promote social reforms, but also to restrict immigration (Wish 1945). Moreover, as many historians have noted, U.S. prosperity did not result only from the accumulation of large individual fortunes and capitalist smartness; the rise of the country to the status of major global economic power was also attributed to a political reconfiguration.[5] The most important political event was the "segregation compromise," which gave Southerners the freedom to deal with the black population at their discretion. The "North abandonment of the Negro," as Beard (1913) states, was consolidated in a juridical statement, the Supreme Court decision to uphold the Southern states' claims that "race relations" belonged to the domain of the private. The compromise that enabled the political unification crucial to the thorough industrialization of the U.S. American space, which facilitated the United States' subsequent global predominance, also entailed deployments of "partial" violations (Jim Crow legislation) and "total violations" (lynchings), which resulted in the first large black movement northward. In short, transregional and intranational migratory movements would become crucial in the writing of the U.S. American text, in the definition of who among the inhabitants of the United States should enjoy the benefits of "progress."[6]

What I find in the statements deployed between 1880 and 1930 is the fashioning of a global/historical consciousness, that is, the writing of the U.S. nation through the articulation of signifying strategies belonging to both regions of modern representation, namely, science and history. Following the prevailing narrative of transcendental poesis, these statements wrote the trajectory of the U.S. American subject as the realization of a transparent I. But to do so, U.S. American writers faced a challenge their European cousins could easily sidestep: the temporal trajectory they mapped took place fully outside Europe, in a global region they had, from the start, shared with "others of Europe." Though the historic signifier, the nation, could sustain statements that construed progress as the actualization of the particular U.S. American Spirit, it could not resolve this challenge because the analytics of raciality situates the American continent before the moment of transparency—a challenge that could be addressed only with the deployment of the arsenal of raciality to write the white ("Anglo-Saxon") body, the body housing the U.S. American mind, as an expression of a European consciousness. What I gather in these writings of the U.S. American nation are statements in which racial difference and cultural difference produced the place of the national subject, for they delimited the inhabitants of this postslavery polity whose ideas actualized and actions expressed the principles articulated in its juridical and economic dimensions, that is, universality and self-determination. On the one hand, whiteness connected bodily configuration to global region, instituting the American strand of the Anglo-Saxon and later Eastern and Southern European immigrants as proper signifiers of a transparent I. On the other hand, the physical attributes of Indians, blacks, and Asian immigrants became, as the text of race relations captures, signifiers of threatening but affectable consciousnesses that were either irrelevant (Indians and blacks), or would certainly perish, as U.S. (European/white) Americans fulfilled their historical destiny, that is, the building of a social configuration governed by universality and freedom (as individual self-determination). With this these physical attributes produced a moral differentiation, the distinction between subjects of transparency and affectability, which does not challenge the view that the U.S. American social configuration expresses post-Enlightenment European principles.

Following the spirit of transcendental poesis and the letter of *productive nomos,* these statements wrote the particularity U.S. American subject as an effect of Anglo-Saxon spiritual (moral) attributes. For instance, Strong (1885) claims that Americans' value of freedom and their religiosity were fundamental expressions of their European inheritance. "The Anglo-Saxon," he claims, "is the representative of two great ideas, which are closely related. One of them is that of civil liberty. Nearly all of the civil liberty in the world is enjoyed by Anglo-Saxons: the English, the British colonists, and the people of the United States" (25). Notice that this claim was not just a defense of a self-attributed racial superiority. When claiming liberty (self-determination) as a monopoly of the "Anglo-Saxon race," Strong establishes who among the inhabitants of the Unites States should be recognized as the proper social (juridical and economic) subjects. Moreover, the writing of U.S. Americans as a current of the Anglo-Saxon race also enabled the particular temporal trajectory of the American subject to be written in its discontinuity with English history without threatening claims of belonging in the moment of transparency.

In *The American People,* Maurice Low (1911) indicates this when stating that, contrary to the opinion shared by most Europeans, the

U.S. American people constituted a nationality that actualized fundamentally European (English) principles. "What the founders of the Republic in the beginning—and these were Englishmen and remained Englishmen until they became Americans—have endured," he argues, remains "fundamentally the same now as it was then, inspired by English training and English tradition; unchanged by other forces than English" (9). What transformed these "Englishmen" into "Americans" was, according to Low, turning away from England and identifying their economic interests with the new land. Against the (European) argument that freedom and equality hindered the development of a U.S. American spirit, Low spells out the particular features of the American spirit, its peculiar contribution to "modern civilization." Unquestionably, he claims, the United States constituted a modern nation. What kind of nation? Low's answer to this question conveys the sense of "essential" unity and individuality Hegel defines as crucial to the "Spirit of a People." The U.S. American nation is not only the passive product of its past; it is also a self-productive thing that strives to maintain and assert itself in the midst of all differences. In his description, Low indicates all the attributes of the U.S. American historical subject. "The elements that go to constitute a Nation are many, and all must be present to form nationality," he argues. Low lists various elements that can be divided into those pertaining to (a) the *scene of regulation,* internal juridical configuring, that is, "an unchallenged possession of the country from which a people derive their national name; a common attachment to the political and social system that they have created or that has descended to them; a belief in their own strength and individuality"; (b) the *scene of representation,* common cultural or moral attributes, that is, "a common language . . . ; a universality of religion or a tolerance of religion, that makes religion a matter of conscience between man and man and not under the control of the state; a literature that is truly national—i.e., that is based on heroic achievement or a struggle in defense of an ideal or to widen an idealistic conception"; and (c) the *scene of engulfment,* which situates the nation in the global space, that is, a "dominant virility that enables a people by imposing their own civilization to absorb and assimilate into themselves aborigines and aliens so that they become a part of, and do not remain apart from, the dominant race; uniform . . . code of moral and manners; so that in language as in thought, men find the same forms of action. Morality is not merely a matter of latitude, and there is no meridian of ethics; he who utters a sublime thought has a Nation for his audience" (230–31).

In other words, Low writes the U.S. American as a historical subject whose particularity is an effect of its liberal spirit. He describes the history of the United States as the actualization of English principles—in its language, literature, and morality—introduced by the first colonists and written in the nation's constitution and that remained unchanged despite contacts with the original natives of the American space, slavery, and later European immigration. "The institutions and ideals of America are English," he claims, "and although there was a simultaneous colonization of America by the English, the French, the Spanish, the Dutch, and the Swedes, it is only English speech and English customs and English ideals that have survived" (424). Low's statement is important because it constructs the U.S. American nation as the outcome of the deployment of English desire in the American space, modified only to meet the specificities of its environmental (geographic) conditions. More important, it deploys the grammar of the U.S. national text, which reappears in other rewritings. The demarcation of the place of this "English" subject, however, would require a construction of other inhabitants of the American space as consciousness that did not participate in the unfolding of the subject of "world history." In the following I show how the deployment of the racial to write Indians, blacks, and Asian immigrants in affectability instituted the logic of exclusion, which the arsenal of race relations so successfully captured and reproduced.

"Wild Woods"

Needless to say, the construction of the American continent as "empty land" has been central in the fashioning of self-consciousness as the liberal subject itself. When indicating how labor constitutes the basis for claims for private property, for instance, Locke ([1690] 1947) constructs "America" as a land that remains in the "state of nature"—"the wild woods and uncultivated waste . . . , left to nature, without any improvement, tillage, or husbandry" (139)—as if its inhabitants had failed to exceed the command of the law of nature (the law of reason) and act upon nature to produce more than that which is necessary for the preservation of human life. From Locke's formulation of property ownership as a requirement for "full participation in civil society" (Bauman and Briggs 2003) through the Enlightenment's, the science of man's, and the anthropological constructions of "civilization" that combine both meanings, the economic and political, to produce yesterday's "natives" as collectivities whose trajectories were oblivious to the determinants of freedom to Turner's deployment of the "frontier" to signify, as C. L. R. James (1993) writes, "the heroic quality of American individualism" (101), the figure of the American Indian wrote particularity, the place of the U.S. American subject in globality, for his obliteration constituted the condition of possibility for the building of a liberal-capitalist social configuration in the American continent.

Not surprisingly, the American "native" has from the outset occupied a troubled juridical position (Wilkins 1997). In the U.S. founding juridical documents, the Declaration of Independence and the Constitution, Indian tribes appear as foreign polities with which the newborn state would engage in the way sovereign collectivities relate to others, namely, trade, treaties, and war. Not long after the institution of the U.S. state, however, it was evident that two (or more) sovereign political bodies would not occupy the same territory, at least not when the economic configuration of one of them increasingly required more and more of the other's lands, natural resources, and exploitable labor. In *Worcester vs. Georgia* (1832) the Supreme Court decided against Georgia's claims of police rights in Cherokee land—the objective was to control white persons' access to mines found in that territory—by recalling that "the Indian nations had always been considered as distinct, independent political communities retaining their original natural rights as undisputed possessors of the soil, from time immemorial, with the single exception of that imposed by irresistible power, which excluded them from intercourse with any other European potentate than the first discoverer of the coast of the particular region claimed, and this was a restriction which those European potentates imposed on themselves, as well as on the Indians." However, as Justice John Marshall had indicated the previous year—when delivering the court's opinion in *Cherokee Nation vs. Georgia* (1831) he asked: "Do the Cherokees constitute a foreign state in the sense of the constitution?"—the Indian would be contemplated in juridical statements only to signify the land itself. For Marshall acknowledges that "the condition of the Indians in relation to the United States is perhaps unlike that of any other two people in existence. In the general, nations not owing a common allegiance are foreign to each other. The term foreign nation is, with strict propriety, applicable by either to the other. But the relation of the Indians to the United States is marked by peculiar and cardinal distinctions which exist nowhere else. The Indian Territory is admitted to compose a part of the United States. In all our maps, geographical treatises, histories, and laws, it is so considered."[7]

Even in the most idyllic moment of U.S. romanticism, the Indian is identified with nature—not Kantian *nature,* which was already a product of "pure reason," but the Lockean version of the "state of nature," that product of divine creation yet to be modified/appropriated by the rational thing. In statements on the U.S. American subject, the Indian is articulated to signify "the frontier," the "empty land" that served as the main trope in the writing of the U.S. subject; that is, the "native American" emerges as the embodiment of the wilderness upon which U.S. American subjects would inscribe their "civilization." That is, "regardless of whether the Indian was savage or noble," as Berkhofer (1979) argues, "he would inevitably be replaced by White civilization. The transition from wild, savage nature to a cultivated, domesticated garden in the American West was believed to be as certain as the westward movement of progress had been in European history" (92). The brief references to Indians in the writing of the U.S. American nation deployed between the 1880s and the 1930s indicate how the "original" inhabitants of the American space were written as those whose obliteration enabled the actualization of the U.S. American subject.

For the most part, these statements rehearsed the mid-nineteenth-century romanticism and referred to the earlier phase of Puritan settlement to construct the native inhabitants of the American space as those who, despite some "unfortunate" wars, had collaborated with the deployment of European power or desire in the "North." However, in the last phase (the middle to late 1800s) of the appropriation of the lands of the native of the American space, the final occupation and incorporation of the West and the Southwest, the "Indian" was articulated to signify the superiority and effectiveness of "Anglo-American civilization." These perspectives are implicit in Low's (1911) observation that, although the "Indian" had "exercised a certain influence upon the civilization of the white man," he was never able to impose his civilization on the Englishman or American, nor did "he in any lasting way modify or temper the civilization of the white man" (239). Certainly here we meet anthropology's "vanishing native." However, unlike U.S. twentieth-century anthropologists, who produced this figure as they traveled about seeking to rescue their "cultures" to include in the mosaic of humanity, these writers of the U.S. nation emphasized the "vanishing"; that is, they wrote the Indians' trajectory as a movement toward certain obliteration. Indians were vanishing, Hill (1933) argues, because they "were doomed from the beginning; yet for almost three hundred years they struggled to push back the white man. Their tragic failure has left with many Americans a curious sense of their unimportance" (17). Indeed, the statements that produced the obliteration of "the Indian" in the U.S. national text also reveal that the American Indian has never been unimportant to the writing of the U.S. American nation (Berkhofer 1979). Because "the frontier" indicated the "ever-rescinding" completion of the engulfment of the world west of Europe by European power or desire, "Indians" signified the boundaries of the U.S. American nation, the condition of possibility for the deployment of U.S. American desire. What I find here is the writing of the European and the Indian in an ontological context, globality, in which the former emerges as always already victorious in the "relationship of force," the contention necessary for the appropriation of these North American lands, because it produces this particular "other of Europe" as intrinsically affectable consciousness. The "vanishing Indian" instituted in the writings of the U.S. American subject has remained a conspicuous juridical-moral figure whose troubling position comments on the primary effect of the engulfment of the descendants of yesterday's American "natives," which has been to produce subjects that, though modern, do not inhabit the moment of transparency, that is, modern subjects that gaze but at the horizon of death.

"[E]masculated by a Peculiarly Complete System of Slavery"

On 2 February 1865, the U.S. Senate passed the bill that created the Bureau of Refugees, Freedmen and Abandoned Lands in the War Department. Before the Freedmen's Bureau was a crucial task, as W. E. B. Du Bois (1986) recalled in 1903: "The United States government definitely assumes charge of the emancipated Negro as the ward of the nation. . . . Here at the stroke of a pen was erected a government of millions of men,—and not ordinary men either, but black men emasculated by a peculiarly complete system of slavery" (378). It was a task whose significance was proved by another compromise; the 1877 Hayes-Tilden agreement, in which Democrats retracted their challenge to the election results in Florida, Louisiana, and South Carolina that guaranteed Hayes's election, ensured the inclusion of Southern Democrats in Hayes's administration and support for the expansion of a railroad system in the South. Bell (2000) describes the effect of this political compact on Southern blacks: "The loss of protection for their political rights presaged the destruction of economic and social gains which blacks in some areas achieved. Blacks lost businesses and farms, progress in the public schools was halted, and the Jim Crow laws that would eventually segregate blacks in every aspect of public life began to emerge" (52).

Earlier in this chapter I argued that to understand blacks' subjection in the United States it is necessary to read statements on slavery beyond the argument that it instituted a contradiction at the core of a polity governed by universality and self-determination. Though I address that U.S. juridical construction of and remedies to racial injustice, I think that the particular U.S. mode of racial subjection is consistent with ruling liberal principles. I also think that the most crucial dimensions of this consistency disappear in arguments such as (a) that whites' self-interest has guided legal and policy decisions regarding the protection of U.S. blacks' civil rights (Bell 2000, 53–63), (b) that civil rights legislation has failed because it was met with whites' mobilization (Lipsitz 1998), and (c) that throughout U.S. history the law has had more than an instrumental role, that in fact it has "constructed race," and that, as Crenshaw and her colleagues (1995) write, "racial power [is] the sum total of the pervasive ways in which law shapes and is shaped by 'race relations' across the social plane" (xxv).

Although racial difference governs the U.S. American social configuration, the writing of U.S. blacks' absence that it enables more crucially indicates how the attribution of affectability institutes subjects that are comprehended in juridical universality. What I gather in statements deployed between the 1880s and the 1930s—precisely the period from the end of Reconstruction to just before the beginning of the dismantling of segregation—is the resignification of black difference, from the construction of blackness as a signifier of property, which was sustained by both natural history's account of "race and the varieties of men" and the religious text in which slaves, like other things of the world, became signifiers of their owners' ability to follow the (economic) divine law of nature, to the writing of blackness and Africanity as signifiers of an affectable consciousness fully outer-determined, that is, to the tools of productive *nomos* and the institutions and actions of transparent subjects of whiteness. Throughout its history both the juridical and the economic moments of the U.S. social configuration have presupposed the bearers of the principles actualized by the transparent I. If in the years preceding the Civil War the Southern (moral-economic) difference indicated how blacks departed from that which had defined the U.S. American subject, the compromise of 1877 marked the moment at which black difference, as racial difference, would signify that departure. Not, however, as the ever-vanishing affectable "others," but as the inhabitants of a moral-juridical place, a region of subalternity, which coexists within social configurations built by the transparent (Anglo-Saxon) I. That is, blacks' affectability would remain, for the most part, tied to Southern difference as long as the racial governing of the U.S. social configuration threatened to disturb post–World War II economic projects that required the resources and labor of others of Europe still residing in their "original" global regions.

What I gather in these post-Reconstruction writings of the U.S. American nation is a resolution of blacks' *presence* in Southern difference, that is, the writing of their *absence* in the U.S. juridical moment, beyond the reach of the U.S. Constitution. Not because these statements did not refer to them, but more precisely because when they did so they placed them in the fundamental split in the American space produced by the two distinct modes of deployment of European power/desire as blacks were incorporated into and conflated with constructions of the Southern difference. That is, the engulfing of blacks in regions of subalternity, the process captured by the sociologic of exclusion, resulted from how, in the early twentieth-century United States, racial difference retained the moral-juridical split initially articulated in statements on Southern difference. In these statements, the moral split between the always already modern Puritan "North" and the always already traditional English cavalier "South" was resignified as a split between white and black U.S. Americans. Hence, although the formulations of the science of man enabled the writing of their fundamental affectability, as indicated in Ross's (1919) comment that "blacks were dying out" after Emancipation because they could not meet the challenges of a "modern civilization," the engulfing of U.S. blacks resulted from the writing of the "Negro problem" as the Southerners' problem in statements that rescued the U.S. South from its moral distance. For instance, Low (1911) argues that "slavery in the South, was no mere social excrescence as it was in the North, where it was not woven into the fabric of society and did not color the thought, political institutions, the daily life and the commerce of a people" (492). More important, blacks' erasure from the juridical place occupied by the U.S. American subject occurred in the writing of segregation, which, unlike slavery, would not concern the U.S. state and was construed as an exclusively Southern question, as Myrdal's ([1944] 1962) classic study on racial relations exemplifies.

No other statement more consistently articulates how racial difference governs the U.S. moral dimension, that is, its political-symbolic moment, than the landmark juridical decision that authorized segregation. In *Plessy vs. Ferguson* (1896), the Supreme Court was called on to rule whether an 1890 act of the General Assembly of the state of Louisiana, which provided for "separate railway carriages for the white and colored races," violated the Thirteenth and Fourteenth Amendments.[8] In its decision the court did more than merely determine whether Louisiana acted within the law when Plessy was charged for failing to obey the railroad official who asked him to move to the car allocated for his group. The court ruling also drew the line separating blackness from whiteness and delineated the domain to which the relations between blacks and whites belonged. When dismissing the petition that Louisiana's ruling violated the Thirteenth and Fourteenth Amendments, the court argued that the designation of distinct railroads accommodations based on existing color distinctions did not constitute an attempt to promote "involuntary servitude," nor did it question the "legal equality of the two races." What, then, were the arguments deployed to support the decisions that would become the basis for all subsequent black civil rights rulings? On the one hand, the court ruling articulated what was implicit, because it was yet to be articulated, in the Declaration of Independence and the Constitution. It deployed racial difference to place the "relations" between blacks and whites rightfully outside the sphere of the state. Its reinterpretation of the Fourteenth Amendment moved the relations between blacks and whites from the civil (legal) domain to the (newly born) social (moral) domain and established that the unequal basis of their relations was a matter of social (moral) distance and not political inequality. "The object of the Amendment," the opinion of the Court states, "was undoubtedly to enforce the absolute equality of the two races before the law, but in the nature of things, it could not have been intended to abolish distinction based upon color, or to enforce social, as distinguished from political, equality, or a commingling of the two races upon terms unsatisfactory to either. Laws permitting, and even requiring their separation in places where they are liable to be brought into contact do not necessarily imply the inferiority of either race to the other, and have been generally, if not universally recognized as within the competency of the state legislature in the exercise of their police powers" (68).[9]

When stating that the state of Louisiana had reasonably exercised its "police powers," the Supreme Court ruling indicates why the deployment of racial difference to separate the moral ("social") from the political (juridical) accomplishes what neither the Constitution nor the Emancipation Proclamation could. It established that, concerning the Fourteenth Amendment, "the case reduces itself to the question of whether the statute of Louisiana is a reasonable regulation. . . . In determining the question of reasonableness [Louisiana's legislature] is at liberty to act with reference to the established usage, customs, and traditions of the people, and with a view to the promotion of their comfort, and the preservation of the public peace and good order. Gauged by this standard, we cannot say that a law which authorizes or even requires the separation of the two races in public conveyances is unreasonable or more obnoxious to the Fourteenth Amendment than the acts of Congress requiring separate schools for colored children in the District of Columbia, the constitutionality of which does not seem to have been questioned, and the corresponding acts of state legislatures" (72). When it placed "race segregation" outside the scope of the U.S. Constitution, the court placed "the Negro" beyond the moral-juridical terrain, the principles of which the U.S. American subject actualizes, and therefore undeserving of the protections and entitlements they sustain.

By naming these matters local, private, or social rather than national, public, or political the court situated blacks outside the ethical terrain occupied by the U.S. American people. In this movement, blackness and whiteness came to signify the moral split of the U.S. American space, but still within Southern difference, which only reinforced the writing of the space of the U.S. social configuration as the actualization of universality and self-determination. "The argument," the opinion of the Court proceeds, "also assumes that social prejudices may be overcome by legislation and that equal rights cannot be secured to the negro except by an enforced commingling of the two races. We cannot accept this proposition. If the two races are to meet on terms of social equality, it must be the result of natural affinity, a mutual appreciation of each other's merit and a voluntary consent of individuals." The *Plessy* court, however, did not need to wait for science to settle the question of whether blacks should be included in the body politic, because the scientists of man had already done so. "Legislation," it proceeds, "is powerless to eradicate racial instincts or to abolish distinction based upon physical differences, and the attempt to do so can only result in accentuating the difficulties of the present situation. If the civil and political rights of both races be equal, one cannot be inferior to the other civilly and politically. If one race be inferior to the other socially, the Constitution of the United States cannot put them upon the same plane" (73–74). Whatever else may have informed the court's decision, in the late nineteenth century, it could be articulated only with the deployment of the tools of raciality.

Nowhere was the writing of blacks' absence from the ethical place the U.S. American subject inhabits more dramatically indicated in the later nineteenth and early twentieth centuries than in the constant threats and episodes of physical violence they endured, which went unpunished; harassment by the Ku Klux Klan, numerous cases of lynchings during segregation, and the race riots of the first decades of the twentieth century terrorized U.S. blacks after the abolition of slavery. Perhaps the violence marking the conditions of enslaved blacks belonged to a mode of power that did not need the tools of productive *nomos* to write its subjects, for the power of slaveholders was consistently engraved onto the rebel slaves' bodies as punishment for refusal to accept their economic and juridical position as chattel labor. But later instances of the use of force to frighten U.S. blacks into a position of subalternity makes sense in the political context of the liberal subject only if one recalls that in Locke's formulation, to name a founding one, the common, consensual decision to relinquish the executive powers of the state of nature—the right to use violence to protect property (life, liberty, and possessions)—characterized those united in a "political society." In the postslavery United States, blacks have been forced into a juridical position that resembles Locke's "state of nature." Not, as the foundational statement has it, because "race prejudice" is a "natural reaction" to substantive difference, but because writings of the U.S. subject place them outside the body politic founded by the Anglo-Saxon.

What we have here is not a desire for domination, for domination requires a living being, as Hegel's lordship and bondsman passage indicates. Neither do the historical versions of race relations help us to understand U.S. blacks' subjection, because even if it were used only as an added element of class exploitation or as a principle of stratification, "race prejudice" would need to keep its subjects alive and able to participate in economic production. Perhaps the key to understanding resides in the first version of the sociologic of exclusion, in its assumption that the solution of "the problem of race relations," the restitution of a transparent social configuration, would take nothing less than the obliteration of the racial "other." Frightening as it seems, the sociology of race relations may provide such a useful toolbox for comprehending a kind of racial subjection in which racial difference operates as a strategy of exclusion because of its own participation in the writing of blackness as the signifier of an affectable consciousness, one that radically departed from the one the U.S. legislative and executive powers were instituted to protect.

THE RISING TIDE OF "COLOREDS"

When earlier writers of the U.S. American nation deployed the arsenal of raciality to construct Eastern and Southern European and Asian (Chinese and Japanese) immigrants as the "threatening immigrants" whose natural ability to withstand a lower "standard of living" gave them an advantage over the native (Anglo-Saxon) population, they did not produce them as "superior races." What I find in these earlier statements is how the arsenal of raciality resolved an economic need, for these earlier immigrants constituted the primary source of cheap labor crucial to foster economic prosperity,[10] which threatens to locate the U.S. American nation further way from transparency. Here the writing of the "others of Europe as affectable human beings, bearers of inferior bodies and minds, more explicitly indicate how globality constitutes an ontological context of articulation of the U.S. national subject. For one thing, not all of these "newcomers" were written as permanently "strangers." Southern and Eastern Europeans would eventually be placed within the boundaries of U.S. Americanness because their bodies communicated an origin in the European space.[11] Early Asian immigrants, on the other hand, would be the "newcomers" whose bodies would always communicate their foreignness in a social configuration built by and for Europeans. They were written as foreigners in the "land of freedom prosperity," even though their presence resulted from juridical acts that attended the needs that ensured the success of early twentieth-century U.S. capitalism. This distinction between Asian and European immigrants indicates how globality guides the mapping of the U.S social configuration as it enables the differentiation between "threatening" and "nonthreatening" foreigners. For a while both Asian and European immigrants shared the space of racial or national others, but the latter would very quickly move out of this position, for the U.S.-born generations had nothing besides their last names to indicate their non-English origins. The initial formulation of race relations describes this process according to a sociologic of exclusion that always already assumes whiteness as a signifier of transparency. My reading, however, indicates that the formulations of the science of man informed the very "natural reactions" Park and his students investigated, their construction of the others of Europe as marked by an affectability that proclaims but never really considers them a serious threat to the transparent U.S. American subject.

My analysis of writings of the U.S. American subject of the period between the 1890s and the 1930s focuses on how the articulation of Asian racial and cultural particularity produced the U.S. American subject as the threatened agent of economic prosperity while at the same time postulating that the Anglo-Saxon particularity would ensure the victory of this subject over "newcomers" who were fundamentally unfit to survive in a modern (liberal-capitalist)

social configuration. Most statements against Chinese immigration deployed the arguments of the science of man, which, just as in
the case of Eastern and Southern European immigrants, produced
Chinese immigrant workers as a menace to the native Anglo Saxon.
As in the case of the former, their difference was also attributed to
the economic situation of their place of origin. When it was combined with arguments that defended the restriction of the extension of citizenship rights and the cessation of Chinese immigration
on the basis of their being "non-assimilative with the whites," the
construction of Chinese workers as a threat would prevail in the
U.S. political context and would later be extended to incorporate
the Japanese and other immigrants from Asia. During the first three
decades of the twentieth century, however, the writing of Asian difference privileged globality, not historicity.

When explaining how immigration would harm the American
"national character," Eliot Norton argued, in 1904, that after the
Revolution and extending to the 1860s there was the beginning of
the formation of a "national or racial type" that provided the specific U.S. moral standards. However, he noted, "religion, rule, laws,
and customs are only the national character in the form of standards of conduct. Now national character can be formed only in a
population which is stable. The repeated introduction into a body
of men of other men of different type or types cannot but tend to
prevent its formation" (cited in Stoddard 1920, 255). What I find
here is not a blurring of the zones of deployment of the cultural
and the racial, but actually an indication of how the former was
deployed in a global-epistemological context in which racial difference had already established the place of the U.S. American subject.
Not surprisingly, the most telling signifying gesture in statements on
Asian immigrants was precisely the apparent reversal of the science
of man's formulations. These statements conveyed two apparently
contradictory arguments. On the one hand, they deployed "white
racial superiority" to write U.S. particularity in terms of economic
prosperity. On the other hand, however, when situating the U.S.
American subject against Asian immigrants, these statements deployed Asian affectability in a version of the thesis of the "survival
of the fittest," which apparently reversed Darwin's statement on the
effects of "modern civilization," in the argument that the dire conditions produced by industrialization and urbanization were adequate

only for the already socially, economically, and mentally "inferior races." For instance, read Stoddard's (1920) argument that the problem with "colored immigration" is that it produces even greater damage than white immigration because colored immigrants are "wholly alien in blood and possessed of idealistic and cultural backgrounds absolutely different from ours. If the white immigrant can gravely disorder the national life, it is not too much to say that the colored immigrant would doom it to certain death" (267–68). What does one read here if not the race relations argument that Asian difference, the (cultural) difference expressed in the bodies and manners of Asians, disturbs the modern social configuration? Here again the place of the U.S. American subject overlaps the boundaries of whiteness, for its particularity resides in the fact that it is successfully carrying out the project of capitalism, as Ross's (1919) comment indicates: "Dams against the color races, with spillways of course for students, merchants and travelers, will presently enclose the white mans' world. Within this area minor dams will protect the high wages of the less prolific peoples against the surplus labor of the more prolific" (170). Accordingly, the problem with the Chinese immigrant resided precisely in that, according to Ross, "the competition of white labor and yellow is not so simple a test of human worth as some may imagine. Under good conditions the white man can best the yellow man in turning off work. But under bad conditions, the yellow man can best the white man, because he can better endure spoiled food, poor clothing, foul air, noise, heat, dirt, discomfort and microbes" (273–74).

What race relations constructs as "instinctual reactions" to "visible" markers of cultural difference emerged in political statements that articulated racial difference to both produce the affectability of the other of Europe and advocate policies that would maintain the boundaries of prosperity. "In the matter of Chinese and Japanese coolie immigration," Woodrow Wilson maintained during the 1921 presidential campaign, "I stand for the national policy of exclusion. The whole question is one of assimilation of diverse races. We cannot make a homogenous population of a people who do not blend with the Caucasian race. Their lower standard of living as laborers will crowd out the white agriculturist and is in other fields a most serious industrial menace. The success of free democratic institutions demands of our people education, intelligence, and patriotism, and the State should protect them against unjust competition and impossible competition. Remunerative labor is the basis of contentment. Democracy rests on the equality of the citizen. Oriental coolism will give us another race problem to solve and surely we have had our lesson (cited in Ringer 1983, 286–87). Before and after Wilson's statement, which indicates, once again, how the racial maps early twentieth-century thought, the highest U.S. juridical body stepped in to ensure that economic needs would not undermine the writing of the U.S. American space as the "indigenous" dominion of universality and self-determination. For instance, in *Chae Chan Ping vs. United States* (1889) the U.S. Supreme Court denied Ping's appeal of the Northern District of California decision that he should be detained for unlawful entrance. Having left the United States before the promulgation of the act of Congress of 1888 that excluded "Chinese laborers from the United States," Ping referred to the acts of 1882 and 1884 that ensured Chinese laborers the right of residence. With its decision the Court upheld Congress's sovereignty over immigration legislation, but not without commenting on the moral correctness of its motive. The Court stated: "If the government of the United States, through its legislative department, considers the presence of foreigners of a different race in this country, who will not assimilate with us, to be dangerous to its peace and security, their exclusion is not to be stayed because at the time there are not actual hostilities with the nation of which the foreigners are subjects." That the court did not feel obliged to specify this "danger" can be explained only by the fact that it considered them well known. And indeed they were, not only by the writers of the U.S. subject, but by high-profile politicians like Woodrow Wilson, by white U.S. laborers, and by others who lived in the United States when racial difference ruled ontoepistemological accounts.

What these statements that produced Asian difference indicate is that Asians were placed in an ontological context, globality, in which the difference between "civilizations" could be articulated to produce a distinction between the transparent U.S. subject and its affectable "others." As Said (1978) has reminded us, the "Orient" has been written as the temporal other of Europe, the place of stationary and/or decadent "civilizations." However, it is in its exteriority to the U.S. prosperity—its ability to fulfill the projects of capitalism—that Asian difference is constructed. Here I locate Asian

Americans' ambiguous placing, which has allowed them to move in and out of the boundaries of cultural difference as either "yellow peril" or "model minority," without ever leaving the place raciality has assigned them. For every time the U.S. political and economic needs has required Asian labor, the borders of Asian difference have been open to whichever favored nationality would be retained, as well as to whichever disfavored nationality would be placed outside. In both instances, the doors would never be fully closed to these particular affectable others, because the U.S. state would promptly unleash juridical acts to attend to the state's most immediate economic needs without threatening to locate the Asian other in the place occupied by the U.S. American subject.[12] Such a magnificent undertaking belongs in globality, for it enables the writing of the Asian subaltern subject both as a threat to and as an excessive signifier of that which only whiteness properly signifies, the subject able to actualize the economic and juridical ends of reason.

THE PEOPLE(S) OF THE UNITED STATES

What I find in these writings of the particularity of the U.S. American subject—the statements that sought to answer the question What is the American nation?—is precisely how globality constitutes a moment of the writing of the transparent I as a (liberal) juridical and (capitalist) economic thing. At the turn of the twentieth century, globality deployed *racial difference* to write the U.S. (Anglo-Saxon) American subject against virtually any other inhabitant of the U.S. American space—American Indians and blacks first, later Southern and Eastern Europeans and Asian immigrants. Most examinations of U.S. strategies of racial subjection focus primarily on the writing of the "other within" and assume that the racial operates solely as a strategy of exclusion. My reading shows, however, that the other of Europe had to be produced as such in representation, as an always already affectable thing, so that it would not be impossible to place the U.S. subject and social configuration in transparency. My reading also shows how this entailed a mode of racial subjection, the assumption of the affectability of the others of Europe, that would inform how they are situated before its juridical moment.

These statements constructed the U.S. American subject's proximity to the European space in two moments. On the one hand, they deployed racial difference to write the U.S. American social configuration as the expression of Anglo-Saxon power-desire. When the body is the primary signifier of particularity, it always already constructs the U.S. American subject as "English," European; the geographic distance is bridged. On the other hand, raciality would map the U.S. social configuration as a small version of globality itself by assigning to the others of Europe a moral position not encompassed by the principles, self-determination (freedom) and universality, that Anglo-Saxons alone actualize. What all this indicates is that racial subjection does not result from excessive strategies of power, but is an effect of the analytics of raciality, the political-symbolic apparatus that has produced in the United States global/ historical subjects, the white transparent (national I) and his affectable "others."

10

Tropical Democracy

What I want to show is that the white man, withstanding the struggle for survival in the Brazilian environment to adapt to his new fatherland, had to strengthen himself with the blood of the tropical races. Thus the crossing and then the mestiço *man, who, as a product of this adaptation, is better fit to the environment and, if intellectually inferior to the white man, he is superior to the latter as an agent of differentiation, as an element in the formation of a national type. In any case it is the white man who will prevail; because it was he who brought the civilization; but to assure this very victory, to construct a nationality strong in this environment, he had to dilute in the miscegenation, had to change the purity of his blood. If in this century that determined the humble origin of the poor humanity, we still need to speak of purity of blood, and other mystifying and empty phrases.*
— SYLVIO ROMERO,
HISTÓRIA DA LITERATURA BRASILEIRA

In 1848, Emperor Dom Pedro II went on his first and perhaps only trip to northern Brazil. Fresh memories of a few uncomfortable weeks spent at sea probably accounted for the grumpiness one senses in the journal entries written in the city of Salvador, in the northeastern state of Bahia. While there, the emperor divided his noble time between visits to unfinished construction sites and attendance at cultural events. Nevertheless, he still found time to observe the local faces. Surprised with the composition of the National Guard, he commented in his diary (1959): "I forgot to say that I have not met as many dark faces as I expected and the National Guard is not so black, yet one can always see at once in the windows the turbans of 3 or 4 Mina Negro women" (48). To be sure, his majesty showed much more concern with the physical appearance of the elites: "The Bulcões," he noted, "have a much better complexion than the Munizes, and the baroness of S. Francisco is a perfect lady" (49). Most probably, when scrutinizing *Bahianos'* faces, D. Pedro II, the young heir of the Brazilian Empire, known for his high intellectual pursuits, had in his mind comments by his frequent European visitors about the danger of "race-mixing." How many times had his majesty heard admonitions from foreign scientists, intellectuals, and government officials about the perilous effects of miscegenation on the disposition and the character of his subjects? How could Brazil ever become a "modern civilization" if even in the bodies of its elite one could perceive evident signs of "race-mixing"? What sort of "civilization" could be built by a people the scientists of man chose as an example of the dangers in hidden European colonies?

His majesty's concern reflects statements regarding the conspicuous presence of blacks and mulattos in the streets of middle and late nineteenth-century Salvador, Bahia, such as that of Count Suzannet, who referred to "the immorality of all classes which has enabled the cross-breeding of race and destroyed the color prejudice." Whether in a tone of excitement or revulsion, most European travelers' journals describe an uncanny sight, the blending of Africa and Europe, the "moral degeneration" they witnessed walking and dancing dangerously loose on the streets of Salvador. On the one hand, this danger was signified in the bodies of the vast majority of the city's population. "In general," Tshudi wrote, "the mulattos are extremely sensual, frivolous, thoughtless, and in great majority lazy, lovers of gambling and liquor, vengeful, sly, and astute" (cited in Augel, 1980, 199). On the other hand, they heard and saw this danger in what "negros and mulattos" did on the streets of Salvador. There is a place in the Campo Grande, William Scully wrote in his 1866 journal, where "African Negroes superstitiously adore, and to which they come frequently to bring gifts of fruits and vegetables" (cited in Augel 1980, 208). Observing the traditional Catholic celebration Festa do Bonfim, Von Martius noted that "the noise and unrestrained joy of many Negroes together" promoted "a special, exquisite effect, which could only be understood by those who had the occasion to observe diverse human races in promiscuity" (cited in Augel, 209). Regardless of the adjective used to describe the "mixing" of Africa and Europe, "civilization" and "savagery," these global travelers' journals singled out an aspect of the Brazilian space to which Brazilian intellectuals would attend in the last two decades of the century. When they seemed to have finally heard the European message that sensuality, joy, and noise, instead of being merely special and exquisite, indicated the presence of a kind of human being that was, as the scientist of man Robert Knox stated in 1850, "a degradation of humanity and was rejected by nature" (497), they actualized an affectable consciousness.

My task in this chapter is to indicate how the arsenal of the *analytics of raciality* enabled the writing of the Brazilian national subject as a *transparent "I,"* a specimen of *homo historicus,* against European commentators' claims that its black and *mestiço* population could not actualize the principles, self-determination and universality, whose emergence *transcendental poesis* locates in the boundaries of post-Enlightenment Europe. My reading of statements on the Brazilian nation deployed between the 1880s and the 1930s describes how they allowed the production of precisely that which Europeans doubted the Brazilian was or could ever become. Moreover, it shows how the fashioning of the Brazilian subject as a democratic I was enabled by the rewriting of miscegenation, the strategy of containment, as a historic (eschatological-teleological) signifier. In other words, I show how miscegenation instituted the Brazilian subject, delimited its particular ethical place, precisely because of how it wrote the trajectory of Indians and Africans in affectability, as consciousness that could not thrive in the transparent social configuration the Portuguese built in these Southern American lands. I also indicate how this resolution would be the predicament of Brazilian culture due to miscegenation's intrinsic instability as a scientific signifier. When describing how the arsenal of raciality informs the prevailing versions of the Brazilian text, the whitening thesis and racial democracy, I indicate how the transformation of this scientific strategy (of containment) into a historic strategy (of engulfment) produced a gendered political text, for Portuguese power/desire could be written only as the force of Brazilian history through the appropriation of the non-European (colonized or enslaved) female subject as an instrument. I am always already pointing out that the productivity of European desire resides not in transcendentality but in the premodern—because, as my reading of Locke's formulation indicates, the conditions of female subjection both precede and are encompassed by the rational polity—relationships with female "others of Europe," the sexual that threatens the boundaries that raciality was deployed to produce.[1] My point is that the sexual fails to fix the boundaries of the transparent I not because, as many would argue, human collectivities are the product of a long history of "race mixture," an argument deployed to undermine the science of man's "typology of races"—but because, as a signifier of exteriority or spatiality, it refers to how the play of engulfment never dissipates the relationships instituted by deployments of European (economic and sexual) desire in other global regions. What I gather in these early writings of the Brazilian nation is how, when deployed as a *strategy of particularization,* miscegenation produced a modern subject that embodied the dangerous intersection where the colonial strategies of power/desire, whose deployment contributed to European "progress," threatened the transparency of the being that modern philosophers write as essentially self-determined. However, precisely because it produced bodies that signify continuity between Europe and other regions of the global space, miscegenation would also constitute a signifier of globality that could be deployed to write a postcolonial zone of deployment of European power in *affectability.*

When Brazilian intellectuals, politicians, and scientists turned their eyes and ears to the streets of Salvador, they deployed signifying strategies that always already presumed that the Brazilian social configuration is situated at the edges of liberal-capitalist globality. To place the nation in transparency, they transformed what the science of man describes as signs of degeneration, noise and sensuality, into music and joy, signifiers of African culture, that is, they turned the things blacks do and say into fragments of the African "spirit." The primary effect of this productive anthropological desire was to rewrite the "others of Europe" in affectability by transforming miscegenation into an ambiguous historical (eschatological-teleological) signifier, a political-symbolic gesture whose crucial effect has been to displace the social as the domain of operation of the racial in Brazil. My point is that the silencing of the racial underclass in Brazil—which is the opposite parallel to the silencing of class under the racial in the United States—relies not on the placing of the racial "other" outside the place of the national subject, but on how the eschatological meanings of miscegenation produced a mode of racial subjection premised on the obliteration of the always-already affectable bodies and minds of the others of Europe. For most of the twentieth century, this anthropological desire would supply the arsenal deployed in statements on the Brazilian subject; it would constitute the privileged locus of production of the scientific signifying strategies deployed in the statements that wrote the Brazilian subject as a particular specimen of *homo historicus,* namely, the subject of democracy.

THE FETISHISTIC POWER OF ANTHROPOLOGICAL DESIRE

No other researcher of the postslavery Brazilian configuration has communicated this need to hold onto an eschatological conception of miscegenation (as a challenge to statements by the scientists of man) than the university professor, coroner, ethnographer, and scientist of man Raymundo Nina Rodrigues, the acknowledged founder of Brazilian anthropology (Correa 1982; Leite 1983; Schwarcz 1993; Skidmore 1995). For this reason, before examining how he would gather the fragments of Africanity later anthropologists would offer to writers of the Brazilian nation, it will be helpful to learn why Nina Rodrigues considered miscegenation problematic. In *As Raças Humanas e a Responsibilidade Penal,* Nina Rodrigues ([1894] 1957) argues that miscegenation had produced in Brazil types of human bodies that house a pathological mind. In this critique of the first Republican Penal Code, he challenges its deployment of the principle of "free will." He introduces a racial map to argue for distinct definitions of penal responsibility according to the racial composition of a given geographic region, which suggests a reorganization of this juridical text that, if adopted, would have created a de facto juridical apartheid. Nina Rodrigues thought "free will" should not be used as the sole basis for determining criminal responsibility in Brazil, because this juridical principle presumes a moral homogeneity the country lacked. When justifying this argument, he deploys the signifier miscegenation to show that the mental (intellectual and moral) inferiority of blacks and the various degrees of mental degeneracy of *mestiços* required that a just application of the penal code include distinct degrees of penal responsibility. "In each phase of the evolution of a people and even better, in each phase of humanity's evolution," he states, "we can compare anthropologically distinct races, with proper criminality, in harmony and accordance with their degree of intellectual and moral development" (47). Blacks and Indians, he argues, should have an attenuated penal responsibility because of the "disequilibrium, a psychic disturbance provoked by an imposed adaptation and force in such backward spirits by a superior civilization; to solicit such great mental effort, required by the struggle for social existence, certainly will create inferior races among us, dressed suddenly as civilized peoples, a fundamentally abnormal type" (122).

Regarding *mestiços,* Nina Rodrigues proposes degrees of penal responsibility to be determined according to their degree of mental instability, asserting that, although "human miscegenation" does not produce hybrid bodies (sterile offspring), it does produce mental (intellectual and moral) hybrids, that is, pathological minds. From *mestiçagem,* he argues, derives the "lack of physical and moral energy, apathy, and the want of foresight" that he sees as a characteristic of the Brazilian population (13435). About the first- and second-generation *mestiços,* he states: "It seems that in the latter precisely more delicate is the *mestiço*'s instability. What they gain in intelligence they lose in energy and even in morality: the disequilibrium among the affective intellectual faculties of the degenerated, the exaggerated development of ones against the others; there is a perfect simile in this improvement in *mestiços* intelligence" (145). This statement is more than the mere reproduction of the science of man's formulations to defend the thesis of "racial purity." Nina Rodrigues introduces a typology of minds, *affectable* consciousness, radically distinct from the subject of (self- and inner) regulation, that the notion of "free will" presupposes. Nina Rodrigues thought that, because miscegenation had populated Brazil with a larger number of people whose bodies expressed an affectable consciousness, those lacking self-determination, self-control, and every attribute assumed under the notion of free will, the Brazilian social configuration could not be thoroughly governed by universality and self-determination. With this statement he rewrote the *mestiço* as the signifier of the Brazilian predicament, which had been pointed out by so many European visitors and still haunts interpreters of Brazil.

Because in the science of man miscegenation is a signifier of containment, what is implied in Nina Rodrigues's construction of the Brazilian people as condemned to degeneracy is a lament not so much about wasted European desire but about its unwanted effect, which is to produce bodies that signify Europe and its "others," modern subjects that can always be articulated to signify other-wise. From a desire to save Brazil from the colonizer's most crucial historical error, Nina Rodrigues offered a solution that would limit this unwanted effect by writing blacks and *mestiços* (the majority of the Brazilian population) outside the domain of universality, a statement that could be supported only by the strategies of *productive nomos*. Though this can be reduced to a version of the "hierarchy of races," as many interpreters of the Brazilian predicament suggest, I read his defense of various degrees of legal responsibility as an attempt to demarcate in the Brazilian space an exclusive terrain of the transparent I. Most critical analysts of racial subjection will immediately read it as an articulation of white supremacy or a project of a Brazilian apartheid, and then, after learning that Nina Rodrigues is a mulatto anthropologist, they would rehearse the Brazilian paradox.

Though I would not disqualify the first reading, I think the paradox thesis has been overstated to irrelevance. Instead, I read Nina Rodrigues's statement as an articulation of the predicament of early postcolonial spaces, which includes South Africa, which at the end of the nineteenth century faced the global (juridical-economic) requirement that it be reconfigured as a modern social configuration in an ontoepistemological context informed by the analytics of raciality, which placed the blacks as the subaltern (affectable) regions of globality. In Brazil's case, the solution was to deploy anthropological strategies in a rewriting of miscegenation that also re-signified whiteness, one in which the temporal trajectory of the national subject is narrated not as the actualization of "racial purity" but as a process of "racial or cultural purification"—that is, the fulfillment of the logic of obliteration. Though it did not eliminate blackness and has, in fact, produced Africanity itself, this solution has constituted a powerful strategy of racial subjection, the effects of which are neither superior nor inferior to but just as efficient as those deployed in the United States and South Africa.

FRAGMENTS OF AFRICANITY

Neither the financing of European immigrants nor the oblivion to blacks' and *mestiços'* dire economic situation in the moments immediately after the abolition of slavery could provide what the writing of the Brazilian transparent I did. For the nation is a *historical* (interior/temporal) thing, the writing of its particularity required an specification of its "intrinsic difference," which would then be gathered in accounts of its be/coming. In the science of man's rendering of this signifier, miscegenation could not constitute the basis for this account; what was needed was a notion of cultural miscegenation, which we saw in the "theory of race and cultural contacts" that informs the text of race relations. In his ethnographic text *O Animismo Feitichista dos Negros Bahianos*, Nina Rodrigues ([1900] 1935) deploys this notion of miscegenation to counter the hopeful argument that Catholicism was the prevailing religion among blacks, *mestiços*, and white Bahians. When delimiting what was African ("anismitic and fetishistic") in Bahian religiosity, he provides detailed descriptions of "rituals and beliefs" that would later become the defining features of *Candomblé*. It was not that practitioners and observers had not called attention to the existence of African rituals in Salvador before, but it was in this text that the noise and the food that blacks and mulattos spread on the street corners of the city were identified, classified, and produced as modified African cultural products, that is, the first time they were apprehended as effects of the play of productive *nomos* (Maggie 1995). "Whole and pure," Nina Rodrigues explains, "are only the sentiments which animate their beliefs, which are as fetishist when they use stones, trees, and shells as when they use Catholic saints. The object of this study was to study how this sentiment survives and reveals itself among the negroes, how it acts in all manifestations of our public and private life. The objective is to deduce the sociological principles usually unnoticed or ignored" (20–21). Not surprisingly, Nina Rodrigues would conclude that the mind actualized in *Candomblé*'s "rituals and beliefs" and in the peculiar Catholicism practiced by Bahians lacked the ability to produce the abstract thought demanded by "civilized" religions.

More than that, however, Nina Rodrigues also provides two contradictory assessments of effects of the presence of African bodies and minds in the Brazilian space. On the one hand, he argues that, through the cooptation of the elites by offering religious service and by placing them in high positions in the religious hierarchy, *Candomblé* practitioners guaranteed the survival of their "primitive religious practices." On the other hand, however, he argues that not only the disappearance of African-born priests and practitioners but racial and cultural miscegenation was leading to the elimination of these practices. "If in the African negro there was and there is the tendency to juxtapose ideas learned from Catholic teaching, and fetishist ideas and beliefs, brought from Africa," he notes, "in the creoulo and the mulatto there is a manifest tendency to identify these [Catholic] teachings" (171). Here miscegenation supports the statement that the presence of affectable others of Europe is a threat to "superior races and cultures," but also that "contact" with them will lead to their disappearance. In the U.S. text, this statement reproduces the logic of exclusion, for racial difference is deployed to signal an unbridgeable "distance." In the Brazilian text, it repeats the logic of obliteration, for the signifier miscegenation already presupposes the affectability of the others of Europe. Later statements by the generation of anthropologists who celebrated Nina Rodrigues as the founder of the discipline in Brazil inherited the writing of miscegenation, and deployed the cultural to map the ways in which the obliteration of blackness and Africanity would produce Brazilian culture, in which the latter remained as fragments that would later be appropriated in writings of the Brazilian subject to circumscribe an "essentially" European subject, namely, the tropical subject of democracy.

In the 1930s, however, what blacks and *mestiços* did on the streets of Salvador was rewritten as "residues" of an African mental configuration, as "authentic" actualizations of African culture that had "survived" and transformed in the Brazilian space, despite the influence of European and Native American culture and the hardships of slavery. The most important figure of this first generation of Brazilian cultural anthropologists, Arthur Ramos, who would chair the UNESCO project that aimed to uncover the "secrets" of the Brazilian racial democracy, describes his own work as an enlightened follow-up to Nina Rodrigues's project. In O Negro Brasileiro, Ramos (1934) argues that anthropological investigation of black Brazilians' "rituals and beliefs" should aim to "identify, with the comparative method, the tribal origins of the Brazilian Negro, to reconstitute his cultural personality, lost in centuries of slavery and modified by social and cultural change" (50). When excavating the "elementary structures" of African culture in the black Brazilians' religious practices, Ramos, like his mentor, also registers the pervasiveness of Yoruba culture, which he singles out to delimit the particular kind of Africanity slavery brought to the Brazilian space. "The Yoruba Negroes," he notes, "were since the beginning preferred in Bahia's slave markets." These "tall, well-built, brave, and hard-workers," he states, had "the best disposition and the smarter among them all." What he captures, however, is not the whole and unchanged Yoruba "spirit." "The description and the examination of Negro Yoruba cultural traits in Brazil can only be done, seriously," he argues, "in terms of acculturation and survivals. In reality, this culture did not remain pure in the new environment; they mixed with each other and with the Amerindian and European cultures they met in Brazil" (75).

Resulting from this charting of "African survivals" was the writing of black Brazilians' "rituals and beliefs" as fragments of Africanity, "residues" of African culture surviving in the midst of the dominant European culture. "There are, however, some aspects," Ramos argues "which should be considered immediately: the direct survival, which resulted from the original inheritance of the Negro in the new habitat. Here there is an interesting phenomenon. In the examination of cultural residues, we noted that, while the material cultural traits almost disappeared completely . . . the non-material traits, primarily those related to the religious culture, remain at some point with an absolute purity" (76). That the anthropological mapping of African residues addresses the national desire to obliterate these signs of affectability to write Brazil's as a transparent social configuration is evident in Ramos's view of the role of anthropological research, which is to "know the types of 'primitive' thought, to correct them, raising them to the more developed states, what will be achieved with a radical educational revolution" (23).[2] The primary effect of this anthropological desire was to offer these residual rituals and beliefs of black Brazilians to be appropriated in the rewriting of miscegenation as a historic signifier.

Regardless of the good intentions, these later anthropological rescuing missions deploy the discipline's tool in a context already mapped by the products of the science of man, one that already presumed that miscegenation was an unwanted product of an uncontrolled desire. The primary product of this anthropological desire was the transformation of the global signifier of containment into an object that could be engulfed in the text that writes the Brazilian subject as a particular transparent I. In the process, however, the predicament of Brazilian culture was reproduced precisely, for miscegenation could constitute a useful historic signifier only because of the instability it produced as the point of "contact" between the consciousness that the analytics of raciality writes as fundamentally—because it institutes "difference" as an effect of the productive *nomos*—irreconcilable and unsublatable. For this reason, miscegenation would continuously threaten Brazil's future, as the discussion of deployments of the arsenal of race relations indicates, for it is always available as a global (racial and cultural) signifier to explain why Brazil has been condemned to remain on the outskirts of capitalist globality.

THE SLIGHTLY (TANNED) TRANSPARENT SUBJECT

In the First Universal Race Congress, held in London in 1911, miscegenation was the theme addressed by João Baptista de Lacerda, the director of the National Museum of Rio de Janeiro. Following the tone of the congress, whose participants roundly condemned the science of man, Lacerda chose to challenge the argument that "race mixture" produced "degenerated types." To prove this point, the Brazilian anthropologist presented evidence that, despite the high numbers of slaves introduced in Brazil, sexual intercourse between masters and female slaves produced a significant number of *mestiços* who had played an important role in the formation of the Brazilian "civilization." In his conclusion, Lacerda listed several factors that indicated that in a hundred years or so Brazil would become one of "the chief centers of civilization in the world"; these factors are *mestiços'* tendency to marry whites, the disappearance of the black population given the effects of "destructive agencies" and lack of resources, and finally European immigration, which Lacerda said "will after a time displace the elements that might retain any of the characters of the Negro" (cited in Spiller [1911] 1969, 381). Not only blacks' *affectability,* but also *mestiços'* "half-white" desire, assured Lacerda that in about one hundred years Brazil would finally join other postcolonial, white, "modern civilizations." What Lacerda's statement indicates is that, in the early twentieth century, an eschatological closure seemed the only possible fate for these modern collectivities that the analytics of raciality produces as affectable (degenerate, undesirable, pathological, and nonproductive) consciousness, the dangerously ambiguous offspring of the European colonial enterprise.

What I gather in the articulation of the figure of the hybrid *(mestiço)* in the writings of the Brazilian subject is the delimitation of the dangerous place where European particularity was threatened by the proximity required by the dislocations that ensured the juridical and economic appropriations that guaranteed the successful trajectory of capitalism. In writings of the Brazilian subject, the refashioning of miscegenation as a historic signifier enabled the narrative of the temporal trajectory of a European subject "adapted" to the conditions in the tropical global regions. The signifier that, like racial difference, connects body, global region, and the mind, would govern the Brazilian text, just as the former established the place of the U.S. American subject. This correspondence, however, should not be read merely as parallel effects of an exterior determinant, as it is constructed in the text of race relations. It can be seen that, by giving globality analytical primacy, miscegenation organized the Brazilian text precisely because it placed certain early postcolonial spaces, such as Latin American countries, on the outskirts of capitalist globality. My point is that an understanding of the two moments of resignification of miscegenation, the whitening thesis and racial democracy, requires attention to how the racial informed the global conditions under which they were deployed. Both versions of the Brazilian text engage the same challenge: how to determine the Brazilian people's "intrinsic difference," to narrate the trajectory of a Brazilian "spirit," as the temporal unfolding of the miscegenated Brazilian subject as a transparent I.

When addressing this challenge, the writers of the Brazilian text constructed the predicament of Brazilian culture as the effect of specific geohistorical circumstances that required not only a large number of mixed-race individuals in the population, but also that Indians, Africans, and the Portuguese together create a language, religiosity, and customs distinct from those of the post-Enlightenment European culture. When attempting to rewrite this predicament as the trajectory of a European subject, they deployed the three basic statements of the Brazilian text: (a) the claim that the "Brazilian civilization" is an instance of European (Portuguese) "civilization in the tropics"; (b) the claim that Indians and African physical traits were disappearing from the Brazilian population due to miscegenation and European immigration; and (c) the claim that, because the Portuguese, unlike the English, lacked "race prejudice," they freely mingled with Indians and Africans, resulting in the constitution of the *mestiço,* a "racial type" well suited to the task of building a "tropical (modern) civilization." Although all three are recurrent themes in rewritings of the Brazilian text, the first two dominated the initial version. In the last quarter of the nineteenth century, the strategies of the science of man governed statements deployed by those engaged in the juridical and economic reconfiguration of this former European colony imposed by the capitalist cyclical crisis of the last decades of the century (Hobsbawm 1987).[3] At this moment, the first version of the Brazilian text, the whitening thesis, resignified miscegenation as a historical-eschatological signifier that rendered the temporal trajectory of an "essentially" European "spirit" in the tropical space the simultaneous appropriation and annihilation of affectable Africans and Indians. By the early 1930s, the second version, racial democracy, would rewrite miscegenation as a historical-teleological signifier that helped to indicate that the Portuguese's intrinsic democratic disposition had enabled the building of a "modern civilization" in the tropics. In this version, which remains the hegemonic account of Brazilian nationality, the arsenal of race relations plays a central role, because it was only when contrasted with racial difference that the eschatological meaning of miscegenation could be rewritten as a benign secondary effect of the deployment of an intrinsically democratic I (Silva 1998).

My objective here is neither to introduce new evidence nor to reveal aspects of statements on the Brazilian nation not yet noted by others. Instead I read statements deployed by the two main articulators of the whitening thesis and racial democracy, respectively, the literary critic Sylvio Romero and the anthropologist Gilberto Freyre, who are perhaps too familiar to students of racial subjection in Brazil, to describe the signifying strategies that enabled the writing of blackness and Africanity to signify Brazilian particularity while producing blacks and *mestiços* as subaltern social subjects.[4] That is, I am interested in how, in these statements, precisely that which renders miscegenation dangerous, the productive violence of the sexual intimacy between the male European colonizer and yesterday's female "natives," was rewritten as the determinant of the trajectory of a historical subject toward transparency. This signification of miscegenation as a signifier of productive violence, one that necessarily renders the Brazilian national narrative a gendered political text, has escaped studies that deploy the arsenal of race relations because it can only capture modes of racial subjection premised on racial difference, that is, the ones that rely on the logic of exclusion, which need to continuously name the racial subaltern "the stranger." As discussed earlier, in the U.S. American text the articulation of the *absence* of the others of Europe sustains their exclusion from the place of the liberal (juridical-moral) subject. In the Brazilian text, the articulation of the *presence* of Indians and Africans more closely rewrites the play of engulfment as the dual temporal movement of obliteration of the others of Europe (eschatological) as the condition of possibility for the realization of a transparent I (teleological). Though both the logic of exclusion and the logic of obliteration require a productive (signifying) gesture, the articulation of the others of Europe in affectability, one that necessarily places the national subject in transparency, the latter more successfully postpones spatiality, ensuring a modern social configuration fully governed by transcendentality. That is, miscegenation more consistently than racial difference writes both versions of the *scene of engulfment,* namely, *transcendental poesis* and productive *nomos.* For this reason, I hope this reading of the predicament of the Brazilian subject will contribute to the confecting of critical strategies for analysis of the present global-political configuration. If anything, attention to the effects of scientific signification will help us to comprehend how in the current neoliberal capitalist remapping of the global configuration the analytics of raciality rewrites the others of Europe as modern subjects whose temporal trajectory is the fulfillment of the logic of obliteration.

"The [Brazilian] National Type"

A few decades before Lacerda's intervention at the First Universal Race Congress, the literary critic Sylvio Romero advised Brazilian scientists to investigate and archive the remaining traits of "authentic" Africanity before they completely disappear. In Romero's statements one observes how postcolonial narratives of the nation combine historic and scientific signifying strategies that, in the Brazilian case, consist in the writing of the temporal trajectory of a subject able to produce a transparent social configuration to counter the argument of the scientists of *man* that this is a doomed project. In his *História da Literatura Brasileira,* Romero (1888) describes how

miscegenation had ensured the successful trajectory of a European
I in tropical lands. Though necessary in this process of miscegenation, he argues, Indians' and Africans' participation in the building
of the Brazilian "civilization" was neither lasting nor determining.
The Portuguese, but mostly their mixed sons, were the agents of
Brazilian history. The Portuguese, Romero argues, with their blood
and ideas, linked Brazil to the "great group of occidental people" to
which "we owe our institutions, our culture, and the contact with
European civilization" (105).[5] In his rendering of the whitening thesis Romero writes the temporal trajectory of the Brazilian nation
as the teleological movement of a (slightly tanned) European subject and the eschatological trajectory of its tropical helpers, that is,
his writing of the *mestiço* as the Brazilian subject is premised on
Africans' and Indians' intrinsic affectability. "The mestiço," he argues, "is the psychological product, ethnic and historic, of Brazil; it
is the new form of our national difference. Our popular psychology
is a product of this initial stage. This does not mean that we will
constitute a nation of mulattos; since the white form is prevailing,
and will continue to prevail; it means only that the European here
allied with other races, and from this union the genuine Brazilian
emerged, the one which does not confound with the Portuguese and
upon which our future rests" (91).

When deployed here as an eschatological signifier to refigure
the historical process that leads to the obliteration of the others of
Europe, miscegenation becomes not only an effect of the Portuguese
colonizer's "inner force" and "intrinsic difference," though its "desire" to rape African and Indian females obviously helped. It also
articulates the affectability of the others of Europe, who enter the
text as always already condemned to perish under the strength of
the "superior race." As many have pointed out, the whitening thesis
did not remain in the books of a few selected writers and scientists;
it was the object of animated debates in the Brazilian Congress as
well as grandiose immigration projects framed in terms of the need
to supply the necessary skilled labor force to the emerging industry
and the necessary influx of European bodies and minds to save the
nation from the ill effects of its past dangerous choices, slavery and
miscegenation. The objective of these projects was to increase the
number of whites in the population, hoping that the mixing with
the native population would accelerate the elimination of blacks

and dark *mestiços* (Vianna 1938). The threat miscegenation holds determined that these writings would privilege two themes: the disappearance of blacks from the population and the fundamentally white, European, Brazilian culture, which would increase further with European immigration (Silva 1989; Skidmore 1995). It did not matter that these immigrants were mostly Italian, Spaniards, and Portuguese, Southern Europeans who, as we saw previously, could easily be written outside whiteness. For the formulators of the whitening thesis, they were white; they would come from Europe, and their presence, in the present and the future, would help to ensure that Brazil constituted a modern social configuration.

In the last quarter of the nineteenth century, Brazil was one of the few former European colonies not configured as a liberal juridical-economic polity; there slavery would be abolished in 1888 and the Republic instituted the following year. In *Doutrina contra Doutrina,* Romero (1894) advocates the need to reorganize Brazil as a liberal polity but refuses to attribute the country's political situation to unrestrained miscegenation. Instead, in it he identifies the marker of the Brazilian populus's intrinsic democratic attributes. Why was Brazil politically unstable? For Romero, it resulted from the influence of positivist intellectuals and politicians who ignored the social reforms necessary to render the newborn Republic viable. He cited the country's backwardness, "where nine tenths of the population are illiterate; where large parts of the Central and Western regions are unknown and not inhabited; where the real organization of education, despite bureaucratic fantasy, is actually primitive; where the people still do not have consciousness of the great ideal it should realize; where the classes are amorphous and indistinct; where public opinion lacks discipline and a secure and rational orientation; where the most advanced still think that the old French Positivism is the last word in human knowledge" (286). The elites' backwardness was also actualized in the country's economic configuration. "Economically," he notes, "we are an embryonic nation, whose important industry is still a rudimentary agriculture, extensive, with two million national workers and some tens of thousands of European colonists. . . . National capitalism is scanty, almost stingy" (274).

For the most part, as the previous statements indicate, Romero's writings target the conservative elites' embracing of positivism as the basis for the political and economic reconfiguration of postslavery republican Brazil. But they also address negative statements on how miscegenation would impact the Brazilian people and the future of the country's newborn democracy. "Brazil," Romero reminds the positivist elites, "is an unavoidably democratic country. Son of modern culture, born in the era of great navigation and discoveries, which is important to say, after the constitution of the plebe and of the bourgeoisie; it is, besides, the result of the mixture of distinct races, where evidently the tropical blood predominates. Well, the two greatest factors in the equalizing of men are democracy and miscegenation. And these conditions we do not lack; to the contrary, they abound among us. And one and the other participate amply in the characterization of modern civilization: in Europe the increasing mixture of all classes, mainly after the French Revolution; in the rest of the world, mostly in the foundation of the colonies in America, Africa and Oceania, an enormous racial mixture" (267). When deploying miscegenation as a political concept, Romero does more than accentuate a liberal position. "In Brazil," he argues, "where the two forces, natural and social, have been constantly active; where the formation of the people was, on the one side, the result of the bourgeoisie, of the plebe, and of the third and fourth estate, and where, on the other side, the melting-pot of the three fundamental races has been enormous, democratization is unavoidable. Among such a mixed people, the *mestiços* of all gradations are the majority and, in democratic governments, the majority makes the law. All great events of our history are other victories of the Brazilian population, new, mixed in blood, feelings and institutions" (268–69). When accusing the positivist elite of ignoring democracy, a fundamental modern principle already actualized by the Brazilian people, Romero repeats Herder's injunctions against the embracers of "sickly reason" to write miscegenation as a signifier of democracy.

When I turn to the late nineteenth-century writings of the Brazilian text, I find the manufacturing of a historical account that would constitute the Brazilian people as a transparent I but one complicated by the prevailing argument that miscegenation produced an "unstable" and "degenerate" "racial type." For Brazilian intellectuals and politicians who, in the 1880s, thought it was time to reorganize the country along the lines of a modern capitalist nation-state, to counter this argument became a central task. In effect, the centrality of miscegenation in the Brazilian national text marks anything but a complete rupture with the nineteenth century's arguments that whiteness signifies the kind of consciousness meant to fulfill the projects of modernity. For that reason, the whitening thesis could not but rewrite miscegenation as an eschatological signifier that would result not in the "degeneration" of the European but in the obliteration of the Indian and the African from Brazilian bodies and minds. Not only was the *mestiço,* the embodiment of Portuguese desire, the privileged agent of Brazilian history; by the end of the nineteenth century, the number of "mixed-race" Brazilians could be used to support the argument that Brazil was ahead on the road to complete *whiteness.* Why was *whiteness* a necessary condition for the constitution of the Brazilian nation? The text of the science of man produced whiteness to signify a consciousness endowed with the productivity that resulted in the building of modern social spaces in Europe and in the United States. Hence, only the writing of miscegenation as a historical-eschatological signifier could enable the view that in the future the Brazilian subject would fulfill a European desire. Indeed, just as the U.S. American had been, the Brazilian is here produced as a racial subject whose "spirit" is European, while the national space—a defect writers of the U.S. American text successfully circumscribed to the South—was not only placed outside the European space but was shared with the others of Europe. Not possible before the 1930s—before the rewriting of racial difference as a substantive signifier of cultural difference—was the rewriting of miscegenation as a historical-teleological signifier to distinguish the temporal trajectory of a tropical transparent consciousness.[6]

Patriarchal "Civilization"

In the text of racial democracy, the appropriation of anthropological and race relations strategies finally enables the writing of Brazilian (historical) particularity. What the logic of obliteration informing these scientific renderings of the cultural allows is a version of the play of engulfment in which the two meanings of miscegenation, the teleological and the eschatological, can be deployed to write the *mestiço* (Brazilian) subject's temporal trajectory as a movement toward transparency. The deployment of these scientific signifying strategies has two primary effects. On the one hand, they enable a narrative that shows that since its "origins" the Brazilian subject has exhibited the attributes necessary for constructing a "modern civilization" in the tropics, namely, the ability to "assimilate" the "inferior races and cultures," to fulfill the "race relations cycle." On the other hand, both the anthropological writing of the "native" as always already "vanishing" and the sociological statement that miscegenation constitutes the only solution to the "problem of race relations" would support the statement that Brazil is a *racial democracy* precisely because the Portuguese's lack of "race prejudice" had the effect that the affectable Indians and Africans had disappeared or were rapidly disappearing from Brazil. For Indians, Africans, and Europeans were already democratically united in the transcendental moment of nation, for miscegenation constitutes Brazil's "intrinsic difference"; it endows the still hopelessly miscegenated Brazilians with their particular (tropical) kind of transparency. That is, the Brazilian text could be rewritten, for miscegenation could be safely deployed to write the teleological—the movement toward transparency—trajectory of the subject of a patriarchal "modern civilization." What does not take place here is an ethical crisis brought about by a celebration of the obliteration of an other, because in globality political subjects always already stand before the horizon of death and, as the foundational statement of race relations establishes, the historical destiny of the (affectable) others of Europe is obliteration.

By now I assume the reader will not cringe at my argument that the writing of the transparent Brazilian subject as a traditional (patriarchal) I has been enabled by the deployment of bona fide post-Enlightenment signifying strategies. If this is not the case, if the reader can read the Brazilian version of transcendental poesis only as contradictory, I think it helps if one recalls two things. First, Herder's account of *interiorized poesis,* in which tradition governs the historical, attempts to protect interiority from the *universal nomos,* and introduces the idea of universality of differentiation. Moreover, in the text of racial democracy, patriarchy marks Brazilian difference only because it is deployed in a modern text, that is, one governed by transcendental poesis. Second, the national text is a historic text (governed by transcendental poesis) in which scientific strategies (the tools of productive *nomos*) play the role of the supplement, for they institute that which the transparency thesis presumes but cannot deliver, that is, they mark the place of the transparent I. As versions of the scene of engulfment, then, national narratives necessarily institute fundamentally modern subjects, for the historic and scientific assume that the realization of the transparent I necessitates the engulfing of the others of Europe, because it also presumes the "other" ontological context, globality (spatiality-exteriority), that the analytics of raciality institutes.

In *Casa Grande e Senzala,* Gilberto Freyre ([1933] 1987) provides a version of the Brazilian text where the arsenals of race relations and anthropology produce a version of the play of engulfment in which patriarchy marks Brazilian difference. Through this version, racial democracy, articulates the presence of others of Europe by specifying their contribution to Brazilian particularity; it writes miscegenation as an effect of Portuguese desire when describing Brazil's history as the temporal process of obliteration of Africans and Indians. The most productive gesture here is the engulfing of racial difference, which takes three moments. First, in the statement that even before unleashing its tropical colonial adventure, due to Moorish dominion the Portuguese already possessed the racial and cultural attributes necessary to become a successful colonizer in the tropics. That is, because Portuguese bodies and minds retained traits, even if faint, of the others of Europe to which they had been subjected for centuries, they could not harbor "race prejudice." Second, the articulation of cultural difference to write the historical process displaces considerations of the juridical and economic dimensions of Portuguese colonization. Hence, Freyre rewrites Brazilian history as the actualization of the "distinguishing mark" of the Portuguese consciousness, its patriarchal values, still inscribed in the post-colonial, postslavery Brazilian social configuration. Further, because neither the Portuguese mind nor the colonial or slavery social configuration actualized "race prejudice," Freyre unproblematically reproduces the race relations view that racial difference does operate in the Brazilian social configuration.

Third, the choice of patriarchy over modern conceptions of juridical authority and economic relations renders "family" and "sexual life" the privileged sites for narrating how racial difference has operated in Brazilian history. This constitutes the most productive statement of the text of racial democracy. Because it renders the adult male slave, the worker in the plantations, absolutely irrelevant in the account of Brazilian history and consequently emphasizes the privileged position of the white European colonizer, the female slave would alone stand as the other of Europe who has aided in the production of that which marks the Brazilian "intrinsic difference," namely, the *mestiço*. With this Freyre writes the others of Europe as twice affectable in that not only is the female slave juridically and economically subjugated, but hers is a particular form of gender subjection, for in a patriarchal or slavery social configuration the family constitutes the center of the prevailing conceptions of morality. In racial democracy, racial difference plays no role in the juridical, economic, and moral configuration of colonial Brazil. Instead, it is resolved in the interiority of the always already slightly tanned subject of patriarchy. From this results a mode of racial subjection the sociohistorical logic of exclusion cannot capture precisely because both assume that miscegenation, as a process and index of the obliteration of racial difference, institutes social configurations where the racial does not operate as a strategy of power.

According to Freyre, unlike the English colonizers, the Portuguese were able to take advantage of Indians' and Africans' familiarity with the tropical environment, even though they never really depended on them to build the Brazilian "civilization." "When in 1532, the Brazilian society was economically and civilly organized," Freyre states, "the Portuguese had had contact with the tropics for a whole century; their aptitude for the tropical life had already been demonstrated in India and Africa . . . ; because there the colonial society had more solid basis and stable conditions than in India and Africa, in Brazil the definitive proof of this aptitude would be realized" (4). This aptitude, which derives from the fact that, because of their "ethnic, or better, cultural past" the Portuguese are an "undefined people" between Europe and Africa (5), produced a tropical civilization. "In tropical America," Freyre argues, "they created a society structurally agrarian, in which slavery provided the technique of economic exploration, hybrid of Indians—and later Negroes—in its composition. A society developed less on the basis of racial consciousness, which was virtually none among the plastic and cosmopolitan Portuguese, than on the basis of a religious exclusivism actualized in a system of social and political prophylaxis" (4). More than violence, Freyre argues, the "ethnic and cultural ambiguity" of the Portuguese responds to the successful colonization of Brazil and to the fact that "Brazil was formed without any concern with racial unity or purity" (29). The concept of the cultural, both as it is articulated in Herder's rendering of universal poesis and in the anthropological version of the concept, thoroughly and consistently organizes Freyre's writing of the Brazilian nation. When describing colonial conditions, he provides a vivid picture of a traditional (patriarchal) social configuration, a religious, family-centered, agricultural society that constitutes the Brazilian "intrinsic difference." "The conservative tradition in Brazil," he argues, "has only been sustained by the sadism of command, disguised in the 'principle of Authority,' or the 'defense of Order.' Between these two myths—of Order and of Freedom, and of Authority and Democracy—our political life, which has left the regime of masters and slave too early, tries to find equilibrium. In fact, the equilibrium remains one between the profound and traditional realities: sadist and masochist, masters and slaves, doctors and illiterates, individuals with a predominantly European culture and others with a primarily Indian and African culture" (52). Regarding the articulation of the presence of the others of Europe, this rewriting of the predicament of the Brazilian culture, which, as we saw earlier, is redeployed in sociological investigations, enables Freyre to all but ignore the violent aspects of colonization and slavery, to privilege their influence on the colonial family. With this he rewrites the affectability of the Indians and Africans by enveloping them in the culinary, affective, and pathological aspect of the patriarchal family life. When describing the place of Indians in this context, Freyre rapidly writes their irrelevance by noting that their "laziness" required an immediate substitution for the African. What remains from the Indian, besides culinary items and folklore, is "the feminine part of its culture, which was only feminine in its technique," because females were responsible for the agricultural labor necessary for the "agrarian economic organization the Portuguese established in these American lands" (159).

Half of Freyre's text, however, is dedicated to an account of the "Negro slave [influence] in the Brazilian sexual and family life." It is precisely here that Freyre's deployment of the cultural difference to write the Brazilian subject as a *traditional* (patriarchal) subject of a democracy is contingent on the articulation of the others of Europe in affectability, which sets up a historical version of their necessary obliteration (as the strategies of scientific reason postulate). The productive signifying gesture, the engulfment, enables the account of miscegenation as a process of productive violence, that is, it recuperates the productivity of the Portuguese subject and narrates its teleology as an effect of the obliteration of the black or slave subject, which is not an effect of the Portuguese violent desire but something is presumed in the scientific signifying strategies Freyre deploys. What this privileging of the patriarchal family enables is the immediate displacing of the adult male slave, which is encompassed in the general references to the "Negro" or the slave, but virtually never enters the text in accounts of the toil on the plantation. "In the tenderness," Freyre says, "in the excessive mimic, Catholicism in which we enjoy our senses, in the music, walk, speech, lullabies for the small boy, in everything which is a sincere expression of life, we bring a mark of the African influence: from the slave or mammy who held us, who breastfed us, who fed us, after softening the food in her mouth; from the old black woman who told us our first scary childhood tales; from the mulatto woman who treated us and the one who initiated us in physical love and gave us, in the noisy air bed, the first full sensation of manhood; and from the black boy who was our first companion" (283).

When dismissing the science of man's argument of "Negro mental inferiority," in his opening quote Freyre cites contemporary anthropological studies of African culture to rewrite blacks' affectability as an effect of sociohistorical processes. Though this statement refers to the effects of slaves' juridical-economic position, for Freyre these moments of the patriarchal social configuration are not relevant to capturing the black Brazilian consciousness. Following the logic of the obliteration deployed in the "theory of racial and cultural contacts," Freyre describes how the African slave would "assimilate" into Portuguese patriarchal social configuration: "In the order of influence the forces of the slavery system acted upon the recently arrived African slave are: the church, i.e. the small one of the patriarchal farm; the slave quarters; and manor itself—i.e. considered as part, and not as the center of the dominating Brazilian system of colonization and patriarchal formation. The method of de-africanizing of the 'new' negro here followed was to mix them with the mass of 'ladinos' or veterans, so as the slave quarters became the practical school of brazilianization" (357).

Though Freyre also spends some time enumerating the non-determining "African cultural influences," culinary contributions, folklore, and so on that the Portuguese colonizer received from his black (enslaved) mammy and his young black companions, for Freyre Africans' only relevant contribution was the body of the female slave. In the statement that writes miscegenation as a *teleological* signifier, the productive power, the "inner force," belongs to the Portuguese because their "inclination" to sexual intimacy produces the slightly tanned Brazilian subject. "In relation to miscibility," Freyre explains, "no other modern colonizer has exceeded or even matched the Portuguese. It was by deliciously mixing with women of color from the first contact multiplying themselves in hybrid sons that only few thousands of intrepid machos were able to take possession of very extensive lands and compete with great and numerous peoples in the extension of the colonial possession and in the efficacy of the colonial action" (9). No doubt this privileging of Portuguese sexuality constitutes a crucial dimension of the writing of the black Brazilians as subaltern subjects in that it provides no account of black male sexuality, which has already been removed from the narrative of Brazilian patriarchy, which is from the outset written as a Portuguese "intrinsic difference." Here, however, I am more interested in how this privileging of sexuality in the writing of Brazilian particularity produces the racial/gendered subaltern subject. In Freyre's statements, gendered/racial subjection is produced in the same movement that articulates blackness as an auxiliary (not a determining) marker of Brazilian particularity.

With the placing of miscegenation at the core of the national text, the gendered/racial subaltern subject is written as exhibiting a double affectability. More important, the writing of the Indian and the enslaved African female bodies as the instruments of the Portuguese desire renders productive the violence that created the Brazilian subject. According to Freyre, the "promiscuity" characterizing colonial society resulted from a combination of the male Portuguese's own uncontrolled lust and the easy access he had to the female slave body. Thus, although the male slave and the white woman had their sexuality controlled by the patriarchal system, the Portuguese male and the female slave appeared as the main agents (rather the agent and the instrument) of miscegenation. "The Negro or mulatto women," he claims, "[were] responsible for the precipitation of the erotic life and sexual dissolution of the young Brazilian male. With the same logic one could hold the domestic animals responsible; the banana tree; the watermelon. . . . Almost all of them were the objects upon which the sexual precocity of the young Brazilian man was, and still is, exercised" (371). The most important effect of this celebration of uncontrolled sexuality was not just to mask the violence inherent to slavery. The gendered-racial subaltern was twice affectable. Neither passion (which, though not determined by reason, instituted a subject as the affected person I determined by a given object), nor love (which also refers to a mode of affection, but one that does not depart from the boundaries of rational morality), nor consent (which is a privilege of the self-determined rational thing) could be deployed to capture the female racial subaltern. Her reasons and passions, the attributes of one who desires, of a subject, were written as irrelevant in the statement that compared her to a banana tree, an object that should be engulfed, an exterior thing whose appropriation was necessary for the actualization of the male's desire, that which the Portuguese needed to release the unrestrained lust that marked their particular productive power.

My point is that the effectiveness of racial democracy as a positive historical account depended on the production of the black (and mulatto) female body as a collective (male) property to which no conception of law applied, neither rational law (the moral law or the law of society) nor patriarchal law (the "natural [divine] law"), which constitutes the primary determinant of gender subjection in modern social configurations. That is, the writing of the black Brazilian female body as an instrument of Portuguese desire instituted a mode of racial subjection that was at the same time the very condition of possibility for the writing of the trajectory of a transparent I. In racial democracy, then, the deployment of race relations' version of (physical and cultural) miscegenation wrote blackness and Africanness to distinguish the national subject, as "residues" of the African "spirit" captured by Freyre's fellow Brazilian anthropologists. That is, they were not determining traits because blacks' racial difference entered the narrative of the temporal trajectory of the Brazilian subject in affectability, as the always-already "vanishing" African culture that provided nondetermining cultural traits (culinary contributions and folklore) and as the female racial subaltern subject was twice affectable, determined from without, namely, by her juridical-economic conditions and by her positioning outside the moral rules of patriarchy.

Put differently, racial democracy could describe the national subjects' temporal trajectory, to write it as a particular subject of transcendental poesis, because in its account of miscegenation the appropriation of black females bodies enabled the deployment of the
Portuguese productive power, which was necessary to the writing of
a teleology. Nevertheless, the eschatological meaning of miscegenation was necessary here to write the *mestiço,* the Brazilian subject,
to signify solely the Portuguese productive power. It is only because
racial democracy is an explicit gendered text, where the affectable female slave writes Portuguese productive power, that the deployment
of the racial in a text ruled by the cultural could write the teleology of
a transparent (European) subject even if he could be articulated only
as a patriarchal I. This successful version of the Brazilian subject had
a price. Because the "spirit" of the nation encapsulated both African
culture and physical traits, in this version of the Brazilian text blackness cannot signify a self-determined and productive, even if subaltern, subject. Nevertheless, precisely because the appropriation of
the black female body was also premised on the idea that only whiteness signifies the transparent I, the blackness and Africanness the
woman's offspring inherit from her remain as dangerous signifiers
of a subject of affectability who cannot but signify Brazil's unstable
placing at the outskirts of the modern global configuration.

HYBRIS

Has this version of the Brazilian text been displaced? In case there is
any doubt regarding the correct answer to this question, in *Guerra e
Paz* Ricardo B. Araújo (1994) offers a "postmodern'" reading of
Casa Grande e Senzala and other of Freyre's texts that indicates
how the predicament miscegenation instituted still haunts Brazilian
anthropologists. In his reading of Freyre's version of racial democracy, Araújo attempts to discern what distinguishes Freyre's sociology,
primarily (but not solely) in terms of his rewriting of the Brazilian
text. He challenges the "accusation" that Freyre had deployed miscegenation to produce the image of Brazil as a "racial paradise"—by
masking the brutality inherent to slavery—by arguing that Freyre
writes the Portuguese colonizers as hybrids facing the task of rec-
onciling their distinct tendencies. There would have been nothing
problematic in this argument had Araújo not placed hybris (which
he translates as excess) at the center of Freyre's sociology. To be sure,

Araújo does capture a crucial dimension of Freyre's version of the "tropical democracy," for he identifies hybris as a consistent trope in Freyre's construction of the Portuguese, the tropic, and Brazilian slavery. But the rhetorical figure Araújo deploys to answer the question of why the disparate tendencies remain in a situation of equilibrium, including that between the despotic and the intimate nature of slave (social) relations, becomes an interpretive correspondent to the violence erased in Freyre's reading of slavery. For Araújo argues that "the sexual excess is, in fact, the main responsible for the creation of 'zones of fraternization' . . . which counterbalanced, up to a point, the despotism typical of slavery" (64–65). That this excess remains a Portuguese attribute, a trope for brutality, becomes irrelevant when Araújo suggests that it is exactly the loss of this dimension of intimacy between masters and slaves that characterizes the modernization of the Brazilian society. More important, because Araújo's project is to recuperate Freyre as a critic of essentialism, a kind of ancestor of the postmodern and cosmopolitan critics of modernity, Freyre's apology for hybridity repeats itself in Araújo's reappropriation, for the "object" of Portuguese unrestrained (excessive) desire remains the condition of possibility not, as Freyre wrote her, for Brazilian *(tropical) modernity* but for writing the Brazilian social configuration as always already postmodern.

In Araújo's reading, the gendered/racialized subject emerges again in her double affectability. In contrast, the recognition of the position of the female slave would have led the author to perceive that this unrestrained libido (the force of miscegenation) is actually another (gendered) moment of violence of the (intrinsically violent) master-slave relation. Although the female subaltern's desire—passion, love, and consent (or lack of these)—cannot be articulated in the text that (re)produces her subjection, her silent position is not irrelevant (Spivak, 1994). Every and each reading of the signifying context of her erasure should aim for its productive effects. If it does not, it will rehearse her obliteration, which in the case of Brazil articulates the desire for the obliteration of that which means conservatively about half of the population. Because Araújo's postmodern reading of racial democracy deploys another version of the ethical demand for eliminating the racial from the modern political grammar, it erases precisely the fact that miscegenation has operated as a solution to the predicament of Brazilian elites only because it signifies the obliteration of racial difference. Only by recognizing that this predicament is a product of the very signifying strategies deployed to unpack it, which wrote both Brazil and its always already slightly darker inhabitants as inhabiting the domain of exteriority, will it be possible to formulate emancipatory strategies that may write a future not only for the larger majority of its inhabitants, whom our strategy of racial subjection has written not as always already exterior but as ever nearing the moment of final obliteration. What many today deplore as unrestricted *violência* (violence) that is haunting Brazilian elites into hiding in their bullet-proof cars and high-security condominiums and hijacking the future of whole generations of black and brown Brazilians is but the latest manifestation of the national desire to obliterate the Brazilian people, who, regardless of its elites' desire for whiteness, insist on signifying otherwise.

Following the grammar of transcendental poesis, the text of racial democracy reproduces the sociological statement that racial difference as a signifier of cultural difference could not operate in the Brazilian social configuration because its obliteration would result in the reinstitution of transparency in social configurations that actualize a European consciousness. From that results mappings of the modern Brazilian social configuration in which the *mestiço* emerges as the Brazilian social subject, which assumes that the causes of his or her social subjection can be apprehended only with the category that more appropriately explains modern social configurations, namely, class. The Brazilian subject is the *mestiço;* the proportion of the markers of blackness in his or her body will determine whether he or she belongs in the present and in the future of the nation. Elsewhere (Silva 1998) I argue that a crucial effect of this political-symbolic strategy has been to preclude considerations of racial difference as a dimension of the Brazilian social space. The effect here is not ideological, in the sense that the "dominant racial ideology" hides how racial difference operates in the Brazilian social configuration, but productive. The strategy of racial subjection it entails does not need racial difference to delimit the place of the national subject. For this reason, this mode of racial subjection could not be grasped by the arsenal of race relations. Not because it proves the universal applicability of the "race relations cycle," but because it deploys the logic of obliteration it institutes. Because racial democracy attempts to resolve Brazil's predicament in a version of the scene of engulfment, where the productive moment is the violent appropriation of black female bodies, the "race consciousness" missed by contemporary students of racial politics in Brazil is not available because it presupposes an excluded other, one not engulfed in the narrative of a particular subject of transcendental poesis, who can be/come the subject of a racial poesis. With this I am not mourning the impossibility of writing the black Brazilian subject as a transparent I; I am merely pointing to how the analytics of raciality consistently produces Brazil, and other polities situated in the global South, as global subaltern subjects.

How does this fashioning of the Brazilian as a specimen of *homo modernus* aid the understanding of the contemporary global configuration? Throughout the twentieth century, across the globe historians, fiction writers, and literary critics produced national (historical) narratives in which scientific signifiers ensured what transcendental poesis can only prescribe, namely, the safe placement *of* the national subject in transparency. Much as in other postcolonial polities now situated in the global South, in Brazil an additional effort was required. Unlike their U.S. counterparts, the writers of the Brazilian nation could not immediately produce an account of the unfolding of a European desire because the analytics of raciality produced the bodies of their country(wo)men as signifiers of an affectable consciousness. What renders miscegenation a global signifier that most dramatically indicates the precariousness, due to its hopeless situatedness, of the transparent I, is the fact that the writing of the temporal trajectory of a *mestiço* subject forces an account of the relationships developed among those to whom the weapons of raciality attribute such a fundamental (irreducible and unsublatable) difference that their encounter would lead to the destruction of the affectable ones or of both. Not surprisingly, I show how in the successful version of the Brazilian text these relationships are eliminated from the moment of transparency (the actual present) and placed in the past, where the affectable other emerges as instrument and raw material of the transparent-to-be consciousness, whose temporal trajectory always already presumes the eventual obliteration of the racial subaltern. The fact that the sociohistorical logic of exclusion cannot apprehend this mode of racial subjection without reducing it to a variation of the U.S. mode of racial subjection should not overshadow its efficacy. Attention to how miscegenation operates as a global signifier would check (postmodern and otherwise) celebrations of hybridity, biraciality, multiraciality, and postraciality, which, by having racial difference as their only target, reflexively renew the foundational statement of race relations that attributes the causes of racial subjection to the inability of the others of Europe to become transparent. More important, because it more explicitly captures the logic of obliteration, it indicates how the signifiers of globality institute global regions that remain perilously at the outskirts of modernity. What prevents Brazil from being viewed as the ("empirical") referent entity of the sociological text other than its population's profile? Only anthropological strategies seemed adequate to comprehend the conspicuous presence of the others of Europe and of a *mestiço* population that signifies Europeaness "other"-wise. Much to the despair of today's policy makers, Brazil's global political-economic positioning differs little from that of those countries in Asia, the Pacific islands, and Africa whose populations dramatically signify "other"-wise. The ever-"vanishing" others of Europe thrive under global economic policies that need to exploit their labor and the squeezing of their limited consuming power through the destruction of their safety nets. My point is that understanding of the consistent juridical and economic placing of countries like Brazil requires an acknowledgement that the analytics of raciality has governed the global configuration for about a hundred years or so.

Precariously situated in the global South, Brazil now faces new deployments of modern and no longer solely European and white (European, U.S. American, and Japanese) power/desire, which no longer needs to occupy the lands or enslave the bodies of their "natives" to exploit them because the always-already affectable global subaltern subjects have also been engulfed by disembodied, virtual, strategies of power that hijack their futures without—thanks to the accumulation of so many scientific writings of their exteriority— having to be held accountable for their past. About sixty years ago, colonial subjects of Africa, Asia, Latin America, and the Caribbean held onto their racial difference organized in transregional emancipatory projects, such as Pan-Africanism and Negritude, in which many postcolonial leaders were formed; about twenty years ago, "others of Europe" everywhere held onto their cultural difference to demand the expansion of the dominion of universality and self-determination in their home countries. How much longer will it take until it is acknowledged that the conditions under which they rewrite their own history is not of their making, that the difference that marks them as subaltern subjects also instituted the place of those who exploit and dominate them? About fifty years have passed already since Fanon's outline of the figures that can emerge only in modern representation, the specimens of *homo modernus,* those whose bodily and social configurations do not spell the proper name of man, that is, the global subaltern subjects.

Conclusion: Future Anterior

*He travels endlessly over that plain, without ever crossing the clear bound-
aries of difference, or reaching the heart of identity. Moreover, he is himself like a sign, a long, thin, graphism, a letter that has just escaped from
the open pages of a book. His whole being is nothing but language, text
printed pages, stories that have already been written down. He is made
up of interwoven words; he is writing itself, wandering through the world
among the resemblances of things. Yet not entirely so: for in his reality as
an impoverished hidalgo he can become a knight only by listening from
afar to the age-old epic that gives form to Law.*

—MICHEL FOUCAULT, *THE ORDER OF THINGS*

*My life had its significance and its only deep significance because it was
part of a Problem; but that problem was, as I continue to think, the central
problem of the greatest of the world's democracies and so the Problem of
the future world.*

—W. E. B. DU BOIS, *DUSK OF DAWN*

What sort of answers would one find if she addressed the founding
statements of modern representation, questions that already presuppose "Other"-wise? If abandoning "discovery," the routine of "nor-
mal science," which all too often repeats "thus it is proved" kinds of
statements (Kuhn 1970), the analyst of the social asks other, disturbing, questions—for example, ones that assume that Don Quixote
is both "right" and "wrong," that windmills were indeed knights,
though knights could never be/come windmills. For such questions

253

to be imagined, the master account should not begin, as it does, "In the beginning, when God created the heavens and the earth was a formless void and darkness covered the face of the deep, while a wind from [the spirit, breath of] God swept over the face of the waters. . . ." Because it would have to assume that the writing of time as "the *interiority* of the subject itself and space [as] its *exteriority*" (7, italics in the original), to borrow Luce Irigaray's (1993) interrogation, has always already presumed, before the logos, the irreducible bar and the ontology it announces, which institutes and unsettles what the modern distinctions of "time and space," "soul and body," "right and wrong," "truth and falsity," "freedom and unfreedom" signify—something the analyst of the social should assume even if she could never recognize it.

When excavating the founding statements of modern thought guided by these questions, I found myself much like the "distracted" sociologist, Avery Gordon (1997) in her pursuit of the strategic naming of a critical sociological position that leaves the pathway of "discovery." Instead of taking the road to literature, I chose a sideway to philosophy, wondering whether my annoyance with historicity and universality, whether my hopeless inclination to ask "other"-wise, had led me astray. For I engaged interventions deployed in a moment when Western thought revered the "truth" of *nomos,* when reason was conceived as a constraining force, expecting to find statements that dismissed the illusions of poesis. What I found instead were statements that protected the mind's self-determination, with a deferential disinterest in rendering it an object of scientific reason, which left the way open for its appropriation in accounts of *universal poesis.* Had I lost my way? Perhaps, but most likely not, because, rather than the contradiction my reading of postmodern and postcolonial critics of modern ontology has trained me to identify, the one their moral embracing of historicity assumes, I met with an intimacy that explains why my rejection of the normative choice has led me precisely to the place where I had begun. For this reason, I abandoned my initial question—namely, What if modern thought had been *"other"*-wise, if it had always privileged exteriority?—because once I missed the contradiction I was destined to find, I learned that nothing much would have changed. My failure to grasp the difference between interiority and exteriority, I think, derives from the fact that this distinction "signifies" always already within modern representation, where it corresponds to the fields of history and sci-

ence and the two accounts of the self-determined thing they autho-
rize. Hence, I could only but return to the least complex formulation
of a more troubling question: If the distinction between interiority
and exteriority does indeed belong to the ontological moment of
globality—for Western thought has consistently accepted the view
that the inside and the outside, the within and the without, are attributes of bodies, of extended (exterior/affectable) things—how is
it possible that this distinction preserves interiority as the exclusive
attribute of the *transparent "I"*?

Chasing the answer to this question, I traced the trajectory of
self-consciousness, the figure who, by the end of the seventeenth
century, had sent astrologers, magicians, witch doctors, and those
engaged in the deciphering of the signs of the world into exile in
the province of superstition, the figure which, because always already assumed, needed not be reasserted in statements that rewrote
universal reason as a regulative or productive force. For had self-
consciousness, the self-determined thing, the only one able alone to
decide on its essence and existence, not shared a profound intimacy
with a regulative or productive logos, universal reason, it could not
have organized the "table of identities and difference," the "space
of order" in the margins of which Foucault (1994) locates two figures that entertain contrasting relations to modern signification: the
madman and the poet. When revisiting this epistemological configuration, moved by the questioning of interiority the racial cannot
but impose on modern representation, I learned that the madman
and the poet are the limits only because they constitute the two faces
of self-consciousness. Never oblivious to the logos, if it is taken to
signify a given order (rule or disposition, connection or word[ing])
of things, the mind that misrepresents, the one that fails to communicate the proper meanings, still assumes that correspondence
between words and things that defines representation; rather than
being without reason and word, the madman represents according
to other rules of signification. Nor does the poet, the mind who attempts to unearth hidden similitude, move beyond the boundaries of
modern representation; otherwise the meanings it produces would
vanish as noise, as a loss, and not as an addition to signification.

What neither the madman nor the poet follows, that which responds to their appeal to modern imagination, is the logic of "discovery," the stipulations (control and instrumentality) of scientific
reason that consolidate but also threaten self-consciousness as a

thing of freedom. Nevertheless, as refigurings of self-determination, of self-consciousness that rubs against the protective constraints of the logos, the madman and the poet represent "pure" interiority only because they announce its (im)possibility. As the previous pages indicate, the figure of self-consciousness could not proceed without the logos, which, in the play of *nomos* or poesis, enables the assertion of the mind's ability to access the "truth of things," its ability to capture the manifoldness of the whole of created things with abstract symbols (mathematical and not). In the guise of a regulative (scientific, juridical) or productive (moral) force, universal reason has governed modern representation even as it has been divided into the themes of universality and historicity in attempts to ensure the privilege of self-consciousness in relation to other existing things. For this reason, the madman and the poet would follow distinct trajectories. The poet, the mind that reveals by rearranging signifiers, self-consciousness facing toward universal reason because—as long as poesis, this human productive yearning, does not aim to replace the divine author (as in the case of Frankenstein)—it remains within the boundaries of universal reason, from which it seeks to expand its ends or to (re)interpret its effects, as in Herder's account of universal poesis, where one finds the mind actualizing the principles it receives from the universal creator but never displacing it. Now the mind that represents according to other rules, self-consciousness facing away from universal reason, peering without the *nomos* and poesis, the madman (as Cervantes' wandering hidalgo) has been pushed to the irrelevant margins of modern representation as the signifier of a mind that comprehends neither space nor time. For what else explains why neither *productive nomos* (which locked away madness with pitiful abjection) nor *transcendental poesis* (for which madness does not even become a problem) has qualms, meeting the madman's admonitions with laughter?

Nor would the critiques of modern thought deployed in the second half of the twentieth century and their postmodern followers listen to the warnings of the madman, even though they owe as much to Nietzsche's attacks on reason as they do to Freud's use of the dreams of the hysteric to map the unconscious, Lacan's deciphering of psychotic speech to map a symbolic economy that does not need transparency, Fanon's account of the psychic effects of colonial violence, and Foucault's politicizing of the insane. For "post" critiques of modernity, whether analytic or hermeneutic, challenge universal reason but embrace universal poesis, remaining well at the core of modern representation. In postmodern critical exercises, this limit appears in the privileging of historicity, which, as strategies of inclusion or ideological unmasking, will fulfill the promises it shares with universality, that is, to reveal a "truth" that is but the other name of justice or vice versa, rendering the latter finally realized. My point here is that historicity cannot dissipate its effects, which, in the case of postmodern strategies, are (a) an account of particularity as the effect of the universality of differentiation that institutes "being" before any possible relationship that counts as political and (b) an account of universality that presumes the operation of ideological strategies that unite particular ("intrinsically different") collectivities at the level of "ideal equality," masking the "real" basis of their social existence, which is that these relationships are necessarily "political" (juridically and economically unequal).

Neither effect of historicity I acknowledge would hinder the formulation of global emancipatory projects, ones that would address the conditions of the racial subaltern subject, if transcendental poesis alone governed contemporary social configurations. In transcendental poesis, "Spirit" resolves particularity and universality, effect and cause, multiplicity and "inner force" in a narrative where temporality becomes the "essence" of universal reason; it reunites man and the things (of nature) by transforming the latter into moments of the trajectory of self-productive universal reason, which knowledge has the task of revealing, in the same movement that it reveals that individuals' actions and consciousness do no more than actualize the will and design of Spirit. From this derives the first effect of historicity, in which the various particular collectivities indicate the contemporaneity of disparate stages of Spirit's trajectory fundamentally united in the transcendental productive force they actualize. Nevertheless, transcendental poesis cannot fulfill the promise of inclusion because neither the transparent social conditions it describes nor the ethical principle they actualize, transdencentality, is global. Following eighteenth-century narratives of human history, Hegel's description of the various stages of human self-development locates the final moment of the realization of Spirit within the spatial-temporal boundaries of post-Enlightenment Europe, when human consciousness and the social (juridical, economic, and moral) configurations reached the moment of transparency—when they realized universal reason as freedom. Hence the second effect of historicity, which, though not immediately prescribed by, is congenial with Hegel's account. For if one begins with the assumption that particularity is but a manifestation of "a nonessential," "nonfundamental" differentiation—that is, if one assumes that all particularity is resolved in universality (regulatory/productive) shape-shifted into transcendentality—any use of difference to justify domination and exploitation does no more than to mask truth, that is, that any collectivity, every human being, constitutes but a manifestation of Spirit.

I am suggesting here that transcendental poesis does not sustain the boundaries it describes. For if the destiny of Spirit is realization, each and every social configuration and shapes of consciousness preceding post-Enlightenment Europe's would in time reach the moment of transparency. For such possibility to be denied, it was necessary to write post-Enlightenment Europe's particularity as something irreducible and unsublatable that cannot be resolved or dissipated in the trajectory of the subject of transcendental poesis, but will be achievable only when the difference between Europeans and yesterday's natives becomes an effect of the tools of productive *nomos*. Precisely because they do not engage scientific signification, postmodern and postcolonial critics embrace the promises of historicity, oblivious to the fact that its limits do not reside on its margins, in the "other," which is another poet, the subject of another poesis, but in the "Other" (im)possible mode of representation that the speech of the madman cannot but signify. For this reason, the first move of this text was to identify in the symbolic moment of modern power the operation of scientific and historic rules of signification. I read modern representation as a text in which scientific strategies "supplement" ruling historicity. When deployed in historic texts, scientific signifiers both add to and supplement, constitute and interrupt, the *transparency thesis*. On the one hand, they simultaneously institute and interrupt the narrative of the transparent I that signifiers of exteriority constitute by adding, by making it possible to equate certain exterior, "objective" conditions to the realization of the transcendental temporal movement. On the other hand, they also delimit and produce the zone of operation of the principle of transcendentality, because, as products of scientific texts, they indicate a moment of signification when "science" coexists with "history," where "space" touches the boundaries of "time," in which interiority comes into being against that which it is not, that is, exteriority.

My argument in this book is that modern representation can sustain transparency, as the distinguishing feature of post-Enlightenment European social configurations, only through the engulfment of exterior things, the inescapable effect of scientific reason's version of universality, while at the same time postponing that "Other" ontology it threatens to institute. To be sure, the importance of an engagement with scientific reason is already indicated by the very text that introduces the ideological argument deployed in postmodern texts. It is in scientific signification that Marx finds the strategies he uses in the critique of the account of transcendental poesis as ideology—namely, the masking of the "material" (as opposed to "ideal") economic conditions that constitute human beings as social (interdependent) things—a critique, it should be acknowledged, enabled by Hegel's limited resolution. For the consolidation of universal poesis as transcendental poesis does not displace the *universal nomos* in its scientific and juridical moments, because self-consciousness could not relinquish that which supports its institutive claim, that is, the ability to know the "truth of things" and determine action. But also because, by resolving reason into freedom, the narrative of transcendental poesis introduces the symbolic, when writing of the nation, as a political-moral moment, one that, along with the juridical and the economic, consists in a moment of actualization (exteriorization) of universal reason, as Spirit, the regulating/productive force, the one that writes *homo historicus* as the subject of transparency by postulating the effect of the deployment of the *nomos* in social conditions as the realization of poesis.

These gestures enable the emergence of scientific projects that introduce an account of universal reason as productive *nomos*, the ones that, by assuming the resolution of regulation into representation (productivity), perform the engulfing of nature with the result that, subsumed to transcendental temporality, universality and exteriority become moments of a productive (temporal) process, respectively universalization and exteriorization. Hegel's resolution, which consolidates modern representation, also offers the point of departure for scientific rewritings of the figure residing in its core, namely, *homo historicus*. I am not saying that it is the only source, though I have yet to locate a deployment of the productive *nomos* that does not in some way, directly or indirectly, engage Hegel's account. Rather, by pursuing this effect of transcendental poesis, I embarked on an analysis of modern representation that fully engages its promises and limits because I am convinced that the critical projects that have done otherwise, the ones that only partially engaged either or both, have but (re)produced its (highly productive) effects.

Perhaps the most crucial obstacle to postmodern critical projects has been the refusal to engage this predicament. If anything, our reflexive refusal to side with the madman betrays the intuition that any critique of modern representation should not abandon its grammar and lexicon lest it fall into risible oblivion. I wrote this text within the same constraint. For the mapping of the *analytics of raciality* results from a critical analysis of that region of modern representation, namely, the field of science, the one consistently dismissed by most contemporary analysts of racial subjection as the moment of "falsification." This mapping is not an easy task. The problem here is that undertaking this project, which is crucial if one wishes to capture the political effects of the racial, demands a dive into the reservoir of available critical strategies while at the same time avoiding their limitations. Far from the madman's but even further from the poet's, this critical position faces modern representation sideways through an oblique—from without but without dismissing (as falsification) the logic of "discovery"—engagement with the scientific projects Hegel's resolution both necessitated and authorized. For to capture the political effects of the scientific texts in which man becomes a thing of nature, the most powerful and efficient modern strategies of power because the most productive, one should recognize that transcendental poesis cannot dissipate their effects because it has rendered their deployment necessary.

When I began this project I had only a vague idea of what I wanted to accomplish. I was unsatisfied with how the concept of race was deployed in sociological studies that attempted to explain the social conditions prevailing in the larger collectivities to which I belong juridically, as a Brazilian national and a U.S. permanent resident, though race is so obviously a crucial dimension of their economic and symbolic moment. I was tired of statements such as "Brazil has a multiple system of racial classification, while the U.S. has a binary one," "Americans are obsessed with race, while Brazilians repress

it," "Unlike African Americans, black Brazilians have no race consciousness," and so on. I wanted to understand, but the sociological arsenal available could not help me. Although in both countries
blacks occupy a subaltern position, one that stands before the principles, universality and self-determination, that govern modern juridical and economic dimensions. And yet, the political-symbolic
moment of racial subjection appeared disturbingly different. Like
other students of racial subjection, I knew that it had something to
do with the relationship between race and nation. But I knew nothing beyond that.

From a sociological point of view—which is important here because that is my official disciplinary corner, I know just as much
now. Yet earlier I failed to comprehend so many events! Events that
are, to be sure, fully explained by what and how I know: another
death of a black or brown youth at the hands of law enforcement,
another death related to drug trafficking, another prison rebellion
where many prisoners die, another suicide bombing, another legal
act whose objective is to place more and more "others of Europe" in
a state of illegality. When I learned about them, I got mad. Because
that which enables my "understanding" explains away these events
(and the fear they entail), resolving them in neat sociological formulations that write the deaths I hear about and the ones I can only
imagine as events foretold. Being mad is not bad, for, as Patricia
Williams reminds us, being mad marks the critical position the racial demands. It is good to have company. I just wished there were
more. When I read Gordon (1997) telling of the distraction that led
her to "see" ghosts, I think of my inability to live with mine. These
ghosts have first and last names: the ones I met as a child, others I
met just after they were born and are already dead, and the numerous ones of whom I will know nothing about either their lives or
their deaths. Haunted and mad, I engaged in the project of mapping
the trajectory of the racial, that modern signifier that delimits all the
murders producing the *place* where the lives, the social trajectory, of
racial subaltern subjects unfold.

My description of the effects of signification of the tools of raciality in narratives of the nation transforms these early modern
political subjects into global subjects, specimens of *homo modernus* produced by signifying strategies confected in both domains of
modern thought. What it reveals is that the writing of the teleology

of the U.S. and Brazilian national subjects in transparency necessitated the deployment of the arsenal of raciality, which enabled the establishment of their political location while at the same time providing symbolic elements that can be used in the mapping of these social spaces. That is, it indicates that modern social configurations are the effects of political-symbolic strategies that defined who among the inhabitants of a given nation-state would inhabit the territory of transparency, the one governed by universality and self-determination. In other words, my mapping of the analytics of raciality shows how the philosophical displacement and negation of the human body in the institution of *homo historicus* was just one moment of the writing of the modern subject, namely, *homo modernus*. Moreover, the consistent deployment of the strategies of productive *nomos* in the delimitation of the place of the transparent I indicates the necessity of writing certain human beings as subjects of *affectability*; otherwise the frontiers between post-Enlightenment Europeans and their "others" would not be maintained.

And yet the transparency thesis has been rather powerful. Such is its appeal that the accounts that constituted the most radical critiques of modern thought have not escaped its logic. As noted earlier, historical materialism itself, which targets both dimensions of *homo modernus,* provides an account of emancipation, which is but the institution of "true" transparency, the moment in which the universally dispossessed proletarian overcomes the alienation imposed by liberal ideologies to seize the means and results of man's productive powers. Marxism's embracing of historicity limits its deployment as a basis for the projects of racial emancipation. For one thing, the assumption of a universal human being outside economic exploitation renders it impossible to account for modes of subjection that write human beings as fundamentally different. What I am suggesting here is that the idea of alienation itself presupposes transparency in that it wishes for a moment when the recognition of the productivity of labor, when the desire, will emerge for determining that the producers should enjoy the benefits it brings. Precisely because of its desire for transparency, historical materialism has been a rather limiting strategy for the writing of the racial subaltern as a subject.

What distinguishes writing of the racial subaltern subject is precisely the fact that the strategies of scientific reason, the racial and the cultural, consistently write its affectability. Here we are before the moment of transparency but already when modern minds claim a particularity derived from interiority and temporality. At this moment, Western thought learns of the universality of law (juridical) and the universality of causality (scientific) which, it postulates, can be captured only by beings with reason. As suggested in Part 1, the liberal account of the emergence of the political is premised on the certainty of the naturality of regulation, for its earlier framers assumed that the divine ruler and creator was the supreme regulator of nature, including that of human beings. But they also assumed—and here I have in mind Hobbes and Locke, not Kant—that the divine ruler and creator endowed human beings with self-determination, that freedom is to act solely according to the determination of the will. It is here that the universality of the "laws of causality" and the presupposition of universal (God-given) freedom clash, a problem that Kant attempted to resolve with the categorical imperative, which establishes freedom as always already determined by interiorized universal reason. What happens here is that universal reason becomes the foundation of a polity, for the authority of the state rests on democracy; and more importantly than playing its dominant role is protecting freedom. That is, as Locke, Rousseau, and Rawls posit, the sacrifice of self-determination is justified only if, before (in both senses) the (creation of or a decision of) law there is no fundamental power differential (unequal ability to affect or be affected by someone) among the framers of the "social contract" that institutes the political society. For this reason, liberal political theory and legal theory continuously deal with the problem of exclusion and universality, for they are consistently called on to establish the grounds and reach of freedom and equality.

We know that freedom and equality have never been all-encompassing, that the poor, slaves, and women were initially left out of the liberal founding "deal." However, this has not prevented us from demanding that justice be based on the idea of universality, that is, as either demands for the actualization of or critiques of its pretended, universalism. Demands for both the economic inclusion of the racial subaltern and the denunciation of racial discrimination (individual or institutional) follow this pattern, for they consistently bring forth the "facts" of racism—that is, quantitative and qualitative sociological evidence of racial exclusion. Numerous sociological studies have shown that blacks share a tiny proportion of U.S.

American economic prosperity. The past and present determinants of this situation are known: the accumulated effects of the abandonment of reconstruction; segregation; the consistent explicit and implicit strategies used to deny U.S. blacks access to adequate formal education, jobs, and home property; and the flight of industries to the suburbs and overseas. Recent attacks on affirmative action, as we know, will just worsen this situation, for in the United States the view that only the descendants of Europeans show the necessary mental (moral and intellectual) attributes to benefit from prosperity has not gone away. To be sure, some Asian Americans have been given a share of it, but their fundamental foreignness helps rather than hurts the prevailing strategy of racial subjection, for now they can be used as examples that blacks', Latinos', and Southeast Asians' economic dispossession results from their own shortcomings, their intrinsic affectability.

Neither the liberal argument (nonsystemic or institutional discrimination) nor the critical field of racial and ethnic studies' focus on institutional racism touches on the most dramatic consequences of economic dispossession, nor can they apprehend recent resignifications of raciality. While recognizing that media-produced terms such as "gang banger" and "welfare queen" refer to the racial/gendered subalterns, they read them as codes for racial difference that mask the racially exclusionary aims of the legislation and policy initiatives these terms are deployed to support. The point here is obviously the relationship between racial and class subjection. How can we reconcile modern modes of subjection that have distinct referents, that is, economic position and racial difference? Surely the sociohistorical logic of exclusion explains this relationship, for it posits that racial subalterns will be maintained in a precarious economic condition, for they will not be able to compete under equal circumstances. The problem, however, is that the "gang banger" and the "welfare queen" do not participate in the U.S. economy, and the legislation (mid-1990s welfare reform and crime bills) and the public policies they enable displace them from the juridical moment as well, just as the *Plessy* decision displaced Southern blacks from the domain of the political, that of the U.S. Constitution and its amendments. What I am suggesting here is that to understand the contemporary effects of raciality it is necessary to address how it operates in all moments of the U.S. political configuration. To do so, one should consider (substantive) racial difference not as the hidden referent of a new racially conservative ideological strategy, which is successful because it hides its racism using codes in the same way the sociohistorical logic of exclusion explains racial subjection away by attaching its political effects to individual bias (liberal) or to cultural (sociological) shortcomings of the racial subaltern subject. What the prevailing strategy of racial subjection in the United States indicates is not that the racial explains class subjection but that the association of criminality and material (economic) dispossession has become the new signifier of the affectability of the racial subaltern. That is, the gang banger and the welfare queen correspond to a rearrangement of the analytics of raciality, one that relies not on the strategies of the science of man but on the very sociological strategies that enable the identification of the *causes* of racial subalterns' juridical and economic exclusion.

Similarly, to comprehend how the racial and patriarchy operate as strategies of subjection requires an account of how racial difference and gender difference signify affectability, that is, outer determination. No other figure indicates their combined effect better than the welfare queen, the single female who engages in unprotected sex and uses her children to remain out of work. Beyond supporting the dismantling of the U.S. welfare state, this construct has produced economically dispossessed black mothers as social subjects entitled neither to the legal protections nor the remedies ensured in civil rights legislation. The attack on these women's reproductive freedom—a right women of color elsewhere have never had, as witnessed by the global population control projects along with the criminalization of black female drug users, enabled by their construction as "social problem"—indicates a juridical position that escapes the protection, now under attack, ensured by the *Roe* decision (Roberts 1997). What is stripped away here is precisely consent, that is, what in Locke's account of the *scene of regulation* ensures that self-determination remains a distinguishing attribute of the modern political subject. The criminalization of reproduction operates before consent because the cultural and economic conditions of these black women become the sole determinant of the way the laws are applied to them. The concept guiding gender studies, patriarchy, does not capture this political position because it assumes a woman who can decide, act, and perform out of her own desire, that is, a transparent female subject who will emerge once the veil of patriarchy is lifted. This is a position that the economically dispossessed black mother cannot inhabit because in the various versions of raciality she is always already an outer-determined subject, one whose social trajectory is an effect of how the productive *nomos* institutes her biological, cultural, and social position.

Neither the sociohistorical logic of exclusion nor the notion of patriarchy can account for this particular kind of social subjection. Because both assume that the black female's subjection is an effect of her substantive difference, which becomes the point of departure for racial and gendered representations that support discrimination, the sociohistorical logic of exclusion and patriarchy fail to grasp how a double affectability locates the female of color before the moral (patriarchal text) boundaries of femaleness and the rational (juridical) boundaries of whiteness. My point is that, although the white female subject has been written in domesticity (as wife and mother) in the patriarchal (moral) domain, which has kept her outside the public (male) domain, the female racial subaltern has consistently been written to inhabit the *public* (non-European or non-white) place produced by scientific strategies where her body is immediately made available to a transparent male desire but where her desire (passion, love, consent) is always already mediated by her double affectability. The result is that she is constructed as the subject of lust; hers is a dangerously unproductive will because it is guided by nothing but that which human beings possess as being ruled not even by the "laws of [divine] nature," the preservation of life. Over the last thirty years or so, since the publication of Daniel Patrick Moynihan's (1965) report *The Negro Family: The Case for National Action,* this construction has rendered the economically dispossessed black female an object of public policy, for she has been constructed as the subject of an unrestrained, unruly sexual desire that thrives in the moral degeneracy that proliferates in the dwellings of the black subaltern subject.

During the last three decades, the racial has undergone another resignification, the consequences of which become more obvious if one analyzes its effects on the juridical moment. With this I am not suggesting that the economic moment is irrelevant. My concern here is with how this reshaping of the analytics of raciality is placing large regions of the social and global space—the ones inhabited by the others of Europe—altogether outside the domain of the operation of the law, with the result that people of color now inhabit a sort of "state of nature" to which the juridical devices that classic liberal theorists saw as necessary for the protection of life and liberty do not apply. My point is that it is an effect of the social scientific arsenal that produces the others of Europe as affectable consciousness, which, outer-determined, cannot but actualize that which is exterior to the domain of justice; that is, an effect of the signification of the sociohistorical logic of exclusion is to keep the political-symbolic determinants of such events behind the veil of transparency.

What I see operating in the present global configuration are symbolic and actual violent acts that follow the letter of the logic of obliteration. Today's racial subalterns, finding themselves struggling for juridical and economic justice in an ontoepistemological context, globality, in which they stand always already before the ruling ethical principle of transcendentality, face the horizon of death: existing in urban spaces marked by urban revolts, suicide bombings, or drug-related violence or troubled by wars for the scarce resources and land riches of Africa, Asia and the Pacific islands, and the United States that insatiable neoconservative capitalists desire. We need to trace every and each articulation of raciality, including those that profess its irrelevance, trace at each moment how it rewrites the racial subaltern subject in affectability, producing statements that not only excuse the violent effects of this rewriting but also redeploy the transparency thesis.

What lies before those who engage this text? Halting our future anterior (what the global configuration "shall have been for what it is in the process of becoming"). Engaging it with critical strategies that will undermine the political or symbolic arsenal—the tools of obliteration—that are remapping the place of transparency by instituting global regions and peoples that can be "rescued" through deployments of "total violence," recently renamed "enduring freedom."

Notes

INTRODUCTION

1. The previous quotes are from the madman parable of Nietzsche (1974, 181).

2. According to Lyotard (1984), changes in knowledge registered the dismantling of the "modern order," "the dissolution of the social bond and the disintegration of the social aggregates into a mass of individual atoms" (15), which resulted in the need to forge a new basis for the social bond and the legitimation of scientific discourse. Social interaction, he suggests, is now based on the acceptance of the heterogeneity and the multiplicity of meta-arguments (argumentation with metaprescriptives) that limit the circumstances of their formulation (66).

3. For these authors, "Such re-crafting would not fall too far from the tenets of anthropological desire. In the effort to improve accounts of the long-sought-after 'native point of view,' these experiments attempt different textual strategies to convey to their readers richer and more complex understandings of the subjects' experience. These ethnographies of experience, as we broadly term them, strive for novel ways to demonstrate what it means to be a Samoan, an Ilongot, or a Balinese to persuade the reader that culture matters more than he might have thought" (Marcus and Fischer 1986, 43).

4. The challenge to the "social order" imposed by intrasociety and extra-societal shifts seemed to require a redefinition of the discipline's unit of analysis, namely, the nation-state (Robertson 1992). Regarding intrasocietal reconfigurations, the challenge is recognized even by those who have welcomed the latter. Nicholson and Seidman (1995), for instance, state that

they "were convinced that shifts in left public cultures, in particular the rise and development of the new social movements and their encounter with Marxist and liberal Enlightenment traditions, are one crucial matrix for understanding the formation of postmodern theories in America and perhaps elsewhere" (7).

5. Among these is Habermas (1984), for whom the solution is a new "social contract": if universal reason no longer constitutes an unquestionable foundation, perhaps it could provide a situated one, as a referee of dissenting speech-acts deployed by diverse communicating communities. Others sought to refashion sociology's object—perhaps the surest sign of resistance—redefining "modern society" as simultaneously highly individualized and spatially unbounded. Illustrative of this is Giddens's (1990) refusal to equate the death of the subject with the "end of modernity," arguing that the latest phase of capitalism emerged from the worldwide expansion of modern institutions and the intensification of modern values such as individuality. But these were the times of the cultural, and any new social ontology was required to include the "histories" that unfolded in so many locales, to address this proliferation of "norms" and "values," and to recognize the globe as a shared space (Robertson 1992). Although he considers postmodern theorizing "anarchic," Habermas (1987) recognizes that it remains under the sway of the Hegelian yoke. Others emphasize the problem of inconsistency. Rosenau (1992), for instance, notes that postmodernism's dismissal of theory building is inconsistent, because "an anti-theory position is itself a theoretical stand," and so is the critique of reason, given that "deconstruction . . . is a highly logical, reasoned, and analytical process" (176).

6. The volumes edited by Featherstone (1990) and King (1997) offer a sample of how sociologists and others have engaged the "global turn."

7. In Silva (2004b), I argue that the racial organizes the present discourse of human rights, for it enables writing certain social spaces, as in the campaign against female genital cutting, as resisting the incorporation of those principles that govern the global polity, in this case gender equity.

8. Although this reorganizing has been playing out in major U.S. cities and elsewhere since the mid-1980s, Brazil and other countries in the global South were already quite familiar with the disastrous effects of the structural adjustment policies imposed by the International Monetary Fund, the World Bank, and the former Group of 7. Only recently, however, have we witnessed the emergence of critical analyses that fully address these political-economic processes and consider its impact on the formulation of emancipatory projects in the global South (Bauman 1998; Touraine 1998; Harvey 2000). Nevertheless, this does not mark a radical rupture, because concerns with the political-economic also appeared in earlier "cultural approaches" found primarily, but not solely, as noted earlier, among anthropologists.

9. When asking this question, as will soon become evident, I do not conceive of the racial, as does Winant (2001), as an element of the "global social structure" or the "global world system." What I am targeting here is the racial as a symbolic strategy, an element of signification that preceded and instituted the configurations these social-scientific concepts address.

10. This is an appropriation of Gramsci's concept of social formation, which he uses—along with other historical-materialist concepts such as hegemony, war of maneuver, war of position, and so on—to situate material (economic) production in a historical totality, that is, one in which the cultural becomes a crucial moment in the political configuration of modern capitalist formations.

11. Later, in chapter 7, I show how this question already troubled early approaches to racial subjection.

12. For instance, in his use of racial formation to examine Britain's "new racism" in the mid-1980s, Gilroy (1987) chooses to deny race any meaning. When examining the emergence of this new "ideological" strategy and the "crisis of representation" it provoked, he introduces an analytical strategy that frames race subjection using the language of historical materialism, where racial difference becomes the effect of racism, a social-historical process, a gesture that displaces its biological referent by constructing "race difference" as an "empty signifier."

13. This discussion addresses primarily U.S. gender and feminist scholarship for two reasons: first, because women of color in the United States have challenged the construction of a universal female subject for a longer time and more forcefully than the white, middle-class scholars who wrote her, and second, because, even though I acknowledge the wealth and critical edge of continental, primarily French, feminist interventions, and while my project is informed by them, my project here departs from theirs insofar as my critique of self-consciousness privileges exteriority as a determining moment in signification.

14. For instance, Scott's 1999 statement that "gender . . . means knowledge about sexual difference . . . [as] understanding produced by cultures and societies of human relationships in this case of those between men and women" (2) seems compatible with her attempt to recuperate the effects of gender in the constitution of the nineteenth-century European working class. That is, "men" and "women" remain here as beings to be found everywhere, for they precede (though representations of them are constitutive of) historical processes.

15. Perhaps this distinction is what Wittig (1981) has in mind when she challenges the idea that "women are a natural group," a "racial group," of sorts.

16. For instance, early feminist anthropologists immediately assumed (without theorizing) the pervasiveness of patriarchy by selecting sexual

difference as the "empirical" referent of gender systems and attributing variations in gender subjection to cultural difference (Ortner and Whitehead 1981). For a critique of how this "naturalization," which assumes a certain conception of the body and reproduction, prevents an understanding of other modes of writing the female as a social subject, see Oyĕwùmi (1997).

17. For instance, De Lauretis (1987) proposes that the social subject "is constituted in gender, but to be sure not as sexual difference alone, but rather across languages and cultural representations; a subject en-gendered in the experiencing of race and class, as well as sexual, relations; a subject, therefore, not unified but rather multiple, and not so much divided as contradictory (1). Nevertheless, as Bahvnani (2001) notes, "Difference has become the pivot through which many feminist scholars have interrogated the fundamental bases of feminist intellectual projects" (2). A dangerous gesture emerges that recuperates other and older "differences" to outline distinct "experiences." As Smith (1991) notes, "At precisely the moment when Anglo-American feminists and male Afro-Americanists began to reconsider the material ground of their enterprises, they demonstrated their return to earth, as it were, by invoking the specific experiences of black women and the writings of black women" (45).

18. In non-Western feminist discourse, the "politics of experience" included attention to political economy. As Bahvnani (2001) notes, "Many women from The North—of color or otherwise—are coming to realize that the anti-colonial struggles and struggles of women in the third world, are critical for understanding how gender subordination is both reproduced and challenged everywhere" (2–3). Some met this challenge with the concept of diaspora, which articulates linkages between their own trajectories and those of other women of color in the third world. Collins (1989), for instance, identifies an "Afrocentric feminist standpoint," an ontoepistemological position, that recognizes how race and gender delimit the black female "experience," one that captures how Afrocentrism constitutes a set of values that emerged out of the material conditions of Africa and the black diaspora and recognizes that women everywhere experience "patriarchal oppression through the political economy of the material conditions of sexuality and reproduction" (756).

19. Crenshaw (1995), for instance, introduces the notion of intersectionality to capture "the various ways in which race and gender interact to shape the multiple dimensions of black women's employment experiences" (358). However, when examining the unequal access to legal and institutional remedies to gender discrimination available to women of color, intersectionality merely describes how each of these dimensions—race, immigration status, and so on—functions to exclude women from accessing existing provisions.

20. A telling exception is Espiritu's (1997) discussion of how changing

U.S. immigration policies have shaped gender relations among Asian Americans through the control of the flux of Asian female immigrants. Her analysis avoids the staking effects of exclusion, however, because she shows how immigration legislation has been productive of (a certain kind of [Asian American]) patriarchal formation.

21. With this, I am not minimizing the fact that these racial or nationalist projects were also victims of the unremitting and systematically violent repression of the U.S. law enforcement apparatus.

22. This "institutionalization" of cultural difference within the frames of cultural pluralism (Parekh 2000) appears in the 2004 United Nations Development Program Human Development Report. See also Silva (2005) for a discussion of how cultural difference operates in the present global configuration.

23. He charges these approaches—specifically Afrocentrism—with reproducing "cultural insiderism," which "typically construct[s] the nation as an ethnically homogenous object and invoke[s] ethnicity a second time in the hermeneutic procedures deployed to make sense of its distinctive cultural content" (3). That is, they claim historical (national, cultural, ethnic) particularity to signal the boundaries of the black subject.

1. THE TRANSPARENCY THESIS

1. This argument has appeared in all twentieth-century reviews of the science of man, but more forcefully in the ones deployed after World War II. In an early critique, Jacques Barzun (1938) argues that "race thinking" is a form of knowledge that derived its "truth" from its general acceptance. In other words, he contends that nineteenth-century anthropology assumed, rather than "scientifically" demonstrated, the common "conviction that mind is the simple correlate of physiological structure" (60). The banishment of race thinking to a corner of human psyche away from the locus of reason continues in later critiques. By rejecting its "objectivity" and emphasizing instead the "emotional" sources of race thinking, these reviews place the racial in a muddy terrain covered simultaneously by science and politics, "truth" and "ideology." "'Race,'" Ashley Montagu (1964) argues, is an unfortunate combination of "interest" and "emotional reasoning"; in sum, a scientific fallacy: "it is artificial . . . it does not correspond with the facts . . . it leads to confusion and the perpetuation of error, and . . . for all these reasons it is meaningless, or rather, more accurately, such meaning as it possesses is false" (71). A decade later, Leon Poliakov (1974) would describe nineteenth-century race thinking as a modern expression of an intrinsically European psychological pattern, where the "Aryan myth"—a

"myth of origin"—found its way into scientific inquiry and became the basis of nineteenth-century political ideologies. Placing race thinking outside the objective (scientific) context of signification—as an effect of subjective conviction, beliefs, and error—these critics construe the term race as a nuisance, something improper and unwanted, an evil stain of error in otherwise blessed "truth-full" modern minds. According to Nancy Stepan (1982), nineteenth-century science was used to support a type of thinking that was explicitly, but mostly implicitly, "racist"—an unfortunate episode in which "unconscious beliefs" dominated an otherwise scientific enterprise. Personal "prejudices," she argues, gave origin not to "pseudoscience," but to "bad science," and led "so many outstanding scientists of the past [to believe] that biological races were the key to the most pressing problems of the day" (xvii). In short, "The language, concepts, methods and authority of *science*," Stepan claims, "were used to support the *belief* that certain human groups were intrinsically inferior to others, as measured by some socially defined criteria, such as intelligence or 'civilized' behavior" (ix, my italics). Guillaumin (1995), for instance, observes that the "causal link between mental and physical facts was subsequently deduced a posteriori, in an overzealous attempt to rationalize the idea, with the result that the assertion of a causal link [was then] presented as the distinguishing characteristic of racist doctrine" (36). Gould (1981), for example, refuses the argument that "race theories" derived from individual scientists' subjective (discriminatory) inclinations and recalls that, rather than being purely "objective," any scientific work is embedded in its cultural and social conditions.

2. In *Hegemony and Socialist Strategy,* Ernesto Laclau and Chantal Mouffe (1985) provide a compelling post-Marxist answer to this question by portraying the (postmodern) social space as a terrain constituted by relationally or differentially instituted subjects engaged in political struggle. They rewrite the social as a discursive (symbolic) field, a contingent "structured totality"—but without a fixing or transcendent foundation—in which the relational "identities" are determined by each other ("overdetermination") and by the open-ended rules ("partial fixations") that institute them as "differential positions." This poststructuralist account of the social introduces a reformulation of the political project of the left, "radical democracy," which, as the authors describe it, aims not to "renounce liberal democratic ideology but, on the contrary, to deepen and expand the direction of radical and plural democracy" (176). Because it recognizes and is committed to "the irreducible character of [the] diversity and plurality," they claim, their account of the social "[forces] the myth of a rational and transparent society to recede progressively to the horizon of the social, [which] becomes a 'nonplace,' the symbol of its own impossibility" (191). When discussing the reconfiguring of the political, they identify a process that "stretches from

the workers struggles of the nineteenth century to the struggle of women, diverse racial and sexual minorities, and diverse marginal groups" (181).

3. "My understanding of hegemony," she explains, "is that its normative and optimistic moment consists precisely in the possibilities for expanding the democratic possibilities for the key terms of liberalism rendering them more inclusive, more dynamic and more concrete" (13).

4. She claims that Hegel's concept of universality cannot "rest easily within the notion of a single culture, since the very concept of universality compels an understanding of culture as a relation of exchange and as task of translation," therefore rendering it "necessary to see the notion of a discrete and entitative 'culture' as essentially other to itself, in a definitional relationship with alterity" (24–25).

5. This body of literature is enormous. I do not claim to have covered it in its entirety. This assessment derives from a reading of historical, social scientific, and literary criticism pieces as well as novels by African American authors.

6. In *The Melancholy of Race*, Ann Cheng (2001) indicates how the writing of the racial subaltern subject in interiority cannot but produce an account of loss. Though she argues that melancholia is an attribute of racial ego, suggesting the view that the racial institutes both the dominant and the subaltern, because she privileges exclusion and interiority, Cheng's question of the "subjectivity of the melancholic object" (14) cannot but rewrite the racial subaltern ego in its nostalgia for a lost transparency, an effect that is even more evident in her argument that the melancholy of race is the psychic version of the U.S. dilemma, a mark of how the presence of non-Europeans contradicts the nation's commitment to freedom, and so on.

7. In "Black Strivings in a Twilight Civilization," Cornel West (1997) argues that the predicament of black culture ensues from the need to survive under ideological and structural conditions built on the exclusion "of black people from the human family in the name of white supremacist ideology" (80). "Black *invisibility* and *namelessness*," he states, capture a condition traversing all levels of black experience—existential, social, political, and economic—which results from "the historic 'Veil' (slavery, Jim Crow, and segregation) that separates the black and white worlds." This "veil" erases "black humanity," "black individuality," diversity, and heterogeneity, for it renders black people objects of white fantasies—"exotic, transgressive entities, hypersexual or criminal animals." Further, not only does it render communication between blacks and whites impossible; the "veil" produces subjects that "live in two worlds to survive [while] whites need not understand or live in the black world in order to survive" (86, italics in the original). From this need for survival, he argues, results a suppression of black rage and the perverse "interiorizing" of white fantasies: "After playing the

role and wearing the mask in the white world, one may accept the white world's view of one's self" (87).

8. In *The Mythology of Modern Law,* for instance, Peter Fitzpatrick (1992) shows how such constructions sustain the myth of progress that institutes the paradoxical construction of law as autonomous and socially bound. This construction of modern law, he argues, relies on a conception of the (social) subject as autonomous and socially bound, a contradiction that in the nineteenth century was resolved in the figure of the "native"—"The unevolved savage [that] continues to reside in the civilized subject as a converse and provocation to a disciplined self-control" (131). That is, the civilized (moral or legal) subject that shares in law's autonomy is also a self-regulating thing continuously called upon to tame the "savage," which both threatens and institutes that which is said to distinguish modern social configurations. Taking a slightly different route, in *Racist Culture* David Theo Goldberg (1993) identifies in founding liberal texts formulations that place the native out of the reach of universality. Tracing the production of statements on the moral difference of the "others of Europe" all the way back to Ancient Greek thought, he points to how they are placed outside liberal morality both in explicit exclusions but also by the implicit rendering of the social moment as outside its scope. In *The Racial State,* Goldberg (2002) provides a more direct examination of how race is deployed by the foremost modern political institution, the state. He introduces the notion of "the racial state" to address the ways in which race constitutes and is constituted by the modern state. Focusing primarily, but not solely, on the state's power to exclude, Goldberg maps the distinct forms of racial rule, which characterizes the ways in which the state deploys raciality as a tool for internal differentiation. "Race," he argues, "is imposed upon otherness, the attempt to account for it, to know it, to control it. . . . But paradoxically, once racially configured with modernity the threat becomes magnified, especially fraught, because in being named racially in a sense that it is named as threat. . . . The racial conception of the state [then] becomes the racial definition of the apparatus, the project, the institutions for managing this threat, for keeping it out or ultimately containing it—but also (and gains paradoxically) for keeping it" (23–24, italics in the original). More explicit racializing of liberal thought and its proper subject has appeared recently. For instance, against the view that it contradicts liberal tenets, in *The Racial Contract* Charles Mills (1997) introduces the "racial contract theory" to describe how a contract between whites has instated "white supremacy" as a system of "racial domination" (3). In *Achieving our Humanity,* Emmanuel Eze (2001) shows how connections between modern philosophy and natural history anticipate later articulations of race that exclude non-Europeans from the conception of

humanity. He argues that Europeans' "travels and explorations," which dismissed medieval fantasies about those inhabiting distant lands, raised ontological questions that "philosophers answered . . . with ethnocentric flair and racial ethnocentrism" (16).

9. What Spivak's account of foreclosure in philosophical texts does not explore is how this signifying gesture opens up a moment in phallic signification in which the "other" becomes a constituent of the "I," whose emergence it marks. Lacan (1977) describes foreclosure as the signifying structure in which the signifier, the Other, fails because it does not exhibit the attributes that would constitute it as a proper signifier of that to which it is supposed to correspond ("Name-of-the-Father"); here the proper signifier emerges as a "mere hole, which, by the inadequacy of the metaphoric effect will provoke a corresponding hole at the place of the phallic signification" (201).

10. Many have noted these exclusions in philosophical representations of Africa as the "heart of a darkness" that should be eliminated, saved, or ignored. As Mudimbe (1988) notes, most modern approaches to Africa follow Hegel's postulate that Europe was the only solution for rescuing Africans from their intrinsic "savagery," through "cultural and spiritual conversion" or continuous subjugation. Moreover, Africa has also been constructed as a place of obvious dangers (cannibalism) or hidden ones (deadly viruses). This is what Brantlinger (1986) recognizes in the nineteenth-century British perceptions of Africa as congenial. "[They] tended to see Africa" he argues, "as a center of evil, a part of the world possessed by demonic 'darkness' or barbarism, represented above all by slavery and cannibalism, which it was their duty to exorcise" (194).

2. THE CRITIQUE OF PRODUCTIVE REASON

1. Unlike Foucault, however, I do not find continuity between the late nineteenth-century concept of the racial and seventeenth-century France's notion of "race struggle," for he describes the social as "basically articulated around two races," that is, organized around the "idea that this clash between two races runs through society from top to bottom" (60). I insist that the notion of race deployed in political statements, such as those of Nazism—where it operates, as Foucault argues, "as a principle of exclusion and segregation and, ultimately, as a way of normalizing society" (6)—is informed by the mid-nineteenth-century scientific reformulation of the racial, the one in which universal reason constitutes the ultimate foundation for statements on human difference.

2. As Eze (2001) shows, the emerging modern episteme not only presupposed but commented on the exploitative relations between Europeans

and the peoples inhabiting already constituted zones of deployment of European desire. Moreover, Stoler (1995) indicates that the colonial space was riveted by anxieties that required the deployment of sexual technologies and mechanisms to maintain the boundaries of Europeanness.

3. In *Race and the Education of Desire,* Ann L. Stoler (1995) addresses the limits of Foucault's mapping of the "analytics of sexuality" by showing how simultaneous workings "of technologies of sexuality" and "racial obsessions" in colonial spaces were crucial in the formation of European bourgeois sexuality. Certainly Stoler's analysis contributes to our understanding of how empire figures in the making of bourgeois sexuality through the regulation of the very effects of sexual desire, which are never too far removed from economic desire. More important, however, her analysis of Dutch, French, and British racial discourses and technologies of sexuality also indicates how "the discourse on race" consistently supports investments aimed at producing an ever-threatened European "self" both in the colonies and at the home. She writes: "The production and distribution of desires in the nineteenth-century discourse on sexuality were filtered through—and perhaps even patterned by—an earlier set of discourses and practices that figure prominently in imperial technologies of rule. Civilization could be defended against transgression by invoking the reasoned logic of race" (194).

4. What I am suggesting here is that though certainly, as Dreyfus and Rabinow (1982) argue, Foucault has sidestepped structuralism, phenomenology, and hermeneutics as he refuses to attribute a foundation (formal or historical) to meaning, his antifoundationalism is not a radical rejection of interiority (as that which marks *man*'s uniqueness), for his conception of productive power (as rules of discursive formation) resembles Kant's formulation of reason as the transcendental interior orderer of things (which I discuss in Part 2). That is, Foucault's account of knowledge as the interior orderer of man, the regulator and producer of desires, still ignores that which the latter shares with the things.

5. Why does transparency resist the critique of modern ontology? In "Can the Subaltern Speak?" Gayatri Chakravorty Spivak (1994) offers a powerful answer to this question. Reading an exchange between Foucault and Deleuze against their (re)formulations of power and desire, respectively, she identifies a double movement, the simultaneous rendering transparent of the oppressed and of the Western critical intellectual, which reintroduces the subject, the irrelevance of which they celebrate. She argues that the hiding of Western critical intellectuals' "geo-political positioning" combined with the "schematic opposition between interest and desire" reveals the conflation of two meanings of representation (the political and the symbolic). While the effacing of the critical intellectuals' position (re)produces

the transparent subject, she argues, the conflation of the two meanings of representation evades an engagement with ideology and political economy, because now it is assumed that the subaltern, the other, has finally come into representation, in transparency.

6. "In modern thought," Foucault (1994) notes, "what is revealed at the foundation of the history of things and the historicity proper to man is the distance creating a vacuum within the Same, it is the hiatus that disperses and regroups it at the two ends of itself. *It is this profound spatiality that makes it possible for modern thought still to conceive of time*—to know it as succession, to promise it to itself as fulfillment, origin, and return" (340, my emphasis).

7. Notice that the notion of spatiality I use is very distinct from the one employed in recent writings that address space, place, and location as social categories. Though these are not necessarily explicit deployments of Lefebvre's (1991) construction of space, they do seem to share in the assumption that the latter is an effect of historical processes.

8. "The (pure) trace," Derrida states, "is difference. It does not depend on any sensible plenitude, audible or visible, phonic or graphic. It is, on the contrary, the condition of such plenitude. Although it does not exist, although it is never present outside all plenitude, its possibility is by right anterior to all that one calls sign" (62). Keeping the possibility of an other within its structure, then, the sign will always refer to another sign, another possible structure of signification, another structure of difference. Hence, there can be no transcendental signified whose being is nonsignification.

9. While acknowledging that "Western societies" have been primary participants in the processes leading to the creation of an increasingly globalized world, Robertson observes that the interaction between different "civilizations," different "cultures" has been determinant in this process. Here he challenges accounts of the global conditions that write globalization as a process of homogenization or heterogeneization: as the moment in which the whole globe has come to be ruled by modern principles, of the disappearing "cultural difference" (the difference between "moderns" and "others") (Giddens 1990); as a scene marked by the coexistence of other historical "beings" (disparate cultural principles and practices), which might indicate (as postmodern accounts have it) the end of the modern project; or as the playground of shape-shifting cosmopolitans. According to Robertson, globalization results not from the juxtaposition of self-enclosed "homogeneous" entities, but conceptions of "collective identity" are largely produced in and through these interactions. Focusing primarily on the European context, Robertson distinguishes between several "phases" of the globalization process, where "degree of density and complexity" were a function of "particularistic" and "universalistic" conceptions, such as

formulations (Habermas 1987) and resolves the oppositions between reason and passion, natural and man, and so on (Taylor 1975).

2. For the Roman philosopher Cicero (1994), moral goodness is possible because "nature and reason" have given human beings the ability to comprehend causality, which they deploy when examining their own conduct, and ensure a morally good soul, one not influenced by "outward circumstances," "free of all passion . . . of every disturbing emotion, desire and fear" (34). For Epictetus, the "virtuous man" chooses mind over body, thus realizing its nature by exercising the will, which is a faculty of the human mind that guides the minor faculties (the senses) of the body. For self-discipline, as a quality of the will, the mind's ability to decide, to choose a course of action, regardless of exterior determinants, is a gift from the divine ruler, Zeus, who gave men a "portion of our divinity, this faculty of impulse to act and not to act, of will to get and will to avoid" (cited in Albert et al. 1969, 85).

3. In "What Is Freedom?" Hannah Arendt ([1960] 2000) argues that Augustine's account produces an interiorization of power and freedom that is absent in ancient Western philosophy and has marked the modern conception of the political as the moment of alienation of freedom. "If man has a will at all," she notes, "it must always appear as though there were two wills present in the same man, fighting each other for power over his mind. Hence the will is both powerful and impotent, free and unfree" (452).

4. Medieval philosophers, such as Thomas Aquinas, Duns Scotus, and William of Occam also dealt with these themes—creation, natural (universal or divine) law, rationality, knowledge and freedom of will, and so on. However, although they asked how the rational soul could move from the comprehension of the universals and the multiplicity of things and attempted to indicate that which distinguishes human beings from other created things, and produces distinctions in the "world of men," for them the mind's access to "truth" was guided by the supernatural creator and ruler of the universe.

5. Though I acknowledge that my discussion in this part of the book addresses a theme touched on by many early and contemporary philosophers and theorists, such as Richard Rorty (1979) and Slavoj Žižek (1999), among others, I have chosen not to engage their readings of modern philosophy and their notions of self-consciousness (subject, the mind, "I") directly, for that would render it virtually impossible to provide a concise account of how the articulation and disavowal of exteriority has been crucial in maintaining the dualism that sustains the notion of the mind—or the mental, as Rorty seems to prefer—that organizes modern representation. The *cogito* has been denounced or rejected to be fragmented and then reassembled in various (non-Western) elsewheres, under various guises and for

"nationalism" and "Humanity," for instance. In contemporary global culture, however, it is the intersection of claims for "universality" with claims for "particularity" that produces complexity: "They have become united in terms of the universality of experience, and increasingly, the expectation of particularity, on the one hand, and the experience and, increasingly, the expectation of universality, on the other" (102). Yet, because he privileges "particularity" and "universality" as the axes around which processes of differentiation occur, Robertson does not inquire into the conditions of production of universality and particularity.

10. Further, my portrait of the present global configuration does not privilege movement, the possibility of moving from here to there faster—the apogee of "presence," perhaps superseded only by the "voice's" access to the transcendental signified—emphasized in accounts of the present global conditions. This is seen, for instance, in the argument that the distance between here and there has become irrelevant and, more important, that being there, in spatial terms, has become irrelevant, rendered insignificant by the near-light speed of abstract systems (Giddens 1991) or that "time and space" have become "heterogeneous" (Harvey 1989, 204). I read these accounts not so much as a universalizing impulse, as Fitzpatrick (2001) argues, but as a redeployment of a modern dichotomy, "universal/time" versus "particular/space," and the transparency thesis it presupposes. For these distinctions between today's "globals" and "locals" do no more than reinstitute the gulf by writing the latter as those who have yet to join the transparent global or the ones who do not wish, or are not allowed, to do so, as in the case of political-economic analysis in which the transparency thesis prevents any examination of how the racial has been crucial in the writing of the particularity of the local (always already spatial) and of the global (always already self-present) (Bauman 1998).

11. Perhaps this project shares in what Marx called the fundamental Hegelian mistake, the belief that (productive) activity is a monopoly of the rational mind (and its products). My contention is that, like economic production, symbolic production—representation—is also a political process, a perspective I inherit from twentieth-century versions of historical materialism such as those of Williams (1977) and Gramsci (1999).

12. When describing the unconscious (symbolic) economy in *Écrits*, Jacques Lacan (1997) indicates that the first two symbolic structures, displacement and negation, refer to a mode of signification that is not premised on the transparency thesis. As descriptors of how the subject emerges in the Symbolic, he shows, each captures a particular moment of failure of phallic signification, that is, moments in which the network of signifiers does not institute the "I" as a transparent subject. In displacement (metonymy), Lacan describes, identification is halted as the connection between signifiers

fails, because the other—as the signifier of the Name-of-the-Father—lacks the ability to resolve the subject's desire (164). In negation, on the other hand, the signifier (the other) is declared nonexistent; according to Lacan, it is "the avowal of the signifier itself that it annuls, that is to say the subject affirms the very thing it denies (201). Each exemplifies Lacan's rewriting of the subject, his critique of the Cartesian and the Hegelian renderings of the I, which describes how the subject of the enunciated—to the extent that speech announces the (im)possibility of (an immediate) signification (of transparency)—and its others, as the effects of signification, emerge simultaneously in a given arrangement of signifiers. What interests me here is that, in Lacan's rendering of these signifying structures, failure itself has a productive effect. It institutes not only the subject but also the other, which, in order to misrepresent the Name-of-the-Father has to be brought into representation (articulated) in its failure (disavowed). Moreover, the subject instituted by the signifying bar that interrupts/produces signification emerges in the Symbolic as a haunted I. Not because an expelled (gendered, cultural, racial) other threatens to return in the real but because, as Žižek (2000) nicely describes it, the "'subject' itself is *nothing but* the failure of symbolization, of its own symbolic representation—the subject is nothing 'beyond' this failure, it emerges through this failure, and the *object petit a* ["other"] is merely a positivization/embodiment of this failure" (119–20, italics in the original). Incidentally, this reading of Lacan's symbolic structures follows Žižek's (2000) argument, contra Butler (2000), that rather than suggesting that the form is rooted in a particular content, the moment of exclusion presupposes already existing particulars. Lacan writes sexual difference as impossible, not "as a firm set of 'static' symbolic opposition and inclusions/exclusion . . . , but the name of a deadlock, of a trauma, of an open question, of something that resists every attempt at its symbolization" (110). With this he renders Lacan's account of signification closer to Derrida's (1976). Still, I think because, unlike Lacan, he does privileges speech, in his rendering of the unstable trace Derrida more successfully accentuates how its irreducibility renders transparency a troublesome ontological presupposition.

3. THE PLAY OF REASON

1. Many have acknowledged his ingenuity, how his rewriting of self-consciousness appropriates previous statements and yet constitutes a unique accomplishment while at the same time grounding it on early foundations of modern thought. Certainly Hegel's genius appears in how with the notion of spirit he provides the moral ground lacking in liberal

many different and sometimes contradictory purposes. To the extent that my project here is also a repetition of the desire to exorcise this specter, I envision it not as another denouncement or rejection of the thinking thing, but more along the lines of Žižek's (1999) project, in which he argues that postmodern critics of modern thought are haunted by the Cartesian ghost and explicitly returns to it to seek to unearth the "forgotten obverse, the excessive kernel of the cogito" (2). Unlike Žižek, however, I am not interested in the psychological or analytic implications or effects of resituating the subject in the scene of death.

6. In Greek formulation, the body has already been introduced as a useful but not indispensable tool of knowledge; in his *Physics,* Aristotle states that "scientific knowledge" results from the uncovering of "principles, conditions, or elements"; already "sense-perception" is seen to deal with generalities.

7. The language and trust of the early scientific discourse and that of the European colonial project—particularly the emphasis on movement, discovery, and control—can only support Foucault's claim of the fundamental relationship between modern knowledge and conception of the political. And yet, for about two hundred years, scientific knowledge would not be deployed to account for the differences between Europeans and other inhabitants of the global space.

8. Though I am sure there is no need to justify my choice of Locke to chart liberal ontology and the refashioning of self-consciousness in the scene of regulation, something must be said regarding why I do not engage Locke's (and other) statements in light of the colonial project about which their formulations are indirect commentaries and in which some (as in the case of Locke actively) participated. Unlike Fitzpatrick (1992), Goldberg (1995), and Eze (2001), I locate the emergence of the notion of the racial as configuring the present global space later, in the nineteenth century. Even if, as Goldberg (1995) argues, Locke's statement that links rationality and equality presupposed a correlation between color and (ir)rationality, which would justify African slavery, such correlation cannot be equated with the connection the racial produces between mind, body, and global location because, as will be discussed in Part 3, the latter required the deployment of the tools of scientific reason to support ideas and practices that kept non-Europeans outside the scope of modern moral principles. That is, I recognize, as Fitzpatrick (1992) argues, that the rational thing—in the guise of the legal subject—necessitated the articulation of a domain of savagery (unconstrained or unregulated violence), which the law addressed and where "natives" were located, up to the nineteenth century, when Europeans and "natives" were apprehended by categories of racial difference, and that later, when the latter came to be called "primitive," "traditional,"

and so on, legal decisions regarding the relationships between Europeans and their others could not rely on statements that presume the necessity (in the Kantian sense) of racial subjection. As Forbes (1993) nicely demonstrates, pre-nineteenth-century usage of certain terms, such as "mulatto," "colored," "black," and so on, does not give us license to assume that they already carried the meanings they would later acquire.

9. By choosing Leibniz to illustrate how a critique of scientific reason highlights morality, temporality, and productivity (as the power to actualize the possible and the potential), I am not suggesting that he was the first modern philosopher to engage these qualities of the mind. As Negri (1991) points out, these themes also appear in Spinoza's metaphysics when he addresses the relationship between freedom and time (190).

In a reading that recuperates the emancipatory potentials of Spinoza's system, Negri describes the *Ethics* as a "modern bible in which the various theoretical levels describe a course of liberation, starting from the inescapable and absolute existence of the subject to be liberated, living the course of its praxis in ontological terms, and therefore reproposing the theory at each successive dislocation of the praxis" (48), a statement that attests to Spinoza's complexity because the *Ethics,* as Taylor (1975) argues, also drew the German Romantics and Hegel, privileged precisely as the "finite subject's" context—"a universal life force," as he puts it (16). Nevertheless, I read Leibniz instead of Spinoza for the simple reason that, when engaging the scientific portrait of the universe to recuperate the divine as a productive force—unlike Spinoza, who starts with the statement that God is the sole substance—he immediately locates this productivity ("inner force") at the core of things. This is a gesture that further displaces medieval appropriations of Aristotle's notion of substance, which, I think, still informs Spinoza's *Ethics.*

10. Leibniz does more than recuperate that which had been forfeited in the scene of regulation. By returning to metaphysics, he introduces the themes of contingency and infinity, which cannot but write force as a boundless creative force—the reason I think they disappear in later versions of universal poesis. Because my discussion of Leibniz's statements has to do with how the central themes of the modern philosophical conversation postpone affectability, I will not discuss his notions of contingency and infinity, for they would lead to a distinct venue for a critique of reason that would focus on the notion of power or force itself.

11. This has been called the "disenchantment of the world," the moment in which "matter would at last be mastered without any illusion of ruling or inherent powers, of hidden qualities" (Horkheimer and Adorno 2001, 6).

12. "Reason," Cassirer (1951) observes in his classic analysis of the

Enlightenment, is now "the original intellectual force which guides the discovery and determination of truth. . . . The whole eighteenth century understands reason in this sense; not as a sound body of knowledge, principles, and truths, but as a kind of energy, a force which is fully comprehensible only in its agency and effects. What reason is, and what it can do, can never be knowledge by its results but only by its function" (13).

13. Kant's attempt should not be overstated. For Taylor (1975), this marks Kant's break with the classical conceptions of space as a "property of things" and as "a substantial reality" (355). Incidentally, later I return to Taylor's comments on the differences between Hegel's and Kant's appropriation of space to indicate how the negation of exteriority occurs in Kant's formulations. "Kant," Taylor argues, "is right in his own way that [space] is a simple form. But he is wrong as usual to think of this in a subjective manner. Space is not just subjective; but it is a form in the sense of pure abstraction, the pure abstract reality of the natural, the external; hence it must be filled" (355). What distinguishes Hegel's notion of space, Taylor suggests, is precisely the recuperation of externality, of exteriority, of space (and time, for that matter) "as conditions of things," which, as we will see in chapter 4, was crucial for his own refashioning of universal reason. Deleuze (1984), on the other hand, suggests that Kant inaugurated a phenomenology which negates that which has all along been the grounds of man, the immediate experience of interiority itself. "For Kant," he argues, "it is a question of the form of time in general, which distinguishes between the act of the I, and the ego to which this act is attributed. . . . Time moves into the subject, in order to distinguish the Ego *[Moi]* from the I *[Je]* in it. It is the form under which the I affects the ego that is, the way in which the mind affects itself. . . . 'Form of interiority' means not only that time is internal to us, but that our interiority constantly divides us from ourselves, splits us in two: a splitting in two which never runs its course, since time has no end" (xx).

14. The late eighteenth century saw a proliferation of critiques of the Enlightenment that, like Rousseau's for instance, advanced versions of man that sought a basis for morality and a social ontology outside the prevailing liberal account. My choice of Herder's critique results not from a dismissal of his contemporaries' views but from the fact that his formulations address the most crucial aspects of the Enlightenment. Herder, Taylor (1975) reminds us, "reacts against the anthropology of the Enlightenment" with its objectified view of human nature, its reliance on scientific reason, and so on (13).

15. He writes human "intrinsic difference" according to scientific reason's rendering of nature. Herder identifies four "laws of human being's nature": (a) "'The human being is a freely thinking, active being, whose

forces operate forth progressively. Therefore let him be a creature of language'" (127); (b) "'The human being is in his destiny a creature of the herd, of society. Hence the progressive formation of a language becomes natural, essential, necessary for him'" (139); (c) "'Just as the whole human species could not possibility remain a single herd, likewise it could not retain a single language. So there arises a formation of different national languages'" (147); and (d) "'Just as in all probability the human species [*Geschlecht*] constitutes a single progressive whole with a single origin in a single great household-economy, likewise all languages too, and with them the whole chain of civilization'" (154).

4. TRANSCENDENTAL POESIS

1. As Taylor (1975) suggests, with this gesture, the recuperation of exteriority, Hegel does not emancipate spatiality from the Kantian interiority. It is just a necessary moment before Hegel resolves space into time. "But," Taylor notes, "this immediate external existence has negativity in it because it cannot exist as just external, hence it is in contradiction. Hegel sees negation first in the point . . . , the attempt to get out of externality to singular self-identity. But the nature of space is such that this is a negation of it, to have no extension, so the point goes into the line, the line into the surface, and this into the whole space. But this negativity has real existence as time. So space is no longer at rest, its parts just coexisting. Now it is in movement. Time is the side of Nothing, of becoming. It is the negation of the exteriority of space, but also in a purely exterior way" (356).

2. According to Habermas (1987), Hegel's critique of the Enlightenment targets precisely what I attempt to capture with the notion of an interiorized *nomos,* which is the fact that "it had falsely put understanding [*Verstand*] or reflection in the place of reason [*Vernunft*]" (24), which is also another way of naming the account of universal reason as form. Why I do not use these terms should become more evident in this chapter as I indicate how Hegel's version of universal reason, though it privileges the scene of representation, cannot and should not be incarcerated in the series of distinctions that communicate the two versions of the play of reason I have identified. Not surprisingly, Hegel's first solution to what Habermas (1987) calls "the problem of unification" (25–27) was a return to the divine author and ruler, which he quickly abandoned. In any case, though I recognize, as Habermas (1987) and Taylor (1975) seem to suggest, Hegel's rejection of the interiorized *nomos* as the proper modern ontoepistemological ground, I think that reducing it to a critique of the liberal "individual" captured with the notion of the subjective prevents us from exploring the (dis)continuities between Hegel's and previous statements, ones that Hegel himself spells out

as he rewrites modern philosophy as or in the trajectory of Spirit. Whether his reconciliation is only partially successful, as Habermas argues, or, as I argue, is successful (productive) only because it avoids the kind of un-reflected unity the figure of the divine produces, it is undeniable that it has displaced neither the universality of regulation nor the universality of representation. That is, Hegel's formulations have been crucial in enabling the coexistence of the two scenes, indicated by the themes of (legal and scientific) universality and historicity, in which self-consciousness could remain protected from universal *nomos*.

3. This, I think, is missed in attempts to signal the erasure of the other of Europe produced in modern texts without engaging the conditions of production of the themes, universality and historicity, that institute this place of silence, the place where the language of man is mute. For instance, Spivak's (1999) suggestion that an alternative to Hegel's reading of the *Gitā* would acknowledge that "the *Gitā* itself can also be read as another dynamic account of the quenching of the question of historical verifica-tion. . . . The *Gitā* is a tightly structured dialogue in the middle of the gi-gantic, multiform, diversely layered account of the great battle between two ancient and related lineages. . . . All around the *Gitā* is myth, history, story, process, 'timing.' In the halted action of the text is the unfurling of the Laws of Motion of the transcendence of timing, the Time of the Universe" (45). Of course, Spivak offers this alternative reading against Hegel's ver-sion of historicity, which transforms Eastern "history" and "culture" into a stop on the road to Europeanness, the account in which "Time graphed as Law manipulates history seen as timing in the interest of cultural political explanations" (43). Now, given that Spivak reads the *Gitā* as a performance of the same gesture, it would be too easy (and mistaken) to say that she ultimately reads the historical—captured in the term "Time graphed as Law"—as ideology ("in the interest of"). The self-defeating gesture here, I think, is to retain time as "timing," as if, by doing away with the transcen-dental (Law), one would also do away with the inherent violent act that time as the signified (the moment) of interiority demands.

4. According to Kojève (1969), the ontological premise Hegel introduces is not only the movement of thought, but the nature of being. Not, however, because thought reveals being as dialectical but because thought is (in/of) being.

5. PRODUCTIVE *NOMOS*

1. What this strategy does, Foucault (1994) argues, is make "it possible to establish two quite distinct forms of continuity in the living world. The first concerns the great functions to be found in the majority of species

(respiration, digestion, circulation, reproduction, locomotion)"; it "establishes in the whole living world a vast resemblance which can be arranged in a scale of decreasing complexity, from man down to the zoophyte" (270), and the "other continuity . . . deals with the greater or lesser perfection of organs" (271).

2. In short, the shift from the examination of visible traits to the uncovering of the law determining the particularity of living things caused a radical reconfiguration of natural history: (a) "animated beings" would become the privileged objects of investigation, (b) the search for the universal determinants would focus on variations in the internal arrangement of the body, and (c) internal, invisible processes would determine the principle of classification, character, and the allocation of being in the grid of classification, their placement in a given "class," "order," "family," "genus," and "species," as well as "variety and race."

3. The references to liberal thought here are too many to comment on; the links between nineteenth-century biology and utilitarianism have been pointed out in, for instance, Stepan (1982). However, I stress the point of the influence of Smith's formulation of the division of labor and its effects precisely because of the view indicated in Foucault's (1994), for instance, of a distinction between a biological, economic, and linguistic model operating in sociology. It seems to me that there is no distinction here. All three models refer to a liberal mode of signification, if you will, the elements of which are more clearly presented in Marx's critique of political economy. In the deployment of the idea of division of labor in Cuvier's biology we find one indication of the centrality of the "economic" (liberal) frame. Now in Marx's ([1857–58] 1993) (historical) engagement with (liberal) political economy, the "linguistic" moment appears in his argument that the "value of a commodity represents human labor in the abstract" (51). For Marx, labor operates as a sort of transcendental signified (against Hegel's "Spirit"), the operations of which define the very nature of capitalism. That is, what one has here is a signifying relationship that cannot be addressed without a theory of signification along the lines of Saussure's project—a reading already suggested, but not fully elaborated, in Spivak (1987).

4. When addressing "human variations," he rejects the religious thesis of separate creation (polygenism), arguing that physical and mental ("intellectual and moral") differences among human beings and between the human and other animals are a matter of degree, not kind. Directly engaging earlier deployments of natural history to address "human variation," he argues that visible traits such as skin color, hair, and facial features have no adaptive function, resulting instead from "sexual selection."

5. One can miss the Hegelian references in Darwin's formulation only if one forgets that Hegel was engaging and reconfiguring liberal thought.

How else can one read the difference between the first encounter between two self-consciousnesses, in the passage on the lordship and the bondsman's struggle of life and death, and the second encounter in the moment of "ethical life," in which the recognition of a common historical (transcendental) foundation enables mutual recognition, the moment of transparency? It is true that "natural selection" privileges competition, but the latter is necessary to the fulfillment of its "End." For what is evolution if not the temporal movement of nature toward perfection?

6. Unlike Foucault, however, I do not consider the science of life just another moment of deployment of historicity in the things of the world.

7. "The structure of supplementation," as Derrida (1976) describes it, "is quite complex. As a supplement, the signifier does not represent first and simply the absent signified. Rather, it is substituted for another signifier, for another type of signifier that maintains another relation with the deficient presence, one more highly valued by the virtue of the play of difference. . . . Thus an indication is not merely a substitute that makes up for [supplee] the absence or invisibility of the indicated term. The latter, it will be remembered, is always an *existent*. An indicative sign also replaces another signifier, an expressive sign, a signifier whose signified *(Bedeutung)* is ideal" (89, italics in the original).

8. Foucault describes the modern episteme as a tridimensional formation formed by mathematical and physical sciences, philosophical reflection, and the "new empiricities" (linguistics, biology, and economics). Human sciences, he argues, are situated in the space constituted by these three poles. That is, "in relation to all other forms of knowledge: they have the more or less deferred, but constant, aim at giving themselves, or in the case, of utilizing at one level or another." It is precisely this location, he proceeds, "that renders the human sciences difficult to situate, that gives their localization in the epistemological domain its irreducible precariousness, that makes them appear at once perilous and in peril" (347–48). Nevertheless, as the case of classic historical materialism indicates, even the effort to capture economic production with formal (mathematical) strategies presumes a notion of "conditions of existence" and "evolution" introduced in the science of life.

6. THE SCIENCE OF THE MIND

1. With this notion the scientists of man displaced the focus on physical traits and the old monogenism-polygenism debate. Most critiques of the science of man cite this debate, which basically identified two views of the origins of racial difference. However, I think that it is precisely because it

rehearses religious concern that by the second half of the nineteenth century it was already displaced. For more about this debate, see Stocking (1968).

2. Though this debate illustrates nineteenth-century statements on the threat of scientific reason, length constraints prevent me from exploring it. For similar contemporaneous critiques of the nineteenth-century "race theories," see Stepan (1982) and Stocking (1968), among many others.

3. This was not lost to nineteenth century thinkers, who deployed the racial in descriptions of political processes and social conditions. For instance, in the mid–nineteenth century the Count de Gobineau ([1854] 1967) argued that race produces diversity among peoples of the world and was the force behind their histories. According to Gobineau, civilizations, nations, and states decay not just due to "luxury," "enervation," "bad government," "corruption of morals," and "fanaticism," but because of the racial mixture that, while initially necessary to the emergence of a "civilization," eventually leads to the weakening of the leading people. He argues that civilization is related to two basically human instincts: the urge to "the gratification of material wants" and that for "higher aspirations," and he classifies the "human races" according to the predominance of these instincts. In the "European races," the "utilitarian" or "masculine races," the first principle predominates, while in the "Negro races," the "speculative" or "feminine races," the second one prevails. Thus, while the ability to create civilization depends on the association and equilibrium of the two principles, not all races are able to reach that stage. Only the "European races," he claims, were able to achieve "civilization," the "state of comparative stability, in which a large collection of individuals strive, by peaceful means, to satisfy their wants, and refine their intelligence and manners" (275). According to Gobineau, the "teutonic," the "aryan race," was the dominant one among the "European" or "white races," and therefore the dominant one among all others.

4. When formulating the basis of eugenics, Francis Galton ([1869] 1925) draws primarily from the conclusions of the texts of the science of man to support the argument that to further improve the intellectual and moral abilities of "civilized men" it is necessary to control the natural abilities of following generations by postponing the marriage of intellectually weak individuals and accelerating the marriage of the more able ones.

5. Another important marker of the emergence of twentieth-century anthropology, which I will not describe here for lack of space, was the introduction of a technique that became necessary to the gathering of the visible (social) traits that would give access to "primitive consciousness." The second statement introduces a method for mapping the "primitive" social configurations, the procedures anthropological observers should de-

ploy to excavate the "vanishing" specimens to be added to the archive of humanity. In *Crime and Custom in Savage Society,* Bronislaw Malinowski (1926) argues that the anthropologist should focus on "primitive" social configurations of juridical and economic dimensions, which would entail accounts of "native" society with "genuine scientific character." As late as the mid-1920s, he warns, anthropology still encountered views of the "savage" as immersed in cannibalism, sexual license, and superstitions, which contaminated the discipline itself. For this reason, he states, such "a subject as primitive economics" is both as "important for our knowledge of man's economic dispositions as of value to those who wish to develop the resources of tropical countries, employ indigenous labor and trade with natives" (1). Similar aims could be accomplished by studying "primitive law," which, he states, would be of greater value for the colonial administration. Unfortunately, he charges, "anthropological jurisprudence" is still guided by the assumptions harbored by French, German, and U.S. American anthropologists, that "in primitive societies the individual is completely dominated by the group—the horde, the clan or the tribe—that he obeys the commands of is community, its traditions, its public opinions, its decrees, with a slavish, fascinated, passive obedience" (3–4). For the most part, at least as long as criticisms from within and outside the discipline did not target its privileged strategies, the cultural and ethnography itself, Malinowski remained the celebrated "father" of ethnography, the intensive, preferably prolonged dive into the social conditions of the "vanishing native." Even though it is true that Lévi-Strauss (1963) charges him with providing his own logic for Trobriand institutions, practices, and ideas when "natives" were not forthcoming. In any event, not only would ethnography, the mapping of "primitive" social configurations, further specify how anthropology would address the peoples the racial had placed before transparency; it would also indicate how its rendering of the cultural differs from how this concept is deployed in sociology and history.

    6. Lowie (1934), for instance, notes that while "every human being has a social and a racial (biological) inheritance" and "the two may be in some measure related . . . they are different" (4). The object of "cultural history," he instructs, "includes *all* these capabilities and habits [acquired by man as a member of society] in contrast to those numerous traits acquired otherwise, namely, by biological heredity" (3, italics in the original).

    7. To attack the thesis of "permanence of characters" and "heredity," Boas brings evidence of how "the stage of development" ("primitive" or "civilized") of a given social configuration determines the physical (size of the skull) and mental characteristics of human "types." Against the argument that "racial characters," primarily head forms, had remained unaltered since the Neolithic, Boas offers evidence indicating that "the

influence of the environment [in the growth of the skull] may be more marked the less developed the organ that is subject to it" (47–48).

8. A distinct version of the notion of structure is Claude Lévi-Strauss's formulation of structural anthropology. He draws from Saussure's structural linguistics to confect a strategy of intervention that addresses the unconscious determinants of the systems of representation actualized in "primitive" social configurations. In *Structural Anthropology*, Lévi-Strauss (1963), among other things, explains the advantages of structural analysis as the strategy of intervention more adequate to the conditions of anthropological knowledge. What his version of the anthropological project seeks is to grasp "the unconscious structure underlying each institution and each custom, in order to obtain a principle of interpretation valid for other institutions and other customs" (21). Unlike the task of history, which deals with the "conscious expressions of social life," he argues, the task of anthropology is to examine the "unconscious foundations" of collective representations (18). This is so because the moral principles and rational justifications of the practices and social configurations of "most primitive peoples" are not immediately available to the anthropologist, and even when explanations are available they are not accurate enunciations of the governing principles. Lévi-Strauss's anthropology is also concerned with capturing the operations of the productive *nomos*. For instance, in explaining his strategy of intervention, Lévi-Strauss revisits Radcliffe-Brown's interpretation of the structure of kinship. Whereas the latter focused on the "terms" and "contents," Lévi-Strauss privileges the signifying "structure" they indicate. So, where Radcliffe-Brown found social relations of opposition and solidarity, Lévi-Strauss identifies three signifying relations that constitute the "unity of kinship": a "relation of consanguinity," a "relation of affinity," and a "relation of descent." What these relations indicate is a universal (unconscious) principle, the "incest taboo," which for him is the condition of possibility for representation and social existence itself. Though for Lévi-Strauss the structure of the unconscious is universal, his structural analysis, as do other anthropological signifying strategies, writes the "native" mind as lacking the attribute that distinguishes the *homo historicus*, namely, transparency (19).

7. THE SOCIOLOGICS OF RACIAL SUBJECTION

1. The "race relations cycle" as well as Park's account of the various moments of "racial and cultural contacts" in "The Nature of Race Relations" ([1939] 1950) indicates that his formulation of race relations is consistent with the general social Darwinism marking his formulation of the socio-

logical project. For a discussion of this moment in U.S. American thought, see Hofstadter (1944).

2. Espiritu (1997) suggests that this logic of obliteration remained central in studies of Asian immigrants in the United States until the 1960s, when Gordon's reformulation of the concept of assimilation led to an emphasis on cultural traits and behavior patterns (1–2). Undoubtedly this reconceptualization of assimilation was also an effect of the reconfigurations of the sociological text of the post–World War II period discussed later in this chapter.

3. In the Jim Crow South, Park ([1937] 1950) finds an example of "racial accommodation" that is similar to India's "caste system." In the post-slavery South, he argues, emancipation, urbanization, and education (i.e., "civilization") gave rise to "social problems" precisely because the former socially subordinate (enslaved) group refused to accept the "old" way of life. Instead of "modern civilization," the emancipation of the slaves prompted a "caste system—caste based on race and color," that defined the "form which race relations took under the conditions which the plantation imposed" (181). He describes the U.S. South as demonstrating a traditional social configuration, a moment of the process of "racial and cultural contacts" where the subordinate "racial group" accepted the "social [moral] order" produced by the dominant group. A situation of "stable equilibrium" warranted by the existence of an "etiquette of race relations," a social (moral) order that, operating at the level of personal relations, prescribed "forms of conduct" and defined "social distances." More than a "principle of social order," it was premised on representations of the relations between the basic "racial groups" that defined the differential status of blacks and whites in the Southern "caste system." As a mechanism of social control, this *interiorized nomos* also preserved "social distance" by prescribing the behaviors and attitudes of "Negroes" and "whites" alike. "Progress," which was benefiting the "Negro population," led to the emergence of "race competition" and "race conflict" in a previously unproblematic traditional social configuration, which indicated that both "the South" and "the Negro" were finally catching up with the "modern civilization" prevailing in the rest of the United States. For Park, the "pre-civilized Negro," the Southern configuration, the traditional social space with its hierarchical "racial accommodation" constituted an optimum social situation because it lacked the troubles "race competition" introduces in modern social configurations.

4. Later, in a statement that indicates the displacing of social Darwinism, Park concedes that "race prejudice" "may be regarded as a phenomenon of status" ([1928] 1950, 232).

5. What is at stake here is not whether race relations provides an accurate

description of the early twentieth-century U.S. configuration and processes but how globality informs the formulation or reformulation of concepts such as "social distance" and delimits the appropriation of others, such as the notion of experience, which have now been appropriated by racial and other modern subalterns. In a discussion of the usage of the latter concept, Park ([1924b] 1950) provides an example of how experience should be deployed in sociological analyses. "The value of 'experiences'" to the sociologist, he says, "is that they are the sources, not the only ones, but perhaps the best, from which the student can gain a knowledge and an understanding of the attitude of strange and unassimilated peoples" (154).

6. "The diaspora," Park (1942) argues, "is no longer merely an area of dispersion. It has become rather an area of integration, both economic and cultural. It is in this sense that this history, I might better say natural history, of the career of the African in Brazil has sought to describe the processes by which the Negro has been assimilated and to measure the success he has had in finding a place in what was the diaspora but now is . . . The Great Society" (iii).

7. For changing trends in the historical literature on Brazil, see Tannenbaum (1946); Degler ([1971] 1986); Toplin (1981); and Andrews (1992), among others.

8. He does so with a Lacanian rendering of stereotype as an ambivalent element of signification that reveals more about those who exclude than about the excluded whom it is deployed to objectify. "Racist stereotypical discourse, in its colonial moment," Bhabha (1994a) argues, "inscribes a form of governmentality that is informed by a productive splitting in its constitution of knowledge and exercise of power. Some of its practices recognize the difference of race, culture, and history as elaborated by stereotypical knowledge, racial theories, administrative colonial experience, and on that basis institutionalize a range of political and cultural ideologies that are prejudicial, discriminatory, vestigial, archaic, 'mythical,' and, crucial, are recognized as being so" (83).

8. OUTLINING THE GLOBAL/HISTORICAL SUBJECT

1. In both Gramsci's notion of hegemony (scene of representation) and Althusser's notion of interpellation (scene of regulation), to cite but two crucial examples, one finds an engagement with modern representation that attempts to rewrite historical materialism in such a way as to allow for an account of the symbolic as a moment of operation of power. Whether these are intrinsically contradictory projects obviously depends on how much one is invested in theoretical purity—though, as noted before, Laclau

and Mouffe (1987) indicate that they can be combined. Whether they are successful or not, however, depends on the theoretical position from which one writes. Each is indeed successful if one recognizes how each retains the promise of historicity, the notion of freedom, emancipation, as economic, juridical, and symbolic self-determination, which guides the historical-materialist project. Nevertheless, neither resolves the uneasiness Marx and Engel's scientific desire instituted at the core of this critique of transcendental poesis, the one responding to one of the accusations—determinism, that is—mentioned earlier. Evidently these accusations, which, at least at the conceptual level, have all but disappeared from contemporary post-Marxist debates, remain ethically or politically crucial in critical theorizing, where they rehearse the constraining choice between universality and historicity.

2. The impulse to produce a homogeneous ("undivided") nation justified both the subordination of culturally distinct peoples within a given territory and expansionists' advances premised on historical rights and cultural similarities (Anderson 1983; Gellner 1983; Hobsbawm 1994a).

3. Chatterjee (1993), for instance, also points to this shortcoming when he observes that in India, with the state under colonial control, "anti-colonial nationalism claimed a sovereignty over national culture," within a project which aimed to "fashion a 'modern' national culture that is nevertheless non-Western" (6).

4. Hobsbawm (1994a), for instance, argues that "visible difference in physique" has been incorporated in narratives of the historical nation both to demarcate national boundaries and to create distinctions among its members. Such difference, he claims, operates as a negative (exclusionary) rather than a positive element in the invention of the national community.

9. THE SPIRIT OF LIBERALISM

1. Although this analysis covers a lot of ground, it not meant to be comprehensive. For I do not address the case of Mexican Americans in this text because it opens up questions regarding intracontinental political processes that I hope to examine at another time, nor do I analyze the trajectory of Eastern and Southern European immigrants whose whiteness and European "origin" ensured that they would very quickly be brought into transparency (Jacobson 1998). The trajectory of Eastern and Southern European immigrants is crucial not only as a point of contrast, for it indicates how whiteness bridges geographical spatial, continental boundaries. Moreover, the statements, such as Madison Grant's, that produce a racial map of Europe to distinguish the "Anglo-Saxon" from other European inhabitants

of the United States also suggest that as a signifier, the racial has never signified the substantive difference the sociohistorical logic of exclusion assumes. For this reason, it is not surprising that they are not contemplated in the text of race relations. Given that, though I recognize the importance of the deployment of raciality to place certain Europeans out of transparency, I do not address it here, for doing so would just move this text, even if slightly, away from its central task, which is to indicate the effects of the deployment of the racial that map the present global configuration. Nevertheless, I hope this reading can contribute to the comparative project of racial and ethnic studies as it addresses a crucial moment in the deployment of the representations that have produced U.S. blacks, Asians, and Indians as subaltern subjects.

2. "The prewar generation," Wish (1945) noted, believed that "there would always be new frontiers of advancement . . . as the road to advancement was kept free of corrupt men and monopolistic schemes" (3). The first two decades of the century, according to Wish, saw national wealth increase by almost 100 billion dollars, accompanied by wage increases and a situation of relatively full employment between 1897 and 1907.

3. According to Wish (1945), this new immigration trend, "which brought in a heavy Catholic as well as Jewish element, inspired a campaign to maintain the domination of a native-white Protestant American" (12).

4. For instance, organized labor lost the battle around the 1914 Clayton Bill, a revision of the Sherman Act, which did not totally exclude unions from the reach of antitrust laws (Kolko, 1963, 263).

5. "The new national prosperity was shown in an increase of national revenue. There was a treasury surplus of 100,000,000 dollars in 1882 and 145,000,000 in 1882" (Paxton, 1921, 79).

6. The 1917 provision requiring literacy tests for immigrants is an instance of this collaboration. The 1921 Emergency Law limiting foreign immigration to 3 percent of those already living in the country was also a result of organized labor pressure. This quota system favored primarily British, German, and Scandinavian immigrants and reflected the popularity that Grant's thesis of Nordic superiority enjoyed in the postwar period. Again in 1924, organized labor's "nationalist" feelings were expressed in the National Origins Act, which "provided that the number of immigrants should be fixed at 150,000 per year, and that national quotas should be determined on the basis of the proportion of the number of American descendants of each nationality in 1920 to the total population of that year" (Wish, 1945, 313). The greatest victory was the placing of federal immigration offices under the Department of Labor in 1913 and the approval of a series of pieces of exclusionary immigration legislation.

7. In fact, such recognition, Wilkins (1997) argues, "creates an exotic

juridical potage seasoned by the Court's innovative development of legal doctrines justifying, on the one hand, the imposition of federal authority over tribal lands and Indian citizens and, on the other, creating a set of legal . . . barriers designed to protect tribes from federal agencies, states, and private parties" (22).

8. All quotes are from Tussman (1963). These two amendments to the U.S. Constitution, along with the Fifteenth Amendment, extended the rights of citizenship to African Americans.

9. The interesting move was to reinterpret *Strauder vs. West Virginia*. "Indeed," the court recalls "the right of a colored man that, in the selection of jurors to pass upon his life, liberty, and property, there shall be no exclusion of his race and no discrimination against them because of color, has been asserted in a number of cases. So, where the laws of a particular locality or the charter of a particular railway corporation had provided that no person shall be excluded from the cars on account of color, we have held that this meant that persons of color should travel in the small cars as white ones, and that the enactment was not satisfied by the company providing cars assigned exclusively to peoples of color, though they were as good as those which they assigned exclusive to white persons" (69).

10. In discussing the two main political movements of the period between 1890 and 1930, Hofstadter (1977) argues that Populism and Progressivism combined to critique great corporations and that immigration laws were written as a defense of earlier American political and economic principles. According to Hofstadter, these movements constructed themselves as a defense of principles of the "rural Yankee," the Anglo-Saxon Protestant, against the modernization of the U.S. American space, which "brought with it what contemporaries thought as an 'immigration invasion,' a massive forty-year migration of Europeans, chiefly peasants, whose religions, traditions, languages, and sheer numbers made easy assimilation impossible" (8). According to Hofstadter, in the first decade of this century there would be a merger of Populism and Progressivism despite internal divisions.

11. In fact, that these European immigrants would later "become white" indicates that the Englishness of the "Anglo-Saxon" could have won the "contest over whiteness" only if the "racial categories" refer to, as race relations supposes, substantive difference. But in the United States "racial categories," as Jacobson (1998) reminds us, "reflect the competing notions of history, peoplehood, and collective destiny" (9), because they are but markers of a collectivity's position in a social configuration ruled by raciality, one that needs to be navigated with the grid of racial difference.

12. As Lowe (1996) argues, "The state's attempts to 'resolve' the economic contradiction of capital and the political contradictions of the nation

state resulted in the successive exclusions of the Chinese in 1882, Asian Indians in 1917, Japanese in 1924, and Filipinos in 1934 and the barring of all these immigrant groups from citizenship and ownership of property" (13).

10. TROPICAL DEMOCRACY

1. The conception of hybridity (miscegenation) introduced in the science of man is nicely described by Robert Young (1995) as that which "implies a disruption and forcing together of any unlike living things" (26). While I would not agree with his statement that it makes "difference into sameness"—the problem for writers of the Brazilian nation was that hybridity produced a difference much more pernicious than that signified in blackness, and Indianness, for that matter—Young does indicate why the "fact of hybridity" should preoccupy those involved in the project of reconstituting Brazil as a modern nation-state.

2. In short, this generation of anthropologists, which included Roger Bastide, Edison Carneiro, Manuel Querino, and Melville Herskovitz, among others, produced accounts of Brazilian culture as resulting from "residues" of the "African Spirit" in the American space. In the same movement in which Africanity was made available to write Brazilian particularity, its influence had to be minimized so as to avoid the placing of Brazil totally outside the moment of transcendentality.

3. According to Carvalho (1990), not only did they appropriate the slogans of the French Revolution, but Positivism provided the creed for a project of reconfiguration of juridical-political structures developed by an elite that saw as its task a radical transformation of Brazilian social conditions.

4. Most analyses of nineteenth-century Brazilian social thought—those of Skidmore (1974), Silva (1989), and Santos (2002), to name a few—identify the early versions of the text of the tropical democracy in Abolitionist statements that combined the idea of Brazil as a "racial paradise" with the formulations of the science of man, primarily those concerning the negative effects of miscegenation. Most certainly, though no one has engaged in such a task, the concern with the effects of miscegenation would affect the future of the nation under construction that implicitly or explicitly informed Brazilian social thought from the mid-nineteenth century until Freyre's formulations put it to rest. I would have gladly included many samples of these earlier statements if an amnesia caused by a sudden craving for "discovery" led me to forget that my project in this text is to map the effects of the deployment of scientific and historical strategies in writings of modern political subjects.

5. In his analysis of writers of the Brazilian national character, Leite

(1969) classifies Sylvio Romero, along with Nina Rodrigues, among the group of racist intellectuals who embraced the formulations of the science of man, while he places Gilberto Freyre among those who had confidence in the nation's future. The point here is that this division between racist and nonracist writers of the Brazilian nation fails to situate these writings in their particular global-epistemological circumstances.

6. In the 1920s, this desire would inform statements deployed by artists and intellectuals identified with the *modernismo,* Brazil's own contribution to the aesthetic transformations of the period, which saw the emergence of artistic movements such as the Futurism, Dadaism, Surrealism, and so on. For instance, in his classic *modernista* text, *Macunaíma,* Mario de Andrade (1986) introduces the figures (of the same name) of an antimodern subject of sorts who moves from blackness—"Macunaíma, the hero of our people ... was born pitch black and was the son of the fear of midnight" (9)—to Indianness and whiteness until, tired of a troubled trajectory through which he meets several figures of the Brazilian folklore, he is rescued by a witch who transforms him into the Big Dipper. Whether Andrade wrote Macunaíma to signify the Brazilian subject is irrelevant because, like others in the previous decades, *modernismo*'s apology of the Brazilian subject consistently attributes the nation's shortcomings to an unruly sexual desire. Also in the 1920s, in his *Retrato do Brazil* Paulo Prado ([1926] 1962) answered the question suggested in the first sentence of the book—"In a radiate land live a sad people" (3)—by stating that an unrestrained sensuality and ambition had produced in Brazil a people marked by *affectability,* by laziness, disease, melancholy, and violence (125).

Bibliography

Albert, Ethel M., Theodore C. Denise, and Sheldon P. Peterfreund. 1969. *Great Traditions in Ethics.* New York: Van Nostrand Reinhold.

Alexander, Jeffrey. 1982. *Theoretical Logic in Sociology.* 4 vols. Berkeley: University of California Press.

Anderson, Benedict. 1983. *Imagined Communities: Reflections on the Origin and Spread of Nationalism.* London: Verso.

Andrade, Mario de. 1986. *Macunaíma: O herói sem nenhum caráter.* Belo Horizonte: Editora Itatiaia.

Andrews, G. Reid. 1992. *Blacks and Whites in São Paulo.* Madison: University of Wisconsin Press.

Appadurai, Arjun. 1990. "Disjuncture and Difference in the Global Cultural Economy." In *Global Culture: Nationalism, Globalization, and Modernity,* ed. Mike Featherstone, 295–310. London: Sage.

Appiah, Kwame A. 1992. *In My Father's House: Africa in the Philosophy of Culture.* New York and Oxford: Oxford University Press.

Araújo, Ricardo B. 1994. *Guerra e Paz.* Rio de Janeiro: Editora 34.

Archer, Margaret. 1988. *Culture and Agency: The Place of Culture in Social Theory.* Cambridge: Cambridge University Press.

Arendt, Hannah. [1960] 2000. *The Portable Hannah Arendt.* New York: Penguin.

———. 1979. *The Origins of Totalitarianism.* London: Harcourt, Brace.

Arnold, Matthew. 1888. *Civilization in America.* Philadelphia: Leonard Scott.

Asante, Molefi K. 1987. *The Afrocentric Idea.* Philadelphia: Temple University Press.

Augel, Moema. 1980. *Visitantes Estrangeiros na Bahia Oitocentista.* São Paulo: Cultrix, INL-Ministério da Educação e Cultura.

Azevedo, Aluizio. [1881] 1973. *O Mulato.* São Paulo: Martins.

Azevedo, Celia M. 1988. *Onda Negra Medo Branco.* São Paulo: Brasiliense.

Azevedo, Thales. 1966. *Cultura e Situação Racial no Brasil.* São Paulo: Cia Editora Nacional.

Bacon, Francis. [1620] 1960. *New Organon.* New York: Liberal Arts Press.

Bahvnani, Kum-Kum, ed. 2001. *Feminism and "Race."* Oxford: Oxford University Press.

Baker, Houston, Jr., Mantia Diawara, and Ruth H. Lindeborg, eds. 1996. *Black British Cultural Studies.* Chicago: University of Chicago Press.

Balfour, Henry. 1906. Introduction to *The Evolution of Culture and Other Essays by the Late A. Lane-Fox Pitt-Rivers,* ed. J. L. Myres, v–xx. Oxford: Clarendon.

Balibar, E., and I. Wallerstein. 1991. *Race, Class, and Nation: Ambiguous Identities.* London: Verso.

Banton, Michael. 1967. *Race Relations.* New York: Basic Books.

Barthes, Roland. 1972. *Critical Essays.* Evanston, Ill.: Northwestern University Press.

Barzun, Jacques. 1938. *Race: A Study in Modern Superstition.* London: Methuen.

Bauman, Richard, and Charles Briggs. 2003. *Voices of Modernity.* Cambridge: Cambridge University Press.

Bauman, Zygmunt. 1998. *Globalization: The Human Consequences.* New York: Columbia University Press.

Beard, Charles. 1913. *Contemporary American History.* New York: Macmillan.

Bell, Derrick. 2000. *Race, Racism, and American Law.* Gaithersburg, Md.: Aspen Law and Business.

Berkhofer, Robert, Jr. 1979. *The White Man's Indian.* New York: Vintage.

Bhabha, Homi. 1992. "Race and the 'Ends' of Modernity?" *Public Culture* 4, no. 2: 47–65.

———. 1994a. *Nation and Narration.* London: Routledge.

———. 1994b. *The Location of Culture.* London: Routledge.

———. 1996. "Unpacking My Library . . . Again." In *The Post-Colonial Question: Common Skies, Divided Horizons,* ed. Ian Chambers and Lidia Curti, 199–211. London: Routledge.

Boas, Franz. [1899] 1966. *Race, Language, and Culture.* New York: Free Press.

———. 1911. *The Mind of Primitive Man.* New York: Macmillan.

Bourdieu, Pierre. 1977. *Outline of a Theory of Practice*. London: Cambridge University Press.

———. 1984. *Distinction: A Social Critique of the Judgment of Taste.* Cambridge, Mass.: Harvard University Press.

Brantlinger, Patrick. 1986. "Victorians and Africans: The Genealogy of the Myth of the Dark Continent." In *"Race," Writing, and Difference,* ed. Henry Louis Gates, 185–222. Chicago: University of Chicago Press.

Brinton, Daniel Garrison. [1870] 1901. *Races and Peoples: Lectures on the Science of Ethnography.* Philadelphia: D. McKay.

Broca, Paul. 1864. *Phenomena of Hybridity in the Genus Homo.* London: Longman, Green, Longman and Roberts.

———. 1879. *Instrucions générales pour les recherches anthropologiques a faire sur les vivant.* Paris: Societé d'Anthropologie de Paris.

Brock, Lisa, and Digna Castañeda Fuertes. 1998. *Between Race and Empire: African-Americans and Cubans before the Cuban Revolution.* Philadelphia: Temple University Press.

Brooks, John G. 1909. *As Others See Us.* New York: Macmillan.

Buffon, G. L. L. 1997. "Geographical and Cultural Distribution of Mankind." In *Race and the Enlightenment,* ed. Emmanuel C. Eze, 15–28. Cambridge, Mass.: Blackwell.

Butler, Judith. 1990. *Gender Trouble.* New York: Routledge.

———. 1993. *Bodies That Matter.* London: Routledge.

———. 2000. "Restaging the Universal: Hegemony and the Limits of Formalism." In *Contingency, Hegemony, Universality,* ed. Judith Butler, Ernesto Laclau, and Slavoj Žižek, 11–43. London: Verso.

Caminha, Pero Vaz de. [1500] 1894. *Carta de Pero Vaz de Caminha a El-Rei Dom Manuel, dando-lhe noticia do descobrimento da terra de Vera Cruz, hoje Brazil, pela Armada de Pedro Alvares Cabral.* Vol. 1 of *Revista Trimestral do Instituto Geographico e Historico da Bahia,* anno 1.

Carby, Hazel. 1987. *Reconstructing Womanhood: The Emergence of the African-American Woman Novelist.* New York: Oxford University Press.

Carvalho, José Murilo de. 1990. *A Formação da Almas.* São Paulo: Companhia das Letras.

Cassirer, Ernst. 1951. *The Philosophy of the Enlightenment.* Boston: Beacon.

Chakrabarty, Dipesh. 2000. *Provincializing Europe.* Princeton, NJ: Princeton University Press.

Chatterjee, Partha. 1993. *The Nation and Its Fragments.* Princeton, N.J.: Princeton University Press.

Cheng, Ann. 2001. *The Melancholy of Race.* Oxford: Oxford University Press.

Cicero, Marcus Tulius. 1994. *De Officiis.* New York: Oxford University Press.

Clifford, James. 1986. "Introduction: Partial Truths." In *Writing Culture: The Poetics and Politics of Ethnography,* ed. James Clifford and George Marcus, 1–26. Berkeley: University of California Press.

———. 1988. *The Predicament of Culture: Twentieth-Century Ethnography, Literature, and Art.* Cambridge, Mass.: Harvard University Press.

Clifford, James, and George Marcus, eds. 1986. *Writing Culture: The Poetics and Politics of Ethnography.* Berkeley: University of California Press.

Collins, Patricia Hill. 1989. "The Social Construction of Black Feminist Thought." *Signs* 14, no. 4: 745–73.

———. 1990. *Black Feminist Thought: Knowledge, Consciousness, and the Politics of Empowerment.* London: HarperCollins.

Commager, Henry Steele. 1950. *The American Mind.* New Haven, Conn.: Yale University Press.

Condorcet, Marquis de. 1995. "The Future Progress of the Human Mind." In *The Portable Enlightenment Reader,* ed. Isaac Kramnick, 26–38. New York: Penguin.

Cope, Edward D. 1870. *On the Hypothesis of Evolution: Physical and Metaphysical.* New Haven, Conn.: C. C. Chatefield.

Correa, Mariza. 1982. "As Ilusões da Liberdade." Ph.D. dissertation, Universidade de São Paulo, São Paulo.

Count, Earl. 1950. *This Is Race: An Anthology Selected from the International Literature on the Races of Man.* New York: Shuman.

Crenshaw, Kimberlé. 1995. "Mapping the Margins: Intersectionality, Identity Politics, and Violence against Women of Color." In *Critical Race Theory: The Key Writings That Formed the Movement,* ed. Kimberlé Crenshaw, Neil Gotanda, Gary Peller, et al., 357–383. New York: New Press. Distributed by Norton.

Crenshaw, Kimberlé, Neil Gotanda, Gary Peller, et al., eds. 1995. *Critical Race Theory: The Key Writings That Formed the Movement.* New York: New Press. Distributed by Norton.

Cuvier, Georges. 1802. *Lectures on Comparative Anatomy.* London: Wilson Fort, N. Longman, and O. Rees.

———. 1863. *The Animal Kingdom Arranged according to Its Organization.* London: Henry G. Bohn.

Darwin, Charles. [1859] 1994. *The Origin of Species by Means of Natural Selection; or, The Preservation of Favored Races in the Struggle for Life.* London: Studio Editions.

———. 1871. *The Descent of Man.* London: J. Murray.

Degler, Carl. [1971] 1986. *Neither Black nor White: Slavery and Race in Brazil and the United States.* Madison: University of Wisconsin Press.

De Lauretis, Teresa. 1987. *Technologies of Gender.* Bloomington: Indiana University Press.

Deleuze, Giles. 1984. *Kant's Critical Philosophy*. Minneapolis: University of Minnesota Press.

———. 1994. *Difference and Repetition*. New York: Columbia University Press.

Delgado, Richard. 1995. *Critical Race Theory: The Cutting Edge*. Philadelphia: Temple University Press.

Derrida, Jacques. 1973. *Speech and Phenomena*. Evanston, Ill.: Northwestern University Press.

———. 1976. *Of Grammatology*. Baltimore: Johns Hopkins University Press.

———. 1994. *Specters of Marx*. London: Routledge.

Descartes, René. [1641] 1986. *Meditations on First Philosophy*. Cambridge: Cambridge University Press.

Dreyfus, Hubert, and Paul Rabinow. 1982. *Michel Foucault: Beyond Structuralism and Hermeneutics*. Chicago: University of Chicago Press.

Du Bois, W. E. B. [1903] 1989. *The Souls of Black Folk*. New York: Penguin.

———. [1940] 1968. *Dusk of Dawn*. New York: Schocken.

Dumont, Louis. 1980. *Homo Hierarchicus*. Chicago: University of Chicago Press.

———. 1992. *Essays on Individualism: Modern Ideology in Anthropological Perspective*. Chicago: University of Chicago Press.

Dupré, Louis. 1983. *Marx's Critique of Culture*. New Haven, Conn.: Yale University Press.

Durkheim, Émile. [1915] 1965. *The Elementary Forms of the Religious Life*. New York: Free Press.

———. [1893] 1984. *The Division of Labor in Society*. Houndmills, Basingstoke, Hampshire: Macmillan.

Elias, Norbert. 1982. *The Civilizing Process*. New York: Pantheon.

Espiritu, Yen Le. 1997. *Asian American Men and Women*. Thousand Oaks, Calif.: Sage.

Eze, Emmanuel C. 1997. *Race and the Enlightenment*. Cambridge, Mass.: Blackwell.

———. 2001. *Achieving Our Humanity: The Idea of a Postracial Future*. New York: Routledge.

Fabian, Johannes. 1983. *Time and the Other: How Anthropology Makes Its Objects*. New York: Columbia University Press.

Fanon, Frantz. [1952] 1967. *Black Skin, White Masks*. New York: Grove.

———. 1963. *The Wretched of the Earth*. New York: Grove Weidenfeld.

Featherstone, Mike. 1991. *Consumer Culture and Postmodernism*. London: Sage.

———. ed. 1990. *Global Culture: Nationalism, Globalization, and Modernity*. London: Sage.

Featherstone, M., Scott Lash, and Roland Robertson. 1995. *Global Modernities*. London: Sage.

Fitzpatrick, Peter. 1992. *The Mythology of Modern Law*. New York: Routledge.

———. 2001. *Modernism and the Grounds of Law*. Cambridge: Cambridge University Press.

Forbes, Jack D. 1993. *Africans and Native Americans*. Urbana: University of Illinois Press.

Foucault, Michel. 1972. *The Archaeology of Knowledge*. New York: Vintage.

———. 1978. *The History of Sexuality: An Introduction*. New York: Vintage.

———. 1979. *Discipline and Punish*. New York: Vintage.

———. 1980. *Power/Knowledge*. New York: Pantheon.

———. 1988. *Madness and Civilization: A History of Insanity in the Age of Reason*. New York: Vintage.

———. 1994. *The Order of Things: An Archeology of the Human Sciences*. New York: Vintage.

———. 2003. *Society Must be Defended*. New York: Picador.

Freyre, Gilberto. [1933] 1987. *Casa Grande e Senzala*. Rio de Janeiro: José Olympio Editora.

Gaines, Kevin. 1993. "Black Americans' Racial Uplift Ideology as 'Civilizing Mission': Pauline E. Hopkins on Race and Imperialism." In *Cultures of United States Imperialism*, ed. Amy Kaplan and Douglas E. Pease, 433–55. Durham, N.C.: Duke University Press.

Galton, Francis. [1869] 1925. *Hereditary Genius: An Inquiry into Its Laws and Consequences*. London: Macmillan.

Gates, Henry Louis. 1986. "Introduction: Writing 'Race' and the Difference It Makes." In *"Race," Writing, and Difference*, ed. Henry Louis Gates, 1–20. Chicago: University of Chicago Press.

Gellner, Ernest. 1983. *Nations and Nationalism*. Oxford: Blackwell.

Giddens, Anthony. 1971. *Capitalism and Modern Social Theory*. Cambridge: Cambridge University Press.

———. 1984. *The Constitution of Society: Outline of the Theory of Structuration*. Berkeley and Los Angeles: University of California Press.

———. 1990. *The Consequences of Modernity*. Stanford, Calif.: Stanford University Press.

Gilroy, Paul. 1987. *"There Ain't No Black in the Union Jack": The Cultural Politics of Race and Nation*. Chicago: University of Chicago Press.

———. 1993a. *Small Acts: Thoughts on the Politics of Black Culture*. London: Serpent's Tail.

———. 1993b. *The Black Atlantic: Modernity and Double Consciousness*. Cambridge, Mass.: Harvard University Press.

———. 2000. *Against Race: Imagining Political Culture beyond the Color Line*. Cambridge, Mass.: Belknap Press, Harvard University Press.

Gobineau, Arthur de. [1854] 1967. *The Inequality of Human Races*. New York: Howard Fetig.

Godelier, Maurice. 1973. *Perspectives in Marxist Anthropology*. Cambridge: Cambridge University Press.

Goldberg, David Theo, ed. 1991. *Anatomy of Racism*. Minneapolis: University of Minnesota Press.

———. 1993. *Racist Culture*. Oxford and Cambridge: Blackwell.

———. 2002. *The Racial State*. Oxford: Blackwell.

Gordon, Avery. 1997. *Ghostly Matters*. Minneapolis: University of Minnesota Press.

Gossett, Thomas F. 1963. *Race: The History of an Idea in America*. Dallas: Southern Methodist University Press.

Gould, Stephen. 1981. *The Mismeasure of Man*. New York: Norton.

Gouldner, Alvin. 1970. *The Coming Crisis of Western Sociology*. New York: Basic Books.

Gramsci, Antonio. 1999. *Selections from the Prison Notebooks*. New York: International Publishers.

Grant, Madison. 1921. *The Passing of the Great Race*. New York: Charles Scribner's Sons.

Guillaumin, Collete. 1995. *Racism, Sexism, Power, and Ideology*. London: Routledge.

Habermas, Jürgen. 1973. *Legitimation Crisis*. Boston: Beacon.

———. 1984. *The Theory of Communicative Action*. 2 vols. Boston: Beacon.

———. 1987. *The Philosophical Discourse of Modernity*. Cambridge, Mass.: MIT Press.

Hall, Stuart. [1980] 1996. "Race, Articulation, and Societies Structured in Dominance." In *Black British Cultural Studies*, ed. Houston Baker Jr., Mantia Diawara, and Ruth H. Lindeborg, 16–60. Chicago: University of Chicago Press.

———. 1996. "New Ethnicities." In *Stuart Hall Critical Dialogues in Cultural Studies*, ed. David Morley and Kuan-Hsing Chen, 441–49. London: Routledge.

———. 1997. "The Local and the Global: Globalization and Ethnicity." In *Culture, Globalization, and the World-System*, ed. Anthony D. King, 19–40. Minneapolis: University of Minnesota Press.

Hannerz, Ulf. 1996. *Transnational Connections*. London: Routledge.

Hardt, Michael, and Antonio Negri. 2000. *Empire*. Cambridge, Mass., and London: Harvard University Press.

Harvey, David. 1989. *The Condition of Postmodernity*. Oxford: Basil Blackwell.

————. 2000. *Spaces of Hope*. Berkeley and Los Angeles: University of California Press.

Hegel, G. W. F. [1807] 1977. *Phenomenology of Spirit*. Oxford: Oxford University Press.

————. [1821] 1952. *Philosophy of Right*. London: Oxford University Press.

————. 1900. *Lectures on the Philosophy of History*. New York: Wiley.

————. 1953. *Reason in History*. New York: Library of Liberal Arts.

Herder, J. G. 2002. *Philosophical Writings*. Cambridge: Cambridge University Press.

Herskovitz, Melville. 1967. *Man and His Works*. New York: Knopf.

Higgibotham, Evelyn B. 1992. "African-American Women's History and the Metalanguage of Race." *Signs: Journal of Women in Culture and Society* 12, no. 21: 251–74.

Hill, Frank E. 1933. *What Is America?* New York: John Day.

Hill, John Louis. 1930. *Negro: Liability or Asset?* New York: Literary Associates.

Hobsbawm, Eric. 1987. *The Age of Empire, 1875–1914*. New York: Pantheon.

————. 1994a. *Nations and Nationalism*. Cambridge: Cambridge University Press.

————. 1994b. *The Age of Extremities*. Cambridge: Cambridge University Press.

Hofstadter, Richard. 1944. *Social Darwinism in American Thought*. Boston: Beacon.

————. 1977. *The Age of Reform*. New York: Alfred Knopf.

hooks, bell. 1984. *Feminist Theory: From Margins to Center*. Boston: South End Press.

Horkheimer, Max, and Theodor Adorno. 2001. *Dialectic of Enlightenment*. New York: Continuum.

Howe, Stephen. 1998. *Afrocentrism: Mythical Pasts and Imagined Homes*. London: Verso.

Hume, David. [1754] 1997. "Of the Populousness of Ancient Nations." In *Race and the Enlightenment*, ed. Emmanuel C. Eze, 29. Cambridge, Mass.: Blackwell.

————. [1777] 1977. *An Enquiry concerning Human Understanding*. Indianapolis: Hackett.

Irigaray, Luce. 1993. *An Ethics of Sexual Difference*. Ithaca, N.Y.: Cornell University Press.

Jacobson, Mathew Frye. 1998. *Whiteness of a Different Color*. Cambridge, Mass.: Harvard University Press.

James, C. L. R. 1993. *American Civilization*, ed. Anna Grimshaw and Keith Hart. Cambridge, Mass., and Oxford: Blackwell.

Jameson, Fredric. 1991. *Postmodernism; or, The Cultural Logic of Late Capitalism.* Durham, N.C.: Duke University Press.

Kant, Immanuel. [1764] 1960. *Observations on the Feeling of the Beautiful and the Sublime.* Berkeley and Los Angeles: University of California Press.

———. [1775] 1997. "On the Different Races of Man." In *Race and the Enlightenment,* ed. Emmanuel C. Eze, 38–48. Cambridge, Mass.: Blackwell.

———. [1781] 1990. *Critique of Pure Reason.* Buffalo, N.Y.: Prometheus.

———. [1783] 1950. *Prolegomena to Any Future Metaphysics.* Indianapolis: Liberal Arts Press.

———. [1788] 1993. *The Critique of Practical Reason.* Upper Saddle River, N.J.: Prentice-Hall.

———. [1800] 1974. *Logic.* New York: Dover.

Karenga, Ron M. 1976. *The Roots of the U.S. Panther Conflict.* San Diego: Kwaida.

———. 1993. *Introduction to Black Studies.* Los Angeles: University of Sankore Press.

Kelley, Robin. 1997. *Yo' Mama's Disfunktional! Fighting the Cultural Wars in Urban America.* Boston: Beacon.

King, Anthony D., ed. 1997. *Culture, Globalization, and the World-System.* Minneapolis: University of Minnesota Press.

Kluckhohn, Clyde. 1949. *Mirror for Man: The Relation of Anthropology to Modern Life.* New York: Whittlesey House.

Knox, Robert. 1850. *The Races of Man: A Fragment.* Philadelphia: Lea and Blanchard.

Kojève, Alexandre. 1969. *Introduction to the Reading of Hegel.* New York: Basic Books.

Kolko, Gabriel. 1963. *The Triumph of Conservatism.* New York: Free Press.

Kroeber, A. L. [1923] 1948. *Anthropology: Biology and Race.* New York: Harcourt, Brace and World.

———. 1951. *The Nature of Culture.* Chicago: University of Chicago Press.

Kuhn, Thomas S. 1970. *The Structure of Scientific Revolutions.* Chicago: University of Chicago Press.

Lacan, Jacques. 1977. *Écrits: A Selection.* New York: Norton.

Laclau, Ernesto, and Chantal Mouffe. 1985. *Hegemony and Socialist Strategies.* London: Verso.

Lefebvre, Henri. 1991. *The Production of Space.* Oxford: Blackwell.

Leibniz, G. W. 1989. *Philosophical Essays.* Indianapolis: Hackett.

Leite, Dante Moreira. 1969. *O Caráter Nacional Brasileiro.* São Paulo: Livraria Pioneira Editora.

Levinas, Emmanuel. 1996. *Basic Philosophical Writings.* Bloomington: Indiana University Press.

Lévi-Strauss, Claude. 1961. "Race and History." In *Race and Science,* ed. UNESCO, 219–59. New York: Columbia University Press.

———. 1963. *Structural Anthropology.* Vo1. 1. New York: Basic Books.

Lipsitz, George. 1998. *The Possessive Investment in Whiteness.* Philadelphia: Temple University Press.

Locke, John. [1690] 1947. *Two Treatises of Government.* New York: Hafner.

Low, Maurice. 1911. *The American People: A Study in National Psychology.* Boston: Houghton and Mifflin.

Lowe, Lisa. 1996. *Immigrant Acts: On Asian American Cultural Politics.* Durham, N.C.: Duke University Press.

Lowie, Robert. 1934. *An Introduction to Cultural Anthropology.* New York: Farrar and Rinehart.

Lyotard, Jean-François. 1984. *The Postmodern Condition: A Report on Knowledge.* Minneapolis: University of Minnesota Press.

Mabry, Philip. 1996. "We're Bringing Them Home: Resettling Vietnamese Amerasians in the United States." Ph.D. dissertation, University of Pittsburgh.

MacGrane, Bernard. 1989. *Beyond Anthropology.* New York: Columbia University Press.

Maggie, Yvonne. 1995. *Medo do Feitiço: Relações entre Magia e Poder no Brasil.* Rio de Janeiro: Arquivo Nacional.

Malinowski, Bronislaw. 1926. *Crime and Custom in Savage Society.* New York: Harcourt, Brace.

Marcus, George. 1986. "Contemporary Problems of Ethnography in the Modern World System." In *Writing Culture: The Poetics and Politics of Ethnography,* ed. James Clifford and George Marcus, 165–93. Berkeley: University of California Press.

Marcus, George, and Michael Fisher. 1986. *Anthropology as Cultural Critique.* Chicago: University of Chicago Press.

Marx, Anthony W. 1998. *Making Race and Nation.* Cambridge: Cambridge University Press.

Marx, Karl. [1857–58] 1993. *Grundisse.* New York: Random House.

———. [1867] 1977. *Capital.* Vol. 1. Moscow: Progress Publishers.

———. 1956. *Selected Writings in Sociology and Social Philosophy,* trans. T. B. Bottomore. New York: McGraw.

Marx, Karl, and F. Engels. 1947. *The German Ideology.* New York: International Publishers.

Mason, Philip. 1962. *Prospero's Magic.* London: Oxford University Press.

———. 1970a. *Patterns of Dominance.* Oxford: Oxford University Press.

———. 1970b. *Race Relations.* Oxford: Oxford University Press.

Mathews, Brander. 1906. "American Character." *Columbia University Quarterly* 98, no. 2: 97–114.

McGrane, Bernard. 1989. *Beyond Anthropology*. New York: Columbia University Press.

Mead, Margaret. 1964. *Anthropology, a Human Science: Selected Papers, 1939–1960*. Princeton, N.J.: Van Nostrand.

Mills, Charles. 1997. *The Racial Contract*. Ithaca, N.Y.: Cornell University Press.

Mohanty, Chandra T. 1991a. "Cartographies of Struggle: Third World Women and the Politics of Feminism." In *Third World Women and the Politics of Feminism*, ed. Chandra T. Mohanty, Ann Russo, and Lourdes Torres, 1–47. Bloomington: Indiana University Press.

———. 1991b. "Under Western Eyes: Feminist Scholarship and Colonial Discourses." In *Third World Women and the Politics of Feminism*, ed. Chandra T. Mohanty, Ann Russo, and Lourdes Torres, 51–80. Bloomington: Indiana University Press.

———. 1997. "Women Workers and Capitalist Scripts: Ideologies of Domination, Common Interests, and the Politics of Solidarity." In *Feminist Genealogies, Colonial Legacies, Democratic Futures*, ed. M. Jaqui Alexander and Chandra Mohanty, 3–29. New York: Routledge.

Montagu, Ashley. 1964. *Man's Most Dangerous Myth: The Fallacy of Race*. Cleveland, Ohio: World Publishing.

Morgan, H. Wayne. 1971. *Unity and Culture*. London: Allen Lane, Penguin.

Moynihan, Daniel P. 1965. *The Negro Family: The Case for National Action*. Washington, D.C.: Office of Planning and Research/U.S. Department of Labor.

Mudimbe, V. Y. 1988. *The Invention of Africa*. Bloomington: Indiana University Press.

———. 1994. *The Idea of Africa*. Bloomington: Indiana University Press.

Myrdal, Gunnar. [1944] 1962. *An American Dilemma*. New York: Harper and Row.

Nancy, Jean-Luc. 1993. *The Birth to Presence*. Stanford, Calif.: Stanford University Press.

Negri, Antonio. 1991. *The Savage Anomaly*. Minneapolis: University of Minnesota Press.

Newby, I. A. 1965. *Jim Crow's Defense: Anti-Negro Thought in America, 1900–1930*. Baton Rouge: Louisiana State University Press.

Newton, Isaac. [1686] 1995. *Principia*. Amherst, N.Y.: Prometheus Books.

Nicholson, Linda, and Steven Seidman, eds. 1995. *Social Postmodernism*. Cambridge: Cambridge University Press.

Nietzsche, Friedrich. 1974. *The Gay Science*. New York: Vintage.

Nina Rodrigues, Raymundo. [1894] 1957. *As Raças Humanas e a Responsabilidade Penal no Brasil*. El Salvador: Livraria Progress.

———. [1900] 1935. *O Animismo Fetichista dos Negros Bahianos*. Rio de Janeiro: Civilização Brasileira.

Nogueira, Oracy. 1985. *Tanto Preto Quanto Branco.* São Paulo: T. A. Queiroz.

Nott, J. C., and R. Gliddon. 1854. *Types of Mankind.* Philadelphia: Lippincott, Grambo.

Omi, Michael, and H. Winant. 1986. *Racial Formation in the United States.* New York: Routledge and Kegan Paul.

Ortner, Sheryl B., and Harriet Whitehead, eds. 1981. *Sexual Meanings.* Cambridge: Cambridge University Press.

Oyĕwùmi, Oyèrónké. 1997. *The Invention of Women.* Minneapolis: University of Minnesota Press.

Page, Thomas. 1904. *The Negro: The Southerners Problem.* New York: Charles Scribner's Sons.

Parekh, Bhikhu. 2000. *Rethinking Multiculturalism.* Cambridge, Mass.: Harvard University Press.

Park, Robert Ezra. [1913] 1950. "Racial Assimilation in Secondary Groups." In *Race and Culture,* 204–20. Glencoe, Ill.: Free Press.

———. [1917] 1950. "Race Prejudice and Japanese-American Relations." In *Race and Culture,* 223–29. Glencoe, Ill.: Free Press.

———. [1923] 1950. "Negro Consciousness as Reflected in Race Literature." In *Race and Culture,* 284–300. Glencoe, Ill.: Free Press.

———. [1924a] 1950. "The Concept of Social Distance." In *Race and Culture,* 256–60. Glencoe, Ill.: Free Press.

———. [1924b] 1950. "Experience and Race Relations." In *Race and Culture,* 152–57. Glencoe, Ill.: Free Press.

———. [1928] 1950. "The Bases of Race Prejudice." In *Race and Culture,* 230–43. Glencoe, Ill.: Free Press.

———. [1931] 1950. "The Problem of Cultural Differences." In *Race and Culture,* 3–14. Glencoe, Ill.: Free Press.

———. [1937] 1950. "The Etiquette of Race Relations in the South." In *Race and Culture,* 177–88. Glencoe, Ill.: Free Press.

———. [1939] 1950. "The Nature of Race Relations." In *Race and Culture,* 81–116. Glencoe, Ill.: Free Press.

———. 1942. Introduction to *Negroes in Brazil: A Study of Race Contact in Bahia,* by Donald Pierson. Chicago: University of Chicago Press.

———. [1943] 1950. "Race Ideologies." In *Race and Culture,* 301–15. Glencoe, Ill.: Free Press.

———. 1950a. "An Autobiographical Note." In *Race and Culture,* v–x. Glencoe, Ill.: Free Press.

———. 1950b. "Culture and Civilization." In *Race and Culture,* 15–23. Glencoe, Ill.: Free Press.

———. 1950c. *Race and Culture.* Glencoe, Ill.: Free Press.

Park, Robert Ezra, and Ernest W. Burgess. 1924. *Introduction to the Science of Sociology.* Chicago: University of Chicago Press.

Parsons, Talcott. 1939. *The Structure of Social Action*. Glencoe, Ill.: Free Press.

———. 1951. *The Social System*. New York: Free Press.

———. 1977. *The Evolution of Societies*. Englewood Cliffs, N.J.: Prentice-Hall.

Pateman, Carole. 1988. *The Sexual Contract*. Stanford, Calif.: Stanford University Press.

Paxton, Frederic. 1921. *Recent History of the United States*. Boston: Houghton and Mifflin.

Pedro II. 1959. *Diário da visita ao Norte do Brasil*. El Salvador: Universidade da Bahia.

Pierson, Donald. 1942. *Negroes in Brazil: A Study of Race Contact in Bahia*. Chicago: University of Chicago Press.

Poliakov, Leon. 1974. *The Aryan Myth*. New York: Basic Books.

Prado, Paulo. [1926] 1962. *Retrato do Brasil*. Rio de Janeiro: José Olympio Editora.

Radcliffe-Brown, A. R. 1952. *Structure and Function in Primitive Society*. Glencoe, Ill.: Free Press.

———. 1958. *Method in Social Anthropology*. London: Asia Publishing.

Ramos, Arthur. 1934. *O Negro Brasileiro*. Rio de Janeiro: Civilização Brasileira.

———. 1935. *O Folclore Negro do Brasil*. Rio de Janeiro: Casa do Estudante do Brasil.

Renan, E. 1994. "What Is a Nation." In *Nation and Narration*, ed. Homi Bhabha, 8–22. London: Routledge.

Reuter, E. B. 1934. *Race and Culture Contacts*. New York, London: McGraw-Hill.

Ringer, Benjamin. 1983. *"We the People" and Others*. New York: Tavistock.

Ripley, William Z. 1899. *The Races of Europe*. New York: D. Appleton.

Roberts, Dorothy. 1997. *Killing the Black Body*. New York: Pantheon.

Robertson, Roland. 1992. *Globalization: Social Theory and Global Culture*. London: Sage.

———. 1995. "Globalization: Time-Space and Homogeneity-Heterogeneity." In *Global Modernities,* ed. Mike Featherstone, Scott Lash, and Roland Robertson, 25–44. London: Sage.

Robertson, Roland, and Brian Turner, eds. 1991. *Talcott Parsons: Theorist of Modernity*. London: Sage.

Rockmore, Thomas. 1996. *On Hegel's Epistemology and Contemporary Philosophy*. Atlantic Highlands, N.J.: Humanities Press.

Romero, Sylvio. 1888. *História da Literatura Brasileira*. Rio de Janeiro: Garnier.

———. 1894. *Doutrina contra Doutrina: O Evolucionismo e o Positivismo na República do Brasil*. Rio de Janeiro: J. B. Nunes.

————. 1906. *O Brasil Social*. Rio de Janeiro: Typographia do Jornal do Comércio.

————. 1978. *Teoria, Crítica, e História Literária*. Rio de Janeiro: Livros Técnicos e Científicos Editora.

Rorty, Richard. 1979. *Philosophy and the Mirror of Nature*. Princeton, N.J.: Princeton University Press.

Rosenau, Pauline. 1992. *Postmodernism and the Social Sciences*. Princeton, N.J.: Princeton University Press.

Ross, Edward A. 1919. *What Is America?* New York: Century.

Ruchames, Louis, ed. 1969. *Racial Thought in America*. Amherst: University of Massachusetts Press.

Said, Edward W. 1978. *Orientalism*. New York: Vintage.

Santos, Gislene Aparecida dos. 2002. *A Invenção de Ser Negro*. São Paulo: Editora da Pontifície Universidade Católica.

Sartre, Jean-Paul. [1943] 1984. *Being and Nothingness*. New York: Washington Square Press.

Schmitt, Carl. 1976. *The Concept of the Political*. New Brunswick, N.J.: Rutgers University Press.

Schwarcz, Lilia. 1993. *O Espetáculo das Raças*. São Paulo: Cia das Letras.

Scott, Joan W. 1991. "The Evidence of Experience." *Critical Inquiry* 17 (Summer): 773–97.

————. 1999. *Gender and the Politics of History*. New York: Columbia University Press.

Seidman, Steven. 1994. *Contest Knowledge*. Oxford: Blackwell.

Shakespeare, William. 1987. *The Tempest*. Oxford: Oxford University Press.

Shelley, Mary. [1818] 1991. *Frankenstein*. New York: Bantam.

Silva, Denise Ferreira da. 1989. "Repensando a 'Democracia Racial': Raça e identidade nacional no Pensamento Brasileiro." *Estudos Afro-Asiáticos* 16: 157–70.

————. 1998. "Facts of Blackness: Brazil Is Not Quite the United States . . . and Racial Politics in Brazil?" *Social Identities* 4, no. 2: 201–23.

————. 2001. "Towards a Critique of the Socio-Logos of Justice: The *Analytics of Raciality* and the Production of Universality." *Social Identities* 7, no. 3: 421–54.

————. 2002. "Re-writing the Black Subject." In *Philosophies of Race and Ethnicity,* ed. Peter Osborne and Stella Sandford, 160–71. London: Continuum.

————. 2004a. "An Introduction: The Predicament of Brazilian Culture." *Social Identities* 10, no. 6: 719–34.

————. 2004b. "Mapping Territories of Legality: An Exploratory Cartography of Black Female Subjects" In *Critical Beings: Race, Nation, and the Global Subject,* ed. Patricia Truitt and Peter Fitzpatrick. Aldershot, England: Ashgate.

————. 2005. "'Bahia Pêlo Negro': Can the Subaltern (Subject of Raciality) Speak?" *Ethnicities* 5, no. 3: 321–42.

Simmel, Georg. 1971. *On Individuality and Social Forms: Selected Writings*. Chicago: University of Chicago Press.

Skidmore, Thomas. 1974. *Black into White: Race and Nationality in Brazilian Thought*. New York: Oxford University Press.

Smith, Anthony. 1983. *Theories of Nationalism*. New York: Holmes and Meyer.

Smith, Valerie. 1991. "Black Feminist Theory and the Representation of the 'Other.'" In *Changing Our Own Words*, ed. Cheryl Wall, 38–57. New Brunswick, N.J.: Rutgers University Press.

Spiller, Gustav. [1911] 1969. *Papers on Inter-Racial Problems*. New York: Arno.

Spivak, Gayatri Chakravorty. 1987. "Scattered Speculations on the Question of Value." In *In Other Worlds*, 154–75. London: Routledge.

————. 1994. "Can the Subaltern Speak?" In *Colonial Discourse and Post-Colonial Theory*, ed. Patrick Williams and Laura Chrisman, 66–111. New York: Columbia University Press.

————. 1999. *A Critique of Postcolonial Reason*. Cambridge, Mass.: Harvard University Press.

Stepan, Nancy. 1982. *The Idea of Race in Science*. Hamden, Conn.: Anchor Books.

————. 1991. *Hour of Eugenics*. Ithaca, N.Y.: Cornell University Press.

Stocking, George. 1968. *Race, Culture, and Evolution*. New York: Free Press.

Stoddard, Lothrop. 1920. *The Rising Tide of Color against White World Supremacy*. New York: Charles Scribner's Sons.

Stoler, Ann L. 1995. *Race and the Education of Desire*. Durham, N.C.: Duke University Press.

Strong, Josiah. 1885. *Our Country*. New York: Baker and Taylor.

Tannenbaum, Frank. 1946. *Slave and Citizen*. New York: Vintage.

Taussig, Michael. 1987. *Shamanism, Colonialism, and the Wild Man*. Chicago: University of Chicago Press.

Taylor, Charles. 1975. *Hegel*. Cambridge: Cambridge University Press.

Taylor, George Rogers. 1972. *The Turner Thesis*. Lexington, Mass.: D. C. Heath.

Theory, Culture, and Society. 1988. Special Issue on Postmodernism. *Theory, Culture, and Society* 5, nos. 2–3.

Tilly, Charles. 1975. *The Formation of National States in Western Europe*. Princeton, N.J.: Princeton University Press.

Tocqueville, Alexis de. 1969. *Democracy in America*. Garden City, N.Y.: Doubleday.

Todorov, Tzvetan. 1993. *On Human Diversity*. Cambridge, Mass.: Harvard University Press.

Topinard, Paul. 1885. *Eléments d'anthropologie générale*. Paris: Adrien Delahaye et Emile Legrosnier.

Toplin, Robert. 1981. *Freedom and Prejudice: The Legacy of Slavery in the United States and Brazil*. Westport, Conn.: Greenwood.

Touraine, Alain. 1995. *Critique of Modernity*. Oxford: Blackwell.

———. 1998. *Beyond Neoliberalism*. Cambridge, England: Polity Press.

Tumin, Melvin. 1969. *Comparative Perspectives on Race Relations*. Boston: Little, Brown.

Ture, Kwame, and Charles V. Hamilton. [1967] 1992. *Black Power*. New York: Random House.

Turner, Bryan S., ed. 1990. *Theories of Modernity and Postmodernity*. London: Sage.

Tussman, J., ed. 1963. *The Supreme Court on Racial Discrimination*. New York: Oxford University Press.

Tylor, E. B. 1898. *Anthropology: An Introduction to the Study of Man and Civilization*. New York: D. Appleton.

UNESCO (United Nations Educational, Scientific, and Cultural Organization). 1961. *Race and Science*. New York: Columbia University Press.

Van den Berghe, Pierre. 1967. *Race and Racism*. New York: Wiley and Sons.

Vattimo, Gianni. 1992. *The Transparent Society*. Baltimore: Johns Hopkins University Press.

Vianna Oliveira, F. J. 1938. *A Evolução do Povo Brasileiro*. São Paulo: Cia Editora Nacional.

Vogt, Karl. 1864. *Lectures on Man: His Place in the History of the Earth*. London: Longman, Green and Roberts.

Von Eschen, Penny. 1997. *Race against Empire: Black Americans and Anticolonialism, 1937–1957*. Ithaca, N.Y.: Cornell University Press.

Wall, Cheryl. 1989. *Changing Our Own Words*. New Brunswick, N.J.: Rutgers University Press.

Wallerstein, Immanuel. 1991. *Unthinking Social Sciences*. Cambridge, Mass.: Polity Press and Blackwell.

Weber, Max. 1978. *Economy and Society: Outline of Interpretive Sociology*. Berkeley and Los Angeles, and London: University of California Press.

———. 1987. *The Protestant Ethics and the Spirit of Capitalism*. London: Unwin Paperbacks.

West, Cornel. 1982. *Prophesy Deliverance!* Philadelphia: Westminster Press.

———. 1997. "Black Strivings in a Twilight Civilization." In *The Future of the Race,* ed. Henry L. Gates and Cornel West, 53–114. New York: Vintage.

White, Morton. [1947] 1964. *Social Thought in America*. Boston: Beacon.

Wilkins, David. 1997. *American Indian Sovereignty and the U.S. Supreme Court*. Austin: University of Texas Press.

Williams, Raymond. 1977. *Marxism and Literature*. Oxford: Oxford University Press.

Wilson, William Julius. 1978. *The Declining Significance of Race*. Chicago: University of Chicago Press.

———. 1987. *The Truly Disadvantaged*. Chicago: University of Chicago Press.

Winant, Howard. 1994. *Racial Conditions*. Minneapolis: University of Minnesota Press.

———. 2001. *The World Is a Ghetto*. New York: Basic Books.

Wish, Harvey. 1945. *Contemporary America*. New York: Harpers and Brothers.

Wittig, Monique. 1981. *The Straight Mind and Other Essays*. Boston: Beacon.

Wolf, Eric. 1997. *Europe and the People without History*. Berkeley and Los Angeles: University of California Press.

Young, Iris Marion. 1990. *Justice and the Politics of Difference*. Princeton, N.J.: Princeton University Press.

Young, Robert. 1995. *Colonial Desire*. London: Routledge.

Yu, Henry. 2001. *Thinking Orientals*. New York: Oxford University Press.

Žižek, Slavoj. 1999. *The Ticklish Subject*. London: Verso.

———. 2000. "Class Struggle or Postmodernism? Yes, Please!" In *Contingency, Hegemony, Universality*, ed. Judith Butler, Ernesto Laclau, and Slavoj Žižek, 90–135. London: Verso.

Index

Stoler, Ann Laura, 25, 278nn2–3
strategy of containment, 129
strategy of engulfment, xvi, 32,
102, 105, 112, 125, 127, 129,
134–35, 143, 146–47. *See also*
engulfment
strategy of intervention, xvi,
100–101, 106–7, 120, 136, 143,
155–56, 161, 169, 291n8
strategy of particularization, xvi,
100, 112, 127, 169, 200, 224
structural adjustment, 270n8
subaltern, 181; as affectable,
262–63; in Brazil, 245; and
culture, xix, xxxii–xxxiii,
xxxv, 134; and elites, 186;
gender and the, xxix; in history,
183–87; justice for, 263–64; as
located by modern representation, xl–xli; and the logic of
exclusion, xxx; and logic of
obliteration, 267; in "post-" and
critical race theory, 2–5, 7–9,
11–12, 166–68, 183–87; and
"natives," 14–15; race and the,
xxiv, 34–35, 154, 158–62, 249;
sexuality of, 266; speech of,
168, 173–75, 178; in the United
States, 200, 213, 218, 296n1
subject, xxxviii–xl, 111; black,
7–8, 161–62; Cartesian, 46,
56, 58, 74, 82, 281n11, 283n5;
death of, xx–xxiii, xxxiv,
xxxvii, xli, 35, 270n5; and the
division of the globe, xvii–xix,
250–51; as gendered, 266;
global, xix, 33, 173–74, 187,
196; liberal, 89, 204, 213; scientific, 46; as self–determined,
xiii; as social, 5; subaltern, 2–4,
7, 14, 160, 165, 168, 186–87,
244, 257, 261–62; and the

symbolic trinity, xxxi–xxxii; as
transcendental, xxx; as unified,
5. *See also* transparent "I"
symbolic trinity, xxxi–xxxvii

Tannenbaum, Frank, 294n7
Taylor, Charles, 57, 79, 282n1,
284n9, 285nn13–14, 286n1
taxonomy, 102, 124
Tempest, 171, 173, 179–81
terrorism, 151
time, 59–61, 63–4, 71, 88, 98, 254
time lag (Bhabha), 166–67
Tocqueville, Alexander de, 197–98
Topinard, Paul, 122, 125, 128
Touraine, Alain, 270n8
transcendental "I," 70–72, 76, 79,
83, 94, 98, 112, 194
transcendentality, xx, 26, 28, 70,
80, 85, 87, 94, 100, 258, 267;
in Brazil, 233–34; in historical
materialism, 193; in literature,
173; in sociology, 154, 160; in
subaltern history, 184; in the
United States, 200
transcendental poesis, xvi, xxxix,
20, 33, 39, 94, 97–99; in Brazil,
223; in Hegel, 68–90; in historical materialism, 187, 194,
256–60; in the science of man,
105, 111–12, 116, 124, 133,
143, 148, 155; in sociology,
175; in the United States, 199
translation, 6
transnationality, xxxii, xxxiv
transparency, xvi, xxxii–xxxix,
xli, 15, 29, 71, 257–59, 267; in
Bhabha, 167; in the Brazilian
national text, 238; as an effect
of politics, 174; and engulfment, 259; Fanon's critique of,
37; in Hegel, 73, 75, 80, 86; in

DENISE FERREIRA DA SILVA is associate professor of ethnic studies at the University of California, San Diego.